LANGUAGE LEARNER'S

FIELD GUIDE

LANGUAGE LEARNER'S
FIELD GUIDE

Edited by ALAN HEALEY

SUMMER INSTITUTE OF LINGUISTICS
Ukarumpa, Papua New Guinea

4

National Library of Australia card Number and
ISBN 0 7263 0356 9

Five articles in the Appendix have been previously published.

John Beekman, "Eliciting Vocabulary, Meaning, and
Collocations" is reprinted from Notes on Translation 29:1-11
(1968), by permission of the author and publisher.

T. Wayne Dye, "Stress-Producing Factors in Cultural
Adjustment" is reprinted from Missiology 2(1):61-77
(1974), by permission of the author and publisher.

Aretta Loving, "On Learning Monolingually" is reprinted from
Philippine Journal for Language Teaching 1(3-4):11-15
(1962), by permission of the author and publisher.

Eunice V. Pike, "Language Learning in Relation to Focus" is
reprinted from Language Learning 19:107-15
(1969), by permission of the author and publisher.

First printing   1975
Second printing   1976

Printed by the S.I.L. Printing Department
Ukarumpa, E.H.D., Papua New Guinea

CONTENTS

PREFACE 7
INTRODUCTION 9
 What do you expect? 11
 Preparing for fieldwork 13
 Surveying where to live 20
 How to use this guide 22
 The first day 28
DAY-BY-DAY GUIDE 29
UNITS:
 1: "What is his name?"; "Who is that?"; mimicry 31
 2: Greetings and farewells; intonation; tape file 37
 3: Dwellings; tracking; "What is this?" 41
 4: Tools; "What is that?"; equative clauses 46
 5: Review; anthropology file; dictionary file 49
 6: Village routines and leisure times; mimicry; verbs 52
 7: Conversation starters; person morphemes; pronouns 55
 8: Clothing; gifts; possessive forms 65
 9: Food; conversation and mimicry; "Whose is this?" 71
 10: "What is he doing?"; "What did he say?"; agreement 76
 11: Review; "Where?"; locationals; CV patterns 85
 12: Adornment; pictures; yes/no questions and negatives 91
 13: Kin relationships; imperatives 95
 14: Workload; genealogies; "When?"; time words; tenses 102
 15: Another hamlet; transcribing; transitive clauses 109
 16: Communal work and authority; numerals; verbs 116
 17: Review; phonetic work charts; verb 'to be' 121
 18: Use of fire; "Whom?"; verb affixes 126
 19: Pets; "Why?"; "Because" 132
 20: Art; emphasis; locationals 136
 21: Gift exchange; "How?"; instrumental phrases 141
 22: Review; gestures; tone 146
 23: Attitudes; intonation contours; prohibitions 149
 24: Recreation; plural nouns; residual pronouns 153
 25: Sickness and health; object pronouns; testing data 157
 26: Review; check lists; pitch, stress, and length 163
 27. Creative work; benefactives; "For whom?" 173
 28: Flora; hortatory constructions; verb stem formation 180
 29: Methods of communication; multi-clause sentences; dependent verbs 185
 30: Analyzing length, stress, and pitch; sentences 191
 31: Visiting; complex sentences in other modes 196
 32: Religion; descriptives; agreement 201
 33: Dancing; demonstratives; comparatives 210
 34: Collecting songs; different subject sentences 212
 35: Review; preliminary phoneme statement 218
 36: Social organisation; accompaniment constructions 222

37: Life cycle; desiderative; purposive; reason   228
38: Daily life in detail; vocatives; connectives   235
39: Work patterns; embedded clauses; verbs of speech;   241
    cognition and perception; kin terms
40: Review; morpheme classes; translation   248
41: How to continue language learning   252
42: Language learning away from the language area   260

APPENDIX   265

ON LEARNING MONOLINGUALLY - Aretta Loving   267

THE MONOLINGUAL APPROACH TO STUDYING AMUZGO   272
                                 - George Cowan
LEARNING CANDOSHI MONOLINGUALLY   277
                - Lorrie Anderson and Doris Cox

LEARNING XAVANTE MONOLINGUALLY - Ruth A. McLeod   281

LANGUAGE LEARNING - Alan Healey   285

LANGUAGE LEARNING IN RELATION TO FOCUS - Eunice V. Pike   297

GRAMMATICAL DRILLS - Amy Chipping   307

PROGRAMED REVIEW CARDS - J. E. Henderson   318

LANGUAGE LEARNING WITHOUT TEARS - Alan Healey   322

STRESS-PRODUCING FACTORS IN CULTURAL ADJUSTMENT   327
                                 - T. Wayne Dye
OBTAINING LINGUISTIC DATA - Alan Healey   344

ELICITING VOCABULARY, MEANING, AND COLLOCATIONS   361
                                 - John Beekman
ON ELICITING TRANSFORMATIONS IN VIETNAMESE   389
                                 - Richard Pittman
TESTING THE RECOGNITION OF UTTERANCE PAIRS - Alan Healey   399

COLLECTING GENEALOGIES - J. E. Henderson   408

USING TAPE RECORDERS - Alan Healey   411

PLAIN CARD FILING - Alan Healey   427

PUNCH CARD FILING - Robert J. Conrad   429

PAGE FILING - Phyllis M. Healey   446

LIST OF WORDS SUITABLE FOR MONOLINGUAL ELICITING   452
                                 - Alan Healey
USEFUL EXPRESSIONS - Papua New Guinea Branch of the
                         Summer Institute of Linguistics   460
PROGRESS CHARTS   465
CLASSIFICATION FOR CULTURAL OBSERVATIONS   477
GLOSSARY   479
INDEX   487

PREFACE

This book has been prepared to help field-workers learn the language of the people among whom they are living and working. It is true that many textbooks are available describing how to design a writing system and analyze the grammar for an unwritten language. However, apart from Larson and Smalley's book *Becoming Bilingual: A Guide to Language Learning,* very little information has been published on the best methods of learning to speak a language in the field. The present volume has been compiled to bridge this gap. It consists of three sections. The first section is concerned with what preparations should be made before a person settles in a community to learn its language; the next section of forty units gives day-by-day suggestions on how to discover and begin to use the basic features of the language; and the appendix contains a collection of articles that are referred to throughout the book.

The original idea and the general plan for this volume was conceived by Orneal Kooyers, and it was his drive and enthusiasm that carried the project through to completion. Those who have contributed directly to the contents of the units are Amy Chipping, Irwin Firchow, Dorothy James, Robert Litteral, Elizabeth Murane, Philip Staalsen, Mary Stringer, Helen Wearne, Jim Henderson, and myself. Many other colleagues contributed their ideas, suggestions, and criticisms both to the first edition and now to this extensively revised second edition with its new title. A considerable number of ladies have shared the onerous task of typing and of preparing the index. My sincere thanks to all who have helped to produce this volume, and especially to Amy Chipping and Jim Henderson for their assistance in editing.

Alan Healey
November 1974

PREFACE

INTRODUCTION

```
**************************************************************
*                                                            *
*                                                            *
*                                                            *
*                                                            *
*                                                            *
*         There is no way to learn a second                 *
*         language without devoting time to it,              *
*         not just a good block of time each                 *
*         day but a rather significant segment               *
*         out of the learner's life.                         *
*                                                            *
*                          --Larson and Smalley              *
*                                                            *
*                                                            *
*                                                            *
*                                                            *
**************************************************************
```

What Do You Expect ?

The first edition of this book was oriented to the specific needs of members of the Summer Institute of Linguistics who learn unwritten languages in monolingual, rural communities of Papua New Guinea. When a team of two settle in a village or hamlet to commence their field work, their prime responsibility is to achieve conversational fluency in the vernacular as rapidly and fully as possible, and to gain an understanding of the ways and thoughts of the people among whom they live. Later on, the emphasis of their field work shifts to research into the phonology, vocabulary and grammar of the language they are learning, and eventually to translating materials into the vernacular.

This second edition is oriented to a wider audience. (a) Even though a field worker may have more limited linguistic goals he can still profit by using the *Guide* to organize his language learning, especially if pedagogical materials or formal instructions are not available. (See "Learning Without Analyzing" on p. 27).

(b) If the language to be learnt is already written, and especially if a dictionary and grammar are available, the learner may simplify his methods as described in "Two Starting Points" on p. 25.

(c) If the community where the field worker lives is largely bilingual and he adopts a bilingual approach to learning, suitable alternative instructions are to be found throughout the book.

(d) If he is living in a thoroughly Westernized community, the suggested day-by-day research into a stone-age culture should be redirected to facets of the community's culture that are of comparable interest, accessibility, and importance.

(e) Although the *Guide* is designed for the person who has had a beginning course in linguistics, it is sufficiently self-explanatory for the person without linguistic training provided he first reads carefully pages 86-199 of Nida's book *Learning a Foreign Language*. (He should also make liberal use of the glossary and index found at the back of this *Guide*.)

(f) On the other hand, professional linguists may find some of the sections on elicitation and analysis elementary and may prefer to use their own initiative at those points.

(g) If the reader is teaching or studying a course in methods of language learning (rather than learning an actual language) he sould read "Language Learning" on pp.285-296.

In this revised edition we have tried to eliminate all features that are unique to Papua New Guinea so that each unit will be sufficiently general to be usable anywhere. For 'village' one should freely read 'community', 'neighborhood', 'town', 'hamlet', 'homestead', 'camp' or the like. For any other cultural, geographic, or linguistic feature that seems to be foreign to the reader we ask his patience.

Preparing for Fieldwork

It is quite a shock to be suddenly surrounded by people who speak a different language, and to start learning to talk all over again. This shock will be lessened if the following procedures are followed. Check (tick) off each point as you complete it.

Linguistics

If you have had no training in linguistics, study pages 86-199 of Nida's book *Learning a Foreign Language*.

Information About the Language

Study the latest and most reliable linguistic surveys of the area around where you plan to settle. Read everything that is available about the language and culture, making notes. Read similar descriptions of nearby peoples and closely related languages.

The language materials available to you could vary from the minimum of a word list and tape collected on a survey up to a good description of the grammar and sound system, a dictionary, and some texts recorded on tape and transcribed. You may even have a set of language-learning lessons. You can make good use of whatever materials you have, even before settling in the village.

If there is no dictionary that you can take to the village, you may be able to type one up from a card file or other unpublished materials. If all that is available is a tape-recorded word list, this can form the basis of your dictionary. You should listen to the recording of the list every day, mimicking the words, until you know the more useful ones and have gained some skill in pronouncing them. You should also write each word down and incorporate it into your dictionary file. Read the three articles in the Appendix (pp.427-451) on "Plain Card Filing", "Punch Card Filing", and "Page Filing", and decide which method of filing you will follow. Discuss these media with experienced linguists to help you decide and to get any additional practical tips you can.

If there is no description of the grammar, you could analyze some texts and compile grammar notes. The recordings of the texts should also be mimicked (see 3.6b). Of

course, if you have language learning lessons, you should
make good use of them before moving into the village, so you
can use the vernacular more and the lingua franca less, even
in the early stages while building your house.

Basic Expressions

If you will be settling in a monolingual area, try to
find a bilingual speaker of the language and elicit the following list of expressions. (Note that some of the questions may appear stupid or embarrassing to the person you
are working with. If so, try to find useful questions that
will be suitable.)

GREETINGS -- English: Vernacular:

_____   _____

_____   _____

_____   _____

_____   _____

What is your name?
(or "What should I call you?")   _____

My name is ------   _____

What is his name?   _____

His name is ---   _____

What is her name?   _____

Her name is ---   _____

What did you say?
(or "Say it again, please.")   _____

Say it slowly.   _____

Where are you going?   _____

I'm going to the river.
(place for getting water.)   _____

What is this?
(or "What do you call this?")   _____

Where do you live?   _____

Yes.   _____

No.   _____

I don't know.   _____

I don't understand.   _____

What are you doing?   _____

I want to try (it).   _____

FAREWELLS -- English: Vernacular:

_____   _____

_____   _____

_____   _____

_____   _____

I want food.   _____

I want to buy food.   _____

How much?   _____

That is too much.   _____

It's good.   _____

I don't have any.   _____

Where is it? (the path?)   _____

When will you go?   _____

Who is going?   _____

I want to eat now.   _____

I want to sleep now.   _____

After eliciting, try out any of the questions that you
can with the speaker of the language; he may have answered
the question instead of translating it. If two speakers of
the language are available, you can avoid this problem by
asking one of them to ask the other one the question you are
eliciting.

Record these expressions on tape so you can learn them
before settling in your village. For each expression, record English meaning, silence, vernacular expression, silence, then vernacular again.

English	silence	vernacular	silence	vernacular

You should speak the English and the native speaker of
the language should say the vernacular expression each time.
Practice with the first few expressions, until your helper
understands what you want him to do. Play back the recording, mimicking the first vernacular utterance during the silence that follows it. Listen to the repetition of the
utterance. When the recording is satisfactory, go on and record the remaining utterances. If you are using a lingua
franca, you could hold down the pause button on the recorder
while you say the lingua franca equivalent of the English.

A longer list of useful expressions is given on pp.460-
464, which you may have time to elicit at this stage.

To learn the expressions, go through the tape morning
and evening. At first, for each expression, mimic the first
vernacular utterance during the gap that follows it, then
listen to the repetition of the utterance. Soon you will be
able to say the vernacular expression straight after the
English meaning. When you settle in the village, use these
expressions from the start, observing the people's reactions.
It may be that some of the expressions are not appropriate--
if so you'll need to learn and use more suitable ones.

If you are unable to find a bilingual speaker before
moving into the language area but there are some bilingual
villagers where you plan to settle, you could devote the
first few days there to recording and learning these expressions, so that your accent will be like those around you. If
another linguist helps you settle into the village, he should
elicit and record the expressions for you, so that you can
concentrate on the language you are learning, not on the lingua
franca.

Lingua Franca

Go through the *Guide* and fill in the lingua franca version of each of the expressions suggested for bilingual eliciting, and have someone who is fluent in the lingua franca check what you have written. If there is an S.I.L. branch in the country where you will be working, they may be able to supply a list of these expressions in the lingua franca of that country.

Reading

Read "Language Learning" on pages 285-296 of this *Guide* for a general preview of the various ways you can go about learning a new language.

A few days before moving into the language area, read Units 1-3 so that you will be alert to some of the problems you may encounter with names, greetings, and pointing.

Equipment

Assemble the following equipment for the first three months of language learning:

A battery-operated tape recorder with earphones

10 3-inch magnetic tapes and 5 3-inch empty spools and/or

5 C-60 cassettes, 5 C-30 cassettes, and 3 loop-tape cassettes of different lengths

Pens and pencils

500 sheets of light bond typing paper 21 cm x 27 cm

10 manila folders

5 exercise books for transcribing texts

A copy of the pre-printed loose-leaf *English-Vernacular Word List* obtainable from S.I.L. Bookroom, Ukarumpa, P.N.G.

3 loose-leaf books to take 21 cm x 27 cm paper

A perforator (punch) for loose-leaf paper

5 small spiral-backed notebooks for carrying in your pocket

200 small (8 cm x 13 cm) filing cards in a variety of colors

Materials for filing (1,000 filing cards; or 1,000 punch cards plus a hand-punch for notching them; or several extra loose-leaf books and extra paper fo fit)

Carbon paper (some for writing and some for typing)

10 large sheets of paper for maps and displays

50 big (43 cm x 34 cm) sheets of lined or graph paper for genealogical charts, etc.

Take with you the following books:

(a) William A. Smalley, editor. *Readings in Missionary Anthropology*. (Tarrytown, New York: Practical Anthropology). 1967.

(b) Ernest L. Schusky. *Manual for Kinship Analysis*. (New York: Holt, Rinehart and Winston). 1965.

(c) Raymond Firth. *Human Types*, revised edition. (London: Thomas Nelson). 1956.

(d) Either of the following books:

Melville J. Herskovits. *Cultural Anthropology*. (New York: Knopf). 1955.

Melville J. Herskovits. *Man and His Works*. (New York: Knopf). 1948.

(e) Any one of the following books:

Eugene A. Nida. *Customs and Cultures*. (New York: Harper). 1954.

E. Adamson Hoebel. *Man in the Primitive World*, second edition. (New York: McGraw-Hill). 1958.

Morton H. Fried, editor. *Readings in Anthropology*, Volume 2. (New York: Crowell). 1959.

(f) Eugene A. Nida. *Learning a Foreign Language*, second edition. (New York: Friendship Press). 1957.

(g) William J. Samarin. *Field Linguistics*. (New York: Holt, Rinehart and Winston). 1967

(h) Kenneth L. Pike. *Phonemics*. (Ann Arbor: University of Michigan Press). 1947.

(i) Benjamin Elson and Velma Pickett. *An Introduction to Morphology and Syntax*. (Santa Ana, California: Summer Institute of Linguistics). 1962.

(j) Eugene A. Nida. *Bible Translating*. (New York: American Bible Society). 1947.

(k) A good grammar and a good dictionary of the lingua franca.

To stimulate conversation in the village, collect pictures of items similar to the artifacts of the culture you
are going into. Simple, accurate line drawings are best.
Gather other pictures of two or three people in different
situations. Possible sources are reading books used in
schools and adult education programs, and illustrated dic-
tionaries. Issues of pictorial magazines such as National
Geographic which deal with the country you are working in,
and some clear, unambiguous pictures from your own cultural
background would also be useful. Photographs of your own
relatives will probably be very popular.

Arrange for a library to send you a couple of novels
each month to relieve the strain of learning a whole new set
of speech and behavior patterns. Assemble some tapes of your
favorite music, for the same purpose.

Tape Recorder

If you do not already have a tape recorder, discuss with
technicians the reliability, servicing and local availability
of parts for different models. Ask several experienced field
linguists to show you how they record texts, conversations,
and drills. Ask their opinions on the best models of recorder for field work.

If you are not familiar with tape recorders, read "Using Tape Recorders" on pp.411-426 of this *Guide* and "Tape
Recorders" in Samarin's *Field Linguistics,* pp. 88-102.

Before settling into the language area, practice using
your recorder until you can:

(a) move back and forth between record and playback with
confidence and without accidentally erasing recordings;

(b) stop and restart a recording without leaving noisy
clicks on the recording;

(c) use the pause button to listen to an individual word or
even an individual syllable;

(d) estimate the position and distance the microphone needs
to be from a person, and what setting of the recording level
knob is needed to get a clear recording--neither too soft
and muffled, nor over loud and distorted;

(e) make tape loops, copy or record a stretch of speech
onto a loop, and erase unwanted material from the loop
without taking off the important material.

Surveying Where to Live

Read any available surveys of the area, and make a map showing the boundaries of the language, population centers and access routes. Read the articles in the appendix by Aretta Loving and George Cowan on monolingual language learning.

Make a trip to the area, visiting its administrative center to meet officials and leaders and to get census figures for each census point. Examine several locations where it seems suitable for you to live, and for each one prepare a page listing both the linguistic and the living factors which will help in your decision. The linguistic factors include:

(a) number of people in the community

(b) do they speak a single dialect or are speakers of several dialects present?

(c) what percentage of the people there
   (i)   are monolingual,
   (ii)   are bilingual in the vernacular and a lingua franca,
   (iii) speak a lingua franca but not the vernacular?

(d) how do the people feel about
   (i)   the vernacular language,
   (ii)   their own dialect of the vernacular,
   (iii) other dialects of their language?

(e) can you arrange housing actually within the community's residential area, and physically close (40 feet or less) to some other house?

The living factors include:

(a) an adequate water supply,

(b) an adequate method of getting food supplies, fuel, and medical help,

(c) adequate housing and toilet facilities,

(d) the community's willingness for you to live there to learn their language and to commence whatever other project you have in mind,

(e) the proximity of other outside agencies, such as missions, plantations or government programs, with which you would be competing for food and labor,

(f) the degree of communication with others of your own cul-
     ture and with those who administer your program,

(g) any possible schooling facilities for one's children,

(h) all other things being equal, a suitable place for swim-
     ming or bathing in a hot climate.

At each place you feel would be suitable, elicit and record the Basic Expressions (pp. 14-16). Add other details to
your map, such as village names and agricultural and hunting
areas.

Try to decide which dialect has the greatest prestige,
and which has the greatest population. Do some areas show
cultural disintegration because of culture contact?

While learning the language it is a great advantage to
live where there are few bilingual people, so you will be
forced to use all the vernacular you can. However, bilingual people can help you to get started very quickly, so consider spending the first few weeks at a place where there
are more bilingual people, from whom you can elicit material
to show the basic structure of the language, especially if
you have not previously elicited and recorded the Basic Expressions. This procedure may give you the best of both bilingual and monolingual approaches to learning the language.

As soon as you have decided where to settle, start
learning and using the expressions you recorded there.

Evaluate the names that have been used for the language
group. If there is a long-established government name, use
it and spell it the same way. If not, is there a long-
established linguists' or anthropologists' name? If there
is none of these of long standing, or if the people who
speak the language strongly resent that name, then use their
name for the language or, failing that, their name for themselves.

How to Use This Guide

The body of the *Guide* is divided into 40 discovery units, each of which will help you to make some discoveries about some aspects of the language and culture. It will then help you to analyze and understand those features of the language, and to practice them until you can use them automatically in conversation.

Each unit is divided into several categories or types of assignments. Before beginning work on a unit you should read through the whole unit, since sometimes there are forward references to other categories in the same unit.

At the beginning of a unit there is often a paragraph of preliminary activities. Following this, the categories are numbered so that a specific category number always relates to assignments of a similar nature. For example, category three in all units relates to eliciting data, category one to observing. Each unit does not necessarily contain an assignment in every category. References are made to parts of units by naming the unit, category, and then the paragraph within that category. For example, the reference 14.5b refers to unit 14, category 5, paragraph b.

The categories found in the units are as follows:

Category 1. Observing:

Here you are directed to observe some specific activity or objects which will help you in other categories of the same unit as well as in learning much of the culture. A classified list of the topics is on p. 469. They are also listed alphabetically in the index.

Category 2. Conversation:

Careful attention should be given to this category from the start. It is designed to help you learn to converse fluently in the vernacular.

Category 3. Eliciting Data:

You should make the strongest possible effort to use what you already know (and half know) in the vernacular to elicit the data in this category, as this will help increase your fluency rapidly. In most units more specific

methods (e.g. miming, and creating social situations) are
given for eliciting material monolingually. It is recommended that in the early months all data should be elicited from
a number of people in a variety of informal settings, rather
than from a single, regular, paid language helper.

In units containing material that is particularly difficult to elicit monolingually, bilingual suggestions are
given, but these should be used only when consistent efforts
at monolingual elicitation have proved fruitless. It is
true that if bilingual speakers are available much information can be acquired from them rapidly by using the lingua
franca. However, there are several disadvantages of working
in this way. Your progress in learning to speak the vernacular is slowed down by failure to use it constantly. Your increasing confidence in the lingua franca will then predispose
you to use it in preference to the vernacular. In the face
of this vicious circle it takes considerable self discipline
to limit your use of the lingua franca to the few situations
where it is really necessary.

Category 4. Description:

After gathering data you will need to process it. You
should file your materials so that they are readily available
to you for further study. In each unit you are also instruct-
ed to partly analyze your data before proceeding. This helps
throw light on the problems being studied in that particular
unit. Taped materials should be transcribed with (or by) a
language helper as soon as possible after recording them. A
massive accumulation of unprocessed data is useless to you.

Category 5. Testing:

When you have described a linguistic pattern in Category four, you should test your description by making up new
utterances based on it and checking them with several different people. Modify your description if necessary. In
later units this category has detailed practice for translators.

Category 6. Practicing:

Set time aside to practice and memorize a selection of
the data you gather. Each area of language learning which
presents special problems to you should be attacked systematically with appropriate kinds of drills.

At the end of each unit there are some questions which will help you to evaluate your progress. Under "Comments" you should indicate how well you achieved your aims in this unit. Also list any sections that were too difficult or which need further attention later.

There are two ways to use the material in the units; consecutively, unit by unit, or in a different order as conversational needs and the structure of the languate dictate. Whichever method you choose you should at least begin by following the *Guide* consecutively.

The Consecutive Approach

As you work through the units your efforts will automatically be balanced without undue emphasis on one area at the expense of other areas that are also important. You will also come across instructions to review drills and decisions made in earlier units.

However, you should not always follow the sequence the *Guide* presents. Since every language and culture is different, there will come a time when some facet is holding back your progress in other areas. Then you should look up that subject in the index and do some sections of later units which concentrate on that point. Mark those sections, with the date you did them, practice that linguistic feature, then start using it in conversation. You should then be able to continue consecutively through the units from where you left the sequence.

If the *Guide* suggests that today you investigate pronouns, but someone wants to teach you the numerals instead, then leave the pronouns and concentrate on what he is interested in. You can ask him about pronouns later, and meanwhile your interest in what he is offering will encourage him to teach you in the future. Back at your house you can look up numerals in the index and check (tick) off any section on numerals that you have completed, marking it with the date.

If a death or marriage occurs, look up that subject in the index and make the appropriate observations, no matter what unit you are working through. File your observations, and go over them again later when your language fluency is better.

The danger of slavishly following this consecutive

approach is that you may not freely and spontaneously mix
with people and learn to converse in the language. So remember, THIS BOOK IS A GUIDE, NOT A STRAIGHT-JACKET!

The Need-Ordered Approach

For the need-ordered approach to be successful, you
must spend a lot of time with people, joining in their activities, and talking with them as much as you can. Make a
note of customs, words and constructions that strike you as
new and interesting. At least every second day you should
copy these words and constructions from your notebook to
your dictionary, anthropology, phonology and grammar files.
When some linguistic or cultural feature is blocking your
progress, turn to the index and find out which sections deal
with it, and work through them, analyzing what you have observed, eliciting more data, analyzing again, checking and
preparing drills. Mark the sections off in the lists of
topics following the Progress Charts at the end of the Appendix. (pp. 465-476.)

With this approach imbalance is a constant danger. It
is your responsibility to keep a balance in your work, and
not to follow some special interest to the neglect of other
facets of language learning. Using the Progress Charts regularly will help you here. You will also need to structure
your own review of earlier drills so that the patterns in
them become thoroughly automatic. For this you should use
the Programmed Review Cards presented in the Appendix
(pp. 318-321).

In summary, in following the consecutive approach you
are daily aiming at set goals in your language learning, and
only as problems arise do you interrupt the sequence of units.
On the other hand, following the need-ordered approach, your
learning is more spontaneous and you refer to various parts
of the *Guide* as you meet cultural and linguistic problems.

Two Starting Points

The *Guide* is designed to help people analyze and learn
a previously unwritten language. It is also useful, though,
in helping people to learn a language that has already been
analyzed.

If the language you will be learning has an adequate
writing system, a dictionary and a grammar, you will need
to do very little analysis for yourself. It will be much

faster for you to look up troublesome points in the grammar
than to try to analyze them yourself; though there may be
some things not covered in the grammar, in which the procedures suggested in the *Guide* will help you. Use the index.

Unless you have a good set of language learning lessons,
you should follow the *Guide's* suggestions in making up
drills so that what you learn about the language can become
automatic habits instead of memorized rules. Even if you do
have language lessons, it will pay you to make up some drills
of your own as well, as this will help you to learn.

Kinds of Learners

People vary in their approach to language learning from
analysts to "sponges". Analysts enjoy describing the patterns of a language but find it hard to put their insights
into fluent speech. "Sponges", on the other hand, enjoy being with people, and just seem to soak up language with very
little effort, and without consciously understanding the
underlying patterns. If two people are learning the same
language, it often happens that one is an analyst and the
other a "sponge".

After a few weeks of language learning you should decide which approach you favor, and then read these remarks
again. Analysts run the risk of spending too much time at
the desk analyzing the language, and not enough time out with
people practicing what they have discovered. If you tend to
be an analyst, keep postponing analysis, and go for trips
with people so you can practice speaking to build fluency.
Use what you hear, even if you don't understand its structure.

If, on the other hand, you tend to soak up language
easily, you will tend to learn new words and constructions
at one or two hearings, without writing them down. This
helps your language fluency, but it doesn't help your partner at all. You should write down your new discoveries, and
copy them into the dictionary, phonology and grammar files
at the end of each day. You should also put your discoveries together and describe the patterns in them. Then make
drills to teach the patterns. This way you and your partner
will both benefit from your quick receptivity.

This difference in learning style can easily become a
source of tension and misunderstanding, so you and your

partner should discuss your discoveries together and help
each other.

Learning Without Analyzing

A note for those who wish to learn a language without
analyzing it. This is the way we learned to speak as children, and as adults we can learn a new language in much the
same way. You will probably find, though, that you will
learn more quickly if you do analyze and describe things you
can't understand. Just use the index to find help when you
need it. Making drills will also give you concentrated practice in difficult areas.

Allocating Your Time

Don't try to have a rigid time-table while you are living in the village. One day there will be a ceremony to attend and another day a feast in a different village. Take
any opportunities to be with people and to help with their
work, even if you seem to make no further progress through
the *Guide* on these days, as these occasions are invaluable
in learning the language and culture. There will be other
days, though, when nothing unusual is happening, and you can
catch up with filing new words and constructions and analyzing your discoveries. But on these days too you should
spend some time with people, talking together, using expressions you have learned recently and mimicking to yourself
when you can't understand the general conversation.

If you have just settled down to analysis or to drill
with the tape recorder and someone comes with vegetables for
sale, don't resent the interruption, but sieze the opportunity to talk and perhaps to make a new friend. Be happy to
"waste" time talking with people; such time is never wasted.

The First Day

Your initial contacts with the people in the community where you are settling are crucial. Despite the large differences of culture, they are going to sense many of your attitudes on the very first day. So you need to settle it in your own mind beforehand that two of your main goals are forming friendships and learning to converse in their language. Then the very day you arrive in the community you should begin implementing these two goals. Try to give the least possible attention to baggage, housing, and food (important as these are) and as much attention as possible to the people who come to meet or help you. Be friendly to them in whatever ways seem acceptable, spend time with them, mimic them, accept their corrections, and write down some of their shorter utterances.

If you are in a monolingual situation and have not been able to learn any of the Basic Expressions before arriving there, then note down as many words and expressions you can on the first day. Several of them may prove to be very useful in daily living. By all means attempt to elicit some of the words and Basic Expressions you need. (A list of words suitable for monolingual eliciting is found on pp. 452-459.)

If you have been able to learn the Basic Expressions, use them right from the beginning in all your contacts with people. Smile, greet people, and learn their names. Start finding out the names of common objects in the village. Mimic them and write them in your data book. And notice how people respond when you use the expressions you have learnt. If any of the expressions don't lead to the kind of response you would have expected, try to elicit and learn new ones. (Units 1-4, 9-12, 14, 16, 18, 19, and 21 give hints for eliciting common questions.)

Now turn to Unit 1. As you work through the units check that any expressions you have learnt are idiomatic.

DAY-BY-DAY GUIDE

30

```
**********************************************************
*                                                        *
*                                                        *
*                                                        *
*                                                        *
*                                                        *
*           Yesterday is a cancelled cheque;             *
*           tomorrow is a promissory note;               *
*           today is ready cash--use it.                 *
*                            --Kay Lyons                 *
*                                                        *
*                                                        *
*                                                        *
*                                                        *
**********************************************************
```

Unit 1

AIMS: (1) Listen, mimic, and make friends.
       (2) Learn the names of the community leader and his family.

READ: (1) "Respect and Ethnocentricism" in Smalley pp. 255-257.
       (2) "On Learning Monolingually" in this *Guide* pp. 267-271.

1.1a   Observing the Ecological Setting

What is the environment of the language group?
Among things to notice are: altitude, general vegetation, population density, accessibility from other areas, degree of contact with other language groups, settled or nomadic, gardeners or gatherers, large villages or small hamlets, dwellings near or distant from gardens.

1.1b   Daily Schedule

From today on notice the times of day that people are actually present in the village. Adjust your daily program so you can be with them as much as possible.

1.2   Listening and Mimicking

1.2a   Walk through the village and observe some activity. As you listen to conversation that is not addressed directly to you, try humming the rhythm and pitch patterns quietly to yourself in such a way as not to attract attention. Do so in order to fix the patterns in your mind. This can also be done in your house, when there are people outside talking to each other and you can hear them through the walls.

1.2b   When someone speaks to you, answer with speech or gesture if you possibly can. If you cannot guess the meaning of what he is saying to you, then mimic what he said.

Do not get bogged down in writing. Do not try to pronounce the vowels and consonants perfectly, as this will slow you down. It is more important in the early stages of your language assimilation to get

good rhythm and intonation patterns established. If
something is short enough to get both the rhythm and
intonation and the right CV articulations, try to do
as well as you can with both. On any long utterance,
try to say it as fast as they do, with the same rhythm contours, and slide over any vowels and consonants you cannot reproduce easily. They will come
later. DO NOT TRY TO GET PEOPLE TO SLOW DOWN FOR
YOUR MIMICRY. You will want them to slow down occasionally so you can write the name of something or a
phrase you feel will be useful. Do this only after
you have mimicked it at the proper speed. Some
people may automatically slow down when you try to
mimic. Do not be discouraged if this happens but try
to work up to normal speed again before you leave
each utterance. If you find that you can only mimic
portions of the utterance, repeat the last section
and you will gradually find that you will be able to
repeat more as time goes by. Spend a mimimum of 50
minutes in this activity, preferably in short
stretches of 5-10 minutes or less at a time.

1.2c   NOTE: Whenever you mimic, be alert to people's re-
        actions. If you find they laugh a lot, be cautious.
        It may mean that what you are repeating is funny or
        vulgar. If they seem unusually reserved, what you
        are saying may be taboo to you.

1.3   Eliciting Names

1.3a   Plan to learn the names of the people in one house-
        hold each day. It may help to put the names for each
        household on a separate 3 x 5 card and pin it to the
        wall for that day. The head man's household would be
        a wise starting place. If you have learnt the Basic
        Expressions, use them to discover people's names and
        to make friends. At the same time, check that your
        questions are suitable.

        If you do not know the Basic Expressions, you may
        elicit names by first pointing to yourself and saying
        your name. Then point to the next person. If you
        think that you have received what you want, try an-
        other person to check. If people grasp what you are
        doing, they will probably also give you the expres-
        sion for "What is your (or his) name?" or a similar
        expression that they would use to find out a person's
        name. If you get an expression try it out with sev-
        eral different individuals at different times to see

if it brings the response you desire. Write the
names or expressions in your data book, but only refer to it when you must. Train your memory from today.

1.3b   Problems With Names

Some people may have several names and change from
one to another. Do not be surprised if a different
name is given later. As you elicit names be sensitive to the reaction of the people especially if
there is any hesitation to reply. Beware of asking a
person his own name directly. In some cultures it is
considered either impolite or dangerous to say one's
own name, so you are less likely to cause embarrassment if you ask someone else to give you the name of
the person you want to know. You may, however, find
people are hesitant to give the name of anybody else
within the village, for fear of sorcery. Also there
may be some taboo relationships in which a person may
not be allowed to say another's name and will give you
the appropriate kinship term instead. Be careful to
respect people's reticence in these matters.

1.3c   Kinship Terms Instead of Names

In some areas it is customary to use kinship terms
rather than a personal name to refer to an individual.
You may only learn whether this is true in your area
by listening to people as they call each other or by
observing whether people use your name or a kinship
term such as 'older brother' or 'younger sister'.
In some areas it is proper to use a personal name for
someone around your own age or younger, but improper
to use a personal name for someone older; in such a
situation a kinship term is usually acceptable. If
you find that kinship terms are preferred, see Unit
13 for help with kinship terms. Try to find the expression:

'What relative is he to you?'

Lingua franca: _____

Vernacular: _____

1.3d   If you have not yet learnt the following expressions,
        or have problems eliciting them monolingually, elicit
        them from a good speaker of the lingua franca, and

from now on listen to see if people use them.

'What is his name?'

Lingua franca: _____

Vernacular: _____

Date used: _____   Date Overheard: _____

'Say his name.

Lingua franca: _____

Vernacular: _____

Date used: _____   Date Overheard: _____

'Who is that?'

Lingua franca: _____

Vernacular: _____

Date used: _____   Date Overheard: _____

1.4   Describing the Language Group

Take a folder and label it "Anthropology" for filing
your observations on the culture of the community
where you live. Always date your notes. On the basis
of your reading, your observations in the village, and
your contact with other areas of the country, write
down your general impressions of the people.

1.5   Testing 'What is his name?'

Beware that in eliciting through another language you
may get a literal translation and not an idiomatic
expression. Elicited material is suspect until it is
checked with several others in the village. Use the
expressions you discovered in 1.3 and watch people's
reactions. Also listen for corrections they make.
The final test is to hear the phrase said by one villager to another in a natural situation. Be particularly alert as visitors from another village of the
same language come to your village. They will probably ask one of your neighbors what your name is, and
you can check in this way both the form of the expression used, and which, if either, of the above

expressions is more commonly used. The expression
may have two forms for inquiring about a man and about
a woman.

1.6   <u>Practicing Names</u>

Later record the names and expressions on tape.
Have one of the people who speaks clearly do this.
Keep a separate tape for names and review them as
often as you need to do so. When recording the expressions, use the procedure recommended for recording the Basic Expressions (p. 16).

Read "Programed Review Cards" (pp. 318-321) and make
out a card for what you recorded today. Review the
recording as indicated on the card.

NOTES: The major emphasis in these first few units is
OBSERVING, LISTENING, AND MIMICRY. Of course, the
more time you spend in these activities, the greater
will be the benefit to you, up to your own satura-
tion point, which will vary from individual to individual. Later, the emphasis will shift to listening,
mimicking and conversing.

It is recommended that 2-4 hours be spent with the
people for each of these first units. At least half
of this time should be spent in active, concentrated
listening, mimicking and observing. DO NOT try to do
it all at one stretch. It will be more beneficial to
you (and easier on your village neighbors too) if you
spend only 10-20 minutes at any one time. Visit several of your neighbors during the course of the day.
Spend some time relaxing in between. Go from fireside to fireside in the evening.

If you find that for any reason you cannot even
spend two hours with the people in one day, then
stretch this unit over two days. If you can spend more
time than that recommended, you will receive the
greater benefit.

Date Unit 1 started: _____   Completed: _____

Hours spent on categories 2 and 6: _____

(Always include all time spent with your neighbors in
casual situations and all time spent practicing
drills, as well as the time spent on the items specifically mentioned in categories 2 and 6.)

Hours spent on all other categories: _____

Comments:

```
********************************************************
*                                                      *
*                                                      *
*                                                      *
*                                                      *
*                                                      *
*                                                      *
*                                                      *
*             A journey of a thousand miles            *
*             must begin with a single step.           *
*                                                      *
*                             --Lao Tzu                *
*                                                      *
*                                                      *
*                                                      *
*                                                      *
********************************************************
```

Unit 2

AIMS: (1) Be with people and practice what you know.
(2) Learn the names or kinship terms for people in another household.
(3) Learn greetings.

READ: (1) "The Missionary and the Evaluation of Culture" in Smalley pp. 258-261.
(2) "The Monolingual Approach to Studying Amuzgo" in this *Guide* pp. 272-276.

2.1 Observing Greetings

Spend time with people and go for a short walk. As people greet each other, watch carefully for any gestures or equivalents of the handshake. Notice farewells also.

2.2 Greetings in Conversation

2.2a If you have learnt any greetings, notice how people react when you use them. Do they use the same expressions? Some groups develop vernacular equivalents of 'Good morning' and 'Good afternoon' because of exposure to English, and use these forms mainly with outsiders. Note down any greetings you hear. Some common forms are:

(i) greeting someone by saying his name or a kin term
(ii) asking an obvious question like 'Are you there?', or making the statement 'You're there.' The reply might be 'Yes, I'm here. Have you come?'
(iii) asking 'Where are you going?'

Sometimes people meet without using any greeting formula. Do not force a greeting where it is not appropriate. In the same way, compare the way people say 'Goodbye' with the ways you have learnt.

2.2b As you move from house to house, greet people and use their names or the appropriate kin terms if you know them. Spend time with them, responding as you are able. People will probably want to teach you the

names of things. Mimic what they say several times at
normal speaking speed and write down some of the
names. It may be easier to mimic children than
adults, but beware of occasional wrong pronunciations
and grammar with children. As you leave a group of
people, try to use the appropriate farewell.

2.2c   If you are supervising the construction of your own
house, try to join in the work where appropriate, and
to use any vernacular expressions you can. You will
probably need to use the lingua franca fairly often,
but keep mimicking what the builders say, and you will
soon know the names of tools and parts of the house,
and be able to give simple instructions.

2.2d   Situations for Variety of Intonation

Today and from now on, be on the lookout for situations where you can hear varying kinds of intonational
situations, such as:

(1)   normal conversation
(2)   narrative - someone recounting an event or tell-
      ing a story
(3)   exhortation - someone telling others what they
      ought to do for the family, village, council,
      government, etc.
(4)   argument - husband and wife, parent and child,
      2 men, 2 women, etc.
(5)   anger - grieved adult venting his wrath in
      public
(6)   scolding - parent to child, older child to
      younger
(7)   excitement
(8)   ridicule - comments of someone to a child
      having a tantrum, etc.
(9)   "play talk" - adult talking to baby, children
      at play, men or women joking back and forth at
      work or play, etc.
(10) complaining
(11) calling out to someone
(12)
(13)
(14)
(15)

Tape-record any of these as opportunity arises. Write
the tape reference numbers against the items in the
list above. The tapes will be valuable now for

listening and mimicry and useful later for analysis.
Be sure to record the date and the situation each
time you add to your tape. Try to keep the same
kinds of material on separate tapes (i.e. elicited
material, conversation, and drills.) If you have
several empty spools you can remove an unfinished
spool from the recorder without wasting time rewinding it and then finding the place again later.

2.3   Eliciting Names

Elicit names or kinship terms for another household, if this is acceptable.

2.4a   Describing Greetings

Write a brief description of the greetings and farewells, and any gestures that are used with them.

2.4b   Phonetic Symbols

If you have forgotten any phonetic symbols, you will
want to review Pike's *Phonemics* p. 5 for the vocoid
chart and p. 7 for the contoid chart. Note the suggestions on p. 6 for further modifications of symbols
if needed. If you find you need to modify a symbol,
or make up a new symbol, try to be as consistent as
you can within the phonetic framework of your language, and write a verbal description of the symbols
so used. Remember to indicate pitch contours as you
write phonetically, and to mark stress wherever you
hear it. Try to be consistently neat in your phonetic writing and keep your pencil sharpened.

2.4c   Tape File

Devise an adequate tape file system so that in the
future you will be able to refer quickly to tapes for
practice in listening, mimicking and drilling. Three-
inch tapes are recommended as they are less cumbersome and with them it is easier to find material you
want quickly. Write the date and contents of each
tape both on the tape and on or in the tape box, and
number each tape (and its box) serially.

You will frequently wish to include in your notes a
reference to where a particular utterance or the start
of a particular text or drill is to be found in
your collection of tapes. A suitable reference could
take the form of a number-letter-number combination,

e.g. 5A-15. The first number, 5, identifies the particular tape (reel or cassette) as number 5 in your
collection. The letter, A, indicates the first side
of the tape (B for the second side). And the second
number, 15, indicates how far through the tape you
have to go to find the particular utterance. For
cassettes, this could be that number on the scale
(moulded on the viewing window) which measures the
amount of tape on the right-hand spindle. For reels,
it could be the thickness of tape wound on the take-
up spool as measured in millimeters. Or if your recorder has a counter on it, this number could be the
reading of the counter at that point on the tape
where the particular utterance is found.

2.6   Learning Names and Greetings

Tape-record the names you elicited today (as you did
for 1.6). Review the names recorded for Unit 1.

Record the greetings by creating appropriate social
situations or by obtaining the help of someone who is
bilingual. Mimic the recording and make a review
card for it.

Date Unit 2 started: _____

Hours spent on categories 2 and 6:   _____

Hours spent on all other categories: _____

Comments:

Unit 3

AIMS: (1) Record and mimic a text.
          (2) Learn 'What is this?' 'This is . . .'
          (3) Learn another household of names or kinship terms.

READ: (1) "Proximity or Neighborliness" in Smalley pp. 302-304.
          (2) "Learning Candoshi Monolingually" in this *Guide* pp. 277-280.

3.1a Observing Dwellings

Make preliminary observations on dwellings using these questions as a guide: What types of dwellings are built? Are there different functions for different types? Who lives in them or otherwise uses them? Does any category of people never approach or enter certain buildings? How do they compare with your own village house? What etiquette, invitation, or other formalities are used when a person enters someone else's house?

3.1b Pointing

How do your neighbors point things out? Do they point with a finger, use a hand or arm gesture, or do something else? Many peoples point with the chin, with a protruding lower lip, or even simply by a glance. As you have opportunity, observe how your neighbors point things out to one another, and how they teach their children what to do and what not to do about pointing things out. Do the older people do something different from younger ones? Are some young people picking up the Western way of pointing with a finger? How is this received by the older generation? Try to train yourself and your children to change your habits to conform to what is acceptable in their culture.

3.2 Conversation

3.2a Visit several of your neighbors for some face-to-face "conversation", mimicry practice, listening and observing. Respond to their greetings.

3.2b   If possible try to record a short stretch of conver-
        sation or narrative no longer than 2-3 minutes. Try
        to record when only one person, or one at a time, is
        speaking. Do not record if there is a lot of laugh-
        ing or other confusion, as this will be nearly impos-
        sible to use later.

3.2c   Tracking

        If you do not have access to a tape recorder or have
        extreme difficulty in obtaining suitable recordings,
        observe a conversation from a distance--close enough
        so you can hear, but far enough away to be as unob-
        trusive as possible. In your house is ideal if there
        are people standing around outside the house chatting.
        Try to track one of the speakers quietly or silently
        to yourself whenever he speaks. That is, mimic every-
        thing he says instantaneously so that you are never
        more than one or two syllables behind him at any time.
        Do this a minimum of 3 or 4 times during the course of
        the day.

        NOTE: It is harder to repeat vowels and consonants
        accurately when you are unable to see the speaker's
        mouth. So concentrate mainly on the rhythm and pitch
        patterns as you track, approximating the consonant
        and vowel sounds as well as you can without losing
        speed.

3.3   Eliciting 'What is this?'

3.3a   If you do not yet know how to ask 'What is this?',
        try to elicit this question now. This may be done mono-
        lingually by presenting someone with a hidden object
        (inside a container) or a thoroughly unfamiliar ob-
        ject. If you are forced to work bilingually have the
        language helper ask another person one of the follow-
        ing questions, and let the person reply, all in the
        lingua franca. Then have both people repeat the verb-
        al exchange in the vernacular. (This procedure should
        avoid the problem of a helper replying to your ques-
        tion rather than translating it!!)

'What is this?'

Lingua franca: _____

Vernacular: _____

Date used: _____   Date overheard: _____

'What do you call this?'
Lingua franca: _____

Vernacular: _____

Date used: _____   Date overheard: _____

3.3b   Once you have obtained either of these questions in
        the vernacular, use it with people and note the re-
        sponses. You should expect to get replies such as:
        'It is ...' or 'This is...', 'That is...', 'We call
        it...', 'We call this...', 'We call that...'. Use
        the same question for asking about plural objects and
        persons in the hope that you will be given the cor-
        rect plural form of the question. Also, if you
        point to two different objects, or a group of two or
        three people you may receive replies with an 'and' in
        them e.g. 'Those are a banana and a pineapple.'

        NOTE: People may react more favorably to the ques-
        tion 'What do you call this?' than to 'What is this?'
        They may not answer the question 'What is this?' be-
        cause they think that you are speaking foolishly
        since everyone knows what it is.

3.3c   Eliciting Names of Things

        Using the vernacular phrase 'What is this?' or 'What
        do you call this?' elicit concrete nouns. Put these
        in a special section of your data book labeled Things
        (nouns). (Also allot sections of your data book for
        Events (verbs), Abstracts (adjectives and adverbs),
        and Relationals (conjunctions, prepositions, etc.).)
        Practice these concrete nouns in your next conversa-
        tion, trying not to refer to your data book.

3.3d   Obtain the names or kinship terms of the people in
        one more house, if this acceptable. By now you may
        have learnt the names of all the people in 3 houses.

3.4   Describing Intonation

Diagram or describe at least two intonational contours that you have heard thus far in your visiting and in the text tape recorded in 3.2b. Indicate where you feel they are used (beginning, middle or end of "sentences") and what you suspect they might mean (statement, question, anger, command, etc.).

3.6a   Practicing 'What is this?'

Tape-record a question-and-answer drill like the following:

Vernacular:	SILENCE	English:	SILENCE	Vernacular:	SILENCE
What is this?		house		It is a house.	
What is this?		dog		It is a dog.	
....		.....		....	
What do you call this?		house		We call it "house".	
What do you call this?		dog		We call it "dog".	
....		.....		....	

The easiest way would be to work with two bilingual people, with one asking the questions and the other answering them. Straight after the question, record a silence long enough to mimic the question, say the English name of the object then record some silence, hold down the pause button and say the lingua franca version then record the answer to the question from your other helper. Leave another silence before allowing the questioner to speak again.

If there are no bilingual people available, try to record the drill by giving your helpers cues: point to the objects or say the vernacular expressions yourself. Hold down the pause button while you are speaking in the vernacular. You should be able to make a useful recording after several attempts.

To use this drill, play the tape through and mimic the question in the first silence, try to answer the question in the second silence, and then mimic the recorded answer during the third silence. Tape-recorded stimulus-response drills such as this should always be practiced in the presence of people who will correct your mistakes. Make out a review card for the drill.

3.6b   Mimicking a Text

In your own house, preferably through earphones so as
not to attract the attention of villagers, go through
the tape at least 8 times as follows:

Step 1:   twice, listen only.
Step 2:   twice, listen to a short stretch, stop the
          recorder and try to mimic that much, play
          the stretch back to listen, mimic again. Go
          on to the next stretch in the same way. Be
          sure you mimic at the same speed as the tape,
          even if you do not get it completely accurate.
          You may want to do this exercise several
          times rather than just twice.
Step 3:   twice, listen to a short stretch, mimic, go
          on to the next stretch, mimic, and so on
          through the tape.
Step 4:   twice, try to track the entire portion while
          the tape runs through at normal speed without
          stopping.

3.6c   Using Tape Loops

When there are no people around to talk with, practice
listening to and mimicking difficult expressions, using tape loops. (See pages 415-416 for instructions
on making tape loops for reel-to-reel recorders.)

3.6d   Names and Greetings

Tape-record the names elicited today and make out a
review card. Review the names and greetings recorded
earlier, as indicated by your stack of review cards.

Date Unit 3 started: _____ Completed: _____

Hours spent on categories 2 and 6: _____

Hours spent on all other categories: _____

Comments:

46

Unit 4

AIMS: (1) Investigate tools.
(2) Learn 'What is that?' 'That is...'
(3) Investigate simple phrase and clause structure.

READ: (1) "Shocks and Surprises" in Nida, *Customs and Cultures* pp. 1-23.
(2) "Learning Xavante Monolingually in this *Guide* pp. 281-284.

4.1 Observing Tools

Make preliminary observations of various kinds of tools. Tools are used in many kinds of activities such as gardening, food preparation, eating, timber-getting, wood-working, weaving and sewing, house-building, hunting and fishing, sorcery, warfare, playing and music. Review the drill on 'What is this?' prepared in 3.6a and use this question to elicit the names of all the tools you see. Practice these names in equational clauses such as 'This is a digging-stick.'

Who uses the tools you have observed? Are some used only by women? By men? What are they used for? Are they easy to use? Try them, then have the owners show you the correct way of using them. Mimic their verbal instructions. These observations can lead you into many useful and interesting areas of inquiry in future. What you can't observe or elicit in the vernacular, leave to a later date.

4.2 Conversation

Practice mimicking what people say at proper speed, concentrating on rhythm and intonation as in 1.2b. Spend at least 30 minutes on this in stretches of 5 minutes or less. You may find that you are able to pick up a few more consonants and vowels more easily by now. Do not worry if you cannot. Do not sacrifice speed and good rhythm for pronunciation attempts.

NOTE: Do not repeat any utterance more than three times in succession, as the value of repetition decreases after this.

4.3 Eliciting 'What is that?'

Try to elicit expressions for 'What is that?' and 'That is a ...'. This may be done by pointing in the culturally appropriate way to things at a distance and asking 'What is this?' Hopefully the people will correct 'this' to 'that'. Alternatively, use the situational method of eliciting described in 3.3a and place the hidden object at a distance from yourself and the language helper. Try again to obtain the plural form of the question, and some replies that use the morpheme for 'and' to join two nouns together (as in 3.3b).

4.4a Identifying Morphemes

If there are any morphemes for which you can make a tentative guess at the meaning, write notes about them. Then try to construct a sentence or utterance containing each one, and see how people react.

4.4b Describing Equative Clauses

Study the expressions you have collected and select out those which seem to be equative clauses such as 'What is his name?' 'What is it/this/that?' 'His name is ...' 'It/this/that is ...' 'They are a ... and a ...' Write a tentative description of any patterns you can find in them and give examples to illustrate what you write.

4.5 Constructing Equative Clauses

Test your description of equative clauses in 4.4b by saying some of them with different nouns substituted, e.g. "It is a house. It is a dog." Check your work with several different people.

4.6a Practicing Equative Clauses

When there are some people around, get your partner to point (in the customary way) at various things and ask you in the vernacular "What is this?" You should give the proper response. If you make a mistake in responding and one of the bystanders corrects you, mimic him immediately to help fix the correct response in your mind. Perhaps someone might even enjoy taking over from your partner and continue asking this kind of question. If so, after he has asked you a few questions and helped you with your responses, you

could then change roles and begin asking him a few
questions and mimicking his responses.

Whenever someone shows an interest in helping you with
such language practice, put aside for a while the
other activities you had planned and cooperate with
him as enthusiastically as you can. In so doing you
will improve your grasp of what is practiced together,
you will probably learn something new, and you will
encourage him to help you again in the future.

4.6b   Tracking

Track the tape you made in 3.2b silently at least
four times. If you find it difficult the first time,
refer to 3.6b and do Step 2 or Step 3 a few times before trying Step 4 again. If you do not have a tape
recorder, try tracking the speech of at least five
people.

4.6c   Learning Useful Expressions

Tape-record and learn more useful expressions as you
discover them. Use the procedure you followed when
recording the Basic Expressions (p. 16), or follow
that used in 3.6a.

Date Unit 4 started: _____ Completed: _____

Hours spent on categories 2 and 6: _____

Hours spent on all other categories: _____

Comments:

Unit 5

AIM: Review

READ: "Language Learning Without Tears" in this *Guide*
pp. 322-326.

5.1 Mapping Your Village

Draw a rough map of your village or neighborhood
with the location of each house you have visited.
Put the names of the householders on the map.

5.2 Conversation

Read again the suggestions for listening and mimicking while visiting, given in category 2 of Units 1 to
4. Visit several neighbors and greet them appropriately. Practice the expressions you have learnt.
Join in any conversation you can, and listen and
mimic at other times. Visit a new household and
make friends.

5.4 Filing Cultural Observations

5.4a Go back through the notes you have made in your anthropology file so far. Have you observed anything
which you have not yet written down? If so, write
it now.

5.4b Read "Making and Keeping Anthropological Field Notes"
in Smalley pp. 361-368, and "Classification for Cultural Observations" on the last page of the Appendix.
Divide your anthropology file by topics, and as you
file new notes, refer to the Classification for
help.

5.4c Starting the Dictionary File

Your Dictionary File may be organized on plain filing
cards, punch cards, or loose-leaf paper (see pp. 427-
451). Whatever method you use, be sure to leave
enough space above each word to add a phonemic transcription later. The dictionary file has two sec-
tions--Vernacular-English and English-Vernacular.
The latter could quite conveniently consist of the
pre-printed loose-leaf *English-Vernacular Word List*
mentioned in the equipment list (p. 17).

5.4d   The Topical File

Use a loose-leaf book (or part of one) as a Topical
File, labeling the top-right corner of each page with
a topic. List words and expressions by topic, adding
new topics as necessary, and keeping the pages in alphabetical order. The Topical File gives you another
way of finding expressions. The following topics are
suggested to start with: bird species, carrying
terms, causative expressions, cooking terms, emotions,
exclamations, gardening terms, "if" sentences, kinship terms, metaphors, questions.

NOTE: You and your partner should both write the
words you discover into the same Dictionary and
Topical Files.

5.6   Review Recordings

5.6a   Review the recording made in 3.2b using the procedure outlined in 3.6b.

5.6b   Check your stack of review cards and review any
drills that are due. Catch up if necessary. If
you find this system unsuitable, read the article
in the Appendix again and try to improve the system.

5.6c   Record Useful Expressions

Look through your data book for any expressions which
will be useful in conversation, and have someone record them, along with suitable responses if possible.
Read 3.6a again for help if you need to. Make out a
review card for this recording, or else try out your
improved review system.

5.6d   NOTE: Some people have found it helpful to write
expressions on small cards or slips of paper for
handy reference during moments which would otherwise
be wasted. Others have found a small notebook arranged into appropriate topics or categories to be
very useful in this way. Especially difficult or
important items could be put on cards and pinned to
the wall in prominent places. For instance, on the
wall near the door of your house you could keep a
list of expressions used in buying food.

Date Unit 5 started: _____ Completed: _____

Hours spent on categories 2 and 6: _____

Hours spent on all other categories: _____

Comments:

```
*****************************************************************
*                                                               *
*                                                               *
*                                                               *
*                                                               *
*                                                               *
*                                                               *
*        Each new venture is a new beginning,                   *
*        a raid on the inarticulate.                            *
*                              --T.S. Eliot                     *
*                                                               *
*                                                               *
*                                                               *
*                                                               *
*****************************************************************
```

Unit 6

AIMS: (1) Record and mimic another text.
      (2) Obtain some verb forms.

READ: "Human Factors in Field Work" in Samarin pp. 7-19.

6.1   Village Routine and Leisure Times

6.1a   Watch the people as they leave the village in the
       morning and as they return in the afternoon and note
       what they are carrying. Who carries bags and by
       what method? Who carries babies and young children?
       Who brings the water and firewood? Who carries the
       garden produce? At what time of day do people tend
       to have leisure and how do they spend their leisure
       time? This time of day is probably a good one for
       visiting and conversation.

6.1b   NOTE: Don't feel bound by the sequence the *Guide* fol-
       lows. When an unusual event takes place, look up the
       index for help in recording observations about it.

6.2a   Record and Mimic a Text

       Record on tape another 2-3 minute stretch of speech,
       preferably of a different kind from that which you
       recorded in 3.2b. Remain at the particular activ-
       ity at which you made the recording for some time,
       observing, listening and mimicking. When you return
       to your house listen to, mimic, and track the tape,
       following Steps 1-4 as outlined in 3.6b. Do Step 4
       another 3 times after an interval of at least an
       hour.

6.2b   If you do not have a tape recorder, try tracking a
       different kind of intonational situation if you can
       do so unobtrusively; otherwise track the same sort,
       or mimic as opportunity arises. Spend a minimum of
       30 minutes in short stretches of 5 minutes or less
       either in tracking or in mimicry.

6.2c   Let People Teach You

       As you are with people be on the look-out for any-
       thing they may try to teach you. Some people will
       act out verbs and then tell you what you should

say. Encourage them by mimicking what they are teaching you and trying to use it again. Write down any
expressions you feel will be useful.

6.3   Eliciting Verbs

6.3a   If you know the Basic Expression 'What are you doing?',
        use it to elicit some verbs. If you don't know it,
        join in some activity using one of the tools you
        learnt to use in 4.1 and ask "What is this?" If
        your friend tells you the name of the tool, say "Yes,
        this is a knife. What is this?" as you cut with it.
        Hopefully his response will be "You are cutting." or
        "Say 'What am I doing?'" Mimic the response and
        write it down. Use it again and try to work out what
        it means. If you are saying "You are cutting" some-
        one may correct you with "Say 'I am cutting.'"
        Mimic the correction twice and write it down. Try
        with different tools and different activities until
        you are fairly sure you have some verbs.

6.3b   Among the verbs which you elicit, try to obtain 'he
        said'. Have your partner say a well known noun such
        as 'dog' and see if this will elicit from someone,
        "He said, 'dog'." You could also use 'What did he
        say?' if you know it.

        If you have difficulty getting people to give a verbal
        response to your mimicking, act out a new situation
        trying to use a verbal expression you have already
        obtained in this obviously wrong context (e.g. Say,
        "I am cutting" whilst digging). Immediately mimic
        any correction that they give you since it may con-
        tain the verb you are seeking. Repeat what you learn
        in your next conversation with someone, and elicit
        two or three more verbs.

6.4a   Identifying Morphemes

        Go through your data book when there is no one
        around to talk to, and try to identify the meanings
        of words and parts of words, especially verb stems.

6.4b   Phrase and Clause Structure

        Study phrases which seem to have a noun and an ad-
        jective. Which comes first? Look at clauses which
        seem to have a subject, predicate (verb) and object.
        What order are they in? File a tentative note in

your grammar folder, with examples. From now on,
when you want to make up a sentence in conversation,
try to use this word order rather than that of your
own mother tongue.

6.4c   Rhythm System

What type of rhythm system does your language seem to
employ? Syllable-timed, stress-timed or some other
system? (Read Pike p. 13.)

6.6a   Revising Drills

If you have noticed that any of the expressions you
have learnt or drills you have made are not suitable,
make new recordings now.

6.6b   Practicing Names

Record any names you have elicited or overheard
recently and add this recording to your review system.
Learn to recognize people by name. Call them by name
or kin term whenever you see them if this is common
or acceptable. If not, say their names to yourself
when you see them. Pay particular attention to pitch,
rhythm and stress as you mimic and use names. People
like to have their names pronounced correctly!

6.6c   Learn Three Useful Expressions

Turn to "Useful Expressions" (pp. 460-464) and choose
three which you have not previously recorded and
which you believe will be immediately useful in conversing. Elicit, tape-record, mimic, practice, memorize, and use them.

Date Unit 6 started: _____ Completed: _____

Hours spent on categories 2 and 6: _____

(Always include all time spent with your neighbors in
casual situations and all time spent practicing drills,
as well as the time spent on the items specifically
mentioned in categories 2 and 6.)

Hours spent on all other categories: _____

Comments:

Unit 7

AIMS: (1) Try out a variety of conversation starters.
       (2) Begin investigating person morphemes.

READ: "Principles of Language Learning" in Nida, *Learning
       a Foreign Language* pp. 13-26.

NOTE: This unit is a particularly full one, since it intro-
       duces the whole matter of pronouns and person affixes.
       Like some other long units, it may take several days
       to complete.

7.1   Observing More on Dwellings and Tools

       As you visit people make further observations partic-
       ularly regarding dwellings or tools. Can you add any
       more items to the list of tools obtained in 4.1?

7.2a   Listening-Mimicking-Conversing

       As you visit people, use the opportunity to mimic,
       track, and listen actively to conversation between
       villagers. Throughout the initial period of language
       learning, not just during the first few lessons, THE
       VALUE OF LISTENING, MIMICKING AND CONVERSING CANNOT
       BE OVEREMPHASIZED. It is important to spend more
       time with people than at your desk.

7.2b   Conversation Starters

       When you go to visit, take with you something that
       might be a point of contact and/or topic of conversa-
       tion. Try different things: your kitten, some knit-
       ting, something you are making or fixing, a magazine,
       or photos of your own relatives. Mimic and write
       down questions that people ask.

7.2c   Listen for Pronouns

       While you are with people, be alert for pronouns. If
       someone doesn't respond to a remark addressed to him,
       the speaker may say "You!" Mimic it and write it
       down.

7.3a   Eliciting Person Morphemes

       In many languages the subject of an action is

obligatorily indicated by a subject-person marker attached to the verb. The occurrence of a free subject
(either a pronoun or noun phrase) in the utterance in
addition is usually optional. In other languages,
there are no such markers on the verb and the occurrence of a free subject in an utterance is often obligatory. Read the paragraph on eliciting pronouns on
page 354.

7.3b   Eliciting Singular Subject-person Forms Monolingually

By now you will have obtained one or more verbs (in
6.3). Choose one such expression and try to build on
it, obtaining other forms as follows:

If you know you have a second or third person form,
try to elicit first person by doing the action yourself and saying the expression, hoping to be corrected.

Response: _____

To elicit second person, get someone to do the action
and say the expression, expecting him to correct you.

Response: _____

To elicit third person, call a villager's attention to
someone else in the village who is doing the action
(or get your partner to do it) and say the expression,
hoping to be corrected.

Response: _____

NOTE: Using a form you know to be good language but
in the wrong context is often an excellent tool for
getting the right form for that context. People tend
to appreciate your attempts to speak their language
even when you speak it wrongly, and if you show your
appreciation for any and all corrections, they will
continue to correct you in this way.

7.3c   Eliciting Singular Person Morphemes Bilingually

If all attempts at monolingual eliciting fail, elicit
the vernacular free pronouns through the lingua franca and then use these vernacular pronouns in monolingual eliciting as described below. Elicit any of the

following pronouns which you do not already have:

English	Lingua Franca	Vernacular
'I'	_____	_____
'you'	_____	_____
'he'	_____	_____
'she'	_____	_____
'it'	_____	_____

Then if you know you have an expression in third person, say to someone the third person vernacular pronoun and then the expression. Carefully note his response. He may correct your word order, putting the pronoun in a more natural place.

Response: _____

To elicit first person, repeat the expression, substituting the first person pronoun for the third person pronoun, expecting your friend to correct you by giving you the correct first person form of the verb.

Response: _____

Do the same for second person.

Response: _____

NOTE: Make it a rule in eliciting always to USE AS MUCH VERNACULAR AS YOU CAN. This may seem slower and less efficient at first than eliciting everything through the lingua franca, but remember that the little extra time you take to elicit in this way is giving you excellent practice in using the language, and is showing people that you really want to learn to talk, not just put their language on paper.

If people do not seem to get the idea of correcting you, find someone who is bilingual and have him tell people your request that they correct you. Also have him translate for you into the vernacular:

'If I don't speak correctly please correct me.'

Lingua Franca: _____

Vernacular: _____

Once you have obtained the vernacular for this request, use it instead of the lingua franca.

7.3d   Eliciting Plural Person Morphemes Monolingually

Try to elicit in at least one of the above ways the
first, second and third person singular forms for the
verbs 'come' and 'go'. You may wish to use the
second method as a check on the first one. Be sure
to check for masculine vs. feminine differences in
each person as well, and for human vs. non-human or
animate vs. inanimate in the third person.

Then go on to elicit plural subject pronouns with
these verbs, by similar methods. Try calling your
helper's attention to two or more people in the village who are going or coming and say the third person
singular forms, encouraging him to correct you. Try
to elicit first and second person dual and plural
forms by acting them out. Be aware of a possible in-
clusive/exclusive distinction. To test this for 'we
two', act out going or coming first with your helper,
then with your partner or someone else, excluding
your helper, to see if the forms are the same or different. Do the same with trial and plural.

Check material elicited from one person with others
in the village by using the expressions in appropriate situations and noting the responses.

7.3e   Eliciting Plural Person Morphemes Bilingually

If all attempts at monolingual elicitation over a
period of a week fail to elicit these promouns, then
use the lingua franca to elicit them. First read the
section on pronouns in your grammar of the lingua
franca.

English	Lingua Franca	Vernacular
'we two (exclusive)'	_____	_____
'we two (inclusive)'	_____	_____
'you two'	_____	_____
'they two'	_____	_____
'we three (exclusive)'	_____	_____
'we three (inclusive)'	_____	_____
'you three'	_____	_____
'they three'	_____	_____
'we (plural exclusive)'	_____	_____
'we (plural inclusive)'	_____	_____
'you (plural)'	_____	_____
'they (plural)'	_____	_____

You may have inclusive vs. exclusive in other than
first persons. You may also have a fourth person
which has various functions, one of which is to
distinguish between two different people being referred to in a discussion. In languages where there are
noun classes, or a system of gender agreement, there
may be separate third person pronouns corresponding
to each class. You may not have all of the above
distinctions in your language. You may have more persons distinguished in verbal affixes than in free pronouns, or vice versa. Be alert to these and other
possibilities.

If you feel you are hitting a blank wall with one approach, drop it and try another. If you feel you are
making little or no headway with personal pronouns,
move on to another unit and come back to them later.

NOTE: A person morpheme which, either alone or together with a case-marking affix, constitutes a
word is called a "pronoun". In the instance of a
person morpheme which is affixed to a verb stem to

indicate the subject, object, or other participant in
the action or which is affixed to a noun to indicate
the possessor, we have followed Elson and Pickett
(p. 21) and called it a "person affix" or "person
marker" rather than a "pronoun" or "pronominal affix".

7.4a   Describing Person Morphemes

Study carefully the data elicited in 7.3 and compare
it with previous data. Isolate and confirm the subject-person morphemes. Write a short note describing
whether pronouns, verbal affixes, or both are used
for indicating the subject.

7.4b   When you are confident of any person morphemes, put
them on the person morpheme charts at the end of this
unit. Use one chart for what you suspect are free
forms (pronouns) and the other for what you think are
affixes. Eventually you may need several more charts.
Also you may have to modify the charts to suit the
language. Be sure to make the most of the help you
can get from descriptions of other closely related
languages.

7.5   Using Person Morphemes

Take a verb you have not worked with in this unit and
construct the forms with singular subject, in first,
second and third person, using pronouns or person affixes as required. Repeat with two other verbs.
Check these forms with several different people as
follows. Read a first person form as you act it out,
then read a second person form to your partner while
he is acting it out. Turn to your friend for correction. For a third person form, read it to your
friend while your partner is acting it out. If you
know how to ask "Is that right?", then do so. Write
down any corrections your friend gives you.

7.6   Learning Person Morphemes

7.6a   Tape-record a drill like the following, all in the
first person singular. Use four or five of the verbs
you found in 7.5 that behave the same way.

English	SILENCE	Vernacular	SILENCE	Vernacular	SILENCE
I am weeding		*Sa naakul*		*Sa naakul*	
I am drinking		*Sa naanum*		*Sa naanum*	
. . . .		. . . .		. . . .	

Now make a similar drill in the second person, using
the same verbs, and then one in the third person. Try
to say the expression in the first silence, then mimic
the first vernacular expression.

7.6b   Person Morpheme Transform Practice

Record a drill to give you practice in transforming
simple sentences with a first person subject into
sentences with a second person subject. To record the
drill have your helper give a first-person sentence in
the vernacular, then after a silence he or another
helper gives the second person form with the same
verb, leaves a silence, then repeats the second person form. Use the same verbs as in 7.6a.

Vernacular for 'I...'	SILENCE	Vernacular for 'You...'	SILENCE	Vernacular for 'You...'	SILENCE
Sa naakul		*O nakul*		*O nakul*	
Sa naanum		*O nanum*		*O nanum*	
. . . .		. . . .		. . . .	

Make a review card for these recordings.

7.6c   Practice with the recording, then use the transform
with some other people. Ask someone what he is doing,
then transform his answer into the second person form
and say it, then ask "Is that right?" if you can. Be
alert for any corrections. If your friend repeats
the first person form, transform it and try it again.
Having heard and said the verb stem twice, you are
more likely to remember it. Write it in your data
book and try it with some other people.

Free Pronoun Chart

		Singular	Dual	Trial	Plural
1st Person Masculine Exclusive	(subj.)				
	(obj.)				
	(poss.)				
1st Person Masculine Inclusive	(subj.)	///////			
	(obj.)	///////			
	(poss.)	///////			
1st Person Feminine Exclusive	(subj.)				
	(obj.)				
	(poss.)				
1st Person Feminine Inclusive	(subj.)	///////			
	(obj.)	///////			
	(poss.)	///////			
2nd Person Masculine	(subj.)				
	(obj.)				
	(poss.)				
2nd Person Feminine	(subj.)				
	(obj.)				
	(poss.)				
3rd Person Masculine	(subj.)				
	(obj.)				
	(poss.)				
3rd Person Feminine	(subj.)				
	(obj.)				
	(poss.)				
3rd Person Neuter	(subj.)				
	(obj.)				
	(poss.)				

		Singular	Dual	Trial	Plural
1st Person Masculine Exclusive	(subj.)				
	(obj.)				
	(poss.)				
1st Person Masculine Inclusive	(subj.)	////////			
	(obj.)	////////			
	(poss.)	////////			
1st Person Feminine Exclusive	(subj.)				
	(obj.)				
	(poss.)				
1st Person Feminine Inclusive	(subj.)	////////			
	(obj.)	////////			
	(poss.)	////////			
2nd Person Masculine	(subj.)				
	(obj.)				
	(poss.)				
2nd Person Feminine	(subj.)				
	(obj.)				
	(poss.)				
3rd Person Masculine	(subj.)				
	(obj.)				
	(poss.)				
3rd Person Feminine	(subj.)				
	(obj.)				
	(poss.)				
3rd Person Neuter	(subj.)				
	(obj.)				
	(poss.)				

Date Unit 7 started: _____   Completed: _____

Hours spent on categories 2 and 6: _____

Hours spent on all other categories: _____

Comments:

```
******************************************************************
*                                                                *
*                                                                *
*                                                                *
*                                                                *
*                                                                *
*                                                                *
*                     If at first you don't                      *
*                     succeed, try again.                        *
*                                                                *
*                                                                *
*                                                                *
*                                                                *
*                                                                *
******************************************************************
```

Unit 8

AIMS: (1) Observe clothing.
(2) Practice using person morphemes.
(3) Investigate possessives.

READ: (1) "Learning by Listening" in Nida, *Learning a Foreign Language* pp. 27-38.
(2) "Person" in Elson and Pickett pp. 21-22.

8.1 Observing Clothing

Describe types of clothing worn by men, by women, by
children. Is some clothing made by the people? Some
bought for cash? Traded for? At what age do children begin to wear clothing? Different age for boys
and girls? Describe any processes that you have observed being used to make clothing. As you observe
and admire the things you see, be alert to the reactions of your neighbors so that you do not offend
them. In some cultures, enthusiastic admiration of
an object is an indication of the admirer's desire
for it, and the owner may feel obliged to offer to
give it away whether he wants to or not. If this
happens, the receiver of the gift should be aware
that he is then obliged to the giver to the extent of
the value the giver places on the gift. This is often the way friendships are cemented, by reciprocal
gifts and mutual obligations kept going over an extended period of time. You may save yourself much
frustration and misunderstanding if you are aware of
this. It may be helpful to adopt this practice yourself as you form close friendships with your
neighbors.

8.2a Person Morphemes in Conversation

First review the transform drill on person morphemes
that you made in 7.6b. Then as you visit people,
sometimes ask what someone is doing and transform his
reply into the second person as in 7.6c. If you know
the expression for what someone is doing, say to him
"You are ....." and notice his reply. It may be the
first person transform, or it may be a correction.
Mimic what he says.

8.2b   Notice Possessive Forms

Listen to the conversation as you are with people,
and if you notice any form which may contain a possessive morpheme, mimic it and write it down. Note
also the situation in which it was uttered. As you
ask the names of items of clothing in connection with
8.1, be alert for any possessive forms such as 'my
shirt'.

8.2c   Mimicking Intonation Patterns

When you cannot understand the general conversation,
track silently, paying special attention to the intonation pattern before each pause. You can also
mimic intonation patterns quietly in your house as
people are talking outside.

8.3   Eliciting Possessive Forms

Try to elicit possessive forms. Use any of the following suggestions you find helpful, supplemented by
innovations you think of as you work.

8.3a   Look through your non-elicited data and note possessive expressions you have written. Pick out one
or two for trying to build on. Body parts are often
useful, as they are easy to indicate, and in many
languages must be uttered with a possessive pronoun
or affix. In some languages, however, possessive
pronouns are not used with body parts--they say "I
head", not "my head". If you suspect that this is
true, try words like 'knife' or 'house'.

8.3b   If you have no possessive expressions in your data,
or if those you have will not lend themselves well to
easy further elicitation, try to elicit the expression for 'his (her) hand' by indicating your partner's
or someone else's nearby and asking "What is this?"

Response: _____

Then indicate your own hand and say the expression
given you above along with the first person singular
pronoun, expecting correction as to how to say "my
hand".

Response: _____

NOTE: SOME CONFUSION MAY ARISE IF A PERSON TELLS YOU
WHAT HE WOULD SAY (I.E., 'YOUR HAND') RATHER THAN
WHAT YOU SHOULD SAY (I.E., 'MY HAND') IN REFERRING TO
YOUR HAND. THIS CAN USUALLY BE CLEARED UP AS YOU RE-
PEAT EACH EXPRESSION, INDICATING THE CORRESPONDING
OBJECT AND ANTICIPATING CORRECTION IF YOU SAY THE
WRONG FORM OR WRONG PRONUNCIATION.

8.3c   Try the same procedure with two more body parts and
         two convenient objects. One of these may prove more
         suitable for further elicitation than the one you
         started with.

         Repeat the two expressions 'his hand' and 'my hand'
         (or substitutes), indicating the appropriate objects
         as you do, then indicate to someone his own hand and
         say one of the above expressions with the second per-
         son singular personal pronoun, expecting correction
         as to how you should say 'your hand'. However, he
         may say 'my hand'.

         Response: _____

         Indicate another person's and your own hands together
         and use the first person dual pronoun with the expres-
         sion for 'my hand', to be corrected for first person
         dual inclusive, if there is one.

         Response: _____

         Indicate your own and your partner's hands together
         and say the form given you for first dual, to check
         on a distinction between inclusive and exclusive
         forms.

         Response: _____

         Use this same technique to elicit the plural posses-
         sives. Choose another body part or easily referable
         object and repeat the entire process.

         Fill in the "vernacular" spaces below with what you
         have discovered above. Fill in any blanks using the
         lingua franca if necessary. You may not have all
         these forms in your language, or you may have more!

'my hand' (Lingua Franca: _____)

Vernacular: _____

'your (masc.) hand' (L.F. _____)

Vernacular: _____

'your (fem.) hand' (L.F. _____)

Vernacular: _____

'his hand' (L.F. _____)

Vernacular: _____

'our (dual exclusive) hands' (L.F. _____)

Vernacular: _____

'our (dual inclusive) hands' (L.F. _____)

Vernacular: _____

'your (dual) hands' (L.F. _____)

Vernacular: _____

'their (dual) hands' (L.F. _____)

Vernacular: _____

'our (plural exclusive) hands' (L.F. _____)

Vernacular: _____

'our (plural inclusive) hands' (L.F. _____)

Vernacular: _____

'your (plural) hands' (L.F. _____)

Vernacular: _____

'their (plural) hands'   (L.F. _____)

Vernacular: _____

8.3d   Check all the possessive forms obtained above with
       several other people.

8.4   Analyzing Possessives

8.4a   Study carefully the material obtained in 8.2b and 8.3.
       How is possession expressed in your language, in
       bound form, word, or phrase? (In some instances it
       may be several months before you can be sure which.)
       Is possession expressed in more than one way? In some
       languages the possessed noun takes a set of obliga-
       tory possessive-person affixes plus a noun or optional
       free pronoun to indicate the possessor. Others have
       a special set of possessive pronouns, with or without
       a possessive affix marker on the object possessed.
       Are there obligatory versus optional elements in
       possessive expressions in the language?

8.4b   Fill in as many possessive spaces as you can on the
       Free Pronoun Chart or the Person Affix Chart in
       Unit 7. Elicit other possessives to fill in the
       other relevant spaces.

8.4c   If possession is shown by a special set of free pro-
       nouns, compare each one with the corresponding subject
       pronoun and object pronoun on the pronoun chart of
       Unit 7. Can you identify some morpheme which the
       three forms have in common? (Read "Morpheme Identi-
       fication Procedures" in Elson and Pickett pp. 8-11.)

       Next, by comparing forms across the chart and also
       down the chart, can you identify any person, number,
       subject, object, or possessive morphemes?

8.4d   If possession is marked by an affix attached to pro-
       nouns and/or nouns, you may find that it will not only
       mark possession, but also indicate the person and num-
       ber of the possessor. If this is the case, use the
       person affix chart to sort out all the possibilities
       of persons marked within the affix or affix set.
       Within the possessive marker(s), can you isolate a
       special possessive morpheme or do these markers con-
       sist of portmanteau person/number/possessive morphemes
       which cannot profitably be further subdivided?

8.4e   Put into writing any generalizations you can make
about the possessive forms you have found. This may
not be the only system used to show possession in the
language. Be aware of and make notes about any alternate system(s). For example, the nouns may be divided
into classes, each of which has a somewhat different
system for indicating possession.

8.5   Testing Possessives

Review the tentative description of equative clauses
that you wrote in 4.4b. Are there any parts of it
that you can now state more accurately or clearly?
Construct some sentences like 'That is his house.'
and 'That is his dog.' Make up other sentences with
the same nouns, but use 'her', 'your' and 'my'
instead of 'his'. Try to make sentences that you
could use naturally in conversation. Check your work
with two or three people.

8.6   Practicing Possessives

Copy the singular possessive pronouns or affixes onto a 3 x 5 card and visit some of your neighbors during their leisure time. When someone is using a tool
of his, such as a knife, ask "What is that?" Mimic
his reply, then say "That is your knife." referring
to the card if you need to. Mimic and note down any
corrections. Turn to someone else and say "That is
his knife." Repeat this with several different
things belonging to different people, and with some
things of your own. Do the same with some body parts
if they are suitable, and with items of clothing.

Date Unit 8 started: _____ Completed: _____

Hours spent on categories 2 and 6: _____

Hours spent on all other categories: _____

Comments:

Unit 9

AIMS: (1) Observe foods.
(2) Continue investigation of possessives.
(3) More practice with possessives.

READ: "Language Learning in Relation to Focus" in this
Guide pp. 297-306.

9.1   Observing Foods

Make preliminary observations on as many of these
and other related topics as you can:

Types of food eaten, types produced, cooking and preparing foods, names of foods, times at which meals
are eaten, amount of the day's time spent in food production, preparation and consumption, how it tastes
to you, who eats where, certain foods for certain
people. Be discreet. Don't insist on being around
if people appear embarrassed. You may find it easier
to add some of this information later. Write up
observations and file.

NOTE: Although this particular topic ìs set in this
unit, any time you see anything new going on you
should observe it as closely as seems acceptable.
Make written notes afterwards and file them away for
when they will be needed later.

9.2   Conversation and Mimicry

9.2a   Visit some of your friends around the fire, and listen
actively for words and expressions you already know.
Join in the conversation whenever you can, using expressions and patterns you have discovered. Respond
as well as you can to everything addressed to you.
Mimic anything you are told to say. Learn to laugh
at your mistakes and try again. When you are not participating in the conversation, try to track one
speaker silently to yourself, or hum the rhythm and
intonation of his speech softly if it will not offend
people.

9.2b   When you recognize a new and interesting object word,
mimic it and try to use it in a number of different
sentences, such as 'This is a comb.', 'This is your

comb.' and 'That is his comb.' Mimic any corrections.
Write one of the sentences in your data book. Having
used the word in several different contexts, it will
be much easier to remember.

9.2c   Ask and mimic the names of foods you see being prepared as you make the observations suggested in 9.1.
If you notice any new ways of marking possession,
mimic them and note them for use in 9.4.

9.2d   <u>Difficulties with Mimicry</u>

You should be sensitive to the reactions of people
when you are attempting to mimic them. If you sense
that this habit offends them, there are 3 things you
can do.

(1)   Mimic only the few fairly close friends who
seem to understand your need to mimic as part
of the learning process and appear not to be
offended.

(2)   As soon as you have some idea of how to ask
this kind of question, put your mimicry into
the form "Did you say 'I will XYZ'?" (see
6.3b) or "You said 'I am going XYZ' and what
is that (=what does that mean)?" (See 4.3.)

(3)   Spend more time in silent tracking and in the
mimicking of tape recorded language when no
one is around.

9.3a   <u>Eliciting 'Whose?'</u>

Try to find the form for 'Whose is it?' or 'Whose is
this?' One possible way would be to indicate possession for 'who' as found in Unit 1 with the third person
singular possessive pronoun. Hopefully someone will
correct you. Check this form by holding up some item
belonging to the person to whom you are talking. If
the form is correct, you should get the reply you expect i.e., "That is my stringbag." or "It is mine."
or "It is my stringbag."

9.3b   <u>Eliciting Possessives</u>

Do 9.4a first. If you find alternative ways of showing possession, elicit all the forms of such alternative ways using suggestions given in 8.3. Check the
material with several other people.

9.4 Further Analysis of Possessives

9.4a Go through your non-elicited data gathered to date
and list all possessive expressions you have written.
Compare these with the data on possessives obtained
in Unit 8. Try to match morphemes and see where each
expression fits into the system as you know it. Do
any new or alternative ways of showing possession occur in these expressions? Are some nouns obligatorily possessed? Do they fall into particular categories such as body parts, kin terms, or others? Do
these show possession in the same way as other forms
do? If you find any new or alternative ways of showing possession, do 9.3b before proceeding further.

9.4b Do you need to modify your description of possession
in the light of any expanded possessive phrases which
occur in your data? If formulas help you, try to construct a simple tagmemic formula showing the obligatory elements for each type of possessive expression
you have found. (See Elson & Pickett pp. 68-69, 74-
75.) Then expand your formula with optional elements
of which you are aware at this time. Check your formulas against each expression. Is everything account-
ed for? Check the description you have written.
Have you included everything that occurs in the formulas in your verbal description? If not, include them
now. Also include statements as to any flexibility
of order you may have found in expanded possessive
phrases.

9.4c Filing

File all data that you have checked and confirmed.
Add person morphemes to the charts of Unit 7, add
words to both halves of the Dictionary File, and add
both words and expressions to the Topical File.

9.5 Testing Possessives

9.5a If you found any alternative ways of showing possession in today's material, choose another item from
your dictionary which can be used in that system and
construct all the forms of it.

9.5b If you did not find any new class of possessives, construct sentences using plural possessives.

9.5c   Construct sentences like 'Whose .... are those?' to go
         with the ones you made in a or b. Check your con-
         structions with several different people and note cor-
         rections and/or alternate constructions.

9.6   Practicing Possessives

         If you have trouble making a good recording, read 3.6a
         again.

9.6a   Practicing Alternate Systems

         If you found different sets of possessives, use the
         sentences you constructed in 9.5a and 9.5c which were
         acceptable, and make a drill as follows:

English	SILENCE	Vernacular	SILENCE	Vernacular	SILENCE
dog		Whose dog is that?		That is my dog.	
pig		Whose pig is that?		That is my pig.	
...		....		....	

         Use about 5 nouns, all of which take the same posses-
         sive marker.

         Make another drill using the third person possessive
         marker.

         Repeat this procedure with another set of possessives
         if there is one.

9.6b   Practicing Plural Possessives

         If you did not find a different set of possessives,
         use sentences you constructed in 9.5b and c to make a
         drill like the one in 9.6a, but using plural posses-
         sives, first with the first person, then with the
         third person.

9.6c   Make a review card for the recording. If your review
         of some drills represented in the stack of review
         cards is overdue, catch up by reviewing two days'
         drills each day.

9.6d   A Game With Possessives

         You should know most of the possessive pronoun forms
         now. Set up a game using the possessive pronouns
         and/or affixes plus a noun, e.g. 'my house', 'your
         house', 'your cat', 'your dog', 'his dog', etc. in

the sentence frame 'This/that is ...' Let your partner give you cues (he may use pictures or 'Whose?'
questions to show the object possessed and point to a
person to show the possessor) and you reply with the
complete sentence. Body parts are often convenient
nouns to use to drill possessives, i.e. 'my ear',
'your hand', 'his head', etc.

Make sure that some people who are good at correcting
you are present when you begin this game. Some of
them, especially older children, may enjoy joining in
to ask you the questions.

9.6e   Using Possessives

Copy 'whose?' questions and possessive markers onto a
3 x 5 card and go for a walk with some friends. Take
an exercise book with you, in which you can draw a
rough map. Use 'whose?' questions to find out who
owns or controls gardens, land, buildings and other
features in the wider neighborhood, and mark them on
your map. Refer to the card only if you need to.

When there is a social gathering and people have arrived by canoe, horse, bicycle or car, use 'whose?'
questions to find out who owns each one. Also try
'whose child is that?' and 'whose wife is that?' Do
not press these enquiries if people are reticent to
answer, or are not interested.

Date Unit 9 started: _____ Completed: _____

Hours spent on categories 2 and 6: _____

Hours spent on all other categories: _____

Comments:

Unit 10

AIMS: (1) Notice your neighbors' interests.
       (2) Discover 'What doing?' and 'What saying?' questions.
       (3) Analyze and practice verbs.

READ: "How to Learn a Language" in Pike pp. 228-231.

10.1 Observing People's Interests

Try to notice which topics of conversation are most interesting to your neighbors. Many ethnic groups are happy to talk at length about kin relationships, and know their family trees in much more detail than we Westerners do. Other peoples delight to tell traditional stories or to discuss the day's events or some items on the news broadcast. Other topics of interest are gardening, hunting, daily work, and trading with traditional artifacts. Try to decide on two or three topics to learn about, so you can make interesting conversation.

10.2a Join in a Common Activity

First review the person morpheme transform drill made in 7.6b and the 'Whose?' drill of 9.6. Then, go with a friend who is good at teaching you and help him with his work. Farming, fishing or clearing land would be suitable, but stalking game would not, as you want to talk together! On the way, ask who owns different things you see. If you know the Basic Expression 'What are you doing?', use it as you watch your friend work. Transform his answer into the second person as you mimic the verb stem. Use the expression 'I want to try it.' so you can start to help him with the work. Mimic his instructions, or transform them if you can.

If you do not know how to say 'What are you doing?', try using inappropriately some of the verb forms you found in 6.3a, in the hope that as well as correcting you, your friend will teach you to say "What are you doing?"

10.2b Listening for 'What did he do?'

When you and your friend return to the village listen
carefully to the conversation, and try to note down
any questions people ask him. Try to record the conversation on tape if you can do so unobtrusively.
One of the questions may be "What did he do?"

10.2c Gathering "Interesting" Vocabulary

Listen closely when people are discussing one of the
topics you chose in 10.1. Mimic and note expressions
and words that are used in discussing the topic. Ask
vernacular questions to find out what the terms and
expressions refer to. Develop an interest in these
topics and try to join in the conversation when you
can. PEOPLE WILL ENJOY TALKING WITH YOU IF YOU CAN
DISCUSS THINGS THAT INTEREST THEM.

10.3 Eliciting 'What?' Questions

Study the questions you wrote in 7.2b and 10.2b
and listen to the recording if you made one. If possible, ask a bilingual person to translate these vernacular questions back into the lingua franca to give
you a check on their meanings. Some of them may be
useful in eliciting other questions in 10.3a to 10.3d
below and should certainly be used.

10.3a Eliciting 'What are you doing?'

If you don't yet know how to say "What are you doing?",
try doing something new or strange, such as carving,
knitting, making or fixing something, in the hope that
someone will ask "What are you doing?" Have your partner ask someone "What did he do?" if you found it in
10.2b. Mimic any questions you hear and write them
down. Then try each one with other people to see if
any of them elicits reasonable responses such as "I'm
peeling taro." If these attempts fail, try to elicit
the question through the lingua franca.

'What are you doing?'   Date overheard: _____

Lingua Franca: _____

Vernacular: _____

10.3b   <u>'What is he doing?'</u>

When you have the question 'What are you doing?', use
it about a third person, using the third person morpheme instead of the second person (if you can identify it) to see if people accept this or correct it for
'What is <u>he</u> doing?' Test the question to see if it
elicits reasonable responses.

'What is he doing?'   Date overheard: _____

Lingua Franca: _____

Vernacular: _____

10.3c   <u>'What did he say?'</u>

If you know the Basic Expression 'What did you say?',
substitute the third person for the second person if
you can, and ask someone this question just after
someone else has spoken. Mimic and note any corrections.

If you don't know 'What did you say?' substitute
'he said' (found in 6.3b) for 'he is doing' in
'What is he doing?' found in b above, and try this
question. If you could not discover 'he said' previously, try to elicit it now using the suggestions
in 6.3b and asking "What is he doing?"

'What did he say?'   Date overheard: _____

Lingua Franca: _____

Vernacular: _____

10.3d   <u>'What did you say?'</u>

If you don't know this Basic Expression, try to elicit
it now by substituting the second person for the third
person in 'What did he say?' found in 10.3c above.

'What did you say?'   Date overheard: _____

Lingua Franca: _____

Vernacular: _____

10.3e   Checking 'What?' Questions

Check these elicited forms with several people until you are confident that you have idiomatic expressions. Each time you use the questions write down the
replies they evoke.

(1)   Check by saying the expression to several dif-
      ferent people and notice whether they respond in
      the expected way.

(2)   Check also by eliciting these questions from
      several different people and comparing carefully
      any differences in the way they say it.

(3)   The ultimate check will be to overhear it said
      by one person to another in a natural situation.
      Keep your ears open for this, and then mark the
      date after each expression written in 10.3a to
      10.3d above.

10.4a   Describing 'What?'

Study the material obtained in 10.2b and 10.3. Compare it with the expression for 'What is this?' and
'What is that?' (3.3 and 4.3). Try to identify the
morpheme(s) for 'what'. Note that there may be a
different form of 'what' to indicate action from that
used to indicate a person or thing. Similarly, a
different term may be used for animate vs. inanimate,
or human vs. non-human. Be alert to these and other
possibilities. Compare the expressions elicited with
previous written data. Identify as many morphemes as
you can and check their meanings.

10.4b   Studying Verb Forms

Study the responses to the questions "What are you
doing?" and "What is he doing?" Identify the person
morphemes and verb stems. If you are sure of the
meanings of the verb stems, file them in the dictionary (both vernacular to English and English to vernacular).

10.4c Study these verbs again to see if they all fit the
       pattern you described and checked in 7.4 and 7.5.
       Expand and modify your description as necessary.
       There may be classes of verbs that behave differently
       from each other. On the other hand, in longer sen-
       tences there may be two kinds of verbs--independent

and dependent--which take quite different subject-person affixes.

10.4d Intonation Contours

Diagram or describe the intonation contour that is most commonly used with information questions (What? Who? What do?) and the contour that is most commonly used with the replies that are given to these questions. Is there any consistent difference between these two contours? Base your conclusions on your experiences in listening, mimicking and tracking and on your tape recordings of drills and of free texts.

Note down any other ideas about intonation that you have developed recently.

10.5 Constructing Other Verbs

10.5a Take some replies to 'What are you doing?' and construct the equivalent replies to 'What is he doing?' and vice versa.

10.5b Choose one of the new patterns you found in 10.4c and construct some sentences using first, second and third person in this pattern.

10.5c Check your work with two or three different people, and modify the descriptions if necessary.

10.6 Practicing 'What?' Questions

10.6a Once you have checked the 4 questions obtained in 10.3 and are confident you have idiomatic, useful forms, record a question and answer drill for each one as follows:

Vernacular	SILENCE	English	SILENCE	Vernacular	SILENCE
What are you doing?		Weeding		I'm weeding.	
What are you doing?		Sweeping		I'm sweeping.	

Use four or five different responses chosen from the ones you have written before or from the sentences you checked in 10.5. See 3.6a if necessary.

Make similar drills with the other questions.

10.6b Make a transform drill using some new pattern you

discovered in 10.4c, using the method outlined in
7.6b. Make a review card for these recordings.

10.6c When you are watching an activity, ask someone 'What
is he doing?' Mimic the reply then transform it into the second person and say it to the person who is
doing the action. Note any corrections. Repeat this
with many different activities until it becomes automatic.

10.6d Agreement

Be on the alert for agreement between a verb and its
noun subject or between a noun and its possessor. If
you observe it, be sure to work it into a drill at
this point (see 26.6b for how to set up the necessary
type of drill for this feature).

10.6e Names

Continue to review names learnt earlier, and to record new names.

Date Unit 10 started: _____ Completed: _____

Hours spent on categories 2 and 6: _'_____

Hours spent on all other categories: _____

Comments:

Use the evaluations of the first ten lessons to make
the following summary:

Number of weeks spent in the village between starting
Unit 1 and completing Unit 10: _____

Total hours spent on categories 2 and 6 during Units
1-10: _____

Hours per week: _____

Total hours spent on all other categories during Units
1-10: _____

Hours per week: _____

After considering the statistics in this summary and
your progress during this period, what changes do you
plan to make in your approach to people and to language learning, or in your use of future units?

```
*****************************************************************
*                                                               *
*                                                               *
*                                                               *
*                                                               *
*                                                               *
*                                                               *
*         Don't be afraid to ask dumb questions.                *
*         They're more easily handled than                      *
*         dumb mistakes.                                        *
*                                                               *
*                            --William Wister Haines            *
*                                                               *
*                                                               *
*                                                               *
*                                                               *
*****************************************************************
```

Unit 11

AIMS: (1) Review.
        (2) Begin preliminary phonological analysis.
        (3) Begin investigation of locationals.

READ: "Rhyme and Reason" in Nida, *Customs and Cultures*
         pp. 24-53
      OR "Cultural Relativism and Cultural Values" and
         "Patterning and Integration in Culture" in Hers-
         kovits, *Cultural Anthropology* pp. 348-366, 411-429.
      OR "The Problem of Cultural Relativism", "The Pattern
         Phenomenon", and "The Integration of Culture" in
         Herskovits, *Man and His Works* pp. 61-78, 201-226.
      OR "The Nature of Culture" in Hoebel pp. 151-173.
      OR "The Content of Culture and the Universal Pattern"
         in Fried pp. 21-38.

NOTE: This is a long unit. Use it to catch up and consoli-
      date as well as working with locationals. IT IS BET-
      TER TO USE FLUENTLY WHAT YOU KNOW THAN TO GET MENTAL
      INDIGESTION BY DISCOVERING NEW THINGS TOO FAST.

11.1   Observing Gestures

As you check the material you elicit in 11.3, observe
any gestures which may accompany answers to questions
involving the interrogative 'where', and add these to
your written notes on the subject. Also note any new
gestures as you visit your neighbors to do the assignments of 11.2.

11.2a   Tracking

Track the tapes you made in 3.2 and 6.2 at least four
times each. Or spend 45 minutes in short stretches
(of 5-8 minutes each) listening, mimicking and tracking speech in live situations. Or do a combination,
spending some time tracking the tapes and some time
mimicking and tracking speech in the village.

11.2b   Listening for 'Where are you going?'

As you visit with neighbors be on the lookout for the
expression 'Where are you going?' Perhaps someone
has already asked you this, or you learnt it as a
Basic Expression.

11.3a Eliciting 'Where?' Questions

If you don't yet know 'Where are you going?' try
to elicit questions containing the word 'Where?'. Begin by miming hide-and-seeking actions, or set out on
an unusual route somewhere, or return from some place
where nobody saw you go. See if this will prompt
such questions as 'Where is it?', 'Where are you going?', 'Where did you go?'

11.3b

Construct 'What are you going?' if you can, and ask
someone this question as he is leaving, hoping that
he will correct it to 'Where are you going?'

11.3c

If you are unable to discover this monolingually,
elicit the following through the lingua franca.

'Where is your house?'   Date overheard: _____

Lingua Franca: _____

Vernacular: _____

'Where are you going?'   Date overheard: _____

Lingua Franca: _____

Vernacular: _____

'Where did you come from?' or 'Where did you go?'

L.F.: _____   Overheard: _____

Vernacular: _____

'Where do you eat?'   Date overheard: _____

Lingua Franca: _____

Vernacular: _____

'Where is she now?'   Date overheard: _____

Lingua Franca: _____

Vernacular: _____

11.3d Eliciting Locationals

Use each question with several different people and
note their responses. The responses to your second
or third question may include the locationals: 'up',
'down', 'up a steep rise', 'up a slight rise', 'to
the west', etc. On the other hand you may only be
given place names. Other questions may have led
to responses containing the location words, 'here',
and 'there', or phrases like 'to the river'.

NOTE: You may have already discovered in 7.3d, or
you may discover now that the verbs of motion in
your language show many more distinctions of meaning
than just 'come' and 'go'. The motion verbs may obligatorily take affixes which indicate the exact
direction (absolute or relative) of motion; or
there may be completely different verb stems to indicate each direction of motion. Since these verbs of
motion already indicate direction, special direction
and location words may be used much less frequently
in such a language.

11.4a Studying Consonant and Vowel (CV) Patterns

In preparation for beginning your work chart for
phonology analysis, go through all data obtained thus
far and list on a separate sheet of paper non-suspect
CV patterns with examples of each pattern listed.
(See Pike pp. 129a, 131, 132a, 136a, 137b for suspect
and non-suspect CV patterns).

11.4b Non-suspect Clusters, Initially or Finally

List on another sheet examples for each of the following if they occur in your data so far:

Utterance initial single C, non-suspect CC, CCC etc.
Utterance initial single V, non-suspect VV, VVV etc.
Utterance final single C, non-suspect CC, CCC etc.
Utterance final single V, non-suspect VV, VVV etc.

11.4c Suspect Sequences, Initially or Finally

List on another sheet any utterance initial or utterance final suspect phonetic sequences which you have
found in your data so far, with examples of each.
These are sequences which may be interpreted either
as a sequence of phonemes or as a complex unit phoneme. Also list any single phones which may act

as two units, with examples.

11.4d Medial Clusters

List on another sheet any utterance medial contoid
or vocoid clusters (either suspect or non-suspect)
which occur in your data thus far, with examples of
each.

11.4e Making Hypotheses

From the examples you have listed in 11.4a and
11.4b above make any hypotheses you can in regard to
(1) interpretation of any of the suspect clusters you
have listed in 11.4c and 11.4d above, and (2) emic
syllable division in any of the clusters in 11.4d.
Write out any such hypotheses on a separate sheet of
paper so they can be tested against future data.   Put
examples with each hypothesis you write.

NOTE: Emic syllable division in medial consonant
or vowel clusters can often be determined by comparing such clusters with that which occurs utterance
initially and finally.

Keep these sheets in a separate folder, adding to
them as you get additional data. Title each sheet
appropriately.

11.4f Studying 'Where?' and Locationals

File any words and expressions obtained under 11.3.
Try to isolate the morpheme or morphemes for 'Where?'.

11.4g Starting a Grammar File

If you are using plain filing cards, copy each spontaneous (non-elicited) clause from your data book onto a
separate card. Devise a set of labels or symbols that
can be written along the top edge of the card to represent the structure and other important features of
the particular clause. Leave room for other labels
or symbols that may be needed later. If you have
several colors of cards, then one color could be
used for clauses, another for noun phrases, etc.

If you are using punch cards you should begin copying
spontaneous clauses onto them. Now is the time to
start planning a scheme for representing the structure of each clause by punching. (See "Punch Card

Filing" pp. 429-445 for ideas on punching codes.)
Again, leave as many holes as possible unused so that
there will be room for adding information or features
that you will discover later.

If you are using page filing, then label sheets of
looseleaf paper in your Topical File (or in a separate Grammar File if you wish) for the various kinds
of clause structure such as transitive active, transitive passive, ditransitive active, ditransitive passive, intransitive, motion, equational, descriptive,
and existential. This file also has separate pages
for important function morphemes such as negatives,
time words, locationals, question words, and various
tenses.

With such a system for filing all your grammatical
data, it will become much easier to look through your
non-elicited data for examples of some feature that
you find yourself studying in later units.

11.4h   Revise Descriptions

Read through your descriptions of grammatical patterns
and cultural features. Add any new information and
modify the descriptions as necessary, illustrating the
changes with examples. Incorporate locatives if
possible.

11.4i   Filing

Bring your filing up to date by adding any words and
expressions you are now sure of to the Dictionary
and Topical File.

11.5   Constructing Sentences with Locatives

Use some of the locatives you have discovered to construct suitable answers to the questions in 11.3c.
Check your work with some friends.

11.6a   Learning Locationals

Choose some of the more useful locatives you have discovered, and make several short drills as follows:

Vernacular	English	Vernacular
Where did you come from?	up there	I came from up there.
Where did you come from?	down below	I came from down below.
Where did you come from?	the East	I came from the East.
....	....	....
Where are you going?	up there	I am going up there.
....	....	....
Where is your house?	up there	It is up there.
....	....	....

(With SILENCE columns between each)

Sometimes use a drill just after it has been made so that your helper will understand what you want. Enter the recording in your review system.

NOTE: In recording such drills use your own voice for the English utterances and a native speaker's voice for all vernacular utterances. To record good flowing utterance without hesitations or slips, hold down the pause button while you tell your helper (in the vernacular or lingua franca) what you want him to say, wait while he says it, then release the pause button and nod to him to say it again. To obtain silences just the right length for mimicry, immediately after recording a vernacular utterance mimic it silently to yourself with the recorder still running, wait one or two seconds longer, and then nod to your helper to say the next utterance.

11.6b Learning Useful Expressions and Names

Look through your data for any expressions which would be useful in conversation or for eliciting. Have someone record them, with some suitable responses for each one, on your tape of expressions. Follow the procedure outlined in 3.6a.

Have someone add the names of the members of any households where you have made friends recently to your tape of names.

Keep adding to your tapes of names and expressions in this way. Enter these recordings in your review system.

11.6c Practicing with Person Markers

Look through the person charts of Unit 7 and note any person markers or sets of markers which you cannot use fluently, but which you are sure you have elicited correctly.

For each of these sets, record drills like the ones in 7.6a and b. In the first drill for each set use four or five verb stems with the same person marker, then with each different combination of person, number and gender in the set. This helps you learn the person markers. The second drill with each set should use a transform between first and second person, third and second person, singular and plural, singular and dual, masculine and feminine, etc. These transforms are needed very frequently in conversation.

First you should make drills with the most useful sets of markers, leaving rare sets until later. Make a card dated for one month ahead and enter it in the review system, and on it write a reminder to make more drills with person morphemes if necessary. Do not enter more than two or three drills in the review system on one day, or their effectiveness will be reduced.

After reviewing the drills on a set of person markers, try to find situations where you can use the markers and transforms in conversation.

11.6d Correcting Pronunciation

Spend extra time visiting your neighbors and practice patterns and expressions as often as you can. Practice more frequently those which are more difficult to pronounce or to remember. Encourage people to correct your pronunciation, rhythm and intonation as you speak. Listen carefully to their corrections and try to mimic as much as you can. Remember not to repeat anything more than three times in succession.

If some point needs correction repeatedly, focus on that point and try to get it right. Take extra time to analyze the problem and make a drill about it. If you don't respond to correction, people will probably stop correcting you.

11.6e Practicing Names

Try to speak by name to each person you know. If people don't use personal names, use the kinship terms or clan names or silently think of the person's name as you speak to him.

STOP: Special Assignment

If there is some part of the grammar which is a real hindrance to further progress, take a few days to try to solve the problem. Look up the subject in the index for help.

Read again "How to use the *Guide*" (pp. 22-27) and decide which approach you will follow in using the *Guide* from now on. Are you and your partner analysts or "sponges"? (See "Kinds of Learners" p. 26.) Discuss together how you can help each other.

Date Unit 11 started: _____ Completed: _____

Hours spent on categories 2 and 6: _____

Hours spent on all other categories: _____

Comments:

****

Memorization without adequate mimicry is a good way to ensure a foreign accent.

****

Unit 12

AIMS: (1) Observe personal adornment.
       (2) Use pictures in conversation.
       (3) Study negatives and yes/no questions.

READ: (1) "Factors Which Determine the Kind of Data
            Obtained" in Samarin pp. 45-55.
       (2) Again "Using Tape Recorders" in this *Guide*
            pp. 411-426.

NOTE: Don't feel bound by the sequence the *Guide* follows.
       Tackle phonological or grammatical problems out of
       sequence if you want to.

12.1 Observing Personal Adornment

Observe and note personal adornment. Is the skin
scarified? How? Are parts of the body pierced?
i.e. nose and ears. Are decorative items worn?
All the time or only on certain occasions? Do
men and women decorate in different ways? Is body
painting done? If so, when?

12.2a Using Pictures in Conversation

Introduce an issue of a magazine with pictures of
people similar to your language group, when there are
only two of your friends present. Record their comments and questions on tape. Join in the conversation when you can.

Listen to the recording with your friends, trying to
find out what some of their utterances mean. Choose
some which would be useful in describing or explaining the pictures, write them in your data book and
add them to your tape of useful expressions.

As you look at the same pictures with other friends,
try to use as many of these expressions as you can.
Gather and learn to use other expressions in the
same way.

12.2b Gathering Yes/No Questions and Negatives

Listen to the tape made in 12.2a with the people who
made it, trying to locate negative statements and

questions which can be answered with 'yes' or 'no'.
For each of these that you find, ask the speaker to
say it clearly so you can write it down.   Use 'What
did you say?' (10.3d or Basic Expression).

If you recorded the conversation in 10.2b, listen to
the recording with someone who was there, preferably
a bilingual person. With his help write down any
negatives and yes/no questions which occur in the conversation.

Listen for yes/no questions and their answers when
children return from errands, and when people return
after being away for a few days. Jot down what you
can, and check the meanings when convenient.

12.2c   A Problem with Questions

In some language groups it is not common to ask many
questions, and in some areas it is considered rude to
do so. Think back over your use of questions to date
and try to recall people's apparent reactions. Be on
the alert in the future and write down notes about the
acceptable and unacceptable time and way of asking
questions. If there seems to be a strong reaction
against the frequent use of questions you will need to
limit your practicing of questions to a few people who
are sympathetic with your language learning program.

12.3   Eliciting Negatives

For each type of clause you have noticed so far, try
to elicit the negative form by using a positive form
inappropriately, then asking "Is that right?" If
this fails, use the patterns you discover in 12.4 to
construct yes/no questions and use them in situations
where the answer should be 'no'.

12.4a   Studying Yes/No Questions

First read "Interrogative Clauses" in Elson and Pickett pp. 115-116. Then look through your data, especially the material gathered in 12.2b, and list yes/
no questions in groups, one group for each type of
clause you are aware of (such as motion, intransitive,
equative, etc.). Compare each group with statements
of the same clause type, and describe the structure
and intonation of the questions and the rules for
transforming statements into questions. File your

description, with formulas and examples.

12.4b   Studying Negative Statements

Compare negative statements with positive, in the same
way as you compared questions and statements in 12.4a.
Describe the structure and intonation of negative
statements. How is a positive statement negated?
Some verbs (e.g. 'having' as in 'He has a ...' or
'existing' as in 'There is some...') may be negated
differently from other verbs.

12.4c   Filing

Look through your data book for locationals. List
these locationals, and identify the morphemes and
their tentative meanings, if possible.

Look through any recently collected text material.
Continue to watch out for non-final verbs (see 10.4c).
Add new expressions, words, and morphemes you are
sure of to your Dictionary File and Topical File.
File non-elicited clauses in your Grammar File (or
Topical File) (see 11.4g).

12.5   Constructing Yes/No Questions and Negatives

For each clause type, take at least four statements
and transform them into yes/no questions. Construct
the negative answer to each question. Check your work
with several people by asking the questions (with the
right intonation) in situations where they should be
answered both affirmatively and negatively. Note any
corrections, and modify the descriptions as necessary.

12.6a   Practicing Negatives and Yes/No Questions

Make a drill with questions and negative answers. For
each clause type, use three or four questions with complete answers, such as:

	Vernacular	SILENCE	Vernacular	SILENCE
Equative:	Is that your dog?		No. It's not my dog.	
	Is that a (food)?		No. It's not a (food).	
	....		....	

	Vernacular		Vernacular	
Motion:	Are you going to the river?	SILENCE	No. I am not going.	SILENCE
	....		....	
Intransitive:	Is the baby sleeping?		No. He's not sleeping.	
	....		....	
Transitive:	Can you see the bird?		No. I can't see it.	
	....		....	

Use vocabulary that you know well, and try to make the sentences as natural and useful as possible. Keep a list of the meanings of the sentences you have recorded, and read it as you mimic the recording if necessary.

Enter the recording in your review system, and practice these patterns with your friends whenever you can. Note any corrections and try to correct your understanding of the patterns.

12.6b Practicing Pronunciation

Have one of your friends put a list of words on tape (about 20-25). Mimic this list twice on 4 different occasions, particularly practicing the individual sounds of the words. Remember to record each word twice with space between utterances for mimicking. If you do not have a tape recorder, make a list of words and go through it with 8 or 10 different people, encouraging them to correct your pronunciation. Listen carefully when they repeat the words and mimic them as accurately as you can.

Date Unit 12 started: _____ Completed: _____

Hours spent on categories 2 and 6: _____

Hours spent on all other categories: _____

Comments:

Unit 13

AIMS: (1) Start investigating kinship terms.
(2) Begin investigation of imperatives.

READ: (1) "Techniques for Collecting a Corpus" in Samarin pp. 75-84.
(2) "Grammatical Drills" in this *Guide* pp. 307-317.

NOTE: This unit has two main topics, kin terms and imperatives. As it is fairly long, you may prefer to work on one of these topics first, then repeat the unit, working on the other topic.

13.1 Observing Kin Relationships

Read through the page in your Topical File for kinship terms to refresh your memory. As you begin to learn some of the kinship terms and relationships, observe how different relatives behave toward one another, how their relationships affect obligations and privileges as regards helping with work projects, looking after children, borrowing and lending, giving and receiving gifts, helping meet obligations to outsiders, etc.

Also observe how relationships affect settlement patterns. Is there any obvious arrangement of kin folk living within a definable area? What sort of relatives live in the same house? Does more than one co-wife live in the same house? With children? At what age do the children move out? At marriage, do they set up their own homes, and if so, is this near the parents?

Begin whatever new sections are needed in your anthropology file as you make these preliminary observations.

13.2a Gathering Imperatives

Look up imperatives in the Grammar File and study their form, so you will be able to recognize them more easily. Join in a cooperative activity where several people are working together. Mimic any brief instructions you are given, and write them down. Then try to follow the instructions!

Watch the others working, and when you hear a command,
ask someone "Did he say ...?" or "What did he say?"
Mimic the command and write it down.

Visit a home when children are present. Write down
some commands and their responses, both action and
speech. Use English to describe the contexts in
which these things are said. Join in the conversation whenever you can.

13.2b   Notice Kin Terms

When someone calls out to attract someone else's attention, does he use a personal name, a kin term of
address or call "My namesake!"? Whenever you notice a
kin term of address, mimic and write it down, noting
who used it, to whom, and if possible the relationship
between them.

When one person refers to another without using his
name, he will probably use a kin term of reference.
Note these when you hear them, again noting who used
each, of whom, and their relationship.

13.3a   Eliciting Imperatives

First check through the data you have obtained up to
now and write into the spaces below any of the corresponding vernacular expressions you already have in
your data.

13.3b   If you do not have the exact expression in your data,
but something similar, try to elicit the expression
called for by using the expression you already have.
For instance, if you do not have 'Come!' but you do
have 'He is coming' and the pronoun 'you', try constructing 'You are coming' and encourage your language helper to correct the expression. Or use the
lingua franca pronoun for 'you' with any form of the
verb 'come' you may have in your data and encourage
your helper to correct you. While eliciting this
command, have your partner stand at a distance, and
actually come to you as soon as you give your incorrect "command".

13.3c   Any of the following expressions which you are unable
to elicit by the above methods, or by pure acting,
elicit through the lingua franca.

'Come here (singular)!'   L.F. _____

Vernacular: _____   Date overheard: ____

'Come here (dual)!'   L.F. _____

Vernacular: _____   Date overheard: ____

'Come here (plural)!'   L.F. _____

Vernacular: _____   Date overheard: ____

'Go (singular)!'   L.F. _____

Vernacular: _____   Date overheard: ____

'Go (dual)!'   L.F. _____

Vernacular: _____   Date overheard: ____

'Go (plural)!'   L.F. _____

Vernacular: _____   Date overheard: ____

'Bring it here (sing.)!'   L.F. _____

Vernacular: _____   Date overheard: ____

'Take it away (sing.)!'   L.F. _____

Vernacular: _____   Date overheard: ____

'Take it and eat it (sing.)!' L.F. _____

Vernacular: _____   Date overheard: ____

13.3d By using the first and second person pronouns along
       with the second person imperative form of the verb
       of the same number, try to stimulate some of your more
       helpful friends to give you the following utterances.
       (Do NOT elicit these through the lingua franca.)

Date Overheard:

'I must go.'   _____   _____

'Let's (dual inclusive) go.'   _____   _____

'Let's (plural inclusive) go.'   _____   _____

'He must go.'   _____   _____

'They (dual) must go.'   _____   _____

'They (plural) must go.'   _____   _____

NOTE: In some languages, verbs with these meanings
belong to the imperative mood; in other languages,
they belong to moods quite separate from the imperative.

13.3e   Check the responses obtained, as outlined in 10.3e.

13.3f   Eliciting Kinship Terms for the Immediate Family

Read Schusky, *Manual for Kinship Analysis* pp. 5-12.
Choose a family you know well and draw a kinship diagram for the man of the house, writing the names of
his parents, wife (or wives) and children beside the
symbols that represent them. Make another diagram
with one of the children as "ego". Make the diagrams
large enough to add kinship terms to them.

From the Topical File and the material gathered in
13.2b, fill in any terms you can which either "ego"
would use when referring to the other people on his
diagram. Write in the terms he would use when addressing them also.

Take your diagrams and visit the family. Use what
you know to elicit the other terms of reference by
asking the head of the house questions such as: "She
is your wife. He is your son. Who is she?" (indicating his daughter). If this fails to elicit the desired response, try asking "Is she your son?" instead of
"Who is she?" Use a pattern like "You call her ..."
"What do you call him?" to elicit the terms of address
you don't yet know.

Repeat this procedure with the other diagram and the

person who is "ego" in it, looking for such terms as 'older brother' and 'younger sister' as well as checking the terms you have just found.

13.4a   Studying Imperatives

Study the imperatives in the Grammar File and those found in 13.2a and 13.3a-d. Try to isolate as many morphemes as you can. In some languages a verb stem without affixes indicates the imperative, and in others, imperative is indicated by intonation. There may be different forms of the imperative to distinguish polite requests, informal requests, and impatient commands; or the language may distinguish between general or future imperatives and specific or present imperatives. Different patterns may be used with motion, intransitive and transitive verbs.

Write tentative descriptions of the different types of imperative in the language, or the rules for transforming statements into imperatives. Diagram or describe the intonation contour(s) used with imperatives. Display any person markers used with imperatives in charts like those of Unit 7.

13.4b   Studying Kin Terms

Add new kin terms to the ones in the Topical File, as they may behave as a separate class of nouns. Study the terms obtained. Can you isolate a morpheme which marks them as kin terms? Is possession shown obligatorily or optionally with kin terms? Is possession marked in one of the ways you discovered in Units 8 and 9, by a variation, or by a completely different system of markers?

Are the kinship terms of address related systematically to the terms of reference, or do they form a completely different system?

13.4c   Filing

Keep filing tested words and expressions--they are much easier to find that way! Add any new CV patterns to the ones listed in Unit 11, with examples.

13.5   Using Imperatives and Kin Terms

Construct as many different types of imperatives as you can (see 13.4a), using five common verbs and the

person-number markers you have found. Use kin terms
of address with these where appropriate. Try to construct sentences using the other kin terms you have
found. Construct useful questions with kin terms instead of pronouns. Test these carefully, and modify
the descriptions if necessary.

13.6a   Practicing Imperatives

For each type of imperative construction and for each
combination of person and number that can be used
with imperatives, record a drill of three imperatives
using different verb stems. Use verbs you know well
if possible.

Then make a transform drill as follows:

Vernacular		Vernacular	
You (sg.) come!	SILENCE	You (pl.) come!	SILENCE
You (sg.) go!		You (pl.) go!	
....		....	

If the transformation from singular to plural takes
several different forms, depending on the person or
on the particular verb stem, make different drills.
Use imperatives in conversation, but be culturally
polite as you do so.

13.6b   Practicing Kinship Terms

If kinship terms use a possession system you have not
learnt before, make six drills each of which has a
useful and interesting frame sentence containing an
important kin term with which you are not yet thoroughly familiar. In each drill substitute all of the
person-number possessors which you have found (see
Unit 7 charts).

If there is a difference between kin reference terms
and kin address terms, make a transform drill in which
the stimulus is a kin reference term, and the response
is the corresponding terms of address.

Record the useful questions you checked in 13.5, and
use them in conversation. For example, ask "What is
your brother doing?" instead of "What is he doing?"

13.6c <u>Practicing Pronunciation</u>

Continue the word drills. You may drop from the list
any words which "come naturally" by now and add to the
list new words with sounds you may find difficult.

Make a list of words that seem to have the same vowel
in them. If you cannot get single syllable words with
the same sound, try to get words with the same sound
in the same syllable (preferably either first or last
syllable) of a word. Put these on tape and mimic
them as closely as you can. Some time during the day
say them to someone in the village and have him correct your pronunciation. If you lack data, refer to
the List of Words in the Appendix or the dictionary
of the lingua franca for ideas for further eliciting.

Date Unit 13 started: _____ Completed: _____

Hours spent on categories 2 and 6: _____

Hours spent on other categories: _____

Comments:

```
**********************************************************
*                                                        *
*                                                        *
*                                                        *
*                                                        *
*                                                        *
*                                                        *
*               Learn by trying.                         *
*               Practice makes perfect.                  *
*                                                        *
*                                                        *
*                                                        *
*                                                        *
*                                                        *
*                                                        *
**********************************************************
```

Unit 14

AIMS: (1) Collect a brief genealogy.
(2) Investigate 'When?' and its temporal responses.
(3) Study and practice tense changes.

READ: "Stress-Producing Factors in Cultural Adjustment" in this *Guide* pp. 327-343.

14.1a Observing Work Load

Continue to observe the full range of people's activities and assess their work load. What tasks do men, women, older children, and younger children each do?

14.1b Investigating Wider Kin Relationships and Terms

Read "Collecting Genealogies" on pp. 408-410. Construct sentences such as 'Who is your father?' or 'Your father--what is his name?', 'Who are his children?', 'Where is his house?', 'Who is his wife?'. If you know the vocabulary, construct other questions such as 'How many children?', 'Who is first?', 'Who is next?', 'What is his clan?'. Write these questions on a 3 x 5 card to take with you.

Visit the family from whom you elicited kinship terms and try to collect a brief genealogy for the head of the house. USE ONLY VERNACULAR QUESTIONS. You will learn to speak much more quickly if you don't use the lingua franca to gather information. If some information is too hard to elicit using the vernacular you know at present, leave it until later. Note and use any questions people teach you, or expressions they use in describing relationships. Note any new kin terms, or people whose names ego will not say.

Collecting genealogies can become a happy and interesting occupation for you and your neighbors. When you first start, though, you will probably be exhausted after asking about ego's parents, his siblings and some of their children. Don't attempt more than that at first.

14.2a Conversation

Spend some of your time in free "conversation" on
some topic, using as much of the vernacular as you
have been able to assimilate up to now, and mimicking whatever people tell you to say.

Spend extra time conversing with each person with
whom you check the material you construct in 14.5.

14.2b Gathering 'When?' Questions and Responses

In situations in which someone is likely to ask a
'When?' question, note carefully the apparent questions and responses that you hear. Such situations
include all leavetakings, what people say to you
near or at the time of your own departure from the
village, and when a community leader announces some
special event such as a census taking or tax collection.

14.3a Eliciting 'When?' Questions and Time Words

From the Grammar File and/or Topical File, find all
the time words and 'when?' questions you can. Use
the Basic Expression 'When will you go?' or any other
'when?' question in appropriate situations to elicit
more time words, and to check the ones you have noticed already. If you don't have any 'when?' questions, construct 'What are you going? Tomorrow?'
and ask people in appropriate situations, so they
will correct the question and thus supply 'when?'.

Use questions like 'When will you go? Yesterday?'
about past events so people will change your questions
into the past tense. Try in this way to find a past
tense form for each 'when?' question you have. Use
these questions about different events until you have
time words or expressions for at least the following:
'day before yesterday', 'yesterday', 'today', 'tomorrow', 'day after tomorrow', 'night', 'day', 'dawn',
'morning', 'noon', 'afternoon', 'dusk'.

NOTE: Be on the alert that some of the time words you
hear may be vague ('long time ago', 'recently', 'now',
'soon', 'later on', 'sometime', 'always') and that
some of the time-of-day words may be much more specific
('early afternoon', 'late afternoon', 'sunset'). Furthermore, the time slot may be filled by uninflected

temporals (that is, time words without affixes, such
as 'tomorrow', 'now'), phrases or inflected words with
a time/location marker ('in the morning', 'at noon')
or by descriptive or idiomatic expressions ('when the
sun is overhead', 'cock-crow').

14.3b   Eliciting Statements in Different Tenses

Use these time words and any sentences in non-present
tenses that you know to make a pattern for eliciting
statements in other tenses. For example:

            Today.   He is going.
            Tomorrow.   He will go.
            Yesterday.
                                _____

If this does not elicit 'He went', try using 'Yesterday. He is going.' as the last line, to force a correction. Try to elicit a statement for each time
word or expression you have.

14.4a   Identifying 'When?'

Study your data and try to find the question word(s)
expressing 'When?'. Does it seem to be uninflected,
or inflected for location like a noun, or inflected
for person and tense like a verb?

14.4b   Studying Tense

Read "Tense" and "Aspect" in Elson and Pickett p. 23.
For each time word in your Topical File examine each
utterance in which it occurs in your data and try to
discover how the verb is marked for tense. List the
tense affixes or particles that have been observed associated with each time expression. If you feel you
understand most of your time words, then these asso-
ciations may help clarify the meaning of certain
tenses, and vice versa.

What tenses do you feel you have discovered so far
and what are the morphemes that seem to mark them?
They may be marked by particles, verb prefixes, verb
suffixes, verb reduplication, or some other technique. Are all tenses that you have discovered so far
marked in the same way? If the subject person is
affixed to the verb, do the affixes vary somewhat for
tense?

Write a tentative description of the system of tenses and give examples.

14.4c   Expanding the Description of Tense Markers

Test to see if the same set of person markers can be used for all tenses. Choose a verb you can use well in the present tense and elicit the form for each person and number of subject in each tense using patterns similar to the one in 14.3b. Repeat this with a verb of a different type (e.g. transitive instead of intransitive).

If the person markers change with tense, take extra time to work on tense. Look up the subject in the index and work through sections that deal with it.

On each of several days before and after an event, record a text about the event. Take part in the event and record a conversation between two people immediately after it. Transcribe the texts each day (see 15.3a) and copy each clause onto a card or appropriate page in the Grammar File. Label or punch the cards for person and number of the subject, and for the various tenses and aspects if you are fairly sure of them. Use these examples in analysis, and keep revising your descriptions until you can construct correctly the different tenses for the common verbs you are using, at least for the person-number combinations you use most frequently. Make extra drills so you can change the tense of the verbs you have been using, without having to stop and think of rules. Verbs are very important in most languages, and are worth extra time if you find them hard to use.

14.4d   Making a Genealogical Chart

Use the data you gathered in 14.1b to draw a partial genealogical chart. Try to identify new kinship terms and to understand any expressions you wrote while collecting the data. Use a bilingual person to help you if possible. File any further observations you have made about kin relationships.

14.4e   Enter all discoveries that you are fairly confident about (because of several instances in your data and consistent reactions from your neighbors) in your Dictionary File. Continue filing both words and expressions in the Topical File.

14.5   Testing the Descriptions of Tense Markers

Choose about 3 recent events and about 3 which will
take place soon. For each one try to construct a
'when?' question for each type of verb you have, both
for 'you' and for 'he', such as "When did your brother
spear the turtle?" and "When did you eat turtle-meat?"
Try to have each tense represented by at least two
questions. Construct a complete sentence to answer
each question, such as "He speared it yesterday." and
"I ate turtle-meat yesterday."

Check your work with several neighbors, and modify
your descriptions if necessary.

14.6a   Practicing With Tense

Unless tense is very easy to mark, do not depart from
the singular in this section. Use one type of verb
first. For each tense record a question and answer
drill such as:

Vernacular		Vernacular	
When will your brother go to the ceremony?		He'll go tomorrow.	
When will he return?	SILENCE	He'll return tomorrow.	SILENCE
....		....	
When will you go to the bush?		I'll go tomorrow.	
When will you return?		I'll return to-morrow.	
....		....	

The English meaning of each question should be filed
so you can read it while using the drill, or else it
could be recorded before the question. If you choose
the latter, leave a silence between the English and
the question.

Repeat this pattern for each tense. Unless it is too
difficult at this stage, record a similar set of
drills for each different verb type you have.

14.6b   Tense Transformation Practice

For each type of verb you have, try to record a transform drill from the present tense to another tense,

or from a near tense to a remote tense. Try to use
yes/no questions as the stimuli.   For example:

Vernacular   Vernacular

Is the baby sleeping? Are you weeding?	SILENCE	No. He was sleeping this morning. No. I was weeding this morning.	SILENCE
or			
Did you bring the timber today? Did the dog kill it today?		No. I brought it last week. No. He killed it last week.	

Try to make a transform drill with each tense as the
response. Only use plural subjects if tense marking
is not complicated.

14.6c   Reviewing Drills

Add the recordings of a and b above to your review
system, and review other drills as they are due.
If more than four drills are due on the one day, divide your reviewing into two or three periods during
the day.

14.6d   Practicing Pronunciation

(1)   Continue drilling pronunciation lists, ex-
        panding it as new sounds are encountered.

(2)   Make another word list using a different common
        vowel. Drill these words concentrating on the
        vowel in focus. Review and drill the vowel lists
        of previous units as they are due.

(3)   Set up lists of different stops for each type of
        articulation, e.g. p, t, k; b, d, g; mb, nd, ng.
        Group words as to initial, medial and final posi-
        tion. Put these on tape, listen to and mimic
        them, concentrating particularly on the stops.
        Pronounce them with someone and have him correct
        you.

Date Unit 14 started: _____   Completed: _____

Hours spent on categories 2 and 6: _____

Hours spent on all other categories: _____

Comments:

```
********************************************************************
*                                                                  *
*                                                                  *
*                                                                  *
*                                                                  *
*                                                                  *
*                                                                  *
*                                                                  *
*             Complacency is the enemy of study.                   *
*                          --Mao Tse-Tung                          *
*                                                                  *
*                                                                  *
*                                                                  *
*                                                                  *
********************************************************************
```

Unit 15

AIMS: (1) Visit another hamlet.
       (2) Continue investigation of transitive clauses.
       (3) Practice names and transitive clauses.

READ: "Learning a Foreign Language From an Informant" in
       Nida, *Learning a Foreign Language* pp. 58-85.

15.1a Visiting Another Hamlet

First review the recordings of greetings you have made,
and the drill on 'Whose?' questions of 9.6. Then
visit a nearby village or hamlet or some houses in
your community that you have not visited much before.
Or take a trip for some specific purpose for a mile
or two along a main trail at a time of day when it is
well frequented by people.

Record and later add to your file any additional observations related to the topics of previous units.
Under the topic 'dwellings', for instance, you may
wish to photograph or diagram the inside of a house
you visit. Or you may notice additional tools or weapons you have not seen before. Continue to map
houses and record names in your own village or nearby hamlets.

15.1b Extending the Genealogy

Collect more genealogical details from the same ego
as in 14.1b, or from another family. If as a result
of your work with tenses in Unit 14 you can now ask
'When did he die?' and 'Where did she live long
ago?', do so where appropriate.

15.2a Using Greetings

As you approach a home in the hamlet you visit or
someone on the trail, practice under your breath the
appropriate greeting, then use it and note the reply.
On other occasions, as you approach a person, practice
under your breath the appropriate reply to the greeting you expect him to give you, then wait and let him
greet you first, note what form of greeting it is,
and give the best reply you can. After greetings
have been exchanged note his next few utterances,

which will usually contain at least one question.
Respond as well as you can. Also note his leavetaking and reply to your leavetaking. Whenever you can
do it without offence, write down any such expressions that you have not written previously. When
writing is not appropriate, try very hard to memorize
any short utterance or part of an utterance that
seems of particlar interest, and write it down from
memory as soon as the visit is ended. In all writing
of people's spontaneous utterances, be sure to note
down your guess at the meaning and/or a brief statement of the context or circumstances in which it was
said.

15.2b   Sharing an Activity

Share an activity (work in the village, hunting, gardening, gathering food or firewood, sitting around a
fire, etc.) with one or more of your friends and mimic conversation relating to the work. Enter into the
conversation as much as you can. Mimic everything
that you are told to say. Listen actively to conversation as it goes on around you and try to follow it,
either by observing activity accompanying it or by
seeing how many familiar phrases or portions of
phrases you are able to recognize. Inwardly try to
track some of the conversation from time to time when
you are not directly involved in the activity. Try
and get next to someone who will repeat utterances
for you and answer your questions such as "What is
he doing?" Transform his answers whenever you can.
Write down some transitive clauses that you hear.

Continue to be alert to new intonational patterns
and add them to your taped collection at every opportunity. See 2.2d.

15.2c   Recording a Conversation

Try to tape-record a conversation or a discussion
between two or three people about the activity you
shared after getting their approval.

15.3a   Transcribing the Conversation

You will need a patient friend to help you, preferably a bilingual person who was present when the recording was made. If the conversation of 15.2c is
unsuitable, use any recent recording. Spend about

1/2 hour (and <u>not</u> more than 1 hour) at a time on
this work.

Read "Transcribing Text" on pp. 424-425 of this
Guide and the four paragraphs on transcription in
Samarin pp. 104-105.

As you transcribe the conversation use the following
procedures:

(1) If you are using an exercise book for transcribing texts, leave the first two pages blank for a list
of contents, then write the transcription on only one
of each pair of facing pages. Leave the other page
of each pair blank for extra notes about words and
expressions in the texts. Head the first page of
each text with a title, the names of the speakers,
dates of recording and transcription and the tape
reference to the recording of the text. Give each
text a code letter, and number each line of text on
each page. Below each line of text, leave a line for
morpheme-by-morpheme identification and another line
for free translation into English.

(2) To get your helper started, play the whole text,
then rewind and play the first pause group. Stop the
recorder and say "What did he say? Say it slowly."

(3) As you transcribe, be sure to mark pause and as
much information about pitch/intonation as you can.

(4) All differences between what you hear on the
tape and what your helper repeats to you should be
noted. Some of these differences will be hesitations, some will be places where the speaker corrects
himself, and a very few will be the speaker's acci-
dental errors.

(5) During the process of transcription and attempted elicitation and explanation of the meaning of the
text, quite often your helper will explain further
details of what is on the tape, or of why someone
did what he did, or of how people do or view a particular kind of activity. Whenever you can understand
even part of what is being said, take down notes.
Do not regard such comments as a nuisance that inter-
rupts your transcription. Listen attentively and follow up with further questions if you can. You will

find these comments very helpful later on in understanding the text better and some of them will give
information that should be added to your anthropology file.

(6) If you cannot find out the precise meaning of an
expression, try to clarify the meaning by asking your
helper 'When?', 'Who?' and 'Where?' questions. Use
the vernacular in preference to the lingua franca
whenever you can.

15.3b Clarifying Meanings

Go though the utterances obtained in 15.2 and mark
each word you are unfamiliar with. Try and enquire
the meaning of each one by questions such as:

'X. What is that?' or 'What is X?'

'He is Y-ing. What is he doing?'

'The man is Z. What is Z? What is a Z man?'

15.3c Eliciting Transitive Clauses

If you do not have many transitive clauses in your
data so far, act out various things and ask "What
did I do?" to elicit expressions such as 'You hit the
dog.' and 'You picked up a stone.' Next, have your
partner do the action so that you can obtain the
third person equivalent, and then both do the action
together so as to obtain a second person dual or
plural equivalent. Some of the things you act out
should be a sequence of two actions.

15.3d If Your Tape Recorder is not Working

If your tape recorder is broken or the batteries are
flat, try to elicit a description of some process by
asking a person what he is doing and having him dictate the reply. Sometimes the reply will be a single
sentence, but sometimes it may be a rather longer
description.

15.4a Studying New Material

Study and compare the new material gathered in 15.2
and 15.3 with that from previous units, isolating as
many morphemes as possible. Determine the meanings
of as many new morphemes as you can and especially
verb stems. Then check through the material for

meaning with a helpful friend. Verify the specific
meanings of as many verb forms as you can. Try to
find out if these forms would change for masculine
vs. feminine.

Study the transitive clauses. Are there any morphemes that mark which part of a clause is the subject, and which part is the object? Does word order
determine these categories? Do the vernacular subject and object match the subject and object in the
English translation? If some (but not all) clauses
seem to be reversed, there may well be some kind of
grammatical emphasis similar to the English passive
or the several types of focus found in Philippine
languages.

Expand or modify the tentative description of transitive clauses that you wrote in 6.4b as necessary.

15.4b   Check for Dependent Verbs

Some of the utterances examined above, and the last
expression in 13.3c will contain two or more verbs.
If you have verb affixes, examine each verb form
which occurs and see if any of them have affixes
that seem to be different from the affixes found on
verbs in sentences of one clause. In some languages
multi-clause sentences often contain several dependent verbs along with one or more independent verbs
(especially in the last clause) and this distinction
is shown by affixation. If this is true of the language you are learning you need to become aware of
it and begin using dependent verbs very early.

15.4c   Check for Agreement

Search through your materials to see if you find
evidence in your language of agreement between the
verb and its subject or object (see 26.6b for an
example of agreement). In quite a few languages at
least some of the transitive verbs obligatorily indicate the person and/or number of the object, and
for third person objects they may indicate size,
shape or noun class.

15.4d   Add expressions and words to your Topical File, new
words to your Dictionary File, and new verb affixes
to your chart. Copy clauses into the Grammar File
from the text you transcribed. Place the names

obtained in 15.1a with the appropriate houses on
your map.

15.5   Testing a New Pattern

If you had to modify your description of transitive
clauses in 15.4 to account for emphasis, medial verbs
or agreement, construct sentences to test your description. Check them with some friends, and modify
the description if necessary.

If you did not find these features, repeat 14.5,
but with plural subjects, and with some plural
objects.

15.6a   Learning Names

Write below 10 names obtained in 15.1.   Add them
to your tape of names and practice, memorize and use
them as outlined in 6.6b.

(1)   (6)

(2)   (7)

(3)   (8)

(4)   (9)

(5)   (10)

15.6b   Practicing Transitive Clauses

If you found different clause structures or markers
to show emphasis, make a drill of several sentences
with the subject emphasized and other drills with
several sentences where each other part of the
clause is emphasized. If you understand the emphasis system well enough, make a transform drill as
well.

If you found a difference between medial and final
verbs in 15.4b make a simple drill with two-clause
sentences you have gathered or constructed and
checked.

If you found agreement in 15.4c, make a drill in
which the agreement class is kept constant for several sentences, but the nouns the verb agrees with

are different for each sentence. Repeat this for different agreement classes.

Repeat your drills in different tenses.

If you did not find these features, repeat 14.6a and 14.6b for transitive verbs using plural subjects and some plural objects.

15.6c   Practicing Pronunciation

Continue the word drill for pronunciation. Add words which have any new or difficult sounds.

Date Unit 15 started: _____ Completed: _____

Hours spent on categories 2 and 6: _____

Hours spent on all other categories: _____

Comments:

NOTE: You should be spending a MINIMUM of 3 hours a day in the combined activities of categories 2 and 6, and in visiting and working with your neighbors. Otherwise you are in grave danger of being tied to your desk. Most units cannot be finished in a day, so spread them over several days, but keep up your mimicry and drills. YOUR MAIN TASK FOR THE FIRST SIX MONTHS IN THE VILLAGE IS TO LEARN TO TALK. This takes practice, practice, practice. Vary your activities, but keep up your mimicry and memory drills and conversation practice. Use everything you know as often as you can. It may be slow and painful, but it's worth it!

Unit 16

AIMS: (1)   Observe communal work and authority.
           (2)   Investigate numerals and intransitive verbs.

READ: "Old Customs and New Ways" in Nida, *Customs and
Cultures* pp. 224-249.
OR "Culture Change" in Fried pp. 372-385.
OR "Cultural Conservatism and Change" in Herskovits,
Cultural Anthropology pp. 443-460.
OR "Conservatism and Change in Culture" in Herskovits, *Man and His Works* pp. 479-491.

16.1a Observing Communal Work and Authority

As you work with people in 16.2 below, note which people work together, and which people give commands. If the work benefits one man or family, how are the workers repaid?

16.1b Using Body Parts in Counting

In 16.3 below you may discover that body parts are used in counting. Be sure to record anything about such a method of counting in your anthropology file.

16.2 Practicing Transitive Verbs in Conversation

When there are people about, spend time with them; book work can come later. Join in some activity with them such as maintenance work, communal projects, or perhaps cash-crop work. Ask "What are they doing?" to find out the names of different activities. Mimic the replies you get then construct several different sentences with the verb stem if it is transitive. Note any corrections. Write one or two clauses containing the verb stem. Join the people doing the activity and say "We are ...", using a transformation of the original answer to your question.

Mimic any intransitive verbs you hear, and note them for analysis in 16.4. Write the whole clause, not just the verb stem.

Mimic any unfamiliar imperatives and write them down. Note who gave the command to whom, and what his response was.

Join in the conversation as much as you can, using expressions and patterns you have practiced, and mimicking to yourself when you can't understand what is said.

16.3a Eliciting Numerals

Elicit any numerals that you do not already have in your data by acting out the counting of stones or other small objects. Note that some peoples don't have numerals above three or four and others form larger numbers by long expressions combining 'one', 'two', 'three', 'four', 'hand' and 'foot'.

16.3b Counting Words and Numeral Adjectives

As you elicit the numerals be careful to elicit them in two ways. Firstly, once you understand the hand gestures used for counting, have someone count a group of stones and note down how he says "one-two-three...eight-nine". These are counting words. Then, when he has finished, point to the stones and ask "What is that?" and note how he says "Those are nine stones." The word in this instance will probably be a numeral functioning as an adjective, and may be a different form from the counting word for 'nine'.

16.3c Check for Noun Classes

Repeat your elicitation for various kinds of objects such as coconuts, sticks, pieces of sweet potato, houses, pigs, men, women, children, brothers, sisters, trees, net bags, eyes and ears.

Some languages have different forms of each numeral according to the type of objects being counted, e.g. round versus long things. Other languages have noun classes or a gender system which seems to be completely arbitrary.

16.3d Eliciting 'How Many?'

While you are eliciting and mimicking numerals, on several separate occasions present to the person with whom you are conversing a group of uncounted items. If you have recently been doing all the counting he may take the initiative and ask you "How many are there?". If not, you could ask him "What are there? Three? Four?" in the hope he may correct you and give the proper form of the question. In some languages people prefer to use the more specific

form of this question, namely, 'How many stones are
there?'.

16.3e   Eliciting More Intransitive Verbs

Expand your vocabulary by using the expression 'What
am I doing?' as you act out various other actions that
are likely to be intransitive, e.g., cough, hiccup,
yawn, laugh, cry, faint, go to sleep, wake up, fall,
jump, run.

Check all your newly elicited material with several
people as outlined in 10.3e.

NOTE: If 'What am I doing?' is difficult to construct,
or if people think it a stupid question, have your
partner ask "What is he doing?" as you do the actions.

16.4a   Studying Numerals

Read "Obtaining Expressions Which Modify Nouns and
Verbs" in Nida, *Learning a Foreign Language* pp. 72-
75 and "Number" in Elson and Pickett pp. 20-21. Then
study the numerals you have found. Are the forms used
when counting different from the forms used as adjectives? Are different numerals used for different
classes of nouns? Are nouns marked for dual or plural?
Is the plural marker omitted from nouns if a numeral
is present? Write a description of your numeral system using these discoveries. List all the numerals in
the Topical File and Dictionary File.

16.4b   Studying Intransitive Verbs

Study the intransitive verbs you have found. Are they
similar to transitive verbs, or are they substantial-
ly different? Is there a consistent difference between motion verbs and other intransitive verbs? Do
some verbs depart from the regular patterns followed
by other verbs? ('Come', 'go', 'do', 'hit', 'eat' and
'be' are irregular in many languages.)

If you discovered a transitive subject marker in 15.4c,
is this also used on the subject of an intransitive
verb? A few languages have an ergative system in
which the object marker in a transitive clause is used
as the subject marker in an intransitive clause. The
subject of a transitive verb then carries an ergative
marker.

Write descriptions of the regular patterns you find, and list irregular forms on a separate page in the Topical File.

16.4c   Keep filing your discoveries in the Dictionary, Topical File, charts and Anthropology File. As you transcribe more text, copy the clauses into the Grammar File. If you are using punched cards, you may be ready now to devise categories for punching information about phrases, sentences or discourses.

16.4d   Studying Suprasegmentals

As you have listened to your word/vowel lists, what instances have you heard of long versus short vowels (or consonants)? What have you discovered about stress or pitch on syllables and words? Write down anything you have noticed, with examples.

16.5a   Testing With Numerals

Test your descriptions of numerals by constructing and checking sentences in the usual way.

16.5b   Testing Intransitive Verbs

Test your descriptions by constructing and checking several sentences using each pattern you have discovered.

16.6a   Practicing Numerals

Record someone counting up as far as will be useful to you. Make a drill with 'How many?' questions and numerals in the answers. Include 'How many children do you have?' and 'How many children did they have?' for use in collecting genealogies. If the numerals have morphemes that mark noun classes, use several nouns from each class in the drills. Keep the members of each class together to give concentrated practice on each class marker.

16.6b   Practicing Intransitive Verbs

Record drills to give concentrated practice with each pattern you have discovered in intransitive verbs. If none of the patterns is new to you, repeat 14.6a and 14.6b for intransitive verbs using plural subjects.

16.6c   Practicing Verbs

Take a verb used in a previous lesson and drill it in
a sentence frame, changing it through all known
tenses and all person-number subjects. Have your
partner give you cues by saying what the subject is.
Respond by giving the complete expression with its
proper verb form. Make sure that someone is there to
correct you. Drill these several times a day, taking
turns. Try to use each form in an appropriate village situation. Practice also with other verb stems.

16.6d   Practicing Pronunciation

Make several lists of words, each list having one
vowel common to all the words in that list and occurring in the same syllable. Give special attention to
any vowels which you find difficult (to hear or pronounce) or which differ from English in their use.

16.6e   Mimicking a New Recording

Track a new short stretch of any intonational tape
you have, following steps 1-4 as outlined in 3.6b.
If you do not yet have any different kinds of intonation (see 3.4 and 10.4d) on tape, try to get a new
one now, or tape a new stretch of a kind similar to
one you have done previously, and track it. If you
do not have a tape recorder, track live conversation
as outlined in 3.2c.

Date Unit 16 started: _____ Completed: _____

Hours spent on categories 2 and 6: _____

Hours spent on all other categories: _____

Comments:

Unit 17

AIMS: (1) Review.
(2) Begin a phonetic work chart.

READ: "Don't Learn That Language!" in Smalley pp. 341-358.

17.1 Review and Update Observations

Again go through all the notes you have taken about
the customs and culture of the community where you
live. Organize under appropriate topics and sub-
topics any information which you have not yet so
organized, and write anything down which you have
observed but failed to put into writing, especially
your recollections of working with people in 16.2.

17.2 Conversation with a Different Group of People

Visit some people, either nearby or in another village, that you have not visited frequently before.
Converse to the full extent of your ability, using expressions and patterns you have learnt. If you find
it helpful, take objects with you to ask about, or
go with questions prepared in the vernacular on some
subject you would like to talk about. See 10.1 and
10.2c again. (Use any topic suggested in category 1
of the units if you lack ideas.) Listen for words and
phrases you know in longer stretches of speech. If
you cannot mimic a whole phrase, try the last word
or two, gradually expanding it at each attempt. Be
careful always to mimic with the same intonation
that people use.

17.4a CV Patterns

Add any new material to the lists of CV patterns,
consonant clusters, and vowel clusters begun in Lesson 11.4.

Test the hypotheses you wrote in 11.4e against the
new data. You may need to modify or delete some
statements, and add others. Put into writing any
hypotheses you have regarding the interpretation of
phones which may be either consonant or vowel (i-y,
u-w, etc). Give examples.

17.4b Making Work Charts

To through all your data and make work charts of
consonants and vowels. List any phonetic cluster
which you are tentatively interpreting as a single
unit with a unit symbol in the chart. (See Pike
p. 68.) On a separate sheet give initial, medial and
final examples of each phone on the work charts wherever possible.

17.4c Initial Phonemic Analysis

(1) Circle phonetically similar pairs or groups of
sounds on the work charts. (See Pike pp. 69-70.)

(2) Write any hypotheses you have for uniting
phonetically similar phones on the basis of either
complementary distribution or free variation. Give
examples.

(3) List phonetically similar pairs or groups of
sounds for which you are unable to formulate a hypothesis for uniting, and write in examples to show contrast where possible. Avoid an over-dependence on
minimal pairs at this stage, as they can be very mis-
leading and difficult to discern in early analytical
attempts. Instead, try to get subminimal (analogous
rather than identical environment) pairs, triplets,
quadruplets etc. for whole groups of similar sounds
showing each phone initially preceding the same phone,
or finally following the same phone, or medially with
the same phone preceding and following. For example:

INITIAL		MEDIAL		FINAL	
pabep	'vine'	*kipo*	'skull'	*molep*	'grease'
bakir	'tree'	*ibon*	'leaf'	*sateb*	'rat'
bama	'river'	*tibol*	'stone'	*ikeb*	'rope'
waleb	'place'	*iwor*	' pig'	*konew*	'lake'

Do not be sparing in your examples. It is better
to have too many than too few. Scan your lists of
vowels and consonants used in pronunciation drills
to see if there are any contrasts of distribution
here. Be on the lookout in the future for further
examples where you lack good contrast.

17.4d   Describing Person Morphemes

Go through your material gathered in the last few
units and see if you have recorded there any additional person morphemes that should be added to your
charts in Unit 7. Then if you have not already done
so, you should try to summarize your conclusions concerning similarities and differences between types of
person morphemes in the total system. Make notes
about the following points: (1) Do person morphemes
have a different distribution according to their use
as subjects, objects, or possessors? (2) Are there
similarities in the phonetic makeup of the various
sets? (3) What are the contrastive features between
the different sets? (4) Are there any sets which
you tentatively want to assign a label to? Please
keep in mind that your analysis is very tentative.
You are not expected to have the final description in
hand at this time by any means!

17.4e   Studying the Verb 'to be'

Search through your data for clauses whose English
translations contain the verb 'be' ('am', 'are', 'is',
'was', 'were'). What different kinds of structure do
the vernacular clauses have? Some languages have
different clause patterns for each of 'He is tall.',
'He is my uncle.', 'He is in the house.' and 'There is
a pig in the garden.'

What do you feel matches the English 'is' in clauses
such as these? Nothing? A particle? A verb? Are
there several different verbs for 'be' for different
circumstances? Write a tentative description of
your discoveries.

17.4f   Reviewing Descriptions of Grammatical Patterns

Review the descriptions made in previous units. If
some of them need revision, take time now to do further analysis and testing, so you will make fewer
mistakes in conversation.

17.4g   Filing

If there is any data which you have checked and for
which you are reasonably confident you have the right
meanings but have not yet filed in your Dictionary
File and Topical File, do so now before proceeding
with further units.

17.6a   Review Practice Recordings

Review drills and groups of expressions and names as
indicated by your review system. Try to catch up
with review if you are behind. Remove from review
any drills or expressions which are so elementary
that they annoy you.

If you are not using a review system, review all the
names, expressions and drills you have recorded.
BREAK THIS REVIEW UP INTO 10-MINUTE SESSIONS, as we
do not learn much from long sessions with drills.
Drop from review any expressions which come automatically in conversation.

17.6b   Practice Other Patterns

If you modified any descriptions in this unit, make
drills to give concentrated practice with the new
features you have discovered.

If there are any patterns you have described and
checked but which you can't yet use automatically,
make drills so you can start to use them. Some of
these may be dual or plural person markers with possessives or with different verb types in different
tenses. You may need to practice other sets of
numerals or the markers for different noun classes.
Make drills to practice vocabulary you need in conversation. Take extra time now to translate your
discoveries into automatic speech habits.

17.6c   Tracking

Review, tracking each of the intonational stretches
you have done, and especially that of 15.2c or spend
at least 30 minutes tracking speech in live situations in the village, in short stretches of 5 minutes
or less each. Some of the more common intonational
patterns should begin to feel more natural to you by
now. If they do not, spend MORE time in mimicry,
tracking and listening and LESS time in analysis and
memorizing. If you still feel quite awkward and
stilted as you mimic, you will probably find it helpful to go back and repeat 1.2, 3.6b, 3.6c, 6.2, 8.2c,
9.2 and 15.2.

STOP: Read through your comments on Units 1-10 and do any
parts you listed as needing further work. Discuss

your discoveries and progress with your partner, and discuss ways you can help each other more in future.

If you are behind in any area, and particularly if you still feel awkward or very stilted as you mimic, take several extra days for review and extra drill, mimicry and conversational practice.

If some facet of the language or culture is blocking further progress, look up that topic in the index and work through some categories out of sequence to solve the problem. Make drills on the problem so your conversational ability can improve.

Date Unit 17 started: _____ Completed: _____

Hours spent on categories 2 and 6: _____

Hours spent on all other categories: _____

Comments:

```
***********************************************************
*                                                         *
*                                                         *
*                                                         *
*                                                         *
*                                                         *
*         Exercise, exercise your powers;                 *
*         what is now difficult will finally              *
*         become routine.                                 *
*                                                         *
*                            --Lichtenberg                *
*                                                         *
*                                                         *
*                                                         *
*                                                         *
***********************************************************
```

Unit 18

AIMS: (1) Elicit and study sentences with two or more verbs.
       (2) Study and start using 'Who?', 'Whom?', and 'Whose?'
       (3) Begin studying aspect and mode/mood.

READ: "Obtaining Linguistic Data" in this *Guide* pp. 344-360.

18.1a Observing the Use of Fire

How do people in your community make fires? What fuel do they use? Where do they collect it--from far or near, from their own land and gardens or just anywhere in the bush? What do they use their fires for--simply to cook, to dry or smoke food, or for warmth and a light to talk by at night? Do they use fires for destroying rubbish? for hunting game (by burning off the grass)? for clearing gardens and fertilizing the soil? for tool making, e.g. straightening the shaft of an arrow or spear? for salt making? for baking pottery? Do they use fire brands for torches? How is fire used in initiation, religious, and magical ceremonies? Is it used for marking the body? From your observations, file as much data as you can on this topic.

18.1b Ask someone to teach you the art of making a fire--how to lay it out and build it, how to light it both with a match and with an ember, how to keep it going. How and where and when would they blow on the fire to keep it burning and how to keep the pieces of wood together in the fire? What do they do to make it blaze for cooking things in a pot, or for producing hot ashes in which to roast food? How do they find dry wood to burn in wet weather? Swallow your inevitable Western pride and let people teach you these skills.

18.2a Conversation

Visit several people or groups and join in the conversation as much as you can. Continue to be alert for any differences between your pronunciation and that of your friends. It is too easy to become careless

in listening as you struggle to expand vocabulary and
handle the grammar in conversation. Beware of this.
Pronouncing with the proper speed and intonation is
far more crucial in your early months than taking on
a great memory load. Once bad habits have been formed, it is much more difficult to break them. KEEP
LISTENING AND MIMICKING.

18.2b   Recording a Descriptive Text

Ask someone to explain something to another person or
to relate what he has been doing, and tape record this
if he is willing. If not, unobtrusively write down
snatches of what is said, and afterwards enquire from
the speaker about what you have written.

18.3a   Eliciting Sentences Containing Two Verbs

Act out sets of actions that can be expected to stimulate people to utter sentences containing 2 to 3 verbs.
Vary the acting so that sometimes (1) you are doing
two things simultaneously, (2) you and your partner
are doing two different things simultaneously,
(3) you do two or more actions one after another
(both with and without an interval between), (4) you
do an action after one by your partner (either as an
interruption, or in immediate sequence, or in delayed
sequence).

If this fails to produce any of the kind of utterances you are looking for, try asking questions of
the type 'Why did he come?', 'When did he come?',
'What did he do?' You may be given some complex
sentences in reply, such as 'He came because you called.', 'He repaired the fence and went home again.'

18.3b   Eliciting 'Whom?'

If you still do not have the words for 'Who?' and
'Whose?' try again now to elicit them (see 1.3 and
9.3). If you have 'Who?' and 'Whose?' but still do
not know 'Whom?' find out what it is. It may be the
same form as is used for 'Who?' in the subject slot.
Try constructing a sentence using the word for
'Who?' in the object position and see if your friends
correct you. (Note: Even if they do not, check with
several people and listen carefully to hear whether
they use this word in this way in their conversation.

Remember that the final check on any elicited material is to hear it in a natural context.)

18.4a Studying Aspect and Mode/Mood

As well as person, number and tense, verbs are often
marked for aspect (kind of action, e.g. begun, completed or incomplete, continuous or punctiliar, habitual etc.) and mode/mood (speaker's attitude to action,
e.g. conditional, imperative, negative, emphatic, interrogative, dubitative, intentive, etc.) ("Mode" is
the American term and "mood" the British term for the
same thing.) Verbs can also be marked for the type of
object (e.g. human or non-human) and for the benefici-
ary of the action. These features may be marked by
affixes, words or clauses. If you have noticed any of
these or other interesting features of the verb,
write tentative notes on them, with examples.

18.4b Studying Dependent and Independent Verbs

Reread 10.4c and 15.4b. Then study the text materials which you have recorded and the multi-verb sentences elicited in 18.3a and note all occurrences in
them of what appear to be dependent verbs. Look at
these verbs and compare them with verbs found in
single-verb sentences and with the verbs found in the
"main" clause of multi-verb sentences in text and in
elicited materials from Units 15-18. In some languages the "main" or independent verb may come in any
position in a sentence depending on the particular
type of sentence. In other languages the independent
verb usually occurs last in the sentence.

Can you see any obvious differences between the verbs
of single-clause sentences and others that only occur
in multi-verb sentences, or between verbs in final
and non-final clauses. For example, do they differ
in how they mark tense, aspect, mood, or subject person-number? Do there appear to be any limitations
as to which affixes can occur on either kind of
verb? Do verbs in non-final clauses have markers
which show that the actor is changing between the
actions? Are there any special affixes in these
verbs which may predict the tense of the following
clause or indicate the relationship between the
clauses, e.g. whether the actions are sequential,
simultaneous, or cause-and-effect?

18.4c Making Paradigms

Process all the data you can. In order to see the
system that is operating within the verb, write paradigms for independent verbs as far as you are able
e.g.

'I went.'	'I'm going.'	'I'm not going.'
'You went.'	'You're going.'	'You aren't going.'
'He went.'	'He's going.'	'He isn't going.'

With what you have in your paradigms and any other
forms you have seen but cannot fit into the paradigms,
make up a tentative chart to show the order of affixes
and how they combine. If there seem to be several
classes of verbs (e.g. ditransitive, transitive, intransitive, and motion verbs) that behave differently,
prepare separate paradigms for each class and separate charts of their systems of affixes.

Prepare a new set of paradigms and make a new order
chart for dependent verbs, if you have discovered any.

18.4d Allomorphic Variation

As you have searched through your materials you may
have noticed some verb stems appear to have two or
more forms (allomorphs). Select some easy-to-elicit
aspect-tense-person combinations which seem to exhibit
the several allomorphs of any such troublesome stems.

On the other hand you may have noticed that certain
affixes seem to have allomorphs. In this instance,
select easy-to-elicit affix combinations which seem
to contain the majority of these troublesome allomorphs.

Now prepare a chart or charts with a column for each
of the affix combinations selected above. Take a row
across the chart for each of the verb stems in your
data and fill in any of the appropriate verb forms
which you actually have in your data.

NOTE: When you have included all the information you
have on the paradigms and charts, put them aside and
add to them as you obtain more information. In later
units you will be returning to look at verbs in
greater detail.

18.4e   Connectives

Look out for any features that seem to be used to join clauses together, e.g. intonation, affixes, clitics (to the verb), separate words (conjunctions) or groups of words (connective phrases) or even nothing (zero). Make a note of any connective devices you observe in the data and indicate what you suspect to be the meaning (some will not be obvious and may even take years to pin down).

18.5a   Constructing Two-clause Sentences

Using vocabulary items you know, try to construct several sentences with two verbs. Construct some with the actor in the first verb (1) the same as and (2) different from that in the second verb.
E.g. 'I saw the pig and I ran away.'
     'I saw the pig and it ran away.'
Check these utterances by using them in conversation with a number of individuals. If they correct you, change what you have written.

18.5b   Testing Aspect and Mode/Mood Markers

Test one or two of the descriptions you wrote in 18.4a in the usual way.

18.6a   Practicing 'Who?', 'Whom?', and 'Whose?'

(1) Make question-and-answer drills using the words for 'Who?' and 'Whom?' in the subject and object slots, and varying the verb or the locational phrase.

Question		Answer	
'Who went to the store?'		'Tom went to the store.'	
'Who went to the market?'	SILENCE	'Tom went to the market.'	SILENCE
....		....	
'Whom did you see?'		'I saw Peter.'	
'Whom did you hit?'		'I hit Peter.'	

(2) Set up drills in which you use the word for 'Whose?' as the attribute of the subject in (a) equative (b) intransitive (c) transitive clauses, e.g.
(a) 'Whose cat is it?'   (b) 'Whose dog is coming?'

(c) 'Whose pig ate the food?' Also (d) use 'Whose?'
within the object slot of transitive clauses, e.g.
'Whose food did the pig eat?'

Record the drills as usual, practice them, then use
the questions in conversation whenever you can.

18.6b Practicing Aspect and Mode/Mood Markers

If in this unit you have adequately described how
an aspect or mode is marked, make a drill keeping the
marker constant in about 6 different sentences. Make
a transform drill from unmarked to marked sentences,
or from one aspect or mode to another. Practice with
the recording, then start to use the feature in conversation. Listen for corrections and for any alternative uses, and modify your description and drill if
necessary.

Date Unit 18 started: _____ Completed: _____

Hours spent on categories 2 and 6: _____

Hours spent on all other categories: _____

Comments:

****
*   *
*   *
*   *
*   *
*   *
*   *
*   *
*   *
*   Rome was not built in a day.   *
*   *
*   *
*   *
*   *
*   *
*   *
****

Unit 19

AIMS: (1)   Start observing the role of animals.
        (2)   Study 'Why?' questions.
        (3)   Continue investigating verb forms.

READ: (1)   "Man and Nature" in Firth pp. 40-70.

        OR "Technology and the Utilization of Natural
        Resources" in Herskovits, *Cultural Anthro-*
        pology pp. 119-142 OR in Herskovits, *Man and*
        His Works pp. 241-265

        OR "Before the Machine" in Fried pp. 147-160

        OR "Food Getting", "Housing", and "Handicrafts"
        in Hoebel pp. 177-238.

        (2)   "The Language Informant" in Samarin pp. 20-44.

19.1   Observing the Role of Animals, Birds and Fish

Start filing notes on the animals, birds and fish
that are important in your area. Which ones are
caught by hunting, trapping or fishing, and which
are domesticated? Are some of the latter kept only
as pets, or do all have economic importance? Do
people seem to regard some as possessions and others
as part of the family? How do people react when an
animal is sick, or when young are born? Which animals do people feed, and which find their own food?
If some kinds are in competition with humans for
food, how do people react to the situation?

Are there any taboos relating to different types of
animal? Are some birds or animals regarded as good
or bad omens, or as a sign of rain? What part do
animals play in ceremonies and social gatherings?

19.2a   Conversation While Collecting Genealogical Information

Continue to collect genealogical details from others
of your neighbors as appropriate. Use new vernacular questions as you are able, and try to follow up
the information people volunteer about their relatives. Mimic names carefully before you write them
down. Stretch your understanding and use of the vernacular as much as you can.

19.2b <u>Listening for 'Why?'</u>

Invest time in conversation with people, and join in
their activities and ceremonies. Be alert for any
questions that seem to contain 'Why?', such as 'Why
is he crying?', 'Why did you hit him?' or 'Why have you
come?' Mimic the question and write it for later analysis. Describe the situation and write the answer
to the question if you can.

19.3a <u>Eliciting 'Why?'</u>

Visit someone who has proved fairly talkative and
helpful in correcting you. If you do not already
know the verb for the particular activity he is engaged in at the time, elicit it by asking, "What are
you doing?" If the reply is "Making twine", construct the sentence 'You are making twine.' and try
it on your friend for correctness. Once he is satisfied say the sentence again preceded by the word for
'What?' in the hope he will correct you by giving you
the expression or construction for 'Why?'. Repeat
this same technique with several different people as
they are doing different kinds of things, especially
activities whose purpose you genuinely don't understand. On each occasion note down carefully the way
in which they correct you.

19.3b Visit people at some unusual times and/or in some unusual places and note carefully their greetings to
you. They may all be a stereotyped greeting such as
'Have you just come?' or 'You are here'. But they
may sometimes ask "Why have you come?". If any of
the greetings appear to contain an unfamiliar question
word, try using it to construct possible 'Why?' questions (as in 19.3a) and note carefully how people correct you.

19.3c If all attempts at monolingual eliciting of 'Why?'
fail, find someone who is bilingual and elicit:

'Why is he doing that?'   Date overheard: _____

Lingua Franca: _____

Vernacular: _____

'Why are you doing that?'   Date overheard: _____

Lingua Franca: _____

Vernacular: _____

By this stage you should be able to detect whether
your bilingual friend is translating the question or
giving you a typical reply!

19.4a   Studying 'Why?' Questions

Study 'Why?' questions discovered in this unit, and
any you had entered previously in the Grammar File or
Topical File. Modify your clause descriptions if
necessary.

How are the answers to 'Why?' questions constructed?
Is there an overt relator 'because'? Do you notice
any new patterns in aspect markers or dependent
clauses in these sentences?

19.4b   Data Processing

Add new forms to your paradigms and charts. Keep
adding morphemes, words and expressions to the Dictionary and Topical File. This filing should be
brought up to date at least twice each week, so that
the items you have discovered can be found when
needed.

19.4c   Kin Relationships

Continue to chart the kin relationships among your
neighbors. If you have noticed any patterns in regard to where people live or who they marry, write
tentative descriptions and file them. In order to
find people on the charts, make an index or a cross-
referenced list for each hamlet or part of the
neighborhood.

19.5   Testing 'Why?' Questions and Responses

Construct 'Why?' questions that will be useful in
understanding people's behavior, such as 'Why did he
do that?, 'Why do they live here?', and 'Why don't you
say her name?' Test them as well as you can, and be
alert for corrections as you use them in conversation.

Construct other questions, and two-clause sentences
using 'because' and test them.

19.6   Practicing 'Why?' and 'Because'

Record a drill with 'Why?' questions and two-clause
answers. Try to make the questions as useful as possible. Practice with the recording, enter it in the
review system and start asking 'Why?' in conversation
(if this is acceptable in the culture).

Date Unit 19 started: _____ Completed: _____

Hours spent on categories 2 and 6: _____

Hours spent on all other categories: _____

Comments:

```
**************************************************************
*                                                            *
*                                                            *
*                                                            *
*                                                            *
*                                                            *
*                                                            *
*                  What you don't use                        *
*                  you will surely lose.                     *
*                                                            *
*                                                            *
*                                                            *
*                                                            *
*                                                            *
**************************************************************
```

Unit 20

AIMS: (1) Observe indigenous art.
(2) Investigate emphasis.

READ: (1) "The Aesthetic Drive: Graphic and Plastic Arts" in Herskovits, *Cultural Anthropology* pp. 234-266 OR in Herskovits, *Man and His Works* pp. 378-413.

OR "Art" in Hoebel pp. 252-278.

(2) "The Eliciting Technique" in Samarin pp. 106-129.

20.1a Observing Art

By careful observation and occasional questions, find out all you can about indigenous art. What art-forms do people use? Do they carve? paint? make pottery? make net bags? weave? In the production of their art objects what instruments and materials are used? Where do they obtain these? From natural resources around them? by trading? To what use do they put their art? For example, do you find it displayed on their weapons, their musical instruments or parts of their houses? Or is it used (only) for religious and ceremonial objects? Is the art work used simply as decoration, or does it seem to have some deeper religious/magical/mythical/totemic significance? Who does the artistic work--specialists or just anyone? What kinds of design do they produce? And what do the art designs represent--people, animals, inanimate objects, actions, or nothing? Do different people/ clans have particular art forms or designs that belong solely to them? Observe all you can, bearing in mind that you will not be able to answer all these things immediately. (It may be several years before you can answer some adequately.)

20.1b Photographic Documentation

From now on, make a project of taking photographs of things and activities in the culture of the people you live among. For instance, you could ask them to bring you all their different kinds of tools or art to photograph, or you could take pictures of the various stages in preparing some food. These photographs will give you an additional opportunity to

show an interest in their culture and way of life,
and will be useful as you prepare literacy materials
later. Assume the role of a learner and talk with
people as much as possible about these things, having
them explain things to you. You will inevitably profit from the conversations and the closer interaction with people that this project will bring you.

You should have one extra print made of each photograph and give it to the most important person involved
in each picture as a way of thanking him for his help
in the project.

20.2a   Effective Conversation Habits

Each day spend at least an hour, preferably not all
at one time, in conversation with your neighbors.
Use the vernacular as much as you can, and mimic
whatever people tell you to say to fill in the gaps.
Ask questions about what is said so you can understand
it better.

Keep using the transformations you have learnt, such
as 'I' to 'you', 'he' to 'they' and statement to question. When you hear a useful or interesting word or
construction, mimic it and write it in your data book.
Try hard to use the new form straight away in three
other sentences.

20.2b   Listen for emphatic statements for analysis in 20.4.
Note interesting examples of the use of conjunctions
and aspect or mode/mood markers to add to your charts
and paradigms.

20.3   Eliciting Emphatic Statements

Try to elicit emphatic statements. To do so, create
a situation in which you throw doubt on something
which is a certainty, so that there will be a strong
possibility of someone repeating a statement in a
more emphatic way to correct your "misconception".
For example in the situation where you know Joe is
going to town, try both of the following:

(a) Say "Joe won't go." You could then expect to
     be corrected with "Yes, Joe WILL go." or in some
     languages "No, Joe WILL go."

(b) Say "Joe will stay." (suggesting a verb which you

know to be wrong). You would then hope to be
corrected with an emphatic "No, Joe will GO."

20.4a Studying Emphasis

Study the examples of emphatic utterances you have
found. Do they constitute a separate mood marked by
an affix or verb auxiliary? Emphasis may be shown instead by a word like 'certainly' or 'completely', or
by a separate clause. Write a tentative description,
with examples.

20.4b

Look through the data you have collected recently,
identifying morphemes and clarifying their meanings
with someone who can help you. File words you are
sure of in the dictionary, and add any new person morphemes to the charts of Unit 7. Add other examples to
the charts and paradigms of verbs. Continue placing
people's names against their houses on your map of the
neighborhood, and cross-reference them to the genealogical charts.

20.4c

Add pages to the Topical File or categories to the.
Grammar File to cover 'How?' questions and instrumentals, prohibitions (negative imperatives), benefactives and hortatory forms (i.e. 'Let's ...'). Record examples in these topics as you come across them.

20.5 Testing With Locationals and Emphasis

Review your work on locationals (Unit 11) and construct sentences with locative phrases such as 'to
the market', 'around the house'. Construct several
emphatic sentences. Try to make the sentences as
natural and useful as possible. Check them with
several friends.

20.6a Practicing Locative Phrases and Emphasis

Record a drill using sentences like the ones in 20.5.
Keep the thing to be learned constant, and use familiar vocabulary.

20.6b Practicing Pronunciation

Make lists of words with contrasting points of articulation but with the same manner of articulation,
e.g. all nasals, all fricatives, or all affricates.
Be sure to have the phones represented in initial,
medial and final positions, if possible. Put on

tape and drill, concentrating on the manner of articulation in focus. Review stops drilled in Unit 14.6d(3).

Date Unit 20 started: _____ Completed: _____

Hours spent on categories 2 and 6: _____

Hours spent on all other categories: _____

Comments:

Number of weeks spent in the village between starting Unit 11 and completing Unit 20: _____

Total hours spent on categories 2 and 6 during Units 11-20: _____

Hours per week: _____

Total hours spent on all other categories during Units 11-20: _____

Hours per week: _____

Considering the statistics in this summary and your progress during the period, what changes do you plan to make in your approach to your neighbors and to language learning, or in your use of future units?

STOP: Special Assignment

Congratulations on finishing the harder half of the
units. Take a holiday for a few days. Get away if
you can and stay with some people of your own culture
or at some resort, and come back refreshed to tackle
the second half. (If you have to be away from your
language area for a longer period of time, read Unit
42 "Language Learning Away from the Language Area"
before you leave.)

```
*****************************************************************
*                                                               *
*                                                               *
*                                                               *
*                                                               *
*                                                               *
*                                                               *
*                                                               *
*              Little strokes fell great oaks.                  *
*                                                               *
*                     --Benjamin Franklin                       *
*                                                               *
*                                                               *
*                                                               *
*                                                               *
*****************************************************************
```

Unit 21

AIMS: (1) Observe gift exchanges.
(2) Begin investigating instrumental forms and 'How?' questions.

READ: (1) "How Do I Adjust to Giving" in Smalley pp. 292-301.
(2) "Making Work Session Profitable" in Samarin pp. 130-150.

STOP: Don't feel bound by the sequence this *Guide* presents. When an unusual event takes place, look up the index for help in recording observations about it. When some linguistic problem is hindering your language learning, look it up in the index for help in solving it.

21.1 Observing Gift Exchanges

Observe when gifts are being given or received. Try to find out the etiquette of these exchanges. To whom are gifts given--uncles and aunts? brothers and sisters? cousins? nieces and nephews? parents-in-law? siblings-in-law? children-in-law? friends who are not relatives? trading partners? aliens or enemies to commence or cement a friendship? What kinds of gifts are given or exchanged? Is the exchange gift regarded as the same in kind or value as the original gift? When is the exchange gift given--immediately, or after a delay of days, months, years? Can you see any evidence for why people give the first gift of an exchange? Is it out of kindness or love? in full expectation of receiving an exchange? because it is etiquette when visiting or being visited? to demonstrate or cement friendship? to gain prestige from one's generosity? to gain power and influence from having a large number of debtors? Note that what may appear to be a gift may in fact be payment for services to a shaman, house-builder, midwife, artist, murderer, grave-diggers, mourners, pig-minders, and the like.

Remember that at first you may only observe "the obvious" about this topic, but as you continue to observe over weeks and years, the deeper motives and

principles will gradually become more apparent to
you.

21.2a Visiting Some Old People

Visit some of the very old people in the area. Go
prepared with a couple of topics to talk about and
several specific questions to ask.

21.2b Using Inner Speech

Make a special effort to hold inner conversations in
the vernacular with yourself while you are engaged in
daily activities requiring little concentration.
Read again "Don't Learn That Language" in Smalley
pp. 349-351. You have learnt many questions by now
with which you can interrogate yourself and frame
suitable replies. Remember Reyburn's comment that
"After having disciplined yourself to employ inner
speech, you will be surprised at how easy it is to
say things in actual conversations."

21.3 Eliciting 'How?' and Instrumentals

If you have some examples of 'How?' questions or instrumentals in the Grammar File or Topical File, study
them first, and try to use their morphemes and structure to elicit these features in other clause types.
If you do not have any examples, try to elicit them
as suggested below.

NOTE: The English interrogative 'How?' has a broad
range of meaning and may lead to responses that tell
the method/procedure, manner or instrument of an
activity. The corresponding interrogatives in the
vernacular and the lingua franca may have different
areas of meaning. The 'How?' of manner is dealt with
in Unit 38.

21.3a Eliciting 'How?' (Method)

Show someone how to do something new (e.g. making
bread) or something that may seem puzzling (e.g.
seeing things at a great distance through binoculars,
tying knots that untie at a pull), or perhaps ask the
person to do something he doesn't know how to do.
Such a situation may result in his asking you
"How ...?" Try to record this in your data book or
on tape, for use in 21.4.

21.3b <u>Eliciting 'How?' (Instrumental)</u>

Try to elicit 'What with?' or 'How?' by using 'What?'
instead, in sentences like 'What did you cut your
hand? knife?' 'What did you do/get and cut your
hand? knife?' Try this on different occasions with
different people, noting their corrections.

21.3c <u>Eliciting Instrumentals</u>

If you have not already found out how to express instrumentality, try to elicit statements such as 'He
cut it <u>with</u> <u>an</u> <u>axe</u>.' If you are able to do so, make
use of your investigations in 21.3b to ask 'How?'.
Alternatively, try acting out the situation, as you
did in earlier units, to see if this will elicit the
desired statement. Do the same kind of action with
several instruments in turn.

If neither of these methods succeeds, construct experimental sentences using vocabulary you know, e.g.
'He cut his hand--knife.' and see if people correct
you.

21.4a <u>Studying 'How?' and Instrumentals</u>

Analyze the constructions you have found. Note that
in some languages the interrogative word for 'How?'
is a verb and 'How?' questions, therefore, contain at
least two verbs. Note also that in some languages
the nouns may take an instrumental affix; in others
the verb is marked for instrumentality; in yet
others an instrument is indicated by a whole additional clause, e.g. 'Axe take wood chop' = 'Chop the wood
with an axe.' And in yet others there may be a separate verb that means 'to chop wood with an axe',
with or without the use of the word 'axe'.

21.4b <u>Transcribing Text and Filing</u>

Transcribe a tape-recorded text, preferably of a dis-
course type you have not yet transcribed. Read 15.3a
again before you start. Ask questions (in the vernacular where possible) to clarify the meanings and
uses of new words and constructions. Enter your discoveries in the dictionary and other files, with
references to the parts of the text they occurred in.

Keep on filing the material you write in your data
book when visiting or working with people.

21.5   <u>Testing Your Understanding of 'How?' and Instrumentals</u>

Check the tentative description you wrote in 21.4a by
constructing 'How?' questions and appropriate answers
containing instrumentals such as 'How did you catch
the bird?' 'I caught it with a trap.' and 'How did
you come here?' 'We came by canoe.'

21.6a   <u>Practicing Instrumentals</u>

Record a drill with sentences like the ones in 21.5
to give practice in asking 'How?' and in using instrumental markers. Enter it in the review system,
and when you can say the sentences easily, start using them in conversation. Extend the sentences to
fit different situations, being alert for any corrections.

21.6b   <u>Practicing Pronunciation</u>

Make lists of words for vowel and consonant sounds
that you have heard and that are not covered in earlier lists. Remember, these do not have to be phonemically analyzed yet. Drill these new sets of
words and have various people check your pronunciation.

Make lists of contrasting points of articulation (see
20.6b) with yet another manner of articulation. Put
these on tape, practice pronouncing them and have
your pronunciation checked.

Review previous lists of vowels and consonants as
indicated by your review system.

Continue pronunciation list drills, adding new
sounds or new examples of difficult sounds.

Date Unit 21 started: _____ Completed: _____

Hours spent on categories 2 and 6: _____

Hours spent on all other categories: _____

Comments:

```
***********************************************************
*                                                         *
*      THIS BOOK IS AN AID.                               *
*      YOUR REAL JOB IS TO LEARN THE LANGUAGE.            *
*      IT IS FAR BETTER TO BE OUTSIDE                     *
*      WASTING TIME WITH PEOPLE                           *
*      THAN TO BE INSIDE                                  *
*      STUDYING THIS                                      *
*      BOOK.                                              *
*                                                         *
***********************************************************
```

Unit 22

AIMS: (1) Review.
      (2) Bring data processing up to date.

READ: again "Language Learning" in this *Guide* pp. 285-296

22.1 Cultural Observations

Bring your cultural file up to date as outlined in 17.1.

22.2a Tracking

Track each of the intonation tapes you have made (see 16.6e and 17.6c) once. Then play the tapes again, listening carefully for words, phrases and expressions you may know. When you recognize something, stop the recorder and mimic it more carefully, trying to approximate the individual sounds as well as you can. If you have difficulty hearing the individual sounds, have someone listen to the tape and repeat the word or phrase for you to pronounce more carefully. Mimic no more than 3 times and then go on. After you have finished going through the tapes in this way, track them each once more. Repeat the entire process after an interval of at least 2 hours has elapsed.

If your tape recorder is not working, spend some time, on at least four different occasions today, in tracking speech in live situations and in listening carefully to and mimicking words and short phrases for practicing individual sounds.

22.2b Visit several people in the village and converse, using the expressions and drills you have learned as much as you can. Listen for familiar phrases, especially instrumental forms, and mimic everything you are told to say. Observe gestures used while people are talking. Some gestures take the place of verbal responses, and others completely change the sense of what is being said. If possible, talk with one or two people you have never conversed with before. Note any facet of the language that is holding you back in conversational ability.

22.2c Make an agreement with your partner that from now on
you will TRY to use only the vernacular--no English
or lingua franca--in talking to each other when vernacular speakers are present. This will help both
your relations with your neighbors and your fluency.

22.3 Learning Useful Expressions

Elicit, tape-record, and learn three more of the Useful Expressions listed on pp. 460-464.

22.4a Bringing Filing Up to Date

If there is any material in your data book which you
have checked out but have not yet filed in appropriate
files or charts, do so now.

22.4b Continuing Phonemic Analysis

Add any new patterns from data obtained in Units 18-21
to your lists of CV patterns and clusters, with examples. Add any new sounds to your work charts,
with examples. Add any new data that provides good
proof for contrast to your contrastive sets of examples. Check the hypotheses you have previously
written down against the new data and modify your
hypotheses as needed.

22.4c Tone

What evidence do you have that the language you are
studying is or is not tonal, i.e., most words contrast
not only in their consonants and vowels but also in
the pitch on individual syllables or in the pitch pattern spread over the word as a whole? (You will be
checking this more carefully in frames in 26.4.)

22.4d Concentrating on Special Topic(s)

Look back at the comments you wrote at the end of each
unit from 11 to 16. If you listed any topics as needing further work, consider spending a few days now on
these topics. If some area of the grammar is holding
up your conversational progress, concentrate on it
for some time so you will be able to use that feature. Look up the topic in the index, work through
the sections, mark them with the date and then resume your work in this unit.

22.6a Practice Gives Fluency

Review practice recordings as indicated by the review
system. If you are not using any review system, you
should set about reviewing all drills and recordings,
doing only about four each day, until they are done.
Drop from review any that you have mastered thoroughly.

22.6b Concentrated Practice

If there are some grammatical patterns you understand
well but cannot use fluently in speech, take extra
time now to record drills to practice these patterns
so you can start using them. Make the sentences as
useful as possible, keeping the feature to be learnt
constant. Then make a transform drill to give practice in adding the feature.

Establish speech habits based on your understanding
of the language before moving on and tackling new
problems.

Date Unit 22 started: _____ Completed: _____

Hours spent on categories 2 and 6: _____

(Along with categories 2 and 6, always include all
time spent with your neighbors and others in casual
situations.)

Hours spent on all other categories: _____

Comments:

Unit 23

AIMS: (1) Observe social interactions.
(2) Continue investigating verb forms and learn seven new verbs.
(3) Study prohibitions.

READ: (1) "On Eliciting Transformations in Vietnamese" in this *Guide* pp. 489-398.
(2) "Principles of Translation" in Nida, *Bible Translating* pp. 11-30.

23.1 Observing Attitudes and Social Interactions

As you attend different ceremonies, observe the attitudes of the participants. For example, at a wedding, are the bride and groom joyful, or very subdued? Do initiates appear frightened or expectant? Do the onlookers share the same attitudes as the participants, or are their attitudes opposite or complementary? Note the behavior that manifests these attitudes. If there are speeches, try to note who makes them, how the speakers are related to the other participants and what attitudes they express.

Make similar observations in ordinary every-day situations where people gather in groups.

23.2a Recording Different Discourse Types

Take the tape recorder with you to a number of different situations such as communal work, recreation, wedding, funeral, political meeting or religious ceremony. Record speeches and stretches of conversation when appropriate.

23.2b Tracking a Recording

Track a recording (about 4 minutes) which contains an intonational type different from any you have done up to now, as outlined in 3.6b. If your tape recorder is not working, spend several minutes tracking live situations, at least five times, with intervals between.

23.2c Visiting

Visit several of your neighbors and spend time

conversing and mimicking with each one. Listen for
pronoun and verbal forms with which you are familiar.
Write any new helpful or useful expressions for which
you can discern or discover the meanings. Particularly write those containing new verbal forms and/or
negatives.

23.3   Eliciting New Verbs

Obtain seven new verb roots. Elicit by asking "What
is he (are you) doing?" or work with some roots you
have heard in conversation or recorded on tape but
have not yet investigated.

23.4a   Listening for Intonation Contours

For each recording made in 23.2a, enter details such
as tape reference, speaker, subject matter and dis-
course type in the tape index.

First read through the list of intonational types in
2.2d. Then listen to the new recordings you made in
23.2a. As you find good examples of familiar intonation types, note the tape references for these
against the items in the list in 2.2d. You will need
these later for analysis and description of intonation contours. If you find an example of an intonation contour you have not noticed before, note the
tape reference against the item in the 2.2d list, or
add more types of intonation contours to the list if
necessary.

Listen to your other recordings of spontaneous speech
and add to the list the references to other good
examples of intonation contours.

23.4b   Describing Intonation Contours

Describe and illustrate any new intonation contour
you have discovered in 2a and 4a above. If necessary,
modify the description of or expand the meaning attributed to any contours you have described previously. Add new examples to the descriptions where appropriate.

23.4c   Describing Prohibitions

Look up 'prohibitions' in the Grammar File or Topical
File, and study the examples collected there. (If
you cannot find any examples that you have heard,

construct some examples by negating imperatives. Do
this for singular and plural commands, both transitive and intransitive. Try these constructions with
some of your friends and note their corrections.)

Study these examples and describe their structure.
Are there any differences in the way imperatives are
negated for different aspects or for transitive and
intransitive? Describe the intonation contour(s)
used with prohibitions.

23.4d   Transcribing, Filing, and Analyzing

Continue the transcription of your (taped) text material, preferably using another or several other persons to help you (see 15.3a).

Study the new data obtained recently. Compare it with
previous data to confirm what you already know and to
isolate as many new words and morphemes as you can.
Check the material for meaning with a helpful friend.
Bring the Dictionary File and Topical File up to date.
Continue to investigate verbal forms. Following the
detailed suggestions given in 18, enter any new forms
on your charts.

23.5   Checking on New Verb Roots and Prohibitions

Construct at least 14 sentences, using the new verbs
obtained in 23.3 in different tenses/modes and with
different person/number/question markers, etc. At
least half of these sentences should contain two or
more verbs.

For each clause type (e.g. transitive, intransitive),
construct two sentences using familiar vocabulary.
From each sentence, construct the imperative form and
then negate it, e.g.
'They came to the house.'
'Come to the house!'
'Don't come to the house!'

Try to make your constructions as useful and interesting as possible. Check them with some friends.

23.6a   Practicing New Verb Roots and Prohibitions

Record a set of sentences similar to those constructed
in 23.5 to give practice with the seven new verb roots.

Use each root in two or three sentences.

Record a drill to give practice with prohibitions.

Record and learn useful expressions as you come across them.

23.6b Practicing Pronunciation

Make lists of words containing each of the vowel glides or clusters that you have noticed and drill these just as you did single vowels. You may not have a lot of these at this stage. Don't worry if you don't. List and drill the ones you have.

If there are any manners of articulation that have not been drilled to contrast different points of articulation, make lists of these and drill with them as you did in earlier lessons. Review previous consonant lists.

Date Unit 23 started: _____ Completed: _____

Hours spent on categories 2 and 6: _____

Hours spent on all other categories: _____

Comments:

Unit 24

AIMS: (1) Observe recreational activities.
       (2) Add more nouns to vocabulary.
       (3) Gain confidence in the use of subject pronouns.

READ: (1) "Eliciting Vocabulary, Meaning, and Collocations" in this *Guide* pp. 361-386.
       (2) "Principles of Equivalence" in Nida, *Bible Translating* pp. 130-148.

24.1 Observing Recreational Activities

As you join with people in village life, observe their recreational activities. What do they do in their leisure time? Do they carve, or make net bags? Do they make music or tell stories/jokes/riddles? Do they perhaps, as a result of European culture contact, gamble/drink/read? Or do they still swing in their hammocks, or just sit and talk around a fire sharing tobacco and betelnut? What games do the children play? What amusements do the people have? Write down any observations you have made and add them in your cultural file.

24.2 Practicing Subject Pronouns in Conversation

Review your descriptions of subject pronouns and mimic one of your drills that gives practice with non-singular subject pronouns.

Share an activity with some of your neighbors and converse and mimic at every opportunity. Try to practice varying subject pronouns as you converse, taking advantage of your grammar analysis to expand your speaking ability. (Remember to laugh with them at your mistakes, and indicate pleasure for any corrections.) Be an alert observer and listener when you are not participating directly in the conversation. Track inwardly to yourself when you are unable to understand what is going on.

Be alert to new useful expressions and write them in your data book. Notice any new contexts for familiar vocabulary or grammatical forms and write them. Be especially alert for expressions from your elicited material which have not yet been confirmed in natural

unelicited contexts, particularly those containing
interrogative words, imperatives and personal pronouns. As you recognize such expressions, note particularly the word order and intonation, and record
them carefully as you write.

24.3   Eliciting More Nouns

Using the vernacular expression for 'What is this?'
elicited and checked in Unit 3, or by asking "What do
you call this?", make a list of 15 more concrete
nouns. (If you are running out of ideas of vocabulary
to elicit see the word list in the appendix.) Elicit
the plurals of these nouns and of any other nouns,
previously elicited, whose plurals you have not recorded.

NOTE: If in Unit 16 you discovered several classes
or genders of nouns which determined variant forms of
the numerals, then be sure to check the plurals of
several nouns from each class, as they may take different plural markers.

24.4a   Checking Previously Elicited Expressions

Compare with their elicited counterparts any expressions you wrote in 24.2 which correspond in any way
to previously elicited material. Are they the same
as, or different from, the elicited expressions? If
they differ, in what ways do they differ? Be particularly alert to small changes in word order and to
intonation differences. As you make these compari-
sons and as you continue to notice such things in
future listening, try to determine whether the elicited form you obtained was a freely used variant, a less
commonly used variant, or an unnatural construction
which you will want to replace with a natural one.
Intonation differences may indicate a different attitude on the part of the speaker while the basic meaning of the expression is unchanged. This will signal
another area you will need to investigate in the
future. For now, write any such examples on a separate sheet of paper labeled "intonation", noting which
was elicited and which was non-elicited, and anything
that would give you a clue as to the speaker's attitudes. File this with your phonology analysis material. If you happened to catch the non-elicited expression on tape, be sure to include a reference to
that tape with the example. Elicited utterances with

a particular intonation can probably be recaptured on
tape at any time. These will give you valuable minimal or sub-minimal pairs for intonation.

24.4b Studying Dual and Trial Forms

Check your descriptions of possessives, the plurals
of different classes of nouns, subject and object
forms, verb forms, etc. Try to extend your descriptions to cover dual and/or trial (if you have found
these distinctions) as well as singular and plural.

24.4c Residual Pronouns

What do you have left in the data that may be pro-
nouns--anything? You may have another set used in
polite speech. You may have a set used to manifest
an appositional relationship. The important factor
is: Can you group them in a single chart or are there
further divisions necessary? Do you have any left-
overs which you cannot yet assign to any specific
set? Until functions are more obvious, remember you
can always label the charts of these: Type a, Type b,
Type c, etc.

NOTE: Unexpected forms may be used in certain kin relationships. For instance, brother-in-laws may have
to use 'you (pl.)' instead of 'you (sg.)' when addressing each other.

24.5a Working with the New Nouns

Take some of the new nouns you have elicited and construct clauses using the nouns in different slots
which were investigated and drilled in previous units:
subject (Unit 2), object (15), possessor (18), location (11, 20), instrument (21). Examples of such
clauses could be:

'The arrow flew up.'
'The boy made an arrow.'
'The arrow's head flew off.'
'He put down his spear beside his arrow.'
'He shot the bird with his arrow.'

Use both singular and plural forms.

24.5b Testing out Dual and Trial Forms

If in 24.4b you modified any descriptions to cover
dual or trial forms, construct new sentences to test

your modified descriptions. Construct other sentences with the new verbs elicited in Unit 23.

Check all your constructions with some friends as usual. Also use your constructions, when checked, in "inner conversation" (see 21.2b).

24.6a   Learning to Use the New Nouns

Make a drill using the nouns elicited in 24.3 in the possessor and/or possessed slots. If this is not possible, then concentrate on drilling them in object position.

24.6b   Practicing Duals and/or Trials

If appropriate, make a drill on duals in which three sentences contain the same dual marker. Repeat for the other dual markers. Repeat for trial. Question-and-answer patterns will probably be most natural.

Make a second set in which singulars are transformed into duals or trials.

24.6c   Practicing Pronunciation

Set up drills for consonant clusters, putting like clusters in one list. Record these and drill them. Have a native speaker check your pronunciation.

Review previous articulation drills which deal with sounds that are still causing you difficulty.

Date Unit 24 started: _____   Completed: _____

Hours spent on categories 2 and 6: _____

Hours spent on all other categories: _____

Comments:

Unit 25

AIMS: (1) Observe sickness and health.
      (2) Expand your knowledge of object pronouns or person affixes.
      (3) Transcribe more text and learn to use some items discovered in it.

READ: (1) "A Method for Eliciting Paradigmatic Data from Text" in this *Guide* pp. 387-388.
      (2) "Terms for Features of Man's Form" and "Terms for Features of the Natural Environment" in Nida, *Bible Translating* pp. 149-167.

25.1 Observing Sickness and Health

What have you observed about health and hygiene among your neighbors? What methods or principles of hygiene do they observe? What do they do as regards washing, or water for drinking? Do they make use of formal or informal toilet facilities? What is their attitude towards pests and insects, especially those that bring disease? How do they tackle problems such as lice or skin complaints? And if someone is sick, what do they do then? Do they quarantine or avoid him in any way, or does this depend on the particular disease? What methods or medicines are resorted to for healing? How is the sick person regarded? Is he pitied? or feared? Is sickness common or rare? And what is the situation, attitude, or treatment for animal diseases and diseases of the main food crops? Observe and enquire as you move around the neighborhood and other villages and take notes for your anthropology file.

25.2a Practicing Object Pronouns in Conversation

Visit some friends and try to use in conversation the object pronouns or affixes that you know. Listen for corrections, and note them for analysis in 25.4.

25.2b Tracking a Discussion

Sit in on some village discussion (informal court case, discussion of economic ventures, welcoming a young man home from contract labor, house building, village clean-up, speech by community leader, etc.)

and silently track as much of the discussion as you
can.

25.3 Eliciting More Object Pronouns or Affixes

Review object pronouns and affixes in the charts of
Unit 7. Work from what you know to find new object
pronouns. Construct a series of utterances like the
following:

Stimulus	Response
'dog'	'He saw it.'
'man'	'He saw him.'
'woman'	'He saw her.'
'I'	....
'you'	....

Work with someone you have found helpful in eliciting,
and read both stimulus and response to him until he
has grasped the pattern and can make the appropriate
responses. Add other stimuli and try to find an object pronoun or affix to correspond with each subject
form you know.

Repeat this procedure using nouns of different
classes as the stimuli, to see if different pronouns
are used with different noun classes. Repeat again
with different verbs to see if any new forms appear.
Investigate transitive imperatives to see if they
take different object forms.

If these methods fail, try constructing sentences
with subject pronouns in the object position, and get
someone to correct them. Only use the lingua franca
for this eliciting as a last resort.

25.4a Studying Object Pronouns or Person Affixes

Study the material obtained in 25.2 and 25.3. Check
out all discoveries. Fill in as many as possible of
the object spaces on the charts in Unit 7. You may
find that further modifications in the chart will be
necessary, especially if the third person has several
forms corresponding to noun classes or genders.

25.4b Transcribing Texts

Continue transcribing any tape-recorded texts that

you have, including conversations. If you do not
have a conversation on tape, try to record two of
your friends discussing some pictures or a forthcoming or recent event.

Continue filing words and constructions as you find
them in text materials.

25.5   Testing Recent Discoveries

(1)   Construct clauses using the nouns elicited in
       24.3 in the object slot. Preferably use transi-
       tive verbs you have recently obtained. (See
       23.3 and 15.3c.)

(2)   Transform these clauses, replacing the object
       noun with the appropriate pronoun, e.g. 'He hit
       the dog' → 'He hit him.'

(3)   Expand these clauses with an instrumental, e.g.
       'He hit him with a stick.'

(4)   Experiment to see if 'hit' can take an inanimate
       subject. Try transforming 'He hit him' to 'The
       stick hit him', by replacing 'He' with 'stick'.
       Watch for any changes in the verb.

(5)   Take the clauses of (2) and replace the third
       person object pronouns by a variety of first and
       second person object pronouns.

(6)   Take the clauses of (2) and add an extra verb to
       make a two-clause sentence. Perhaps the easiest
       verbs to add will be motion verbs such as 'go'
       and 'come', e.g. 'He came and hit him.'

Check out these constructions thoroughly and use them
in your conversation as opportunity arises.

25.6a   Practicing Object Pronouns or Affixes

Record a series of sentences concentrating on the object pronouns you cannot yet use easily. For each
pronoun (or affix) record three or four pairs of question and answer sentences like the following:

       'Did they see you?'   'Yes, they saw us.'
       'Did they take you?'   'Yes, they took us.'
       ....

As you plan the sentences, think of the situation

where each could be used, so they will be as useful
as possible.

If different noun classes require different pronouns
to stand for them, record several sentences using
each of the pronouns, e.g.

    'Did you see the shark?'   'Yes, I saw it.'
    'Did you see the tuna?'   'Yes, I saw it.'
     (same class)
    ....

Next, record a set of sentences where the class of
the noun in the object changes from one sentence to
the next, e.g.

    'Have you seen my spear?'   'No, I haven't seen it.'
     (class 1)
    'Have you seen my dish?'   'No, I haven't seen it.'
     (class 2)
    ....

Set up a similar type of drill if there is agreement
between the verb and object.

25.6b   Learning Useful Vocabulary and Constructions from Text

Choose some of the words you discovered while transcribing text in 25.4b. For each word, record three
or four sentences that contain the word. If the first
sentence can be a vernacular definition of the new
word (e.g. '"Boar" is a male pig.') and the other
sentences use familiar vocabulary, there need not be
any English meanings on the tape. If this cannot be
done, each sentence should be preceded by its English
meaning and a pause. Record each sentence twice,
with silence between.

Choose some construction(s) that you discovered and
understand at least partially. For each construction,
record the English meaning, silence, then the clause
or sentence from the text, silence, then the expression again. Record variations in the construction,
each preceded by a vernacular stimulus (if possible)
such as 'two people', 'many people' or 'I', 'you'.

25.6c   For all recordings you make for practice like this,
have one or two people who speak clearly record the
vernacular utterances, while you (or your partner)

should speak the English meanings. Leave periods of
silence for mimicry after the vernacular utterances.
Also leave a period of silence between the stimulus
and the response (or between the English and the vernacular) in which you can try to say the vernacular
before you hear it from the tape. This self-testing
increases retention.

Enter each recording in the review system.

25.6d Learning Useful Expressions

Choose three of the Useful Expressions listed on pp.
460-464, elicit them, check them, record them on tape,
practice them with the tape and a native speaker, add
them to your system for regular reviewing, and use
them in conversation with someone today.

25.6e Practicing Pronunciation

Have you noticed any vowels which you would consider
to be long? (See 16.4d). If so, set up word lists
having these long vowels and drill them as you did
with other vowels. If you don't have length, look
for nasalization, laryngealization or any other modification of the vowels and do the same with them.

Set up contrastive phonological drills to help you
control any of the above features. For instance,
suppose you wished to contrast English d and θ in
word initial position you could adopt the following
procedure.

(1) List your words (preferably in a frame) with your
contrasted sounds occurring in the same position in
the word.

Illustrating d: Illustrating θ:
It is this.   *It is thin.*
It is that.   *It is thick.*
It is theirs.   *It is thought.*
It is thine.   *It is third.*
It is there.   *It is thread.*

Have someone tape-record these expressions, reading
down the lists in turn. Listen and mimic.

(2) Next practice the difficult contrasts by drilling across the lists, e.g. *It is this, it is thin;
it is that, it is thick,* etc., putting these on tape
also.

(3) For further practice of these contrasts make other recordings to drill the words in random order, e.g. *It is this, ...that, ...thin, ...thine.*

(4) Finally put a drill on tape in which the contrasted sounds occur anywhere in any words, e.g. *It is a thread, ...feather, ...breath, ...thong,* and practice with this.

Work with a native speaker in all of this, having him tell you whether your mimicry is correct or not.

Drill previous vowels that still give you problems.

Continue to set up lists of consonant clusters, record them, practice them and then have a native speaker check your pronunciation. Practice earlier drills.

Date Unit 25 started: _____ Completed: _____

Hours spent on categories 2 and 6: _____

Hours spent on all other categories: _____

Comments:

```
********************************************************************
*                                                                  *
*                                                                  *
*                                                                  *
*                                                                  *
*                  A word in the mouth                             *
*                  is worth ten in the book.                       *
*                                                                  *
*                                                                  *
*                                                                  *
*                                                                  *
********************************************************************
```

Unit 26

AIMS: (1) Review.
       (2) Add to phonetic work chart and hypotheses.
       (3) Begin sorting words for their pitch, stress, and length patterns.

READ: (1) "Testing the Recognition of Utterance Pairs" in this *Guide* pp. 399-407.
       (2) "Terms for Features of Material Culture" in Nida, *Bible Translating* pp. 168-177.
       (3) "Analytical Procedure One Amplified for Special Application to Problems of Pitch" in Pike pp. 105-115.

26.2a Tracking Recordings

Review the intonation and text tapes 3.2b, 6.2a, 15.2c, 16.6e, 18.2b, and 23.2a following the tracking and mimicking procedures outlined in 3.6b. Do one or two sections, take a break of at least an hour doing a different activity, then come back and do a different one or two sections. Do this several times each day that you are working on this review unit.

26.2b Extra Conversation

Try to spend an extra amount of time in conversation with your neighbors during the course of this unit, putting into practice all of the expressions, drills and vocabulary that you have learnt. Do not spend too long at any one time, but vary your activities and visit different people doing different things from time to time, talking, mimicking and listening. Don't wear yourself out; take a break when you need it and as long as you need and then go back and try again. Remember always to mimic using the same intonation you hear. English intonation habits are one of the hardest things to break as you learn a new language. It takes conscious thought and effort.

26.4a Bringing Filing up to Date

Process any material (vocabulary, phrases, or grammatical data) that has been checked but not yet filed in appropriate charts or files.

26.4b   Reviewing Anthropological Notes

Review observation topic suggestions and questions in
category 1 of Units 1-7. Then read on through all
your notes and written observations on these topics.
Are there things you have observed on any topic
which come to mind now but have not yet been written
down? If so, write them and file them with your
other notes. If you have not already done so, take
time now to bring your file up to date and organize
under appropriate topics and sub-topics (see p. 477)
all the notes you have written.

26.4c   Phonemic Analysis

Add any new sounds from data obtained in Units 21-24
to your consonant and vowel work charts, and new CV
patterns and clusters to your lists. Continue to be
on the lookout for contrastive sets of words to add
to your proofs of contrast between two or more similar sounds. Add new words to your present sets which
give further or better contrast. Put into writing
any further hypotheses you may have by now for uniting phonetically similar sounds. The hypotheses may
be either that the two or more sounds are in mutually
exclusive distribution or that they are in free variation. Once you have put this into writing, keep your
eyes and ears open for new data which may conflict
with any hypothesis, and adjust your hypotheses accordingly. Or, if there seems to be only one exception to a hypothesis, put the conflicting example
with the hypothesis, to be checked later against further data.

If there are sounds of which you are still not sure,
make use of check lists at this time to tune up your
hearing as to whether they are the same or different
from sounds that seem similar.

NOTE: Check lists are very useful for length, stress,
and pitch, as well as for other phonetically similar
pairs and triplets. Preparing such lists forces you
to sort your phonetic data and check hearing, as well
as giving pointers for areas where phonological drills
should be made (cf. 25.6e). They can also give valuable clues for your phonemic analysis, by revealing
patterns of distribution and points of contrast in
phonetically checked data.

26.4d   How to Make and Use a Phonetic Check List

(1)   Make a list of your hard-to-distinguish similar
sounds in a given analogous environment, e.g. word
initial in a stressed syllable.

(2)   Give your language helper a list of the words,
in the lingua franca if he can read, in picture or
object form if he cannot.   Take the first word (Word
A) as your point of comparison, and have him say the
first two words.   Note down whether the initial sound
is the same or different in both words.   Then have
him repeat the first word with the third word, the
first word with the fourth, etc., each time noting
down whether the initial sound is the same or different from that in Word A.

If you hear all the initial sounds of these words as
the same, then assume that you only have one phonetic
item in this context.   (Nevertheless, later on you may
hear words which make you wonder at the correctness
of your decision.   At that time re-check all the pertinent data by this same method.   If by then you have
several words which may be either minimal pairs or
homophonous pairs and you aren't sure which, then apply the Pair Recognition Test to them.   See pp. 399-
407.)

(3)   If you have heard some of the initial sounds of
the words as different from Word A, reshuffle your
items into two lists of "same" (as Word A) and "different".   Then have your helper go straight through
the list you have noted as the same as Word A, to
check that it is really uniform.   (If it is not, the
odd word will probably stick out like a sore thumb,
and should be duly amputated!)   Do the same with the
list of words different from Word A.   If all in this
list are uniform, then you have demonstrated that
there are only two sounds in these two separate lists.

(4)   It is quite possible, however, that in the "different" list you still have more than one sound.   If
this is so, repeat the procedure in (2) with this
shorter list of words, this time comparing each item
with Word B, the first word of this "different" list.
Continue repeating procedures (2) and (3) until you
are satisfied that all your lists are uniform.

This procedure can be used effectively to sort out
all your different phonetic sounds, even when you
still cannot analyze them exactly. New words containing these hard-to-distinguish similar sounds
should be checked against the consistent lists,
while pairs of words (sub-minimal pairs at first,
and later minimal pairs where possible) can be taken
from the lists to practice hearing and speaking control.

26.4e   Noting More Examples of Intonation Contours

Work through all spontaneous recordings made since
Unit 23, and study intonation contours following the
procedures outlined in 23.4a and 23.4b.

26.4f   Analyzing Pitch, Stress, and Length

Go through your data and begin making lists of words
having the same number of syllables which seem to
have the same rhythm (stress and length) and pitch
when pronounced in isolation. Begin by making separate lists of one-syllable words, two-syllable words,
three-syllable words, etc. You may find it more
flexible to begin by writing each word on a separate
piece of paper (3 x 5 or smaller) and sorting the
words into piles having the same number of syllables.
If your Dictionary File is on cards, these can be
used without re-writing. Each pile or list should in
turn be sub-grouped for similar CV patterns, vowel
and consonant content, etc., to facilitate hearing
the pitch and rhythm patterns without interference
from widely differing vowel quality or consonant articulation. NOTE: To check and sort these for stress,
pitch and length, frames must be used (see Pike p.
107). Then go through each sub-group with your language helper, sub-dividing the words according to
your first impressions as to whether they are "same"
or "different" in pitch and rhythm within a given
frame, as he pronounces them, grouping and regroup-
ing them until you think each pile or list is uniform as to rhythm and pitch.

Clip each pile of such words together and set them
aside to listen to again later when you are fresher.
If it helps you to give each group a tentative label
according to what you think its distinguishing feature is (i.e. stress on first syllable vs. stress on
third, long-short vs. short-short syllable lengths,

high-low vs. rising-low pitch, etc.), do so. If you
are using punch cards, you may wish to punch them to
reflect this classification. At this stage, however,
it is more important to determine whether words in
fact sound different from others in pitch and rhythm,
and how many such different groups there are, than to
put specific labels on the differences.

You will probably have some words which are particularly difficult to determine, either because of unusual CV structure or because the pitch and/or rhythm
seems to fluctuate. Put these under a separate category labeled "residue" to be handled after the rest
have been sorted out, or defer punching these cards
until later.

26.4g   Expanding Topical File

Add pages to the Topical File or categories to the
Grammar File to cover the following topics: (a) same
subject and (b) different subject multi-clause sentences, descriptives, comparative constructions,
demonstratives and indefinite morphemes. As you find
examples of these in conversation and while transcribing spontaneous texts, file them for use in analysis.
Add other categories as appropriate.

26.6a   Reviewing Practice Recordings

If you are using a review system, bring your programmed review of recordings up to date. Review any other
drills which are not becoming automatic.

If you are not following any review system, review
previous recordings of drills and expressions. Leave
out any which come automatically now. Break this
practice up into 5 minute segments.

Check the accuracy and acceptability of the recordings made in Units 8 to 11, and replace any that are
not really natural speech. Try to use more of these
expressions and grammatical patterns in conversation.

26.6b   Practicing Agreement

If you have observed agreement in your language between a subject and its verb or an object and its
verb make up a context-forcing drill (see p. 167) to
master this. Construct your drills by substituting

in turn one or more representative nouns of each
gender/class in a suitable sentence frame.

For example, in Kikuyu where there is agreement between the verbal prefix and the subject noun, one
could set up a context-forcing drill thus (the trouble
spot for agreement is underlined):

	SUBJECT: nouns from various classes	SENTENCE FRAME: Tense: Action: 'is' 'going'	
'teacher'	*murutani*	*ni*	*a-radie*
'crocodile'	*kiŋaŋi*	*ni*	*ki-radie*
'fire'	*moaki*	*ni*	*u-radie*
'foot'	*ikiña*	*ni*	*ri-radie*

To use this drill have your partner act as a prompter
and give you an item which forces your choice of the
other item(s) in that utterance: e.g.
Prompter says: *"Kiŋaŋi"*
Learner says: *"Kiŋaŋi ni kiradie"*
In this way, if your language has agreement between
the subject, or object, and the verb, then the particular class or form of the noun your partner gives
you will be the item which forces you to make the correct choice of verb agreement. Always have a vernacular speaker present to correct your pronunciation,
and let him expand the drill by giving more stimuli
as you progress.

When you think you are ready for it, try to make a
game of this drill with some children. Let them take
turns in giving the stimuli, and when anyone picks a
word you can't handle, reward him with a token such
as a match-stick. The one with the most sticks after
ten minutes wins.

26.6c   <u>Practicing Pronunciation</u>

Review word lists that give attention to words or
sounds which you still find difficult to pronounce.
Go over these with various neighbors, having them
say the words and correct your pronunciation as you
mimic them.

QUIZ: From memory, write below six different kinds of question you have learnt, together with their meanings
and two appropriate answers for each. If you cannot
do this yet, review the various kinds of questions and
answers until you can.

Q1: _____

  A: _____

  A: _____

Q2: _____

  A: _____

  A: _____

Q3: _____

  A: _____

  A: _____

Q4: _____

  A: _____

  A: _____

Q5: _____

  A: _____

  A: _____

Q6: _____

  A: _____

  A: _____

List five cultural discoveries you have made in recent
weeks.

(1)

(2)

(3)

(4)

(5)

List the sounds which you feel are still giving you
difficulty in pronunciation:

List the sounds which your partner feels you frequently mispronounce:

List the sounds for which your neighbors most frequently correct you:

List the sound pairs which you believe to contrast
and you have difficulty either in hearing or pronouncing:

Write below conclusions you have reached or points
which have been clarified for you as you reviewed,
under any of the following topics:

(1)   Cultural observations.

(2)   Intonation.

(3)   Phonology.

(4)   Subject nouns and pronouns.

(5)   Object nouns and pronouns.

(6)   Indicatives.

(7) Imperatives.

(8) Interrogatives.

(9) Negatives.

(10) Locationals and Instrumentals.

(11) Verbal forms

(12) Vocabulary.

STOP: If you feel at all overwhelmed at this stage, take as
many days as you need to review and catch up. If you
still feel awkward with the sounds of the language,
drop everything else and spend considerable time in
mimicry. Children aged 8-12 years are often quite
helpful for this. If you still have difficulty using
any of the expressions and patterns which you have
practiced, review them until you can use them with
confidence, before adding new ones to your load.

It is of far greater importance in these early months
to keep at your language learning--mimicry and memory,
conversation and drills--than to make great analytical
advances. DO NOT GET BOGGED DOWN IN DESK WORK. Take
more time for each unit if necessary, or omit parts
of the units and come back to them later. For the
parts you do do, process your materials as you go.
Discuss with your partner how you can help each other
more.

GET OUT OF THE HOUSE. DO NOT TAKE PAPER AND PENCIL.
VISIT YOUR NEIGHBORS. TALK. Try to use the words,
phrases, drills and intonation patterns that you know
as often as you can.

UNIT 26

Date Unit 26 started: _____ Completed: _____

Hours spent on categories 2 and 6: _____

Hours spent on all other categories: _____

Comments:

```
*******************************************************
*                                                     *
*                                                     *
*                                                     *
*                                                     *
*                                                     *
*                                                     *
*           You will learn more from people           *
*           than from a tape recorder.                *
*                                                     *
*                                                     *
*                                                     *
*                                                     *
*                                                     *
*                                                     *
*******************************************************
```

Unit 27

AIMS: (1) Participate in a creative activity.
(2) Increase facility in the use of subject and object forms.
(3) Begin investigating benefactives.

READ: "Terms for Features of Social Culture" in Nida, *Bible Translating* pp. 178-202.

27.1 Participation in Creative Work

Observe a creative activity such as house building, canoe making, making string, rope, clothing, tools, weapons, etc. Mentally note new things which you will later write down in your anthropology file. Attempt to join in the activity if possible. Note people's reactions and write them down later. Do they try to teach you how to do it? Are they teaching their children? Who is doing it - only men, only women, or both? If children help, what ages are they? How much do they do?

Do 27.2 at the same time.

27.2a Conversing While Participating

As you observe and participate in the activity of 27.1, enter into the conversation as much as you can. Try to use expressions you know, especially 'What are you doing?' (Unit 10), 'Why are you doing that?' (Unit 19), and put your subject and object pronoun drills to use as you try to recognize and use new expressions. Mimic things you cannot understand or answer. Pay careful attention to all corrections, either of your pronunciation or grammatical usage.

27.2b Gathering Spontaneous Speech Forms

Be on the look-out to hear expressions which you have elicited being used in actual conversation, as a check on their correctness and usefulness. Also try to memorize some of the new expressions which are spoken directly to you or which you are told to say. If you hear expressions which seem to pertain directly to the activity you are participating in and which are new to you, ask questions about them to discover their

meaning and help fix them in your memory, so that
later you will be able to recall them and write them
down or re-elicit them by re-enacting the situation
with someone. Be alert for any intonation patterns
you are not yet familiar with.

Afterward get someone to tape-record an account of
the activity for transcription or, if your tape recorder is not working, get a patient friend to relate
it for you to write down. Here (hopefully) you may
again come across some of the expressions you noted
earlier while you were busy. Do not forget to include
intonation contours and pauses in your transcription.

NOTE: Texts such as this are particularly valuable
because you already have a good idea of the meaning
of the text before you begin transcribing it.

27.3a   Eliciting Benefactives

The benefactive in a clause shows who benefits from
the action (e.g. 'He bought it for me'; 'Go to the
river for him'; 'Speak on my behalf'.) It may be
shown by verb affixation or by an affixed noun or
pronoun. It may be the same as the indirect object,
or indicated by a special set of pronouns. It may
be expressed in the possessive, e.g. 'I brought his
water.' = 'I brought water for him.'

27.3b   Look up benefactives in the Grammar File or Topical
File and try to find some pattern(s) in the examples
recorded there. Build on these examples to find more
instances of benefactives, using a procedure like
the one outlined in 25.3. Try to fill out the pat-
tern(s) you have noticed.

Alternatively, have your partner ask you for something, then go and get it for her. Say "I bring
water" and add "her". Repeat the action of carrying to another person and say "I bring water" and
add "you". Carry it to a third and say, "I bring
water" and add "him". See if the onlookers will
correct you and give a benefactive.

As a third alternative you could experiment with
'because' (possibly learnt in 19.3 with 'Why?').
For example, try "I brought water because the woman"
and see if anyone corrects you.

27.3c Eliciting 'For Whom?'

Using what you have just discovered, try to construct 'Did you bring it for whom?' or 'You brought
it--who?'. Use these expressions in appropriate situations and ask people to correct you. Try to find
the most natural way of asking "Who did you bring it
for?" Then ask this question several more times and
note the answers to compare with the benefactives
you have found so far.

27.4a Describing Benefactives

Study the examples of benefactives you now have, and
try to formulate the rules for adding a benefactive
to a clause. Elicit more examples if necessary.

27.4b Checking and Filing

Study the new data obtained in 27.2 and 27.3, comparing it with known data and noting familiar pronouns,
verbal forms, vocabulary, etc. Check unfamiliar
items for meaning with a helpful friend. Check any
previously elicited expressions against corresponding
non-elicited phrases you have written down and make
any necessary corrections in your elicited data.
Keep filing your discoveries so that you can find
them again.

27.4c Transcribing Text

Transcribe the text material suggested in 27.2b. Or,
if this is completed, continue some earlier unfinished transcription.

27.5a Constructing More Benefactives

Think of some situations where you would need to use
benefactives in conversation, and make up a sentence
for each situation. Use the description you made in
27.4a. Check the sentences with several people as
usual, and modify the description if necessary.

27.5b Translating the English 'of' Construction

Words (and morphemes) usually carry more than one
meaning, and function words (e.g. prepositions, conjunctions) and affixes especially so. For instance,
the English word *of* and its allomorph -*'s* are used
with a large number of different meanings. Day by
day as you are constantly expressing yourself in the

vernacular notice how often you need to translate an
English *of* or -*'s*. If you first decide the exact
meaning of the particular *of* construction you wish to
translate, then it is much easier to decide upon the
best vernacular equivalent.

Review possession (8.4 and 9.4) and locationals (Unit
11). Then try to translate the following types of
English *of* and -*'s* phrases. (There are many more
types.) If any of the words are not cultural, substitute something that is more appropriate in your area.

(1) Manufactured Aggregate:

'a roof of leaves' _____

'a fence of stakes' _____

(2) Natural aggregate:

'a bunch of bananas' _____

'a swarm of bees' _____

'a herd of cattle' _____

'a group of children' _____

(3) Measure:

'one sheet of paper' _____

'seven loaves of bread' _____

'two kilos of rice' _____

'three meters of rope' _____

(4) Contents and Measure:

'a cup of cold water' _____

'a bag of sugar' _____

'a handful of stones' _____

'a boatload of people' _____

(5) Quantitative Part-Whole:
'one of the sheep' _____

'a piece of the dress' _____

'half of the food' _____

'the rest of the people' _____

(6) Specific Part-Whole:
'the door of the house' _____

'the point of the arrow' _____

'the man's hand' _____

(7) Positional Part-Whole:
'the top of the mountain' _____

'the back of the boat' _____

'the inside of the box' _____

(8) Location:
'a city of Greece' _____

'the lakes of England' _____

'a village of the Highlands' _____

'the tallest mountain of Tibet' _____

(9) Identification:
'the village of Greenwich' _____

'the city of Jerusalem' _____

'the state of Arizona' _____

(10) Reference:
'the story of Jonah' _____

'the song of Norway' _____

'some news of the (missing) plane' _____

(11) Role:

'the President of Mexico' _____

'the manager of the shop' _____

'the chairman of the committee' _____

(12) Kinship:
'Peter's mother-in-law' _____

'James' brother' _____

'the woman's son' _____

(13) Ownership:
'John's boat' _____

'my dog' _____

'the woman's money' _____

27.6a Practicing Benefactives

Record a set of sentences containing benefactives.
For each of the more common person-number combinations record three question-and-answer pairs such as:

'you' 'Who did you bring   'I brought it for you'.
          it for?'
       'Who did you get   'I got it for you.'
          it for?'
       'Who did you do   'I did it for you.'
          it for?'

'him' 'Who did you bring   'I brought it for him.'
          it for?'

The question could be changed sometimes for variety,
e.g. 'Who did they build it for?' If the vocabulary
is all familiar, there need not be any English meanings on the tape. Enter the recording in the review system, practice with it and start using benefactives in conversation.

27.6b Learning Useful Expressions

Continue to record and learn useful expressions.
Elicit some more from the list on pp. 460-464.

27.6c Practicing Pronunciation

Set up drills for any areas of consonants or vowels
that are still giving you trouble or have not been
adequately covered earlier.

Take your groups of two-syllable words from 26.4f,
put them in a suitable frame and tape-record them.
Practice pronouncing them, being on the lookout for
pitch or stress differences. You don't have to have
your stress or tone analyzed to be able to mimic what
is said.

Review any previous drills which need more practice.

Date Unit 27 started: _____ Completed: _____

Hours spent on categories 2 and 6: _____

Hours spent on all other categories: _____

Comments:

```
*******************************************************************
*                                                                 *
*                                                                 *
*                                                                 *
*                                                                 *
*                                                                 *
*                                                                 *
*                    To learn, you must want                      *
*                    to be taught.                                *
*                         --Prov. 12:1 LB                         *
*                                                                 *
*                                                                 *
*                                                                 *
*                                                                 *
*                                                                 *
*******************************************************************
```

Unit 28

AIMS: (1) Observe flora.
(2) Investigate hortatory forms.
(3) Expand vocabulary.

READ: (1) the first half of "Problems of Linguistic Equivalence" in Nida, *Bible Translating* pp. 241-263.
(2) again "Language Learning Without Tears" in this *Guide* pp. 322-326.

28.1 Observing Flora

As you spend time with people at work or on the trail, observe the flora of the countryside--trees, bushes, grasses, vines, ferns, flowers, fruit, fungi, etc. Observe all you can about how these things are used: which ones grow wild, which ones are planted, which are used for food, for medicine, for housebuilding, for making or decorating things, or for magical ceremonies. If it interests you, make a collection or draw pictures of flowers and leaves, adding notes as to where they grow or were found and what people tell you about their names, uses, etc. (You may find such vocabulary lists of little use in conversation, but they will be valuable for your phonemic analysis and perhaps useful in literacy work later.)

You can do the same for fauna (fish, snakes, reptiles, mammals, birds, and insects) too if you are interested.

28.2a Conversation

Keep using the vernacular as much as you can in conversation. Make good use of patterns and expressions you have learnt recently. Ask questions and try to understand the answers. Ask further vernacular questions to clarify what people have said. Use each useful new vocabulary item that you hear in several different sentences and write down a sentence containing the new item. When you can't understand the general conversation, keep tracking and humming intonation patterns.

28.2b Noticing Frequency of Pronouns

Observe how often your neighbors use pronouns. More

than you do? Less than you do? In the same way as
you do? Take notice, and endeavor to model your usage on theirs.

28.3a Eliciting Hortatory Constructions

Look up hortatory forms or first person imperatives
in the Topical File or Grammar File. (See also 13.3d.)
Try to discern the pattern(s) in these examples and
decide what other forms you need to elicit. Use the
forms you know for eliciting new forms by analogy,
e.g.

             'I will go.'   'Let's go.'
             'I will stay.'   'Let's stay.'
             'I will use his canoe.'   ....

If you have not yet found any hortatory forms, try
using a first person inclusive with a future tense to
convey, for example, 'Let's go to the river'. See if
a corrected form is given to you. Mimic it and write
it down. Then use it again with the same and other
verbs. If you are using it correctly, it should result in people doing as you urge them, or declining.

Try to elicit a negative form of the hortatory, e.g.
'Let's dig.' → 'Let's not dig.' If necessary, put your
usual negative device with the positive hortatory and
note any corrections.

28.3b Expanding Vocabulary

In this unit, try to become familiar with five new
verbs and five new nouns, and practice using them so
they will become part of your working vocabulary.
They can be chosen from expressions you have written
down recently or from the list of words suitable for
monolingual eliciting on pp. 452-459. Try to choose
words that will be useful in conversation.

For each word, try to assemble two or three sentences
using it. Elicit more if necessary, using the vernacular as much as possible.

28.4a Studying Hortatory Forms

Compare the hortatory forms you now have. Are there
differences between motion verbs, intransitive verbs
and transitive verbs in the way hortatory constructions

are made? Are aspects such as continuative/punctiliar
significant? Write a tentative description of hortatory formation, or expand a previous description to
include hortatory constructions.

28.4b Studying New Vocabulary Items

Identify the stems of the verbs and nouns of 28.3b,
decide what classes they belong to, and file them in
the dictionary. If any of them show unusual behavior
as they are used in sentences, elicit more expressions containing them and try to understand the different behavior.

Continue checking and filing new discoveries as usual.

28.4c Formation of Verb Stems

Write a brief description of how transitive and/or
intransitive verb stems are formed. Intransitive
stem + affix = transitive stem? Noun or adjective +
affix = verb stem?)

28.5a Expanding Hortatory Constructions

Construct expanded sentences using the hortatory
forms with additional phrases or slots. For example:

	'Let's dig.'
With object:	'Let's dig the yams.'
With benefactive:	'Let's dig (the yams) for him.'
With locational:	'Let's dig (the yams) in my garden (for him).'
With instrumental:	'Let's dig (the yams in my garden for him) with our digging sticks.

By checking these expanded constructions with several
people, try to get an impression of how long a clause
the language would normally allow. Be especially
careful in mimicking the intonation and rhythm of
these expanded sentences, and notice any changes as
the sentences get longer. Check in your Grammar File
or transcribed texts to see if you have any clauses
as long as this in spontaneous utterances.

28.5b Translating Hortatory Constructions

Translate the following and then check your translation with some of your friends, mimicking and writing
down any corrections given to you.

'Let's go to town now.'   _____

'Let's build three shelters.'   _____

'Let's kill it.'   _____

'Let's both mend the fence.'   _____

28 5a Practicing Hortatory Forms

For each type of hortatory construction (e.g. transitive, intransitive, motion) record about five hortatory sentences. Each should be preceded by its English meaning or an indicative equivalent, e.g. 'I am
going.' 'Let's go.'

Make a second recording of indicative-hortatory pairs
where the clause type changes from one pair to the
next, e.g.

'I'm staying.'   'Let's stay.'
'I'm going to eat   'Let's eat the food.'
  the food.'
'I'm going to shoot   'Let's go and shoot birds.'
  birds.'

Try to make all the sentences as useful as possible.
Review the recording systematically as usual, and use
what you learn in conversation.

28.6b Learning the New Verbs and Nouns

For each of the new vocabulary items of 28.3b, record
three interesting sentences containing the new item.
Use familiar vocabulary for the other words in each
sentence where possible.

Review the recording systematically as usual.

28.6c Expansion Drill

Beginning with a hortatory form as your frame, set
up an expansion drill to gain control of longer
utterances containing several slots. (See pp.

313-314.) Tape the drill, expanding one slot at a
time. In drilling these expansions, do not expand
more than one stage beyond what you can utter with
reasonably correct segments, intonation and speed.
Base this drill on your elicitation (28.3a) and
checked construction (28.5a).

28.6d Practicing Pronunciation

Review lists of two-syllable words from 27.6c. Take
groups of three-syllable words, put them in a suitable frame and tape-record and mimic these as was
done for two-syllable words. Concentrate mainly on
pitch, accent, and rhythm, secondarily on segmental
sounds.

Drill areas of consonants and vowels where you have
pronunciation problems.

Date Unit 28 started: _____ Completed: _____

Hours spent on categories 2 and 6: _____

Hours spent on all other categories: _____

Comments:


```
***********************************************************
*                                                         *
*                                                         *
*                                                         *
*                                                         *
*                                                         *
*                                                         *
*                                                         *
*        Listen, or thy tongue will keep thee deaf.       *
*                  --American Indian proverb              *
*                                                         *
*                                                         *
*                                                         *
*                                                         *
*                                                         *
*                                                         *
***********************************************************
```

Unit 29

AIMS: (1) Observe methods of communication.
     (2) Continue conversing and studying intonation.
     (3) Continue investigating multi-clause sentences.

READ: (1) "Intonation" in Nida, *Learning a Foreign Language* pp. 116-118.
     (2) "Survey of Sentence Types" in Elson and Pickett pp. 121-126.
     (3) Second part of "Problems of Linguistic Equivalence" in Nida, *Bible Translating* pp. 263-279.

29.1 Observing Methods of Communication

Observe all you can about methods of communication
and make a note of any stylistic features you may
have noticed in how people talk when they are together. How much do they communicate by whistling?
What gestures have you observed and what are their
apparent significance? There may well be gestures to
express pleasure, amazement, disgust, approval, disapproval, threat, joking, sexual invitation, greeting,
failure, success, uncertainty, etc. (See also 22.2b.)
Do people use any form of picture writing, or have
they bushcraft symbols? How do they send messages to
distant places? by runners? by drums? or by paper
and pen as a result of European influence? Write
down anything you have observed on this topic and be
alert for opportunities to discover more.

29.2a Tracking

Make a tape-recording in another kind of social situation with the hope of obtaining some new intonation
patterns (see 2.2d and 23.2a). Track it as outlined
in 3.6b. Do step 4 at least six times.

Whenever you hear an extended speech by a single person, try to track quietly to yourself portions which
you cannot yet follow. Learn to use time which otherwise might be spent in frustration to good advantage
by practicing intonational patterns this way. Remember, "Proper intonation is not just a linguistic ele-
gance. It is a basic part of making oneself understood." (Nida).

Continue to build up your recorded library of intonational types. If possible, include several examples
of each type you observe. Remember also to record on
the tape the date and cultural context of each example
as it is obtained, as later on this may help you guess
at the meaning of some of the intonation contours.

29.2b Conversation

Spend extra time visiting and chatting with the neighbors from whom you elicit material in 29.3, and as
you check the materials constructed in 29.5.

While talking with people, write in your data book
any new expressions you feel will be useful, or which
correspond with material you have previously elicited.
Particularly be alert for hortatory expressions. Remember to indicate intonation and rhythm, and to include clues about the context of each expression.

29.3a Gathering Multi-clause Sentences

Continue the study of multi-clause sentences and
especially of sentence medial or non-final verbs
(sometimes also called dependent verbs or participles). Look again at your data elicited in 18.3a,
then check thoroughly through all your unelicited
data and transcribed text to find examples of multi-
verb sentences. You are very likely to find many such
sentences in your text materials. Add them to the examples in the Topical File or Grammar File. (If necessary, repeat the elicitation procedures of 18.3a.)

For this unit pick out the examples you have of sentences where the actor (subject) of both or all the
clauses is the same. E.g. 'Having come, he sat down'
= 'After he had come, he sat down.' 'When we see you,
we will talk to you.' Work only with the indicative
mode as other modes will be studied in Unit 31.

Do not use sentences in which the actor of the
clauses is different. E.g. 'When he comes, I will go'
or 'She came and I saw her.'

29.3b Eliciting Variations of Multi-clause Sentences

When you have found examples, try to elicit the same
sentence forms with other subjects. For example:

(1) If you find 'He came and saw it.' in your materials, use that form with different subject pronouns.
(E.g. 'You came and saw it.', 'I came and saw it.',
etc.) As you use them, be sure to encourage people
to correct you, and when they do, mimic and write
down the corrected form.

(2) Try also to get examples of as many aspects and
tenses as possible. (E.g. 'He'll come and see it.'
'He (always) comes and sees it.')

Do not forget, however, that the subject of both
clauses is to be the same for this investigation.

29.3c Repeat 29.3b for each of the different kinds of inter-
clause relationships described in 18.3a: general sequence, briefly delayed sequence, lengthily delayed
sequence, one action interrupting another, and simultaneous actions.

29.3d If possible, tape-record sentences with these multi-
verb-same-actor types of construction in them.

29.4a Analyzing Dependent Verbs

Process your verbs in non-final clauses by working
through the instructions given in 18.4c and 18.4d.
Write paradigms for each tense and aspect, etc., and
make charts of their affixes. To refresh your memory
as to things commonly found in verbs and their affixes,
reread 18.4a. You may find you need to start more
verb charts to handle all the data you are likely to
obtain by such a systematic attack on dependent verbs
as is suggested in 29.3.

NOTE: If you observe that for a given person or tense
there are two or more ways of expressing a sequence
of actions by the same person, then you should consider the possibility that these may distinguish between actions that are regarded as a part of a single
process, actions that are cause-and-effect, and actions that occurred in significant time sequence
rather than coincidentally.

29.4b Studying Collocations of Tenses and/or Aspects

If, in the material examined so far, the dependent
clauses appear to employ exactly the same range of
verb forms as the independent clauses do, then go
through all of your multi-clause sentences and determine which tense and aspect may occur in a dependent
clause preceding a given tense and aspect in the independent clause, and which conjunctions may occur
with such a combination of clauses.

29.4c Noting Positions of Time Words and Free Subjects

Search through all your materials and determine where
in the sentence the time word, if any, occurs and
where a noun or pronoun occurs as a free subject.
Is the subject optionally, obligatorily, or never repeated as a pronoun in the rest of the sentence, or
only indicated by verb affixes?

29.4d Indexing Intonation Patterns

Work through the procedures of 23.4a and 23.4b, applying them to the recording made in 29.2a and any
other uncatalogued recordings.

29.5a Testing Complex Sentences for Aspect and Tense

Take three fairly full/long sentences of the same-
subject type from your data and, keeping the subject-
person constant, change each sentence to all of the
tenses and aspects you know to be possible. Try them
out with someone you do not normally work with. When
you are satisfied that he has made all the corrections he wishes, tape-record the utterances for mimicry later and also mimic three times on the spot. It
is very important to mimic at full speed.

29.5b Translating Same-subject Sentences

Translate the following, and check you translation
around the village, making corrections where necessary.

'The girl got up and walked away.'

_____

'The child went into the house hopping.'

_____

'As he came near the house he heard music.'

'A woman carrying a vessel of water met me.'

29.6a   Practicing Multi-clause Sentences

For each of the inter-clause relationships that proved important in 29.3c record about four sentences
using familiar vocabulary. Keep the subject constant
(e.g. 'he' or 'we') so you can concentrate on learning the way each relationship is marked.

29.6b   Transforming Tense and Aspect

Make and tape-record a transform drill in which you
take a multi-clause sentence with a time word and, by
changing the time expressions and verb affixes, shift
the sentence through all known tenses and aspects.
In preparing this drill it is important to ascertain
carefully the best free English translation you can
for each sentence, and also to ensure that the meaning relationship between the two or more clauses in
the sentence remains constant, despite your transforming the tenses.

29.6c   Transforming the Subject

From the materials of this unit select a sentence of
the same-subject type which contains between 10 and
15 syllables and has a pronoun as free subject. Make
and tape-record a transform drill in which the subject is varied to all persons and numbers. For instance, 'I shot the pig and cooked it and ate it.'
'We shot the pig and cooked it and ate it.'

29.6d   Practice and Review

Practice with the above recordings until you can anti-
cipate the correct responses fairly well, and then
enter them in the review system. If any earlier
drills need more review than the system allows for,
give them extra attention. Remember, speaking must
become automatic.

29.6e   Practicing Pronunciation

Review previous recordings as necessary.

Take lists of 4-syllable words. Tape-record and mimic
them as a drill in frames in the same way as for two-
and three-syllable words.

Date Unit 29 started: _____ Completed: _____

Hours spent on categories 2 and 6: _____

Hours spent on all other categories: _____

Comments:

```
*****************************************************************
*                                                               *
*                                                               *
*                                                               *
*                                                               *
*           Language communication involves                     *
*           a relationship between individuals                  *
*           and not merely the memorization                     *
*           and repetition of phrases and the                   *
*           practicing of structures.                           *
*                            --Wilga Rivers                      *
*                                                               *
*                                                               *
*****************************************************************
```

Unit 30

AIMS: (1) Review.
       (2) Extend phonology analysis.

READ: (1) again "The Monolingual Approach to Studying
            Amuzgo" in this *Guide* pp. 272-276.
       (2) any book you have describing the culture of the
            area,
            OR the cultural notes you made from your reading
            before beginning your field work.
       (3) "Procedures in Field Analysis" and "Phonology"
            in Samarin pp. 175-194.

30.1 Filing Observations

Catch up on your filing of cultural observations, if
you have not already done so. As you flip through
your file, notice the various topics and events that
are described. Try and recall any customs or events
which you have observed but which have not yet got
into the file, and write up something on them now.

30.2a Tracking

Review all the intonation tracking tapes you have collected, following the procedures outlined in 22.2a.
Spend more time reviewing the tapes from Units 16,
18, 23, and 29, and give the others time according to
their relative difficulty. Vary your activities between practices with the tapes. Remember to do your
tracking at times when there are no people around to
talk to. It is always more profitable to spend time
with people than at your desk. When away from the
language area you will still have a desk but not all
the people to talk to.

30.2b Conversation

Do 30.6 first. Then spend a minimum of 3 hours (in
several broken stretches) conversing with and listening to your village neighbors, participating in any
of their activities and taking careful note of corrections they may give you as you try to talk. Be
sure to show your pleasure at their helpfulness to
you in this way.

30.2c   Make a firm agreement with your partner to use only
        the vernacular and no English or lingua franca at all
        in talking to each other when vernacular speakers are
        present. In addition, set a specific 30-minute
        period each day when the two of you are alone for
        talking to each other only in the vernacular.

30.4a   Filing

        Catch up on the processing of checked grammatical
        material and vocabulary.

30.4b   Analyzing Length, Stress, and Pitch

        If there is any material in your data book that you
        have not yet processed for phonology, do so now, fol-
        lowing the suggestions in 26.4c and 26.4d, and adding
        to groupings begun in 26.4f. If you have found evi-
        dence that your language has contrastive tonal or com-
        plex stress patterns, you should list every word in
        your Dictionary File in its appropriate pitch-stress
        group as well, after testing it in a standard frame.
        If the dictionary is filed on punch cards, code the
        pitch-stress information and punch it onto the cards
        instead of making lists.

        Add new hypotheses and/or modify previous ones on the
        basis of the new data. On the basis of the pitch-
        stress groupings you have made, put into writing one
        or more tentative hypotheses (guesses on the basis of
        present evidence) about such features. Is stress pre-
        dictable? Do you hear only one high pitch per word
        or do many words have two or more? How many pitch-
        stress groups do you have for two-syllable words?
        For three? For four? For one? Do you hear more
        than one stress on words of three or more syllables?
        If so, are the multiple stresses equal in force and/
        or length or is there primary vs. secondary stress?
        Re-listen to your groupings with such questions in
        mind, and try to put your conclusions into writing.
        Put several examples with each hypothesis.

        If you find tone or stress particularly difficult to
        hear, concentrate on listening for "same" versus "dif-
        ferent" as you categorize your lists of words, without
        trying to attach labels to the different groups unless
        you find it helpful for your own use. Your having be-
        gun the groupings will mean a great saving of time
        and effort both for yourself and any consultant who

will help you in the analytical conclusions.

30.4c Beginning Sentence Analysis

Go through all of your tape-recorded spontaneous text
materials (excluding elicited sentences, useful expressions and pattern drills) which you have transcribed and try to identify sentences. On the average,
how many clauses does a sentence contain in narrative
materials and how many does it contain in non-narra-
tive materials? What are the longest sentences you
have in these two types of materials? As you converse with people, try to make your average sentence
length more and more like theirs.

In multi-clause sentences, do you find special intonation features which occur only in non-final clauses
and never in a final clause? If so:

(1) Go through your spontaneous texts to identify
several examples of these medial contours not
already indexed, and index such examples, as suggested in 23.4a and 23.4b.

(2) Try to elicit a few utterances which contain
these features and tape-record them for mimicry
practice.

(3) Choose a social situation in which the talking
is of a style that is likely to contain these
medial contours and spend as much time as possible tracking all that is said. Pay most attention to getting intonation and rhythm correct.

30.4d Transcribing Text

Transcribe more (tape-recorded) text, then study it
carefully for any further new data which you can analyze and add to your files. Remember to mark in
pitch, stress, and intonation patterns, not only to
help you in your conversation, but for analysis and
study. Remember also to jot down cultural observations each time you obtain and transcribe text material (see 15.3a(5)) and add them to your anthropology
file.

30.4e Concentrating on Special Topic(s)

Read 22.4d again and apply its instructions to the
comments you wrote on Units 17-20.

30.4f Expanding Topical File

Add categories to the Topical File and Grammar File
to cover time clauses, accompaniment constructions
and other moods the language may use, such as desiderative, causative, purposive, reason, conditional.

30.6a Reviewing Earlier Recordings

Review all previously recorded useful expressions
which do not yet come automatically to your mind and
lips when appropriate situations arise. Spend extra
time on those you find more difficult. Make tape
loops for drilling any expressions from Units 27-29
which you feel need such intensive drill. Check the
accuracy and acceptability of the recordings made in
Units 12-16 and replace any that you now realize are
not really natural.

30.6b Practicing Grammatical Patterns

Mimic previous practice recordings, especially those
made in Units 27-29, trying to say each expression
after the stimulus and before you hear the response
from the tape. Make a special effort to use these patterns in conversation. Try to relate yesterday's activities to a couple of friends, and mimic their corrections. Choose some events that make you use a different tense again and relate them to your friends.

Try to start a game with some children in which you
read out a multi-clause sentence and the children take
turns to give time words or aspect indicators as cues.
You then try to transform the sentence to fit the cue.
(Read the last paragraph of 26.6b again.)

30.6c Learning Useful Expressions

Go through the whole list of Useful Expressions found
on pages 460-464 and mark all the expressions that
you have not yet learnt or that you cannot construct
and utter fairly readily. Elicit each one of these
expressions, record them, practice them with the tape
and a friend, practice them in conversation, and make
a review card for them. If there are more than ten
of these expressions, continue the eliciting and recording in the next couple of units.

30.6d Reviewing Pronunciation Practice

Review your pronunciation drills and spend extra time
on any features or sounds which you have not mastered
yet. Particularly review the pitch and rhythm lists
from Units 27-29. You should be able to mimic these
without hesitation.

Date Unit 30 started: _____ Completed: _____

Hours spent on categories 2 and 6: _____

Hours spent on all other categories: _____

Comments:

Number of weeks in the village between starting
    Unit 21 and completing Unit 30: _____

Total hours spent on categories 2 and 6 during
    Units 21-30: _____

Hours per week: _____

Total hours spent on all other categories during
    Units 21-30: _____

Hours per week: _____ _____

Considering the statistics in this summary and your
    progress during this period, what changes do you
    plan to make in your relationship with people in
    the community where you live, in your methods of
    language learning, and in your use of future
    units? (Read "Two Approaches" again on pp. 24-
    25.)

Unit 31

AIMS: (1) Observe the giving and receiving of hospitality.
       (2) Investigating other modes in multi-clause sen-
            tences.

READ: (1) "Putting Words Together" in Nida, *Learning a
            Foreign Language* pp. 163-184.
       (2) "Morphology and Syntax" in Samarin pp. 194-204.

31.1a Observing Visiting

Observe visitors to your village. Deliberately take
time to do this as often as you can. If possible,
find out where they come from, to whom they are related in your village, and what the relationship is.
Begin learning the names of frequent visitors. Keep
track of how often they visit and how often your villagers visit them, the purposes of the visits, how
hospitality is shown, how guests act, etc. Is hospitality shown in different ways for different kinds of
visitors? Do different relationships call for different behavior in visiting and receiving visitors?

NOTE: In some cultures, everybody's business is public enough so that this kind of information will be
given easily, with people being happy that you are so
interested in them. However, in all such gathering
of information, be very sensitive to your neighbors'
reactions, and if they seem reluctant or uneasy in
answering any questions, do not push on unduly or un-
heedingly, but rather investigate areas where information is happily given. Some things may not be discussed either through fear, embarrassment (if outsiders
have ever laughed at their customs), or taboos. Some
things which they may hesitate to discuss freely now
may be shared later when they know you better and
trust you more.

31.1b Going Visiting

As you have opportunity, visit other villages. Observe hospitality shown to you, and compare it with
what you have observed. Make notes of similarities
and differences. Utilize your observations to be a
good guest according to their culture. Be a good host
in the same or an equivalent way.

31.1c Mapping

Keep adding to the map started in 9.6e. Show the village where you are living, nearby villages, and other
important landmarks. Expand the map in detail as you
personally visit places. Make it to scale, keeping
it as accurate as possible as to distances. Eventually you will want to make larger copies of the village
and area maps, and put them in a convenient display
spot to begin giving people an interest in maps and
to teach them to read them. A large wall map of the
world and one of Biblical areas would be good additions to such a display.

31.2 Talking with Visitors

Listen carefully to conversations between your neighbors and any visitors who come. What are the most
common topics of conversation? Can you tell whether
the visitors speak the same or a different dialect?
If feasible, use appropriate question forms such as,
'Where have you come from?' to learn about the visitors.

Enter into the conversations as much as you can, but
remember that in any language, a good conversational-
ist is also a good listener. Learn what their main
interests are and capitalize on these in new vocabulary you choose to learn.

Write several expressions pertaining to the main
topics of conversation as you listen to and participate in conversations with your neighbors and visitors. Also be alert for new verb forms and for opportunities to check elicited data as similar expressions arise in conversation. Are you remembering
always to write the intonation contours?

31.3a Gathering Complex Sentences in Other Modes

Continue your study of multi-verb-same-actor types of
construction by investigating verb modes other than
the indicative (investigated in Unit 29). Assemble
examples from your files and by further eliciting.
Base your elicitation on constructions that you have
already worked on, attempting to transform them into
different modes by the use of markers, affixes or
free words which you have discovered earlier, such as
negative, yes/no interrogative, information

interrogatives ('Who?', 'What?', 'Whose?', 'Where?',
'Why?', 'When?', 'Whom?', 'How?'), imperative and
hortatory. Thus, if you have the statement, 'We'll
go and tell them' (indicative mode) you should be
able to transform it into the following:

(1) negative: 'We won't go and tell them.'

(2) yes/no interrogative: 'Shall we go and tell
     them?

(3) information interrogative: 'When shall we go
     and tell them?'

(4) imperative: 'Go and tell them!'

(5) hortatory: 'Let's go and tell them.'

Note any corrections that people give you. Mimic
them, then write them down.

31.3b When you have a corrected form, then try to obtain
       other persons and tenses of that mode, using the
       methods suggested in 29.

31.4a Checking and Filing

       Study, compare and check material obtained in 31.2
       as outlined in 27.4b.

       Process your verbs as in 29.4 by writing paradigms
       for each different mode and charting their affixes.

31.4b Describing the Formation of Other Verb Modes

       Write down the rules you can see for transforming in-
       dicative/declarative clauses into the various other
       modes, and give examples.

31.5a Testing the Rules for Forming the Other Modes

       Take two or three multi-clause-same-subject indica-
       tive sentences from your data and use the rules for-
       mulated above to transform them into the other modes
       (such as those listed in 31.3a). Check them as usual
       and modify the rules if necessary.

31.5b Translating Complex Sentences in Other Modes

       Translate the following, checking your translation
       with several people. Mimic and write down any cor-
       rections they give you.

'They didn't wash their hands before they ate.'

'Go and search carefully for the child.'

'Why are you standing there looking up into the sky?'

'Call the workmen and pay them.'

'The girl isn't dead; she is only asleep.'

'When did he see that you were sick and give you medicine?'

31.6a   <u>Practicing Multi-clause Sentences in Other Modes</u>

For each of the modes in the language (such as those listed in 31.3a) record about three pairs of multi-clause sentences. The first member of each pair should be indicative and the second should be its equivalent in the mode being learnt. Thus the indicative sentences are the stimuli or cues, and the sentences in the other modes are the responses. E.g.

'They bought the food.'	SILENCE	'Buy (pl.) the food!'	SILENCE
'They cooked the food.'		'Cook (pl.) the food!'	
'They ate the food.'		'Eat (pl.) the food!'	
'We mended the fence.'		'Let's mend the fence.'	
. . . .		. . . .	

Make a second recording to give practice in transforming indicative sentences into the other modes. E.g.

'She saw a bird.'	yes/no	'Did she see a bird?'
'She saw a bird.'	'When?'	'When did she see a bird?'
'She saw a bird.'	'What?'	'What did she see?'

'She saw a bird.'	'not'	'She didn't see a bird.'
'She saw a bird.'	imperative	'See (look at) a bird.'
'She saw a bird.'	hortatory	'Let's see (look at) a bird.'

After practicing with the above recordings, try to involve a friend in giving vernacular cues so you can make appropriate transformations. You may be able to make it into a game with some children.

31.6b Practicing Pronunciation

Review lists of 2- to 4-syllable words in frames.

Set up and record lists of 5 or more syllable words, if you have such. Drill these as you have done previous lists, remembering to give chief attention to pitch and accent.

If you have found that any particular consonant or vowel combinations slowed you down as you mimicked the pitch and rhythm lists, set up drills containing these combinations, and practice them until they come more easily to you.

Date Unit 31 started: _____ Completed: _____

Hours spent on categories 2 and 6: _____

Hours spent on all other categories: _____

Comments:

Unit 32

AIMS: (1) Focus on religion,
       (2) Begin investigating descriptives,

READ: (1)   "Reason and Unreason in Human Belief" in
               Firth pp. 152-185.
            OR "Religion: the Problem of Man and the Uni-
               verse" in Herskovits, *Cultural Anthropology*
               pp. 210-233.
            OR "Religion: the Control of the Universe" in
               Herskovits, *Man and His Works* pp. 361-377.
            OR "Religion and Magic" in Hoebel pp. 523-555.
            OR "Devils and Doubts" in Nida, *Customs and
               Cultures* pp. 134-180.
       (2) "Terms for Features of Religious Culture: in
            Nida, *Bible Translating* pp. 203-240.

32.1 Noting Religious Beliefs and Practices

What have you observed that might be classed under the
broad heading of religious beliefs and practices?
What indications have you come across of a belief in
spirits and the supernatural? Any overt evidence such
as spirit houses, or fertility figures, or ceremonies?
Or less tangible things such as taboos, or fears,
spoken and unspoken, about them? Have you been permitted to attend any festivals or funerals where
people perform any of their ceremonies/ritual/magic?
What customs have you noted associated with birth,
sickness, death, or coming of age?

This topic covers a very wide field. It is unlikely
that people will take you far into their confidence
about such things in your early days of living with
them. However, you should observe all you can and
make notes about anything that seems pertinent to
your investigation of these subjects.

32.2a Increasing Conversational Ability

In addition to the time spent checking the material
elicited and constructed in 32.3 and 32.5, spend at
least two hours visiting with friends and conversing
with them, preferably in 5-15 minute stretches at a
time. Practice your expressions, and wherever possible use what you have been drilling as you converse.

Remember, the drills are of little value unless you are using the material you have drilled in everyday conversation.

32.2b   As you visit your friends, pay particular attention to the most common topics of conversation. Write down several expressions pertaining to these topics so that you can learn them and enter into their conversations, activities, and interests more directly. Remember also to be alert for expressions similar to those you have elicited, both for checking the accuracy of your elicited data and for gathering alternative ways of saying things.

32.3a   Gathering Descriptives

Look up descriptives and indefinite quantifiers in the Topical File and try to elicit more of them through pantomime and your knowledge of the vernacular.

Place ten objects in one person's hand, three in another and none in another, and try to obtain words for:

many   _____

few   _____

all   _____

none   _____

both   _____

32.3b   Eliciting Color Words

To obtain words for colors, show materials or paper of different colors, e.g. red, blue, black, white. Remember that the people's spectrum of colors may be divided up differently from the way we have learnt to regard it, so that they may make fewer or more distinctions in color than we do, and have very different groupings. Often, too, a particular color may be described by two or more terms. Repeat this elicitation with several people to ascertain the range of variation of the various terms you discover.

32.3c   Antonyms

Two contrasting items can be used to try to obtain some of the other probable common descriptives such

as a long vs. short stick, a big vs. small stone, a
round vs. flat stone, an old vs. young person, a thin
vs. fat person, sweet vs. bitter-tasting food, hot vs.
cold liquid, a clean vs. dirty garment, new vs. old
material, thin vs. thick cloth, etc.

32.3d   Gathering Comparative Constructions

Look up the Topical File and Grammar File for the vernacular equivalent of the English comparative and
superlative (e.g. *good, better, best*). If you cannot find any among your data then try to elicit them
by comparing three or more similar things, and hoping
that you will be told that A is bigger than B but that
C is the biggest of all three. You may find that the
comparative is expressed by an affix such as English
-er, a word such as English *more*, or a sentence such
as 'This one is big, that one is small', or 'This one
is big, that one is very big.' Once you feel you
have found a vernacular equivalent, test it out with
several people in the village to see how they respond.

32.4a   Checking and Filing

Study, compare, and check the material obtained in
32.2 as outlined in 27.4b.

32.4b   Studying Descriptives

Study the material obtained and checked in 32.3.
Look through your data for any of these descriptives
and see how they are used. Note that if your have
previously discovered the existence of noun classes
or genders within the language, it is likely that the
descriptives will also indicate these classes by
agreement in their affixes or some similar device.

By comparing these elicited materials with data and
texts you have obtained previously, try to identify
instances of descriptives being used in a descriptive
clause such as 'The dog is black' and instances of
descriptives being used in a noun phrase in the subject or object slot of a clause, e.g. 'The black dog
came.' Write a tentative description of these constructions.

32.4c   (1) Write notes on any new observations or conclusions you may have made about agreement, especially
between descriptives and nouns in a noun phrase.

(2) What different constructions are used to express the English verb 'be', e.g. 'He/this is a man' (Unit 3), 'He/this is here' (Unit 11), 'He/this is big' (Unit 32)? Give examples with the description and file it.

(3) Describe the comparative construction(s) discovered in 32.3d.

32.4d Work on some more text transcription.

32.4e Process all your new data, both from tape transcription and other sources.

32.5 Checking on Descriptives

Take the descriptives elicited in 32.3 and try to construct phrases with a noun and one of the descriptives in them. Use both singular and plural forms of these phrases, and use them in different slots in the clause such as subject, object, and possessor. If you have this kind of phrase in your unelicited data or transcribed text material, base your construction work on it. Check your constructions with several people and make any necessary corrections.

32.6a Joining in Common Topics of Conversation

Choose three of the expressions written under 32.2b and record at least three variations of each one (e.g. singular and plural, present and remote past). Precede the first variation by its English meaning and the others by vernacular cues. Leave a period of silence each side of each vernacular sentence. It does not matter if you cannot understand the structure of the sentences completely, it is enough to learn them and to be able to modify them a little to fit other circumstances. Practice with the recording and try to use the expressions in conversation.

32.6b Learning New Descriptives

For each descriptive you have discovered but cannot yet use automatically, record three different sentences containing the descriptive. Use familiar vocabulary for the other words, and try to make the sentences as natural as possible.

NOTE: In some languages a noun phrase tends to have

only one stress or one high pitch; and in some languages a phrase, in the object slot for instance,
takes up about the same span of time as a single noun
in the same slot. So mimic noun phrases carefully.

Practicing With Descriptives

Using a limited number of the descriptives elicited
in 32.3 (e.g. 'good', 'bad', 'little', 'big'), set up
a drill for noun phrases with a noun and a descriptive
in them. Drill these phrases in the object slot of a
sentence with a transitive verb (e.g. 'see', 'touch',
'hold', 'feel', 'know', 'approach', 'leave', 'hit'),
keeping the subject the same. Then, keeping the object the same, use in the subject slot those phrases
which are based on animate nouns. When you have mastered these drills using one verb, vary the verbs
also. Drill by having your partner give you cues,
but with a vernacular speaker present to correct you.
Then have some of the utterances put on tape and mimic them until you get the correct stress, rhythm, and
intonation.

If you have agreement between nouns and descriptives
in your language, make a context forcing drill to
practice this feature in sentences. To set up this
kind of drill, read again 26.6b and see the Portuguese
drill given below for mastering agreement between
masculine or feminine nouns and their articles and
adjectives. The trouble spots for agreement are
underlined.

	Prompter says: (Nouns from different classes)	Learner says: 'I bought a new ...'
'book' m.	*livro*	*comprei* <u>*um*</u> *livro* <u>*novo*</u>
'ruler' f.	*regua*	*comprei* <u>*uma*</u> *regua* <u>*nova*</u>
'map' m.	*mapa*	*comprei* <u>*um*</u> *mapa* <u>*novo*</u>
'suit' m.	*terno*	*comprei* <u>*um*</u> *terno* <u>*novo*</u>
'pen' f.	*carneta*	*comprei* <u>*uma*</u> *carneta* <u>*nova*</u>

32.6d Practicing Pronunciation

Listen again to your lists of words as suggested in
30.4b. Then add to your lists and tapes of 2, 3, 4
and more syllable words, new words discovered since
each list was prepared. (Go through your data book
for these). Especially add any examples you can to
those pitch or accent patterns which have few examples.
If you have found as you mimicked the tapes that you
needed to re-group your lists to have words with the
same pitch or stress patterns in the same lists, re-
tape your lists of words in their more consistent
groupings.

32.6e Learning a Text

Your intonation practice for this unit is to try to
learn one of the short texts used in the tracking
drills. Work on it a phrase or sentence at a time.
You may not be able to do all of it but do as much
of it as you can.

Date Unit 32 started: _____ Completed: _____

Hours spent on categories 2 and 6: _____

Hours spent on all other categories: _____

Comments:


```
******************************************************************
*                                                                *
*                                                                *
*                                                                *
*                                                                *
*                                                                *
*          Applying is also learning, and the                    *
*          more important kind of learning at that.              *
*                              --Mao Tse-Tung                     *
*                                                                *
*                                                                *
*                                                                *
*                                                                *
******************************************************************
```

Unit 33

AIMS: (1) Observe dancing.
       (2) Continue investigating descriptives.
       (3) Investigate demonstratives.
       (4) Elicit vocabulary monolingually.

READ: (1) "Lexicon" in Samarin pp. 205-217.
       (2) "Discovering the Meanings" in Nida, *Learning a Foreign Language* pp. 185-199.

33.1 Observing Dancing

Try to find out all you can about dancing in the area where you are living: what the purpose is, how long in advance dances are planned, who participates in them and in what roles, when (what time of year and day) they take place and how long they last, whether feasting accompanies them, and the like.

NOTE: Whenever you observe the same kind of event on different occasions, record the highlights and compare the events, as this will enable you to determine what are the basic features and what are the variations peculiar to a specific event. Try to obtain a description beforehand of what is going to happen and a description afterward of what did happen as this also will be helpful in determining the basic features.

33.2 Conversation

SPEND TIME IN FREE CONVERSATION, LISTENING, AND MIMICRY. Remember that this is the most important area of your language learning program.

Spend extra time just visiting and conversing with those in the household from whom you gather the material in 33.3. Visit other neighbors as well, spending as much time as you can building your conversational skills.

As you visit, listen particularly for any phrases which might include demonstrative pronouns or adjectives and, if possible, write these phrases down.

33.3a <u>Gathering Constructions With Two or More Descriptives</u>

In English we readily use phrases with more than one
descriptive (e.g. 'big black dog' or 'small white
flower') but in other languages these may sound forced and unnatural. Look up descriptive phrases in the
Grammar File or Topical File, or else scan your tran-
scriptions of spontaneous texts for them. Do you find
any phrases with more than one descriptive? If so,
there may be sub-classes and orders of adjectives
(determining which ones can occur where in a sequence)
or limitations on how many can occur in one phrase.
Elicit more examples to help discover these rules.

If there are no phrases with more than one descriptive
in your non-elicited data, it may be that extra descriptives must be introduced in separate phrases or
clauses. Try to elicit sentences in which the one
noun has two or more descriptives referring to it,
following the natural usage of the language.

33.3b Try to elicit and record expanding sentences such as
'I saw a pig', 'I saw a big pig', 'I saw a big black
pig'. Do not use more descriptives with one noun than
you have found in spontaneous speech.

33.3c <u>Eliciting More Demonstratives</u>

Use the vocabulary you know to construct sentences
for 'This is ...', 'That is ...' and point to objects at different distances. You may find there are
different forms referring to something in the hand,
close by, a little distance away, a long distance
away, and out of sight. You may also find distinctions made between whether it is nearer the speaker,
nearer the hearer or at a distance from both. One or
more of these demonstratives, or perhaps a special
demonstrative, may be used to refer to something previously talked about without any implications as to
where it is. You may find that some of the forms
which you have so far regarded as 3rd person pronouns
turn out to be part of the system of demonstratives.
There is also a strong possibility you may find similarities in shape and meaning distinctions between
some of the demonstratives and some of the locational morphemes identified in Unit 11.

Remember to elicit possible dual, trial, and plural
forms as well as singular ones.

33.3d Eliciting Vocabulary Monolingually

Turn to the list of words suitable for monolingual
eliciting on pages 452-459 and put a mark against
each item of vocabulary that you do not yet have in
your Dictionary File. Now elicit 50 of these items
including those in the lists of size, shapes, descriptives, and colors. Any item that you are not able to
elicit within a couple of minutes should be left for
another occasion. When you have finished, erase the
marks from the items on the list which you have been
successful in eliciting.

All of this eliciting should be done monolingually.
If you have not yet got into the habit of conducting
your linguistic research in the vernacular, this is
an easy project to start with. And as you constantly
extend youself to try and communicate in areas that
are not very familiar to you, you will soon find an
improvement in your general willingness and ability
to talk with people.

33.4a Studying Expanded Descriptive Constructions

Modify your descriptions of phrases and/or clauses to
account for the way(s) extra descriptives can be applied to a noun. Read 33.3a again. When deciding
the maximum number of descriptives that can be applied
to a noun in any one construction, you should describe
the examples of spontaneous speech you have recorded,
rather than constructing longer phrases to see how
many descriptives native speakers will accept.
People usually like to be helpful, and will probably
accept your constructions because they can work out
what you mean, even if what you say sounds unnatural.

33.4b

Study the recording made in 33.3b to see if there are
changes in rhythm or intonation as the descriptive
constructions are expanded. File a note on this if
appropriate.

33.4c Checking and Filing

Check with one or two people the expressions elicited
in 33.3c and the new vocabulary gathered in 33.3d and
in conversation, and file your discoveries as usual.
Continue transcribing texts and copying each clause
into the Grammar File, and copying interesting examples into the Topical File.

33.6   Concentrated Practice

Remember drills are to help you overlearn. Don't
stop using a drill until the things taught in it have
been overlearnt and are automatic. Break up your
drill time into 3 or 4 periods during the day.
Don't do it all at once. Try to convert some of
your drills into games. Language learning can be fun.

33.6a   Practicing Expanding Descriptive Constructions

Make up expanding drills based on category 33.3b and
tape-record these. Use this drill for mastering any
orders of adjectives in the language, for practicing
any agreement in these expanded constructions, and
for overlearning stress and rhythm patterns in these
types of constructions.

33.6b   Practicing Comparative Constructions

If you found a way of expressing comparatives and
superlatives in 32.3d and could describe it adequately (32.4c), make a drill on this feature. Record
about five sentences such as:

'This tree is straighter than that one.'
'This soil is better than that.'
....
Repeat this for the superlative (e.g. 'biggest').

33.6c   Practicing Demonstratives

If you found more demonstratives in this unit, record
a drill to give practice in using them correctly.
Try to make up a game in which you have to choose the
right demonstrative to make statements about different
nearby objects named by the other players.

33.6d   Practicing Pronunciation

Review word lists and practice using words from the
various groups of 2-, 3-, 4-, and 5-syllable words in
phrases within a short sentence frame. Notice any
changes which may occur in pitch, stress, and rhythm
when the isolation forms are used in these phrases or
sentences.

Continue working on the memorization of texts for
intonation practice as suggested in 32.6e.

Date Unit 33 started: _____ Completed: _____

Hours spent on categories 2 and 6: _____

Hours spent on all other categories: _____

Comments:

```
***********************************************************
*                                                         *
*                                                         *
*                                                         *
*                                                         *
*                                                         *
*                                                         *
*         A single conversation across the table          *
*         with a wise man is better than                  *
*         ten years' study of books.                      *
*                                  --Longfellow            *
*                                                         *
*                                                         *
*                                                         *
*                                                         *
***********************************************************
```

212

Unit 34

AIMS: (1) Investigate music.
(2) Improve conversational ability.
(3) Investigate further how temporal ideas are expressed.
(4) Investigate multi-clause sentences with different actors.

READ: (1) "Descriptive Procedures" in Pike pp. 174-206.
(2) "Folklore, Drama, and Music" in Herskovits, *Cultural Anthropology* pp. 267-286 OR in Herskovits, *Man and His Works* pp. 414-439.

OR "Drums and Drama" in Nida, *Customs and Cultures* pp. 181-197.

34.1a Observing Musical Instruments

Note musical instruments. Who makes them? Who plays them and when? Are all instruments played as solo instruments? What other activities does the playing of instruments accompany? Singing? Dancing? Work? Healing ceremonies? Mourning? Sketches of instruments would be useful for your file.

34.1b Collecting Some Songs

Try to tape-record some of the songs the people sing. Inquire to find out which individuals in the village are recognized as good singers, and try to arrange for them to sing for you. Prefer solos or duets, as they will give clearer recordings than a large group. Try to minimize background noise in the recording. Before each song briefly announce your name, the name of the language, the name of the singer, the topic and purpose of the song, and the date and occasion of recording. This will make the recording much more valuable to you or anyone else who might wish to study the music and songs in more detail later on.

With the help of someone who knows the songs, transcribe the words of each one. Get one of the older folk to explain to you the meaning of the words and any hidden implications of the songs. (You may find obsolete or special song vocabulary in them). Also ascertain the contexts in which each song would be sung, e.g. at dances, funerals, etc.

UNIT 34

NOTE: Be cautious about recording (men's) sacred
songs. Tape only such songs as everyone is happy
to have played back publicly.

34.2a Keep Talking (as well as Listening)

Spend time relaxing and chatting with your neighbors
as you seek to obtain information, whether cultural
or linguistic. In your conversation try to use constructions you have been working on, remembering that
the more you use what you know, the more fluent you
will become. As you check elicited material with
your friends, try to spend 5-15 minutes with each one
who helps you. Continue to track and mimic when you
cannot join in a conversation.

34.2b Gathering Non-elicited Data

Begin to gather most of the new expressions and idioms that you need from the conversations you hear
when you are with people. If you can't get the meaning at the time, write down the new phrase or word
and ask someone about it later.

Continue to collect short texts on tape, including
conversations, accounts of events the day they happen,
how-to-do descriptions, explanations of why people do
something, and community discussions.

When the recorder is not in use, keep a tape on it,
ready to record at a moment's notice, in the hope of
catching some exciting piece of news as it is being
told for the first time. If the speaker is imparting
information which he knows is new to the hearers,
some of the grammatical structures may be different.
For example, descriptive phrases may have more adjectives.

34.3a Eliciting Sentences With Time Clauses

If you have not already done so, find out how the language expresses temporal ideas that are based upon
clauses, such as 'After/before/when he came, he shot
a pig.' Or 'When/while/as he was coming, the people
called to him.' Some of these more complicated time
expressions may have been obtained in 14.3 or you may
have found some while transcribing tapes. If you
have not, and you have difficulty in eliciting
sentences expressing these ideas, try the techniques

described in 14.2b, 14.3a, and 18.3a.

NOTE: You may find that these temporal ideas are
expressed by a clause plus a specific word for
'When/while/after,' etc. On the other hand, you may
find that these ideas are expressed by a clause in
which the verb itself expresses distinctions of the
'When/while/after' type.

34.3b   Gathering Multi-clause Sentences with Different Sub-
         jects

In this unit continue your investigation of multi-
verb sentences, and look for sentences in which the
actor (subject) of the first clause is different from
the actor of the second clause, e.g. 'After he left,
I went to sleep.' or 'When he comes, we will eat.'
Once you have found such constructions in your files
or your transcribed texts or by elicitation, then
begin to elicit paradigms of each possible person
and number as subject of the first clause in combinations with each person and number as subject of the
second clause. Thus, if you have found 'He'll come
and then we'll eat', elicit:

(1)   'He'll come and then they/she/you (etc.) will
      eat.'

(2)   'They/she/you (etc.) will come and then we'll
      eat.

Then work through various aspects and tenses of the
verbs (see 29.3b), the different kinds of inter-
clause relationships (29.3c) and investigate the different verb modes given in 31.3a.

NOTE: You will not achieve all this in one elicitation session! Even if it takes one or two weeks
and cross checking between different people, it is
very important that you elicit and check the naturalness of all these combinations very carefully, as
this area of inter-clause relationships is one of the
most crucial in your language learning and translating.

34.3c   Eliciting Vocabulary Monolingually

Elicit monolingually another 50 vocabulary items from
the list of words you have marked on pages 452-459
(see 33.3d). Check them with one or two different
people.

34.4a Checking and Filing

Look through your material gathered in this unit and
enter all new and tested words in your Dictionary
File and words and expressions in your Topical File
if appropriate.

34.4b Process all your new verb material as you have done
in earlier units on multi-verb sentences (see 18.4).

34.4c Write down any new conclusions you have reached about
multi-clause sentences as a result of your work in
this unit and Units 29 and 31. Are the verbs used in
clauses expressing the more complex temporal ideas investigated in 33.3a independent verbs, or dependent
verbs of the type found in multi-clause sentences, or
a new kind of verb form not previously noted?

34.5 Translating Different-subject Sentences

Translate the following sentences in which the actor
of the first clause differs from that of the second
clause.

'While he was speaking, John arrived.'

'At that time the sun will grow dark, the moon will
not shine, and the stars will fall from the sky.'

'Your younger brother has come back home and your
father has killed the fattened calf.'

'Sit here while I work.'

'When you repaired the fence, how many poles were
left over?'

'He watched them going along the road until they
went behind the hill.'

34.6a Learning Useful Expressions and Vocabulary

Continue learning useful expressions and vocabulary
as in 32.6a and 28.6b.

34.6b Practicing Sentences with Events in Sequence

Set up a drill for a series of sentences describing
a sequence of actions by one person. In each sentence include a temporal expression based on a clause
and use the same actor (subject) in both the time
expression and the main clause.

E.g. 'After I had come, I ate.'
     'After I had eaten, I slept.'
     'After I had slept, I got up.'

Get your partner to act out the next action in the
series as your cue, and you then give the next sentence. Be sure to have a vernacular speaker present
who will encourage and/or correct you as you attempt
these. See also "Tail-head linking drills" on p. 313.
Repeat this drill using a different person throughout
as subject and a rather different selection of verbs.

34.6c Practicing Different-subject Sentences

Set up a similar drill describing a sequence of actions done by two different people alternately.

'After we had eaten, he spoke.'
'After he had spoken, we slept.'
'After we had slept for a while, he woke us.'
'After he woke us, we got up.'

Transform both drills into different tenses. Note
that you should be drilling for up to 3 hours per
day, and you can work on these (and similar) drills
for many days to come.

34.6d Practicing Pronunciation

Review any consonant and/or vowel drills involving
words you still stumble over.

Quickly drill lists of 2-, 3-, 4- and more syllable
words. Then continue with the assignment of 33.6d
putting words in various sentences. If you find any
changes taking place in pitch or rhythm, put as many
words from the various groups into that sentence as
will logically fit in with the meaning of the sentence. Put each word on tape by itself, then in the
sentence, and practice, mimicking the tape.

34.6e Learning a Song

Choose one of the songs of 34.1b and record it on a
tape loop. Listen to it for a few minutes several
times each day and then start learning to sing it.
You will probably find it harder than normal speech
to learn, but keep trying.

Date Unit 34 started: _____ Completed: _____

Hours spent on categories 2 and 6: _____

Hours spent on all other categories: _____

Comments:

```
*****************************************************************
*                                                               *
*                                                               *
*                                                               *
*                                                               *
*                                                               *
*                                                               *
*                                                               *
*            We have not really budged a step                  *
*            from home until we take up residence              *
*            in someone else's point of view.                  *
*                                --John Erskine                 *
*                                                               *
*                                                               *
*                                                               *
*                                                               *
*                                                               *
*****************************************************************
```

Unit 35

AIMS: (1) Review.
(2) Begin drafting preliminary phoneme statement.

READ: (1) again "Eliciting Vocabulary, Meaning, and Collocations" in this *Guide* pp. 361-386.
(2) "The Formation of Practical Alphabets" in Pike pp. 208-226.
(3) "Orthography" in Nida, *Bible Translating* pp. 100-129.

35.1 Filing Observations

Catch up on writing notes and filing of observations for the topics covered in Units 31-34 and anything new you have observed this week on any previous topics.

35.2 Conversation

Spend considerable time in actual conversation with your neighbors and friends, listening, mimicking and talking to the best of your ability. As you converse, use every opportunity to review expressions and drills you have learnt. If you find you don't often use many of them in everyday conversation, you should make an extra effort in choosing new expressions and vocabulary to choose those which will be most useful to you in conversation.

35.3 Eliciting Meanings

Choose three words heard recently the meaning of which you do not yet know. Then choose from your Dictionary File or Topical File three words with meanings that have proved difficult to understand over a period of several months. Take these six words and elicit their meanings by following the procedures described in "To Discover the Meaning of Words" on pp. 375-383 of this *Guide*.

35.4a Checking and Filing

Catch up on processing any materials you have checked adequately but have not yet filed in appropriate places.

35.4b Describing the Phonemes

Begin the first draft of your preliminary description
of the phonemes. By now you should be able to attempt at least the Interpretation section and the
Consonants and Vowels sections of the description,
unless the language you are studying presents
particular problems in one of these areas.

Make your statements of conclusions as clear as possible, with many examples of each allophone and of
each contrast. Err on the side of too many rather
than too few examples. If there are things which seem
ambiguous, or which you find particularly hard to
hear, write as clearly as you can where the difficulty lies, and give as many examples as you can find to
illustrate each problem area, so that you can receive
maximum help from a consultant in the shortest possible time. (See "Recording Phonological Data for
Analysis" on page 420.)

This assignment should be continued over the next
few weeks, so do not labor long over this write-up
now as this takes valuable time in the village that
should be spent in learning to talk. Do only as much
as you have time for in this review unit and during
the next few weeks, and you can complete it when you
need to be out of the language area for some reason.
However, making this beginning will show you topics
on which you need to gather more evidence or do additional checking in your village situation.

35.4c Reviewing Previous Descriptions

Review the comments you wrote at the ends of Units
21 to 25 and follow up any sections you listed as
needing extra work. If you feel that any of your previous descriptions are inadequate, go over them and
modify them to fit the data you now have. If some
area of the language is holding up your progress, concentrate on it for a while and try to solve some of
the problems. Use the index.

35.4d Expanding the Topical File

Add topics to the Topical File and Grammar File to
cover vocatives, exclamations, adverbs (descriptives
that modify events), intensifiers (e.g. 'very'),
vernacular equivalents of 'but', 'and' and 'or' (not

necessarily conjunctions) and clauses embedded within other clauses.

35.5a   Checking on Tense Changes

Review the different tenses you have learnt. Then choose out seven sentences from your recent data and transform each of them through all of these tenses.

35.5b   Translating Descriptives

Review descriptives (Units 32 and 33) and then translate the following:

'We sat down on the green grass.'

'They sang a new song.'

'He rolled a large stone across the doorway of the tomb.'

'How many loaves do you have?'   'Seven, and a few small fish.'

'They saw a young man dressed in a long white robe.'

'He picked up five small smooth stones.'

35.6a   Reviewing Useful Expressions

Review expressions from Units 31-34, making tape loops of any which may be more difficult to master.

Review any previous expressions which do not yet come automatically to mind in appropriate situations. Check the accuracy and acceptability of the recordings made in Units 18-21 and replace any that you now realize are not really idiomatic.

35.6b   Review demonstratives. Repeat and extend the game suggested in 33.6c. Review previous names which you still find hard to remember when you see the person. Try to spend extra time with people whose names you find harder to recall, using their name (if this is cultural) in appropriate situations as you talk to them.

35.6c   Practicing Multi-clause Sentences

Review the drills of Units 31-34 dealing with multiverb sentences and agreement problems. Spend at least an hour in 15 minute stretches at a time or less, drilling with your partner giving you cues and vice versa. Drill until your responses come quickly and easily.

35.6d Reviewing Memorized Texts

Review intonation texts. Do as much as you have been able to commit to memory, then go back over the whole text, tracking and mimicking. Review other intonation tracking tapes as well. Review any word list drills that still need work. Keep working on the song that you began learning in 34.6e.

Date Unit 35 started: _____ Completed: _____

Hours spent on categories 2 and 6: _____

Hours spent on all other categories: _____

Comments:

```
************************************************************
*                                                          *
*                                                          *
*                                                          *
*                                                          *
*                                                          *
*                                                          *
*                                                          *
*          Slow and steady wins the race.                 *
*                          --Aesop                         *
*                                                          *
*                                                          *
*                                                          *
*                                                          *
*                                                          *
************************************************************
```

Unit 36

AIMS: (1) Observe social organization.
        (2) Investigate accompaniment and locational phrases.
        (3) Add new nouns, verbs, and descriptives to
            vocabulary.

READ: "Social Organization and the Educational Function"
       in Herskovits, *Cultural Anthropology* pp. 166-190.

      OR "Social Organization: the Structure of Society"
       in Herskovits, *Man and His Works* pp. 289-309.

      OR "Some Principles of Social Structure" in Firth
       pp. 98-127

      OR "The Family" and "The Extension of Kinship" in
       Hoebel pp. 318-354.

      OR first part of "Friends and Frustrations" in Nida,
       Customs and Cultures pp. 92-116, plus Schusky
       pp. 64-69.

36.1 Observing Social Organization

Observe anything you can about tribal groupings and
organization. For example, do all members of the language group feel a sense of oneness? Or is there competition and hostility between members of the same
language group? Are there functional groups based on
dialects? Or are there pertinent groupings based on
place of residence? If so, what are these groupings--
household, hamlet, village, district? Are some of
these groups based on remote kinship that can no longer be traced? Do clan groups live in coherent geographical areas in one or more villages or are they
scattered and often intermingled with other clans in
a village? What do each of these kinds of units do
as a group--join together and fight other residential
groups? Is age a factor in social groupings, e.g. do
all the young men who are of the same age or are initiated together form a group? Are there any significant groups based on sex--activities in which men
may participate and from which women are excluded, or
vice versa?

What have you noticed about the position of women in
the community? And that of children? How and by

whom are the latter trained and disciplined and how
are tribal teachings passed on to them? (What qualities of character appear to be encouraged, what behavior is frowned upon, what standards are demanded in
obeying parents, sex behavior, industriousness, generosity, and in being a good citizen?) In the household,
who is the head? Who in the village? Who of the language group? How are these positions attained?
Through birth, influence, or character? How do all
these things affect the organization and daily life
of the people? Make notes of anything you consider
relevant to this topic, and add them to your cultural
file.

36.2   Clarifying Meanings in Conversation

Select 5 of the words elicited in 36.3c (perhaps 2
nouns, 2 verbs, 1 descriptive); select those which
are unfamiliar to you and those whose meaning is
still rather uncertain. Memorize these words thoroughly and then make a series of visits, without writing materials, to people you usually have little contact with and ask them to explain the meaning and
usage of each word. Use again the techniques of pp.
375-383. By one method or another (see 9.2d) make
sure that you mimic or re-use the various expressions
and illustrations that you are given. When you return home, write down all that you have learnt. During these same visits take the opportunity to check
your constructions in 36.5a.

Continue to collect data while you are with people,
noting down the context in which it was spoken, or
a possible meaning. Always let people know that you
appreciate their help and corrections.

Remain on the lookout for opportunities to collect
text material on tape (see 34.2b) as the further
analysis of sentences and the investigation of paragraphs will require such materials.

36.3a   Eliciting Accompaniment Constructions

Find out the forms for accompaniment/association.
You may discover these as you work through your texts
and unelicited data. If not, try using miming and/or
vocabulary you know. To elicit the phrase expressing
the concept 'with me' say or act "come" and add "me",
hoping that someone will give you the whole phrase.

See whether the form is the same in a transitive
clause such as 'He made it with me' and a motion
clause 'He went with me' by using the phrase you are
given in both types of construction.

NOTE: In a few languages there may be no distinction
made between 'He came with me' and 'He and I came.
In some other languages, although there is no distinction between the morphemes for 'with' and 'and',
there may be distinctions in the order/position of the
'he' and 'I' in the sentence, and there may be a
distinction between singular and plural forms of the
verb. In very few languages are the accompaniment
and instrumental markers the same morpheme, as they
are in the English *with*.

36.3b   Expanding Locational Phrases

Try to discover the full range of positional morphemes
used in locational phrases of the type first explored
in 11.3c.

(1) In sentences containing a verb of motion, locational phrases may express ideas such as 'toward',
'away from', 'through', 'into', 'out of', 'across',
'along', 'over', 'under', and 'around'.

(2) In sentences expressing existence (being or remaining) locational phrases may express ideas such
as 'at', 'near', 'at a distance from', 'in' (house,
bush, pot, stomach), 'outside', 'beside', 'above',
'on the surface of', 'on the side of', 'at the edge
of', and 'underneath'. In some languages the morphemes expressing these ideas are possessed nouns,
some of which are commonly body parts.

(3) In sentences containing a transitive verb,
phrases which indicate the location at which the
action takes place may use many of the same morphemes
or they may more frequently use a rather more general
morpheme for 'at'.

The phrases in (1) may be elicited by you or your
partner walking in various directions to and from
various places and asking, "Where is she going?"
Those in (2) may be elicited by placing a stone in
various positions relative to a box and asking,
"Where is the stone?" The phrases in (3) could be

elicited by performing a particular action in various
different locations and asking, "Where is she doing
so-and-so?" Try to elicit these positional morphemes
with both nouns and pronouns, e.g. 'near the tree',
'near me'.

NOTE: Although in English and other European languages position morphemes (prepositions) are also
used to indicate an object-like participant in certain actions (e.g. 'Give it *to* him', 'Take it *from*
him', 'seen *by* him', and 'angry *with* him') location
morphemes are probably not used in this way in the
language you are learning.

36.3c   Expanding Vocabulary

Elicit 10 new verbs by asking, "What am I/is he doing?"
and 15 new nouns using the phrase, "What is this/that?"
or your newly learnt demonstratives from 33.3c. Also
elicit 5 new descriptives by comparing two or more
similar objects that differ by the attribute being
sought, e.g. a thick versus thin piece of bark.
These vocabulary items should include any marked words
still remaining in the list on pp. 452-459. This
eliciting should be strictly monolingual.

36.4a   Checking and Filing

Compare the data obtained in 36.2 and 36.3 with previous findings. Isolate new morphemes and check for
meaning with a helpful friend. Continue to enter all
new tested words in your Dictionary File and new expressions in your Topical File as appropriate.

36.4b   Accompaniment or Coordinate?

Is there a difference, and if so what is it, in the
grammatical structures equivalent to the two English
clauses 'Tom came with Joe' and 'Tom and Joe came'?

36.4c   Pronouns in Locational Phrases

In locational phrases in which a pronoun is the point
of reference (e.g. 'near me', 'towards me') what form
of pronoun is used? If it is one not previously recorded, obtain all persons and numbers and list them
in the chart of Unit 7.

36.5a   Checking on New Verbs

Take 2 of the new verbs elicited in 36.3c and, on
your own, try to conjugate them through all the tenses,
modes, and dependent forms of the verb that you know.
Check your constructions with several people by using
these verbs in complete sentences, and correct your
forms wherever they tell you.

36.5b   Translation Practice

Review motion clauses (Units 11 and 16), instrumentals
(21), and benefactives (27). Then translate the following, remembering to check your translation with
several vernacular speakers.

'He sat down by the fire.'

'Peter stood outside the door.'

'She stretched out her hand toward the food.'

'Seeing a spring by the side of the road, he stopped
and drank some water.'

'Take this and give it to them for me.'

'Should I hit it with this stick?'

36.6a   Practicing Locative Phrases

Set up drills using accompaniment expressions (e.g.
'with me', 'with Joe', 'with my old friend') in transitive and intransitive clauses. First say a simple
sentence. Then have your partner give you a pronoun,
noun, or noun phrase as a cue. Repeat the sentence
you said earlier including this cue in an accompaniment expression. For example: You: 'I am going to
the village.' Your partner: 'Your brother'. You:
'I am going to the village with your brother.'
Always have a native speaker present to correct you
during this practice.

Set up drills using constructions that include a
locational phrase in different kinds of clauses.
Have your partner ask questions, e.g. 'Where are you
going?' 'Where is it?' 'Where did you put it?' and
you respond with sentences containing locational constructions in them.

36.6b   Practicing Descriptive Phrases with Numerals

Set up drills incorporating noun phrases in which
there is a numeral and a descriptive (e.g. 'I see two
big dogs', 'I see one thin cat'). Limit the number
of descriptives and numerals used but use a larger
number of nouns. Drill these, taking cues from your
partner as to numeral and descriptive. First use
these with a constant noun in your frame. Then, if
the language has agreement in this area, take a cue
from your partner as to the noun and use a constant
numeral and descriptive in your frame. Use these
same phrases in both transitive and intransitive
sentences.

36.6c   Learning to Use New Vocabulary Items

For any of the new words gathered in 36.3c that you
cannot use automatically, record three interesting
sentences for each word as in 28.6b and review the
recording systematically.

Date Unit 36 started: _____   Completed: _____

Hours spent on categories 2 and 6: _____

Hours spent on all other categories: _____

Comments:

****
Errors like straws, upon the surface flow:
He who would search for pearls must dive below.
                                          --Dryden
****

Unit 37

AIMS: (1) File observations on the human life cycle.
        (2) Continue investigating different modes in multi-clause sentences.

READ: (1) "The Life Cycle" in Hoebel pp. 369-383.
        (2) "Selective Mating and Preferential Marriage" and "Marriage" in Hoebel pp. 281-317.

     OR "Kinship and Marriage", "Cousin Marriages", and "Sections and Subsections" in Schusky pp. 57-64 PLUS "Family Stability in Non-European Cultures" in Fried pp. 219-228.

37.1 Observing the Life Cycle

NOTE: Do not spend time trying to elicit this information. For this unit you should record all you can recall having seen or heard relating to these events since you settled in the village. Then in future months continue to jot down observations and add these to your file.

37.1a Birth

Observe a birth, if permitted, and the events preceding and following it. How does a family prepare for a new child? Where is the child born? Who attends the birth? What is the role of the father at this time and in succeeding weeks? When, how, and by whom is the child named?

37.1b Initiation

Find out as much as you can about initiation: Who is initiated and by whom? At what age? Why and by what means? Is another name given at the time of initiation? Who is excluded from attendance and how do people regard any individuals who don't become initiated? Are there several stages of initiation at various ages?

37.1c Marriage

What are the preparations for this? What sort of groups are involved in bride price payments and what and how much is paid? Who initiates the marriage,

and when is it considered final? Is it then regarded
as irreversible?

37.1d Death

Death: What customs can you observe surrounding
death? How is a corpse prepared for burial? Who
wails, for how long and why? Does wailing begin before death? When is death considered final? How is
the corpse disposed of? Are there any ceremonies connected with the death of a person, and if so do they
take place at the time of death or months afterwards?
What is the purpose of such ceremonies? Is there a
ghost, and is it important or feared?

There are various circumstances associated with
death--childbirth, illness during infancy or when
grown up, epidemic, sudden death without apparent illness, old age, accident, warfare, suicide or murder
(secret and open). Try to discover in which of these
death is regarded as the result of natural causes,
the result of sorcery, the result of action of supernatural beings, or the result of other causes.

37.2 Gathering Spontaneous Expressions

Spend 1 or 2 hours out with people. Go somewhere or
do something where you can be with them without causing embarrassment or being the center of attention.
Perhaps sit on the verandah of the men's house or
sharpen an axe with them. Write down everything you
can which you hear that is interesting and ask people
about it later. Use part of this time to listen and
jot down notes, and part to track and converse.

37.3a Gathering Expressions in Other Modes

In your transcribed text or taped materials, you may
have already come across other moods than those mentioned in Unit 31, e.g. desiderative ('I want to ...')
or causative ('He made me eat') or, in multi-clause
sentences, purposive/intentive ('... so that ...'),
reason ('... and therefore'/'because ...') or conditional ('If ...'). If you have found these, make use
of the forms you have to elicit the other persons and
numbers, aspects and tenses of the verbs.

If you do not have any such forms to refer to, then
try to elicit them. Some suggestions for doing this
are given below.

37.3b   Eliciting Desiderative Sentences

The desiderative mode is expressed by a sentence of
just one clause in some languages and by a sentence
of two clauses in others.

Act out a situation with your partner where she
wishes to do something and you prevent her;   then get
someone to comment on the situation.   E.g.

A. says: "I'm going to eat this mango."
B. says: "No, I'LL eat the mango."
A. says: "No, I'LL eat it," and A. eats it.

Then ask your friend, "What did B. do?"   In his response see if he gives you, "She wanted to ..."

NOTE: This may give you a form for frustrated desire instead of an ordinary desiderative.   If you can
get the comment before the actual eating of the mango,
you may avoid this.

You may be able to obtain a desiderative by asking
someone why he is going to do a certain thing (use a
future tense).   In his response he may use a desiderative mode (or a purposive, or a reason).   So note down
the response you obtain, after you have mimicked it,
and later compare it with the forms you elicit in
37.3c and 37.3d.

37.3c   Eliciting Purposive Sentences

Say to your partner in the presence of a vernacular
speaker that you are going to do something such as
go to the river.   Have your partner ask you "Why?"
Reply: "We are going to the river.   We will get
water."   See if this elicits a correction containing
a connective device.

Look at your vernacular expression for 'Why are you
doing that?' and notice the part which means 'Why?'
It may consist of a verbal form or noun with a purposive or reason marker.   If so, you may find it possible to replace this verbal or noun form with a
clause and attach the purposive or reason marker
to it.

If you have succeeded in eliciting a desiderative,
you may find the purposive is based on this, as it is
in quite a few languages, e.g. 'I am cutting the tree

so that I can collect the sap from it' = 'I want to
collect the sap, therefore I am cutting the tree.'

37.3d   Eliciting Reason Sentences

Ask why someone did something in the past. For example, "The man kicked the dog. Why?" The response
may be a reason sentence, but you should also compare
it with what you found in 37.3b.

37.3e   Eliciting Conditional Sentences

Try making a statement about something in the future
which is not yet certain and something that will follow from it as a consequence. Give one possibility
and its consequence, then another and its consequence.
For example:

'We will sell yams and get money. We will go to Wewak.
We will not sell yams. We will stop here.'

OR 'It will rain. We will not go.
    It will be fine. We will go.'

See if people give you a construction uniting the two
clauses. Not that some languages have no equivalent
for 'if', but use a pattern like 'It rains. I'll
stay home.', relying on the juxtaposition of two different tenses to signal the conditional relationship.

37.3f   Eliciting Causative Sentences

Tell your partner to do something and have her reply,
"No, I won't." Repeat your request two or three
times, and her negative reply. Then become more
forceful in your request and give the impression of
anger or imminent violence. (During all this exchange,
make full use of all gestures appropriate to such a
situation.) Your partner should then grudgingly perform the required action. Then ask a bystander to
comment on what you have just done, with the expectation that he will make a statement to the effect,
"You made her do it."

NOTE: In some languages 'You made her do it' is a
single clause with a special causative affix on the
verb; in other languages the meaning is conveyed by
two clauses such as 'You compelled her and so she
did it.' Some languages again do not have a general

verb of causation such as 'compel' and so have to indicate the specific action used to compel the other
person, e.g. 'You got angry with her and so she did
it.'

37.3g Filling out Sentence Patterns

For each of the constructions above elicit (1) several different subject-person/number combinations and
(2) as many aspects and tenses as possible.

NOTE: For each of these multi-clause categories, instances where the two clauses have different subjects
may employ a somewhat different construction from
those in which the clauses have the same subject.

37.3h Bilingual Eliciting of Modes

If you are unable to find the different modes in text
materials or by monolingual elicitation, try to elicit
them bilingually using the suggested forms below.
Because the constructions may be rather difficult to
elicit, it is especially important that you check
what you obtain with several people from your own and
other villages. In particular, each question form
should be checked by presenting it to several people
in turn and noting carefully the replies you receive.
This will give you a better understanding of what the
questions mean or imply to the person questioned.

(1) Desiderative:

'What do you want to do?' 'I want to go home.'

L.F. _____

Vern. _____

(2) Purposive:

'Why have you come?' 'I've come to visit my father.'

L.F. _____

Vern. _____

(3) Reason:

'Why have you come?' 'My food ran out so I came.'

L.F. _____

Vern. _____

(4) Conditional:
'If you get rice, give me some.'

L.F. _____

Vern. _____

(5) Causative:
'He made the boy chop the firewood.'

L.F. _____

Vern. _____

37.4a Describing the Formation of These Modes

Try to write a description (with examples) of the way
each of the modes elicited in 37.3 is expressed. Are
conjunctions used? Are some of the verbs marked to
show the modes? Does the juxtaposition of different
tenses indicate the mode?

37.4b Checking and Filing

Look through your material gathered in this unit and
enter any new tested words in your Dictionary File
and expressions in your Topical File. Continue transcribing texts and filing interesting constructions
found in them.

Process all your new verb material thoroughly as
suggested in 18.4c-18.4e.

37.5a Checking Descriptions

For each mode described in 37.4a, construct several
sentences to check the accuracy of the descriptions.
Choose vocabulary which will make the sentences as
natural as possible. Check them as usual, and modify
the descriptions if necessary.

37.5b Translating Other Modes

Translate the following. Then check you translation
with various villagers and make any corrections
that are necessary.

'Your brothers are standing outside wanting to talk
to you.'

'Come and give her medicine so she will recover.'

'She put it in the box because there was no room for
it in her bag.'

'If you have taken it away tell me where you have put
it.'

'Go out there and make the children come inside.'

37.6a Practicing the New Modes

Select the tenses and aspects which people seem to
use most frequently and readily in each of the constructions elicited in 37.3. For each construction
base a drill on the particular form you have chosen,
by varying that form for person and number.

37.6b Practicing Pronunciation

Write down a list of 20 English words and 10 English
sentences for which you know the vernacular. Choose
a selection of items that includes some that are
easy, some that are difficult and some of intermediate
difficulty. Without looking at your language materials or consulting a vernacular speaker, tape-record
the vernacular equivalent of these 30 items with
your best attempt at normal speaking intonation and
speed. Play it back to a particularly helpful friend
and have him correct you on each item until he is
satisfied.

Date Unit 37 started: _____ Completed: _____

Hours spent on categories 2 and 6: _____

Hours spent on all other categories: _____

Comments:

Unit 38

AIMS: (1) Observe daily life in detail.
       (2) Investigate how vocative, exclamatory, adverbial, and conjunctive ideas are expressed.

READ: (1) again "Language Learning in Relation to Focus" in this *Guide* pp. 297-306.
       (2) again "Stress-Producing Factors in Cultural Adjustment" in this *Guide* pp. 327-343.

38.1 Observing Daily Life in Detail

Find out as much as you can about the daily life of the typical family in the community where you are living. On two or three occasions over a period of several weeks, arrange to spend a whole day with a different family. This will give you a much better idea of what their life is like, affording you an opportunity to see activities which you may not have known about before, and to recognize parallels with your own pattern of daily living. However, it will be necessary that you have the good will of your hosts to accomplish this project. You might suggest to a family you know well that you would like to join them so that you can write and tell your parents what their life is like. But be sure then that you do write afterwards, and, when your parents' letter returns, tell the family any of their comments which are appropriate.

If you are to see all that a day in their life entails, you will need to get up early in the morning (before first light), and remain with them until the evening when they retire to sleep. As the family will probably split up during the day to go to different tasks, you and your partner must be prepared to split up also.

Make a record of everything each member of the family does and when (note down the times). Observe such things as how much time is spent in food preparation and what foods are eaten, how much time the people spend conversing around their fires. When you accompany them to their gardens, note the time they spend in fencing or weeding, harvesting or

replanting. What do they do when rain comes and how
do they cope with it? When and why do people leave
the working group and when do they return? Try to
get a real picture of what makes up their lives in all
its component parts. You will find it very profitable in
gaining insight and understanding to discover these
things.

38.2a Conversation

As you spend time with people in 38.1, take every opportunity to listen, track and ask questions concerning things they are talking about.

38.2b Gathering Vocatives and Exclamations

As you are with people on the occasions suggested
above, listen carefully for words, morphemes, and expressions with which you are already familiar. Also
be alert to hear and note down exclamatory and vocative expressions. For example, during the day when
anyone calls another or begins addressing another
person, note whether special vocative affixes or
particles are used, or intonation in conjunction with
a second person pronoun, a kinship term or a personal
name. Circumstances in which exclamations are likely
to be used are surprise or astonishment, sudden
fright or pain, sudden danger, extreme exertion or
fatigue, seeing something vast in size or number,
approval and pleasure or disapproval.

As far as other new data is concerned do not spend
all your time writing down new expressions, but write
down only expressions which strike you as pertinent
to what you already know.

38.3a Eliciting Manner Words

Consult your files for any manner words that they may
contain and use them in eliciting other manner words
below.

Elicit manner words by performing various actions in
two contrasting ways, e.g. walking quickly and slowly, talking loudly and quietly, jumping high and low,
putting things down carefully and clumsily. (Choose
something in which speed is not a crucial factor
here, or you may get words for speed). Some other
contrasts are listed below; some you will find easier
to elicit than others:

'secretly' : 'openly'
'easily' : 'with difficulty'
'eagerly'/'readily'/'willingly' : 'unwillingly'/
  'reluctantly'
'successfully' : 'unsuccessfully'/'in vain'
'boldly'/'bravely' : 'fearfully'/'hesitantly'
'always' : 'frequently' : 'sometimes' : 'rarely'
'temporarily' : 'permanently'
'definitely' : 'probably' : 'possibly'/'perhaps' :
  'unlikely' : 'definitely not'

Note that in some languages words representing manner concepts are adverbs, but in other languages
manner concepts are represented by adjectives, and in
other languages by verbs.

38.3b Eliciting Intensifiers

Try to elicit, by contrastive acting, morphemes that
intensify or weaken the meaning of descriptives and/
or manner expressions and words elicited in 38.3a.
(Cf. English adverbs of degree such as: *exceedingly;
very; moderately = fairly = rather; slightly = somewhat; almost; just; only; merely.*) Compare your
elicitation with 32.3d where you were investigating
comparative and superlative concepts. You may find
the degrees suggested above are part of the same
system.

38.3c Eliciting 'How?' (for Manner Questions)

When you have collected a number of manner words as
suggested in 38.3a, have your partner repeat an action
previously mimed, for which you now have the manner
expression, and, with some vernacular speakers
present, ask him a question using 'How?' (Unit 21),
e.g. 'How did you hit it?' Have your partner reply
something like 'I hit it hard.' Repeat the same
technique with several actions and see if people allow this usage of 'How?' or correct you, giving you
another question form for inquiring about manner.

38.3d Eliciting 'But'

Try to elicit vernacular equivalents for linking two
contrastive statements (like the English *but*), by
creating or miming two contrastive situations, or by
making two separate sentences and hoping your friends
will correct you. E.g. 'She went (but) I stayed

behind' = 'She went (but) I didn't go.'

Note that many different devices are used to indicate
contrast between two clauses. In some languages
there is a contrast marking affix or particle with one
or more of the words which actually contrast, in
others there is an adversative conjunction or suffix
that links the two clauses, and in others the juxtaposition of two clauses without any conjunction at
all is the normal way of expressing such contrasts.

38.3e Eliciting 'And'

Elicit the vernacular equivalent that is used to link
two descriptive statements (like the English *and*).
Try to elicit this by presenting a friend with two
separate sentences and asking him to correct you,
e.g. 'My father is an old man (and) he has grey hair'
= 'My father is an old man (and) he is a grey-haired
man.' Make sure the two sentences could not be regarded as a sequence of action in time, or cause and
effect. These have been investigated in earlier
units.

38.3f Eliciting 'Or'

Elicit the vernacular equivalent for linking two alternative questions (like the English *or*) by presenting
the two questions separately and appealing to a friend
to correct you, e.g. 'At the feast will they eat taro
(or) will they eat rice?'

38.3g By careful choice of examples for 38.3d-38.3f, put
together pairs of clauses in which the verbs are identical and only the nouns or pronouns, or descriptives
differ (as suggested in some of the examples given).
In these cases notice if, when people correct you,
they convert the sentence to a single clause (e.g.
'She, but not I, went.' 'My father is an old (and)
greyhaired man.' 'Will they eat taro or rice?'),
thus giving you coordinated phrases rather than coordinated clauses.

38.4a Describing Grammatical Patterns

Study the data obtained in 38.3 and write descriptions of the various ways these relationships are expressed. Check and file all data as usual.

38.4b Studying Vocatives and Exclamations

Describe or diagram intonation contours that you have
observed used with vocative expressions. Also list
all exclamatory morphemes you have heard and the intonation contours associated with each. Describe any
other features associated with vocatives and exclamations.

38.4c Filing Unwritten Vocabulary

Quickly scan your English-Vernacular Word List (or a
child's English dictionary) and notice any common
English words for which you do not have any vernacular equivalent entered, and which you either know or
are sure you have heard. After checking 'these items
with a village friend, enter them in your Dictionary
File.

38.5 Translation Practice

Translate 6 of the following passages, selecting one
passage from each pair of alternatives. Check all
your translation very thoroughly and correct it whenever necessary.

(1) 'Zacchaeus, hurry and come down, for I must stay
     at your house today.' Luke 19:5.

OR   "Paul, you are mad!"
     "I am not mad, most excellent Festus; I am speak-
     ing the sober truth." Acts 26:24-25.

(2) 'She went and called her sister Mary secretly
     (quietly).' John 11:28.

OR   'They departed quickly from the tomb with fear.'
     Matt. 28:8.

(3) 'The devil took him to a very high mountain.'
     Matt. 4:8.

OR   'When he heard this he became sad for he was
     very rich.' Luke 18:23.

(4) "The disciples of John fast often ... but yours
     eat and drink." Luke 5:33.

OR   "My father's hired workers have bread enough and
     to spare (= much) but I perish here with hunger."
     Luke 15:17.

(5)   'It had a great high wall with twelve gates, and at the gates twelve angels.' Rev. 21:12.

OR   "Cornelius is a good and God-fearing man." Acts 10:22.

(6)   "Are you saying this of your own accord or did others say it to you about me?" John 18:34.

OR   "Which one do you want me to set free for you, Jesus Barabbas or Jesus called the Christ?" Matt. 27:17.

38.6a   Practicing Manner Words

Record a drill with manner words and their opposites in the same sentence, if possible. For example:

'Don't ask openly but ask secretly.'
'Don't tell it openly but tell it secretly.'
'Don't show him openly but show him secretly.'

'You can do it easily but I do it with difficulty.'
....

38.6b   Practicing Manner Questions-and-Answers

Go around the village with your partner and observe people doing things. As you do so, take turns in asking one another and replying to the questions 'How is he doing so-and-so?' Be careful to select activities that do not all elicit the same adverb in the response given. Make sure that there is a vernacular speaker there to correct you as you practice.

Date Unit 38 started: _____   Completed: _____

Hours spent on categories 2 and 6: _____

Hours spent on all other categories: _____

Comments:

Unit 39

AIMS: (1) Observe work patterns.
(2) Investigate multi-clause sentences with embedded clauses.
(3) Continue investigating kinship terms.

READ: (1) "Work and Wealth of Primitive Communities" in Firth pp. 71-97.

OR "Economics and the Fulfillment of Wants" in Herskovits, *Cultural Anthropology* pp. 143-165 OR in Herskovits, *Man and His Works* pp. 266-288.

OR "Property and Politics" in Hoebel pp. 429-463.

OR "Hoes and Headaches" in Nida, *Customs and Cultures* pp. 73-91.

(2) "Part One" and "Patterned Behavior in Kinship" in Schusky pp. 5-51, 55-57.

OR "Kinship Systems" in Hoebel pp. 355-365.

OR "General Observations Upon Systems of Relationship" and "Classificatory Systems of Relationship" in Hoebel pp. 229-245.

39.1 Observing Patterns of Work

Observe patterns and methods of work among the people you live with. Do the people do the same work all the time, or are there seasons of the year (or work cycles comprising more than a year) in which specific work is done? For example, if the people mainly practice agriculture, observe whether they work in the gardens all the time or only seasonally, whether the gardens are planted at a specific time and, if so, how this time is determined. Notice where the gardens are, how near they are to the place of residence, what kind of ground they are on and how often the site is changed. Discover who does the work in the garden, whether there is a division of labor by sex, and, if so, what sorts of work the men do as opposed to the women, and how their daily routine differs.

What other kinds of work projects do the people

undertake, if any? Is there any co-operation in
them? For example, in housebuilding, who helps a
man, and how is he paid--by food, valuables, cash or
work in return? Are there some types of work limited
to only a few people, e.g., healing, magic, mid-
wifery, or certain manual skills? If so, how does
one become a specialist, and is he rewarded for his
work? On the other hand, is there any sort of work
that is never done by a single person? How does
one arrange to get help for these projects?

File as much information on this topic as you are
able to obtain through your observations and enquiries in the vernacular.

39.2a   Conversation

Continue mimicking people as they talk, whenever you
can, and listen to their conversations. Make a special effort during this unit to spend more time conversing. Specifically set aside time when you know
your friends will be free, and join them. Have definite things prepared in your mind to talk about with
them.

39.2b   Gathering "New Information" Structures

During this unit make a point of taking every opportunity whenever anyone calls on you--for whatever
reason--to converse with him for as long as he is
willing. Do not resent these times as interruptions
to your work; seize them as golden opportunities for
improving your conversational ability. Start tape-
recording as each visitor approaches and record at
least the first part of each conversation. Review
the recordings at the end of the day, to see if you
have caught any structures characteristic of a speaker
imparting new information to his hearers which you
have not encountered before. (See also 34.2b last
paragraph.) Repeat this procedure on other days if
it proves helpful.

39.3a   Eliciting Sentences Containing Embedded Clauses

First do the work directed in 39.4a and 39.4b. If
you are successful in discovering sentences in which
one clause occurs within another clause (as modifier,
possessor, object, subject or location) elicit more
examples of these constructions.

39.3b If you have not discovered any sentences of this type
in your unelicited data or transcribed texts, try to
elicit them as follows. This will involve yourself,
your partner and a helpful friend who will observe
your game and check and correct you. The aim is to
make up sentences with given items as the object of
a verb, such as 'I helped ...'. Your partner will
give you a series of personal names or nouns, noun
phrases (of increasing length) and eventually a
whole clause for you to use in the object slot. For
example,

Prompter says:	Learner says:
John	*I helped John.*
a little boy	*I helped a little boy.*
the man with the red shirt	*I helped the man with the red shirt.*
the man chopped wood	*I helped the man who chopped wood.*

When you stumble in your answers (particularly at the
embedded clause) note down carefully what you are
told to say as a correction.

Follow the same procedure for eliciting embedded
clauses in the subject slot, with a verb such as
'... died'. For example,

Prompter says:	Learner says:
the dog	*The dog died.*
the fat pig	*The fat pig died.*
you planted it	*What you planted died.*

You can use a verb such as 'I am standing' to elicit
embedded clauses in the location slot. For example,

Prompter says :	Learner says:
the log	*I am standing on the log.*
the big black rock	*I am standing on the big black rock.*
the children play	*I am standing on (the place where) the children play.*

NOTE: One of the above slots--object, subject,₁ loca-
tion--will be in the interior of the clause structure
(e.g. Location in a clause which has the order Sub-
ject-Object-Location-Verb). When a clause is substituted in an interior position, it should be possible
to distinguish between an embedded clause (acting like
a noun, say) and a juxtaposed clause on the same level
as the "main" clause.

NOTE: In the corrections you are given you may discover that the embedded clauses function as nouns,
e.g. 'I helped whoever chopped wood.', 'What you
planted died.', 'I am standing where the children
play.' Or you may find that they function as modifiers, e.g. 'I helped the man who chopped wood
(= the wood-chopping man).', 'The thing that you
planted died (= your planted thing).', 'I am standing
on the place where the children play (= the children's
playing place).'

39.3c Eliciting More Genealogical Data

Continue gathering genealogical data about other
households. Use the vernacular as much as you can and
ask questions about the people whose names you record.
Try to find out how husband and wife were related
before their marriage (if at all). Continue to elicit
kin terms by asking "ego" how he addresses and how
he refers to his relatives. (This will be easier
after the genealogical details have been charted and
you can see a diagram of the relationship referred to
by each kin term.)

39.4a Gathering Embedded Clauses

Consult the Topical File or Grammar File and look
through your transcribed texts for any multi-clause
sentences whose structure does not fit into any of the
sentence patterns or types you have examined hitherto.
See if any of the unanalyzed structures contain an
embedded/included/nested clause (a clause construct),
that is, a clause that is not at the same level as
the other clauses in the sentence but instead functions in the way that a noun or adjective does. In
most languages it is possible for an embedded clause
to function as a possessor, modifier, subject, object,
or location, and in this usage it usually takes the
same slot marker as a noun (or adjective) does in that
slot.

In some languages embedded clauses make use of a
special form of the verb and/or a nominalizing affix
attached to the verb or verb phrase. In other languages embedded clauses may be signalled by specific
markers at the beginning and/or end of the clause.
Again in other languages an embedded clause may be
characterized by a change in the normal order of its
slots. You may find embedded clauses difficult to
elicit because your language normally avoids embedding, preferring to express such ideas in coordinated clauses.

39.4b   Gathering Verbs of Speech, Cognition, and Perception

Go through the data abstracted in 39.4a (and if necessary through your unelicited data and transcribed
texts again) and pick out instances of the verbs
'say/tell', 'ask', 'see', 'hear', 'know', and 'think'
which are accompanied by a clause giving details of
what was said, seen, heard, etc. List these examples,
using a separate sheet for each verb.

For any one verb you may find that there is just one
structure employed with it, or you may find several
different structures, as in English:

tell: { *I told him, "I will come tomorrow."*
        { *I told him that I would come tomorrow.*
        { *I told him about my coming tomorrow.*
        { *I told (= instructed) him to come tomorrow.*
        { *I told him that he should come tomorrow.*

ask: { *He asked me, "When will you come?"*
        { *He asked me when I would come.*
        { *He asked me, "Will you come?"*
        { *He asked me whether/if I would come.*
        { *He asked (= invited) me to come.*
        { *He asked that I should come.*

see: { *I saw the man chopping wood.*
        { *I saw that the man was chopping wood.*

hear: { *I heard him singing in the bath.*
        { *I heard his singing in the bath.*
          *I heard (= a report) (that) he was singing
          in the bath.*

know: *We know (that) he came.*
         We don't know whether/if he came.
         We don't know when he came.

think: *I think (that) he will come.*
         I thought (mistakenly) (that) he would come.
         { *I don't think (that) he'll come.*
         { *I think (that) he won't come.*
         I thought about his coming.
         I thought, "He will come."

You may find that several or all of these verbs employ
basically the same grammatical device (e.g. direct
quotation) for introducing the clause which specifies
what was seen or heard or told, etc. You may also
find in these constructions that the clause describing
the action seen or heard, etc., may have the same
grammatical form as the embedded clause investigated
in 39.4a.

39.4c Describing Clause Embedding

Analyze all the data you have extracted and elicited
in 39.3-39.4b above, and write a tentative brief
description of each of the constructions you have discovered.

39.4d Analyzing Kin Terms

For each kin term, start a list of the relationships
the term covers, e.g.

Ego	Kin Term Relationship	Relative
John	BrSo	Peter
John	SoSo	James
Mary	DaDa	Lucy

Make a composite chart of a hypothetical male "ego"
who has one of each relative (see Schusky, p. 9).
Mark in the kin terms you have observed being used
with each relationship. Repeat for a female "ego".

39.4e Checking and Filing

Check the meanings of new words and expressions with
one or two friends and file as usual.

39.5   Translating Embedded Clauses

Translate the following sentences and check them with your friends.

'They saw that the child was beautiful.'

'He placed the body (= corpse) in his own tomb which he had recently dug out of the rock.'

'The man said to him, "Don't be afraid, friend."'

'The children asked their father if they might take the meat and roast it.'

'The pig ate the food scraps that fell through the bamboo floor.'

'Prepare plenty of food, because we don't know how many guests your father will invite.'

39.6a   Practicing Embedding Clauses

Make a drill using patterns like those of 39.3b to practice embedded clauses. Extend it to your conversation, modifying sentences you hear and repeating them with embedded clauses.

39.6b   Learning New Kin Terms

Make up a drill where the stimulus is a relationship (e.g. father's brother) and the response is the kin term of reference and then the term of address. Try to start a game where one person is designated as "ego" and the others take turns to point to or name ego's relatives. You try to give the appropriate kin terms.

Date Unit 39 started: _____ Completed: _____

Hours spent on categories 2 and 6: _____

Hours spent on all other categories: _____

Comments:

Unit 40

AIM: Review.

READ: (1) again "Plain Card Filing", "Punch Card Filing",
             and "Page Filing" in this *Guide* pp. 427-428.
        (2) again "Ways to Process Data" in Samarin pp. 153-
             174.

40.1 Updating Observations

File any observations from Units 36-39 which you have
not filed already, and also any other observations on
old or new topics of which you should have a record.

40.2 Listening, Tracking, Mimicking, and Conversing

Always be prepared to spend time with people, listening to them, talking to them, sitting with them,
tracking and mimicking their speech. As you do so
you will probably find that they become more communi-
cative and take you further into their confidence and
friendship. If you do not make this effort, you will
find it extremely difficult to get close to them when
you want to.

40.4a Analyzing and Filing

Catch up on the analyzing and processing of any materials you have not yet handled and file them appropriately.

Read through (by skimming) all of the material in your
Topical File, Grammar File, and Anthropology File.
Decide how you could change each filing system to make
it more useful to you and/or easier to operate. You
may wish:

(1) to put two topics together as one because of
     interconnections you had not previously recog-
     nized,

(2) to subdivide a topic because it has become too
     large,

(3) to analyze and subdivide a topic because it has
     become too complex, or

(4) to investigate a topic further because your lack

of understanding is hindering your learning the
culture and language.

This reading of your materials will also refresh your
mind on many earlier discoveries that you have long
since forgotten all about.

40.4b Determining Morpheme Classes

Review all the grammatical analysis you have done so
far and make tentative conclusions as to what word or
affix classes you have and any subclasses you have
observed, based either on morphophonemics or on agreement. Indicate how you can distinguish between
nouns and adjectives, adjectives and adverbs, adverbs
and verbs, nouns and pronouns, pronouns and demonstratives, demonstratives and locationals, if they are
in fact distinct.

As you have opportunity, add to your existing entries
in your Dictionary File some kind of symbols to indicate these classes and subclasses. Continue to do
this with all new vocabulary items you enter in the
future.

40.4c Transcribing More Texts

Transcribe at least 5 minutes of tape-recorded text
material. Refer back to 15.3a for help.

40.5   Translating Simple Narratives

Translate one or more of the following passages.
Preferably use the T.E.V. version to translate from.

Luke 19:2-6   The story of Zacchaeus

Luke 7:11-15   The raising of the widow's son

John 6:16-21   Jesus walks on the water

Acts 28:2-6   Paul shipwrecked on Malta

40.6   Practicing Expressions, Grammar, and Pronunciation

Continue to drill and review old expressions, and
keep adding new expressions to your repertoire. Whenever you hear a new expression that you feel would be
helpful to know, put it on tape with several variations and learn them. Check the accuracy and acceptability of the recordings in Units 23-25 and replace
any that you now realize are not really natural.

Review grammar drills, particularly those in areas which are still causing you to stumble in conversation.

Review all your lists of words dealing with length, pitch and stress until you are fully familiar with all the changes that occur in different contexts.

Date Unit 40 started: _____ Completed: _____

Hours spent on categories 2 and 6: _____

Hours spent on all other categories: _____

Comments:

Number of weeks in the language area between starting Unit 31 and completing Unit 40: _____

Total hours spent on categories 2 and 6 during Units 31-40: _____

Hours per week: _____

Total hours spent on all other categories during Units 31-40: _____

Hours per week: _____

Considering the statistics in this summary and your progress during this period, what changes do you plan to make in your approach to your neighbors and to language learning, or in your future work?

READ: "Progress in Language Learning" in this *Guide* pp.
       291-294 and try to objectively assess what stage of
       language proficiency you have reached: _____

STOP: <u>Special Assignment</u>

       Congratulations on finishing the units. Take a holi-
       day for a few days. Get away from the village and
       language area if you can and stay where you can enjoy
       the company of people of your own culture. If you
       expect to be away for an extended period read Unit 42
       before you leave.

```
***********************************************************
*                                                         *
*                                                         *
*                                                         *
*                                                         *
*                                                         *
*        Science may never come up with a                 *
*        better office-communications system              *
*        than the coffee break.                           *
*                                                         *
*                               --Earl Wilson             *
*                                                         *
*                                                         *
*                                                         *
*                                                         *
***********************************************************
```

Unit 41

How to Continue Language Learning

AIMS: (1) Attain good conversational fluency.
(2) Continue to observe and investigate the customs and attitudes in your area, including cultural change, trading practices, the traditional religious system, and the former and present legal systems.
(3) Investigate various areas of the grammar as they come to your attention, including reciprocal actions, reflexive actions, passive voice, negation of all moods, and the expressing of emotions.
(4) Select and train several assistants for language research.

41.1 Observing

Continue to observe at all times and in all places. Detailed suggestions for four more topics are offered below.

41.1a Observing Culture Change

Observe people's acceptance of outside ideas--both values and attitudes. With improved communications and contact with Western culture, what changes have occurred in the traditional patterns of living? For example, in their beliefs about the supernatural, how far has Christian teaching (if any) been accepted, synthesized with the old, or rejected? In their attitudes to sickness do they still rely on the shaman and the old medical cures, or do they try to mix Western medicine with indigenous magic and ceremonies? In regard to the ties of kinship, its responsibilities and interrelationships, how have outside ideas, going away to work, and other changes from the outside world affected them? Have things such as choosing a marriage partner, family obligations, or the place where one lives become a matter of personal choice? Is the old system of sharing between distant relatives being replaced by a greater desire for private ownership? As far as methods of farming, housing standards, possession of material goods, and manner of living are concerned, what changes are there?

Have they adopted Western standards of hygiene, desire for privacy, use of insecticides, and the like?
Or have only a few things (e.g. clothes, watches, and
radios) been adopted because they are regarded as
status symbols? Have ideas about music, art, and
beauty been affected? Do the young people differ
from the old folk in their attitude to "progress"?
Try to learn as much as you can about the sense of
values held by the people you live with.

Read again the readings on cultural change in Unit 16.
If you are interested in changes due to the influence
of Christian missions, then read William A. Smalley,
editor, *Readings in Missionary Anthropology* and Marvin
K. Mayers, *Christianity Confronts Culture: A Strategy
for Cross-Cultural Evangelism*, (Grand Rapids, Michigan:
Zondervan), 1974.

41.1b Observing Trading

Observe all you can about the indigenous exchange system: the types of money in use, what they are (European coins, shells, stones, etc.), and the purposes
for which they are used (e.g. what sort of things are
bought and sold for cash and from whom, and who trades
with whom in non-cash trading?). What is the source
of indigenous money and how are business transactions
remembered? E.g. how much was given as a bride price
for a certain woman? What is the attitude to borrowing? Within what social groupings is it practiced?
What traditional goods are imported and exported in
your locality? Is this trading initiated by specifically organized trading parties who travel to the consumer? Or is it channelled through regular trading
partners? Or is it handled by a group of middlemen
living between the source and the consumer?

41.1c Observing the Religious System

Read again the readings on religion in Unit 32. A
more detailed investigation into the indigenous religion is now suggested.

Find out all you can about local deities, ritual,
magic, sorcery, and attitudes towards Christianity.
Try to learn what sort of non-human beings people
believe in, whether they are of different types, have
names, help or harm people, can be manipulated by
humans, are feared or loved. What rituals do people

engage in? Healing, propitiation of deities, control
of nature (to bring or stop rain) or of other people's
actions? What are the purposes and forms of their
magic and does it work? Why or why not? Who per-
forms it and toward what or whom is it directed? Do
they believe in the efficacy of sorcery, practice it,
suffer from it? What is the effect of sorcery? Is
all death attributed to it? How can sorcery benefit
the sorcerer? Or is it worked by non-human agencies?
And if people have any knowledge of Christianity, how
has this affected their old views and attitudes? Is
God or man the center of their universe? Why do they
think Christ died? How do they think man pleases God
or what do they consider God's attitude to men? Can
God be manipulated for man's benefit? How much syn-
cretism is there in their current religious attitudes?

41.1d Observing the Indigenous Legal System

Read "The Regulation of Conduct" in Firth pp. 128-
       151,
OR   "Law and the Social Order" in Hoebel pp. 467-485.
OR   "Law and Anthropology" in Fried pp. 296-310.

Try to discover what things are considered to be offences in the society and how they are dealt with.
What ideals of behavior do you find? What happens
when these standards are broken? How were offences
against individuals regarded in the old days? As a
misconduct against the community? And what were the
measures adopted to deal with them? How have these
measures been affected by the laws and attitudes of
the government? What methods are used now to deal
with infringements of laws and standards? How have
the ways and the reasons for disciplining the young
people changed? And how are differences and disagree-
ments between people settled in the present day
situation? How do these methods differ from older
ones?

41.2a Building Conversational Fluency

Continue constantly listening to and mimicking people
talking. CONTINUE TO CONVERSE AT EVERY OPPORTUNITY.
WHENEVER PEOPLE ARE ABOUT, TAKE THE TIME TO TALK WITH
THEM. Be on the alert for new expressions, constructions and intonation patterns even when your understanding and fluency in the language increase. What

you learn in this way will provide a constant check against the novel constructions and collocations you will inevitably produce in your spontaneous use of the language.

41.2b Gathering Interesting Expressions and Vocabulary

Whenever you go out for an extensive period of time (e.g. for a long walk, or to a community project or gathering), maintain the habit of taking a small note-book and jotting down new things to inquire about afterwards. Or, when new vocabulary items and grammatical constructions occur in conversation, write them down, and their context, whenever possible. (However only do these things when it would not offend people or interfere with your conversation). Then ask the person what these things mean after the conversation has ended. He may not even remember he used the word or construction and so may give it to you in another context. Ask several other people individually about these new items. This will probably give you yet more contexts, as well as confirm some meanings that others have given you.

41.2c Collecting Texts

From time to time, when circumstances are particularly opportune, continue to collect texts (see 34.2b for the best kinds) for transcription and explanation later. Particularly useful are texts of which you already know the meaning--stories about events which you have also observed or in which you have participated, etc. Try to balance the amount of text you tape with what you can transcribe, as texts are really only valuable as they are transcribed. Be ruthless in erasing "useless" tapes.

NOTE: Remember that the men may use a secret language to conceal things from the women or from you. Be considerate if they do not wish to explain all this to you at first, or if they do not wish this material to be recorded.

41.3 Eliciting Data

As long as you study and use a language you will be constantly discovering new things about it. However, some areas which you would do well to investigate with thoroughness are listed below.

41.3a Expressing Emotions

Find out the various ways emotions are expressed--
hunger, thirst, anger, pain, sorrow, love, pride and
such feelings. Be alert that some of these expressions may use body parts (liver, intestines, stomach,
neck, etc.) and an unusual clause structure.

41.3b Other Relationships Between Actor and Goal

Some of the relationships between actor and goal which
need to be investigated are the Reciprocal, Reflexive,
and Passive voices.

41.3c Negating Non-indicative Modes

Find out how to negate the different modes investigated in Unit 37.

Desiderative: 'I don't want to go.'

Purposive: 'We're not going to the river to get
                water.'
                'We're standing under the trees so that
                we won't get wet.'

Reason: 'The man hit the pig because it didn't
                move.'
                'The man didn't kick the dog although
                it bit him.'

Conditional (contrafactual): 'If it had rained we
                would not have come.'

Causative: 'He didn't make her do it.'
                'He made her stop doing it.'
                (= He prevented her from doing it.)

41.3d Kin Terms

Elicit kinship terms from more households. Investigate the meanings of the various in-law terms especially.

41.3e Select and Train Assistants

Soon you will be wanting to begin the field work for
which you undertook to learn this language. In many
instances this work will be language related: for
instance, anthropology, descriptive linguistics, comparative linguistics, literacy, lexicography, translation, dialect geography, or psycholinguistics. It
is now time that you considered finding and training

several research assistants. Read again "Obtaining
Linguistic Data" in this *Guide* pp. 344-360, and "The
Language Informant" in Samarin pp. 20-44.

From among the many people who have helped you infor-
mally during these early months of language learning,
choose several who seem to have the qualities needed
for your research project. Approach them, and if they
are interested, employ them for a short trial period,
to be extended if they like the work and prove suitable.

Right from the start you should spend considerable effort in training each assistant, and you should expect
that some of them will eventually become researchers
in their own right. These will be able to dig much
deeper into their own culture and language than you
can ever hope to do as an outsider. But only if they
are taught how.

41.4   Analysis and Description

41.4a   Continue with text transcription. See 15.3a.

41.4b   Continue work on your Phonemics Statement begun in
Unit 35. Refer to Pike's *Phonemics* if you meet any
analytical problems.

41.4c   If you have not already done so, commence grammatical
files that seem to be appropriate for your language.
If you have special problems such as morphophonemics,
affix combinations, agreement clause types or conjunc
tions, a filing system can be a great help in solving
them.

41.4d   Investigating Other Styles of Language

Investigate the different styles used in different
degrees of intimacy between people, along the continuum: intimate - personal - consultative - public.

Study the written style employed by people literate
in the language and compare it with transcribed
speech.

It may be helpful to investigate the speech of another close dialect or social stratum.

41.4e Further Reading

As you progress in language analysis and applying the
results to your specific research project, you should
continue to read books and articles that are pertinent to what you are doing. A few suggestions are
listed below:

(1) Robert E. Longacre. *Grammar Discovery Procedures:
     A Field Manual*, (The Hague: Mouton). 1964.

     OR D. Terence Langendoen. *Essentials of English
        Grammar*, (New York: Holt, Rinehart and Wins-
        ton). 1970.

(2) Dow F. Robinson. *Manual for Bilingual Diction-
     aries: Volume 1, Textbook*, (Santa Ana, Califor-
     nia: Summer Institute of Linguistics). 1969.

(3) William A. Smalley and others. *Orthography
     Studies: Articles on New Writing Systems*, (Lon-
     don: United Bible Societies). 1964. [especial-
     ly pp. 22-52].

(4) Sarah C. Gudschinsky. *A Manual of Literacy for
     Preliterate Peoples*, (Ukarumpa, Papua New Guinea:
     Summer Institute of Linguistics). 1973.

(5) Eugene A. Nida and Charles R. Taber. *The Theory
     and Practice of Translation*, (Leiden: Brill).
     1969.

     OR John Beekman and John Callow. *Translating the
        Word of God*, (Grand Rapids: Zondervan). 1974.

41.5a Checking Descriptions

As you work on your analysis continue to make up your
own constructions and check them with several people.
Always be sensitive to their corrections and investigate the reasons behind any changes that are made.

41.5b Adapting Texts

When you have transcribed a short text about an
activity you have participated in, change it so that
you can narrate the events from your own point of
view. Check your changes, then read the account to
several different groups of people. Try to dispense
with the written copy. If the language has near and

remote past tenses, repeat this procedure, transforming the text into each tense as the days go by. Try
it with an event that has not happened yet as well.
Repeat with other texts as appropriate.

41.5c   Translating Simple Narrative Passages

Try translating more simple narrative passages like
those suggested in 40.5.

41.6   Keep Practicing

Keep reviewing drills, following the review system.
Keep recording new and useful expressions and vocabulary, always using about three sentences for each one
as before. Whenever you notice people are correcting
the same mistake frequently, do some analysis on this
point and work the patterns you discover into a drill.
If there is any pattern you understand but cannot use
automatically, make drills to give concentrated practice with the pattern. (See "Grammatical Drills" on
pp. 307-317.)

Keep using in conversation the things you learn by
drilling.

****
"When I use a word," Humpty Dumpty said
in a rather scornful tone, "it means just
what I choose it to mean--neither more
nor less."

"The question is," said Alice, "whether you
can make words mean so many different things.

                                    --Lewis Carroll
****

Unit 42

Language Learning away from the Language Area

AIMS: (1) Concentrate on analysis and filing rather more than is usual in the village situation.
       (2) Spend enough time in conversation and drilling to keep your spoken fluency increasing, not just at the status quo.

READ: All anthropology, phonology, and grammar materials written about the languages within the same family as the language you are learning.

NOTES: Taking Research Assistants Away From Their Village

This unit is intended especially for members of the Summer Institute of Linguistics, who usually take one or two vernacular speakers with them to their headquarters or workshop center from time to time to attend linguistic workshops and for other purposes. It may not be relevant for other users of the *Guide*.

If you take your research assistant away from the village for a period of several months he is likely to have problems of homesickness. This can be minimized by bringing or finding a companion for him--a spouse, a younger brother, another research assistant--who can speak his own vernacular language.

While you are away from the language area it is likely that you will have various other commitments in addition to language learning and research. If you are too preoccupied with these there is a danger that your research assistant will become bored and disgruntled. It is your responsibility to make sure that his normal working hours are fully taken up with activities that are both profitable and reasonably satisfying.

One way is to set him to work on research projects for which you have trained him and which he is now capable of doing by himself. However, you should take care to consult with him fairly frequently lest he be frustrated

by some problem that he can't solve and that prevents
his working.

Another way is to teach him, or have him taught, some
new skill that he values. It is important that you
allow adequate time each day for training and practice
in this skill, and that you always help and encourage
him in every way you can until he becomes reasonably
proficient.

(1) You may teach him a skill with tools, such as
carpentry or automechanics for a man, or using a sewing machine and dressmaking for a woman. When he returns to his village he can share what he has learnt
and also use it himself, perhaps even for a measure
of self employment.

(2) If he is illiterate you should certainly teach
him to read and write, and you could also teach him
how to operate a tape recorder. Then later he may be
able to record valuable text materials, often in more
natural circumstances than if you personally were
present operating the recorder.

(3) If he is already literate you could teach him to
transcribe text from tape recordings, and you could
teach him to type.

42.1 Observing Research Assistants' Reactions to Travel

Observe your research assistants' attitudes to the new
things they meet when they are away from the village
with you. Notice their comments and see what insight these can give you into their own standards and
traditional upbringing, as they react to new customs,
different standards of living, other ethnic groups,
and things they have never seen before.

42.2a Improving Conversational Fluency

Take every opportunity to talk with your research
assistants. Share jokes, stories, descriptions of
customs, daily radio news, and devotions with them.
Keep a list of topics you could talk about whenever
the opportunity offers. Make occasions to do things
together each day (e.g. go for a 30-minute walk each
afternoon) and converse constantly.

Use drills and texts taped while in the village, for
listening, tracking and mimicking.

Have an agreement with your partner never to talk
English or the lingua franca but only vernacular for
some set period each day. This period should include
most or all of the time that your language helpers
are with you.

42.2b   Collecting Spontaneous Texts

Share an activity with your research assistants
such as a picnic, watching house building, or a visit
to any local industries or places of interest, and
afterwards have one of your assistants recount what
has been done. The trip out of the village and all
the many new experiences in an unfamiliar situation
will give stimulus for many narratives and comments
which you can also record. Get at least one text
each week and transcribe it.

Occasionally record your research assistants' comments about an activity that is due to take place
soon; then obtain his comments immediately after the
event; and several days later obtain his comments
again. This should give you various tense forms.

42.3a   Eliciting Data

Plan and elicit material suitable to solve particular grammatical or phonological problems with which
you are faced.

Texts gathered in 42.2b can be used as the basis for
further investigation of new vocabulary items or
grammatical structures by asking your helper to give
you further examples, usages, and paradigms.

42.3b   Toward a Written Style

Get your assistant to dictate to you an untaped text
of some interesting event in which you have both participated. You may find this helpful for absorbing
words, idioms, collocations and natural grammatical
patterns in a style that will probably be closer than
normal rapid speech to the style which will later
prove acceptable in primers, readers, translations,
and other written materials. (If the language you
are learning already has some published indigenous
literature and an established written style, then
select a variety of texts from this literature and
read, study, and absorb them instead.)

42.4a **Analyzing Texts**

Work at text transcription and understanding what
the text says in its entirety, until all the new
vocabulary and strange forms are mastered in that
particular text. Do this work through the vernacular,
not in the lingua franca. Although you may feel this
will limit you, in the long run you will find it
helps your ability to communicate.

42.4b **Filing**

Continue with phonemic and grammar filing and catch
up on any not done previously.

42.4c **Balanced Analysis**

Make the most of your time away from the language
area for doing analytical work. But nevertheless
limit this book work to a definite period of time
each day, so that you can allot adequate time daily
for language learning to balance against your analysis. See 42.2a for specific suggestions.

42.5a **Checking Analyses**

As you investigate and come to understand new grammatical constructions, make up sentences (1) which
utilize these vernacular constructions and (2) which
contain vocabulary items discovered during the past
week. Have your research assistants check and correct them for you.

42.5b **Developing Ability in Translation**

Also translate some sentences or short narrative passages that are appropriate to the level of your grammatical knowledge.

42.6 **Keep Practicing**

Use taped drills to revise structures learned
earlier.

Use texts elicited in 42.2b as a basis for new drills
for mastering new constructions and vocabulary items.

Each day set yourself one construction and three vocabulary items that you deliberately plan to practice
in your conversations with your research assistants
or any other vernacular speakers you have contact
with.

APPENDIX

On Learning Monolingually

Aretta Loving[1]

0. Introduction

We were once faced with an entirely monolingual language-learning situation among the Awas in the Eastern Highlands of the Territory of New Guinea. From that experience a few hints and helps have been drawn up which may give aid to someone facing a similar situation. We have therefore attempted to set forth in this report a few points that we found helpful in language learning. A time schedule of our method of attack concludes the paper.

1. The importance of repetition

We began, of course, the only place anyone could begin — by learning the names of concrete objects. Our method was to point. We were relieved to find pointing in the manner familiar to us was accepted. We did not have to learn to point with the elbow, the foot — or worse yet, the lower lip! We pointed, listened and repeated, and pointed some more, listened some more and repeated some more. We used what we knew even though it was just words like *poeraq* "pig" and *iya* "dog." By doing this we would hear the word repeated over and over again. We are convinced that this repetition from the native speaker of a language is necessary; for it was only after many weeks of hearing the word "pig" that we actually heard and were able to repeat it correctly.

A person learning a foreign language is always advised to "use what you know even though it may be only a few words." On the other side of the fence of the "use what you know" admonition, a word of caution could be added. It is possible to consistently use what is known incorrectly so many times that although it is incorrect usage, the people understand and therefore cease to give corrections. The continual incorrect usage of this word or phrase becomes set in the mind so firmly that the hearing of the correct phrase is dulled. This does not grow less a problem as progress is made in the language, but rather becomes more and more a snare.

---

[1] Summer Institute of Linguistics, New Guinea.

Reprinted from Philippine Journal for Language Teaching, 1 (3-4)(1962): 11-15, with the permission of the author and editor.

2. The importance of listening

Our method of obtaining some of the key phrases was simply listening. This is not always as easy to do as might be imagined. So much unintelligible talk is going on that difficulty may be experienced in picking up an important phrase. So although key phrases are repeated many times within hearing, they are not easily discerned.

We were especially on the lookout to learn to say "What is this?" After two weeks we were tired of pointing and we wondered if the Awas were not equally tired of seeing us point. Evidently they were not, for they continued to be gracious enough to give us new words as we continued to point. One day we were cooking some greens around an open fire. I pointed to the food directing my "question" to an elderly man standing, looking into the pot. He turned to the man next to him and said *anepomo*. I repeated this thinking this was the name of the greens. He and several others smiled and then leaning toward me he said, *tura*. Several others chimed in, but I realized that if I allowed the name of the food to divert my attention I would forget the phrase which must mean "What is this?" I therefore called out, *anepomo, anepomo, anepomo*. This delighted the people, and I began to point to various objects using the new found phrase. But the question came to mind, "Were they so conditioned by our pointing that they would respond correctly if we said, "Abracadabra?" I actually tried this and received a blank look for my efforts. Switching back to *anepomo* I again received object words with pleased grins from those around the fire.

"What are you doing?" was discovered shortly thereafter. We were told by one liguistic team that they had labored to obtain this phrase by one of them making some strange noise in the house while the other listened to see if the people nearby would say, "What is he doing?" We would perhaps have tried this if the phrase had not been forthcoming at about the time it did. One day I was in the house making bread, and a little girl peeked in my door and said, *aneq marimirono*. I repeated the phrase silently to myself a couple of times to insure I did not forget it and then surprised the little girl by not answering but rather turning and going outside. Dick was sharpening some knives for a few of the village men. I looked at him and said, *aneq marimirono*. Several of the men said *sogi insanugeuno* to Dick. "Say, 'I am sharpening a knife.' " We were relieved to see that this was indeed the correct phrase, as several times previously, thinking we had obtained it, blank looks from the people had been our reward when we looked into their faces and repeated it. This was especially so when I tried to use *aboya,* thinking I had discovered the phrase. *Aboya* was later found to be the name of a food made from grated taro. The young men in particular gave me amazed looks since this is a taboo food for them.

We later learned to say, "What is your name?" and "Who is that?" after a few weeks of just pointing to people. (We now wonder why we did not point to people and say, "What is that?" depending on someone to give us the correct phrase.) Sometimes our pointing was not understood and to make them understand that we wished to know their names, we would first give our own names and then the names we remembered of those around us. This gave them the idea we wished to know the name of the one at whom we were pointing. We heard the phrases one night when we were sitting around the fire playing the "What is your name?" game. The people were delighted to see how many names we knew and entered into the game with real enthusiasm asking us "Who is *that?*" and "What is *his* name?" Perhaps these phrases had been asked us before, but we understood them for the first time after about seven weeks after our arrival in the village.

We found it helpful to not answer questions too quickly. To delay in answering gives opportunity to hear the question repeated again, again, and perhaps again. We heard the question "Where are you going?" a number of times before learning it ourselves, simply because we answered too quickly. We knew the query was about where we were going, because this was the logical thing to ask in the given situation. Sometimes when we were just going over the hill to visit another home we would answer, "To America," or "To Kainantu," in order to hear them again say, "No. Where are you going?"

Sometimes the question being asked may be known but what to answer is not. The answer might be conveyed by some non-verbal means, but it could prove best to just look and listen depending on someone to supply the corrcet phrase.

3. The importance of using what is known

There are times when "using what is known" even with the awareness that this is incorrect, is justified. One day I was showing some photographs to a man. *Teawo,* he said pointing to another man nearby. I realized this must mean, "Show him." I took the photographs and showing them to the man I repeated, *teawo, teawo.* The man who had originally told me, "Show him," realized I wished to communicate to the man, "Look!" He corrected me and said, "*Tagano.*" This was an encouragement to use this trick more often. We knew how to say "soon" and "now." We had tried to obtain the word or phrase for "a while ago." We had been unsuccessful and had even been told, "Our language doesn't have that." We were sure there was a way to say it. One evening I was sitting around the fire and observed the oft repeated drama of a pig grabbing a piece of pork and absconding with it. What excitement! The screams brought my husband running out to our group. I attempted to tell him in the language, "*Soon* a pig ate some pork." After I had repeated this at least three times, I was corrected and given the phrase, "*A while ago* a pig ate some pork." Although this may often seem to be displaying ignorance, it will yield important phrases, if the fear of appearing ignorant is overcome. There is no limit to the ways this can be useful. Knowing how to say "He is going," and "yesterday," an attempt could be made to obtain a past tense form by saying, "Yesterday he is going." We successfully learned to say "When?" by saying, "*What* will they go? Tomorrow?" More recently we desired to be able to relate the more difficult phrase, "If we had not been here, he would have died." Our informant was confused when we told him, "When we were not here, he died," (since the one we were discussing was alive). He soon realized what we wished to say and corrected us.

4. The importance of taking advantage of anything that will help obtain language

We found we had many things in our possession which were foreign to the culture into which we entered. Hairpins, buttons, magnets—any objects unknown to the people—became tools to obtain new words and phrases. When we first pointed to the buttons some wore in their noses, and heard, *iregarioq*, we thought this could be their own word for button. But once we heard this repeated about other objects strange to them, we knew we had the phrase for "I don't know." Likewise the phrase, "...doesn't have" was obtained. The answer often came, "Our village doesn't have that."

To some foreign objects the people gave names. Our pencils became *saira seikara*, literally "a pricking or writing stick." My kitchen grater became a *kontigara* since they use a thorny stick by this name for grating taro. They readily accepted the name "tree tomato" from us as being grammatically correct usage since they have a "tree sweetpotato."

Books are an invaluable source of language as well as being excellent reading - readiness materials. We watched the Awas progress in their ability to "read" as we first gave them scrap books with large pictures in them and then gradually introduced them to magazines and catalogues. At first we had to tell them what the pictures represented, but in a short time they were explaining even complicated pictures to us in the language. I observed one woman explaining two pictures to a friend. One was an advertisement of a man taking a photograph and the other was an African woman carrying a load of bananas on her head. These were on opposite pages and one was in color, the other in black and white, but nevertheless her explanation was, "He is taking a picture of the woman carrying the bananas."

5. The importance of spending time with the people

The first five months in the village we found it advantageous to spend our time mainly in conversational environments. Therefore, we spent hours watching every phase of native life we could: the mundane activities of life-like cooking and gardening; the festive activities like feasts and dances; the religious, like puberty initiation ceremonies and garden sprinkling ceremonies; the more unusual, like family or village feud. Those first months we wrote very little — only an occasional card-full to jog our memories and to insure we did not lose any important phrase which could not be so easily obtained again. Circumstances forced us to spend the next seven months away from our village home. However two teen-age Awas served as informants for us during this period. We spent approximately four months of this time in concentrated language work analyzing text material and eliciting paradigms. We still felt it advantageous to spend time in conversational environments and therefore spent as much time as possible with our informants, hiking, working, eating, or merely sitting on the back porch talking about village life.

Our return to the village was a year to the month after our initial entrance. The next four and a half months our time was equally divided between the informal language learning situation of talking with the people and the formal study situation of sitting at a desk with pencil and paper analyzing data with an informant.

Almost a year and a half after we first began studying Awa, we made our first attempt at analyzing some of the grammar of the language and completing the phonemic analysis. This analysis has served to help in increasing conversational fluency as we have continued to study the Awa language.

The Monolingual Approach
to Studying Amuzgo

George Cowan

Introduction

During the first month that my companion and I were living in the Amuzgo town of Xochistlahuaca, a colleague helped
us to settle in. He used bilingual speakers to obtain a vocabulary of Amuzgo words and phrases, and at least one form
of certain abstract verbs, so that I could carry on monolingually. After that, Spanish was never used in actual linguistic work, and was only resorted to when it was imperative
that there be no misunderstanding, and in such cases always
by my companion who spoke Spanish. This enabled me to adhere
strictly to the monolingual approach. As it was impossible
much of the time to obtain a language helper, I was forced
to mingle with the people themselves, and since there was a
high percentage of monolingualism, this made it impossible
to use any other approach.

I am deeply indebted to my companion, Mr. Cloyd Stewart,
for his willingness to be the scapegoat whenever Spanish had
to be used, for instance in dealing with sickness, town and
government officials, and in postal matters. This definitely
increased his difficulty in learning the language. Mr. Stewart realized this but, since he was expecting to go on to
South America soon afterwards, he was willing to be the loser
by this arrangement in order that I might be left free to
pursue the monolingual approach at all times. It goes without saying that if Mr. Stewart had not been there, many difficult situations would have been perpetuated through my
inability to make myself understood in Amuzgo. In this respect the monolingual approach is a serious barrier to maintaining the good-will of the people, until such time as the
language is mastered sufficiently to enable the investigator
to make himself adequately understood on questions of morals,
principle, and the like.

Procedure Followed With Monolingual Amuzgo Speakers

When I had a language helper the morning hours were
spent in going over material already recorded, checking for
tone, getting plurals, and possessives of nouns, conjugations
of verbs, and, when possible, checking for minimal pairs.
This was slow, difficult work, and not too productive considering the time involved, but invaluable in simply drilling

oneself in Amuzgo, for all was carried on in the native language, the language helper being totally monolingual.

The afternoon hours were usually spent tramping the
trails in every direction out from the town, seeking mainly
to develop conversational ability in the language, getting
vocabulary of things seen and done, noting as far as possible standard forms of greeting and other expressions used
by the people among themselves on the trails as they met and
conversed with my language helper. A cheap, bound copybook
was carried in the pocket for recording such data; three-by-
five slips proving quite impractical. On such trips to
places such as ranches, mountains, and rivers, little attempt was made to work over the data obtained, this being
reserved for the morning hours. Thus the time was spent in
a more natural conversational way with few interruptions for
checking tone, plurals, and other grammatical features.

When no language helper was available, which was a
large proportion of the time, I just drifted around town, or
on the trails, seeking to enter into conversation with everyone encountered, whether plowing, butchering, weaving, or
simply travelling. I USED WHAT I KNEW, HOWEVER IMPERFECT,
drilling on it even to the point of monotony to myself. In
this way I gradually acquired more Amuzgo, as oft-repeated
answers began to sound familiar and were adopted for use in
replying to the inquiry of the local people. When possible,
data obtained in this way was written down. But frequently
this was too annoying to the Amuzgos, or held up operations
too much, so the copybook was put away and only what could
be recalled later was written. Much valuable material was
undoubtedly lost but the welcome and interest of the Amuzgos
was not worn thin and I was free to try again on other occasions. I found it was better to pitch in and help the
Amuzgo in his work than to stand aloof with pencil and book
in hand, interrupting his work to get words from him. Conversational ability was forced upon me, for the Amuzgo himself was talkative and seemed to get real enjoyment out of
telling me all about things, even though much, if not most
of it, was not understood.

Contact With Spanish Speakers

I refused to converse in Spanish at all, and in most
cases refused to let on that I even understood it. This
principle was adhered to, not only with the Amuzgos but
also with Spanish-born speakers, for two reasons. First,
Amuzgos were always around when Spanish-born speakers were

present. Second, almost all Spanish-born speakers also
spoke the vernacular, for monolingualism was so high in the
town that business could not be transacted without it. In
fact, even the school teacher who was there to teach the
children in Spanish, on both playground and in the class-
room, had to resort to speaking Amuzgo to make himself
understood.

The wisdom of this strict adherence to the monolingual
principle was demonstrated in later weeks, for whenever a
Spanish-born speaker, or an Amuzgo who spoke Spanish, talked
to my companion, whom they knew understood it, they did so
in Spanish in spite of every attempt of his to carry on the
conversation in Amuzgo. But, at the same time, they would
often turn to me and give the Amuzgo translation of what they
had just said in Spanish. Even Spanish-born speakers soon
came to the place where they themselves would open the conversation with me in Amuzgo. At first I had to play a part,
so to speak, letting on I understood nothing when I actually
did. Later, however, my vocabulary and speaking ability in
Amuzgo so far outdistanced my Spanish that it was no longer
a part to be played but was actually the easier method of
understanding and being understood.

Linguistic Results

The vocabulary was more limited, but was obtained in
the actual situations where I and the Amuzgos were at the
time. Such situations were of course limited. At first
the vocabulary gained was to a large degree, of course,
only concrete words. The actual significance of words often
remained uncertain for a period of time, until enough occurrences were heard to more or less accurately define its
use and meaning. The temptation was strong at times to re-
sort to Spanish to discover meanings of new words. Only
where imperative (see Introduction) was this done. Often
meanings, so obtained, were found to be inaccurate and unreliable due to the bilingual's inability to properly define
words in his own speech.

Conversational ability went ahead faster, for although
the vocabulary was limited, it was a known and used vocabulary, in service constantly, not just fading away on a three-
by-five slip. Much information and data had been in use
for some time before I ever got around to filing it away or
recording it on paper for analysis.

Linguistic analysis was frequently aided by the fact

that it was in actual conversation and use of material in conversation that correlations were discovered. The clerical task of filing material was in the long run, however, most fruitful and accurate, for only then was it possible to isolate and check the significant features one against the other.

Analytical conclusions (for example, proof of phonemes) were delayed by strict adherence to the monolingual approach because meanings all too often could not be established. Also, minimal differences were hard to manipulate because I had to use the very words involved to get the idea across to the language helper, and all too often I failed to do this, or put the language helper on the wrong track by faulty pronunciations. However a little was accomplished in this direction, though at a very slow pace and with many reservations as to its ultimate accuracy.

Social Results

The Amuzgos liked it. At times they took delight in explaining to strangers that I did not understand Spanish but only their language.

The Spanish-born speaker did not like it, in some cases definitely resenting it, for it meant that he had to descend to using Amuzgo in speaking with me. He could not understand in the first place why anyone would WANT to learn Amuzgo, and in the second place, it galled him somewhat that I should insist on learning it before I learned Spanish. And in the third place, it seemed that I was putting the Amuzgo in the preferred place, which was almost an affront to the Spanish-born person.

I found that, once the first surprise and bewilderment had worn off, and my blundering attempts to use the language were taken seriously, not just as something to be laughed at, the people accepted the fact. Often they went out of their way to be helpful in giving words and phrases, and I was more and more accepted as one of them. The monolingual homes were open to me, and the Spanish homes where ONLY Spanish was spoken, were only visited for necessary purposes. Bilingual homes were also open, but I used Amuzgo when I visited.

Basic Recommendations

(1) Train yourself to listen critically and with an eye to the cultural situation in which things are said, whether you are a party to the conversation or not.

(2) Use what is known, no matter how imperfect the pronunciation or arrangement. Test what you are uncertain about by
controlling the situation to isolate essential meanings.

(3) If possible, USE THE VERNACULAR EXCLUSIVELY FROM THE
VERY BEGINNING! Never give the bilingual speaker a loophole
for trying to foist the lingua franca upon you. He will do
it enough without any help from you.

(4) Be willing to be laughed at or to be called a fool for
adhering to these principles. You will have plenty of
opportunity to prove such willingness.

Learning Candoshi Monolingually

Lorrie Anderson and Doris Cox

The notorious Shapras, a subgroup of the Candoshi
tribe, lived in a remote corner of Peru, and here we were
in a small float plane landing on one of their jungle-clad
rivers to settle among them and learn their language. But
how could we communicate with them? All we had was a list
of about 20 Shapra words that the survey team had obtained
when they contacted the tribe and got permission for us to
come.

From the first moment our bags and boxes touched the
shore, our ears were bombarded with different forms of the
expression "What is it?" We couldn't miss it. So we used
it to elicit names for body parts, baskets, fires, or anything in sight. We tried using it on action words. We
would run, walk, or jump and say "What is it?", knowing that
this phrase was probably very inadequate and that we should
be saying, "What am I doing?" But we merely said, *"Maya?"*,
"Mashta?", or *"May ini?"*, all of which we picked up from
them, not knowing whether or not these forms contained tense,
person or aspect. (We would caution new women workers to
note first the behavior of the women of the tribe before
they do any lively demonstrating that might be considered
unladylike. We might have been accepted by the women sooner
had we been a bit more sedate and proper.)

But the Shapras are always responsive in one way or
another. In this case they were delighted at our desire to
learn their language, and whatever our way of expressing
ourselves lacked, they made up for in imagination and gave
us a good many action words.

However, as the days went by we found that there was a
limit to the amount of demonstrating we could do and we began to listen.

We listened to greetings and farewells, wrote them
down and tried to use them. Our use of any of the language
usually brought correction of some kind from them, or else
they would give us alternate forms.

We listened to conversations and wrote down what we
could. If they were merely talking among themselves, we

wrote as much of the conversation as we could with an attempted translation or a description of the context in which
the speech occurred; that is, the activity at the moment of
comment.

Women often came to our house and sat on the floor,
and looked at books or magazines. We joined them with notebook and pencil and wrote down everything we could with a
tentative translation, if we could figure it out at the moment. If not, we noted a reference to the picture at which
the speaker was looking when she commented.

We filed the material, and sometimes we would have
several 3 x 5 slips for a word, containing brief descriptions of each context in which we had found it. When we became quite sure of the meaning of a word we made just one
slip for it, taking the old slips out and putting them into
a separate file.

Securing the meaning of affixes was even harder. We
filed many examples of each one, with different stems, again
with an attempted translation or description of the context
in which the form occurred. We would concentrate on two or
three affixes at a time and find ourselves being acutely
conscious of them when we heard them in a word. Out of
hundreds of instances of an affix that came to our ears, we
selected examples in which it occurred in minimal contrast
or in which the context was especially clear. Or, if we
could get no clue to the meaning, we filed and filed indiscriminately. Then sometimes, with a big backlog of filing
on an affix, the meaning would suddenly become clear to us,
as we heard it in a conversation.

When we were together we always found it helpful to compare notes and discuss what we thought was the meaning of a
word. It usually gave us more clues. We always regretted
that sometimes we both got so busy that we did not take time
to compare our materials.

The first five-month period that we spent among the
Shapras was extremely discouraging as far as the language
went. We felt we had gotten nowhere--the language was one
big crossword puzzle with almost none of the blanks filled
in.

In particular we were confused over seemingly homophonous morpheme alternates for first and third person.

maar-i	'I sleep'
maar-o	'he sleeps'
maar-i-ya	'he is sleeping'

The final *a* of *maariya*, 'he is sleeping,' was often dropped
in fast speech and so at first we confused it with *maari*.

The Chief of the Shapras, Tariri saw our difficulty and
exclaimed one day, "Don't say *maariya* when you're talking
about yourself. My ears don't happily listen to it. If
you're talking about someone else, you say *maariya*. Or you
say *maaro*. Don't say 'I *maariya*' again. I don't want to
listen to it." He went on with different stems to give us
full examples of the person endings, till we understood it
clearly. Though we were still just barely into the language, his monolingual explanations were so good we were
able to understand. He began to explain other things to us
too. We had long prayed for an opening into the maze, and
the understanding of the person endings was just that, because most verbs had person endings, and the same endings
occurred on nouns also.

As we continued to hear new affixes we decided to try
to ask Tariri what they meant. We could explain fairly
well in the language what we were looking for. We would
cite different forms with and without the affix, and ask
him what difference the use of the affix on a form made to
its meaning. He was always helpful, and usually gave examples of contexts in which the various forms could be used.

To determine meaning, we filed like forms together,
whether complete words or recurring partials. At the time
of taking down the form--a word or a phrase--we usually
put what we thought the meaning was and when we got these
filed together it helped a lot. We concentrated on one or
two at a time, listening and listening for them in conversations, trying to get a clue to their meaning. As soon as
we could we compared minimal differences. We did this by
comparing the way they were used in context, since we could
not get a translation of the form in either Spanish or English. More than anything, we looked for many examples of
occurrences of an affix, not only in relation to other
affixes, but the same sequences of affixes with other stems.
The more blanks we were able to fill in, the more obvious
the rest became.

Text, except for conversation, was very hard to get
because no one would repeat enough, or talk slowly enough,
for us to get a story down. We had lots of conversation

text, but only a few short stories, about fifty words a-
piece, up to the time we got the use of a tape recorder,
the third time we stayed with the Shapras. After that,
text was much easier to get. A tape recorder is a must.

Later on there was the problem of finding the words
and phrases that we needed for translating the Scriptures.
We got our best material not by eliciting, but by listening
to the Indians' prayers and witness. We learned a lot also
when they repeated things we had told them about God. They
used more idiomatic expressions when THEY explained it to
someone else. We always noted these down as soon as we
heard them. When Tariri told the story we had been translating to others, we could tell from the questions and remarks of the others what was lacking, or if we were giving
some wrong impressions.

After about sixteen months, there was no doubt we were
communicating with them, but we still had a long ways to go
before we spoke idiomatic Candoshi. There was still so
much of the language for us to learn.

Learning Xavante Monolingually

Ruth A. McLeod

The following notes deal with the way in which we handled the monolingual language-learning situation on the Indian Protection Service (S.P.I.) Post of Simoes Lopes in Mato Grosso, Brazil, the pitfalls we found, and what we would do differently should we be starting afresh. The Xavante on this Post number two hundred, or less, and all are almost completely monolingual. Although we have had the occasional informal help of a man, our assistants have been almost exclusively women.

When we first arrived at the Post (December 1958) we asked for a Xavante woman to help us with the housework as well as doing language work with us. The Post official sent us a different woman each week, some of whom were quite unsuitable as language helpers, and so after a few weeks of frustration we asked if we could have the first girl to help us indefinitely, as she had been quite helpful (when we could persuade her to sit still). We learned later that this was a bad policy, for two reasons. First, the other Xavante women became jealous of her weekly earnings of cloth and thread. Second, by keeping to the first reasonably helpful person, and neglecting to try out other women, for many months we failed to discover those women who were really capable of being good teachers. The fact that we have monthly linguistic goals made us feel rather desperate at our lack of progress. It would have been better if we had been prepared for a slow start, prepared to try out lots of people, prepared to spend only a little time per day at the desk with a paid helper, and prepared to spend much more time at the village with the people there, trying to learn names of things, simple action words, and the like, in a natural context, instead of trying to create situations within the four walls of our house.

We made the mistake of expecting the helper to adhere to our timetable, instead of finding out at what times the Xavante worked and when they rested. As soon as the dishes were washed after the noon meal we would seize our helper and try to extract more information from her, but she was disinclined to work. It was only much later that we discovered that the reason was that the Xavante customarily

work from dawn until about 10 a.m. and do not resume work
until mid-afternoon.

After the experiment of one woman for both housework
and language work we asked for two women, one for each job.
Although we had some trouble when each woman brought along
a squalling baby, we benefitted by being able to listen to
Xavante dialogue.

We found that it was not good to maintain too rigid a
dichotomy between language work and housework. We learned
from the Post official that those who did only language
work were becoming reluctant to do manual work for the
Post! So now we send both women to the river for water,
and sometimes give the language helper other odd jobs to do.

During our first six months out here we made two trips
with our assistant to the fields where the Xavante were
working. The trips would have been more valuable if we'd
taken two women with us, as we'd have had good opportunities for listening to the language.

Although there are usually one or two people in the
village at all times, yet we've found the best time for
visiting to be round about 4 p.m. when the women have
finished work and the afternoon meal is over, and everyone
is relaxing. It is important to sit down when visiting,
whether invited to do so or not. To stand implies that we
are simply onlookers, critical perhaps, without much real
interest; to sit down implies interest, friendliness and
a desire to get to know the people. I've found that the
Xavante accept us much more as one of themselves when we
sit with them and spend time asking questions and giving
them little pieces of information.

It is important to listen to people talking in order to
learn question words and phrases and to notice what people
say when one is going anywhere--most likely a question is
being asked.

It is good to write down everything possible even
though the meaning is not fully understood. It is most
important to make a note of the context, as this often
throws light on the meaning of a morpheme or morphemes in
the clause or phrase. It is good to keep a morpheme file
of phrases containing unknown morphemes, on 3 x 5 cards.
This collection should be maintained, even after the
meaning of a morpheme is learned, since the morpheme may

have a much wider area of meaning than is apparent at the
moment.

Some very useful pieces of information have been
acquired in the course of trying to explain something to
someone. For example, my companion found a mirror of hers
broken and she tried to find out who was the culprit. I
tried to explain to our assistant that my companion was not
angry, she just wanted to know who had broken the mirror.
Our assistant gave me in reply an expression meaning, 'If I
had broken it, I would have told about myself (= confessed)',
containing new usages of known morphemes for 'if' and 'would'.
It is helpful to listen to comments of one person to another
on one's explanation of something, if you are able to make
a note of the comment.

Pictures are useful. I learned how to say 'become'
when showing someone a picture of the Royal Family. I
tried to explain to her that our "chief" was a woman, and
when she died her son, Charles, would be the new "chief".
She responded with the expression, 'When his mother dies,
he will become chief.' A well-known reflexive morpheme had
here appeared with a new area of meaning.

Sketches are useful, when the people get used to the
idea of meaning conveyed by a drawing on paper. For
example, the contrast between a big mouth and a small
mouth (nose, ears, eyes) can be shown by a sketch, and an
intelligent person will soon realize what is wanted.

The use of objects such as stones, sticks, etc., can
be useful in eliciting modifying words. It is dangerous to
create artificial situations and objects, however. I was
trying to find the words for 'thick' and 'thin' (liquid and
solid), and I concocted a flour and water paste to find the
word for 'thick' (liquid). I later discovered that the
word given was *waio ti* 'like phlegm'!

It is good to make sure that the other person knows
what you are indicating, when trying to elicit names of
objects. For example, I pointed to a white cloud and asked
its name. The word given later proved to be the name of a
bird which was sitting on the roof in the direction of my
pointing!

We have found it dangerous to rely heavily upon elicited
material. Verb paradigms and possessive constructions should
be checked thoroughly before being accepted as correct. We

have had helpers who have readily agreed to certain forms
suggested, which have later proved to be incorrect or incomplete.

Those of us working in tribes in Brazil are required
to fill in a vocabulary list for the National Museum. I
have found the list very useful as a guide to the kind of
vocabulary I should know. I have come across some interesting constructions through working on the verb section. I
found that certain words in the list were not easily elicited
(such as blood, seed, tail) although these words are freely
used within a natural context. It seems better to either
omit the word altogether, or learn it in its context, if
its eliciting seems likely to cause offence.

Our battery-operated tape recorder has been an invaluable asset in this monolingual set-up. Even when we were
having difficulty getting suitable helpers, we did manage to
get some text on tape, and we were able to spend time trying
to ascertain meanings. We had some difficulty in getting
people to record at times. The situation was helped by suggesting topics of everyday things such as the snake in the
wood-box or the coming of the plane. Later on, the helper
recorded something that had already been told her, which
gave us some idea of the subject-matter!

Language Learning

Alan Healey

Learning a language involves learning a large integrated
set of speech habits that enable one to communicate with
other speakers of the language.

Practice Makes Habits

A habit is something we do automatically in the appropriate circumstance, often without thinking. For an action
to become automatic it must be practiced until it is over-
learnt. Notice how often and eagerly a small child practices
new sounds and words. But for an adult such constant practice is much harder because he has a previous set of language
habits firmly entrenched within him. While he is learning
the new set he has the two problems of overcoming his natural
preference for his old set of habits and of trying to keep
them from interfering with his use of the new set. In such
circumstances a mere intellectual understanding of the new
language is hopelessly inadequate; automatic speech habits
can only be achieved by relentless practice.

It is a common misconception to think that memorizing
vocabulary and the rules of grammar, and some ability in
the phonetics involved, are all that a person needs to learn
a language. We tend to despise mechanical repetition as dull
drudgery which makes no demand on our intellect. We consider
that we have the intelligence to think out the mechanical
features of phonology and grammar as we talk. But this is
trying to do what the native speaker does not have time to
do when he speaks. If the native speaker has to focus all
of his conscious attention on getting the meaning of his
message across, how much more the non-native speaker.

Language learning involves acquiring a set of automatic
habits that will enable us to communicate successfully. In
programmed language learning, the drills are the scales and
arpeggios, the gear-changing exercises. Each feature must
be mastered thoroughly before any real victory is possible.
Effort is involved, but it need not be drudgery. If drills
are sensibly planned they can be made both interesting and
good fun. Tackle them enthusiastically.

Listening

A field worker's primary need is to learn to hear and
speak the new language. The success of his field project
depends on his being able to talk with the people among
whom he is working. Only if the language has a traditional
non-phonemic writing system will he need to give much effort
to reading and writing, and these should be tackled only
after his listening and speaking skills are well developed.

It is vital that he spend almost all of his waking
hours in situations where he can hear people talking constantly. One cannot learn to understand what one hears in
a new language without actually listening to it being spoken
for thousands of hours. Listening to tape recordings or
the radio is not enough; he needs to spend most of his listening time in face-to-face situations where he can see what is
going on and much more effectively guess the meaning of
what he hears.

Mimicking and Tracking

At every opportunity he should mimic short utterances
to try and improve his intonation, rhythm, and pronunciation of words. Where mimicking aloud might offend, he should
mimic silently with inner speech. One particularly rewarding
form of this is the instantaneous inner mimicking known as
'tracking'. Mimicking whole short sentences at normal
speech speed is better than mimicking isolated words, or than
mimicking sentences over-slowly to try and pronounce each
syllable meticulously. Natural fluent speaking should be
the aim right from the beginning.

Speaking

From the very beginning the learner should convert as
many social situations as possible into conversations. He
should talk, talk, talk, using what he knows and eagerly
receiving corrections. Shy people should go out of their
way to make several friends with whom they chat frequently.
One should become sensitive to what topics of conversation
are of interest to other people--genealogies and local customs often are. All but the born chatterbox will need to
discipline themselves to spend time talking with several
different people every day, searching for or creating
situations that demand communication. This will take quite
an effort at first, but once the conversation gets on to a
topic of mutual interest the strain will lessen and the
learner will find himself thinking more about the messages

being exchanged than about words or grammar. In such a relaxed atmosphere he can learn quite a lot without even being
aware of it. He may also practice inner speech, to prepare
something suitable to say in specific anticipated or imagined
circumstances. This may eventually finish up as thinking in
the vernacular.

Understanding Customs and Attitudes

The learner should make vigorous and sincere efforts to
become a functioning part of the community where he lives.
He should make a considerable number of friendships, taking
care that the relationships are reciprocal and enjoyable to
both parties. And he should learn all he can about the community's customs and attitudes, and then respect them. As
a result he will be a more sensitive member of the community
and a more sympathetic friend. In addition, his understanding of the meaning of words and sentences will be enlarged;
and he will have added freedom in talking, with the assurance
that what he says is socially and culturally appropriate.

No Lesson Books or Teachers

The learner will have to analyze the language a little
so that he can design his own language learning lessons and
record them on tape; in the process he will learn a lot about
the language. Then, when he works through these lessons for
practice he can absorb their patterns and vocabulary and
develop appropriate speech habits fairly quickly. Where no
trained language teachers are available it is good for a person to get his language experience and practice in informal
ways with as many different people as possible. He should
completely avoid the method of employing a single regular
helper (formerly called an "informant"). There are far too
many problems. When the time eventually comes that an employed helper is needed, it is best to employ several (on
different days of the week, for instance) and the period of
employment should be limited to a few months by prior
arrangement.

The Learner's Prior Orientation

A Westerner comes to the learning of a second language
with several handicaps. One is that, if he had studied a
language at school or university, it was probably studied
bilingually and with the main emphasis on reading. Often,
such a person feels helpless when he starts to learn another
language in the field by a basically oral-aural method.
It is essential that he be given a little bilingual help

at the very beginning, and that his living quarters be
located where he can get maximum exposure to monolingual
speakers.

Another handicap is that Westerners are thoroughly
oriented to learning through reading, or through lectures-
plus-notetaking-plus-reading. Take away his pencil during a
lecture and he feels very insecure. He has not been trained
to remember all that he hears. However, he can develop his
memory somewhat by practice, by constant review of what has
been learnt previously, and by the consistent association of
a cultural item or situation with the new utterance to make
its meaning more real to the learner. Constant mimicry,
repeated listening to taped utterances or longer discourses,
and inner speech can all aid the memory.

But perhaps the worst side of this handicap is that a
considerable number of field workers are predisposed to enjoy paper work at a desk. This keeps them away from people,
from forming friendships, from learning about the culture,
and from hearing and using the language intensively.

For most people, the total avoidance of writing down
language materials for the first few months is probably
too drastic an approach to this problem. However, writing
should certainly be limited in the early months and much
attention should be given to mimicry, oral practice, and oral
production from memory.

Conditions for Successful Learning

To learn a language successfully in the field a person
must be strongly motivated. He must really WANT to learn
it. And his determination to learn it must be strong enough
to keep him going when he is battling on alone with no
friend or consultant around to encourage him.

He must also be self-disciplined, able to shut out most
of the things that sidetrack him from his learning. He must
set his goals and priorities at the start and then stick to
them. It is very easy for the ultimate goal or project in
the field work to suddenly assume greater importance than
the language learning that is necessary as a tool for carrying out that project.

On the other hand he must learn to take advantage
of many kinds of learning situations. If he sees a chance
to observe or participate in some new cultural activity,

he should do so enthusiastically for it will provide many opportunities to learn. If a good opportunity arises to converse with someone, it should be given priority over the mere following of daily routines. Or if he hears some new word or expression, he should pause in what he is doing long enough to follow it up to try and discover how it is used and what it means. He must be adaptable in his attitude towards local customs, daily routine, and learning methods. And if any of his methods of learning seem to be ineffective he should brainstorm for new methods and try them out.

He must have an outgoing friendly approach to people, and be willing to spend much of his time with them. No matter how much he uses tape recorders or books, his most important avenue of learning is through his daily face-to-face contact with people. Only people can explain his mistakes to him, give him the right words to say in the particular circumstance, and encourage him to keep trying. But the learner must be careful that the friendships he forms are genuine, that he treats each individual with real love and thoughtfulness. Otherwise people could easily think that he makes friends merely to use them as tools in his language learning program.

He must have heavy exposure to the spoken language, constantly hearing people talk, and talking with them himself. Without these he cannot become fluent. He should choose living quarters which have many vernacular speakers living in the immediate vicinity. He could buy his food supplies from them and spend some of his recreation with them. He should arrange his place of work during the day so that there are always two or three people within speaking distance. He should become involved in as many mini-conversations as possible each day. He should spend his time with a variety of people, not just with one or two individuals.

Furthermore, he should seek out situations for living, working, and visiting where as many of the people as possible are monolingual speakers of the language, rather than bilingual speakers. Admittedly, these situations provide the learner with more strain than bilingual situations where both the people and the learner know the same lingua franca; but monolingual situations let the learner hear more of the language and force him to try speaking it more often.

He should have a reasonable ability in pronunciation

and in other language skills. However, more important is a
sensitivity to his own mistakes and a willingness to laugh
at them and correct them. That is, he should be teachable.

Methods and Techniques

Many different methods may be used in language learning. Each has its particular advantages and degree of effectiveness for people in general, but its appeal and value
varies considerably from one individual to another. For this
reason it is good for the learner to become familiar with a
wide variety of methods and techniques and to use as many of
them as he finds effective for him personally at his stage
of learning. Below is a list of many of the techniques
that have been used and an evaluation of their general effectiveness as learning devices. All of these techniques are
worth using from time to time, even those classed as generally "low".

Source of language information for the learner	Technique that contributes to learning to hear and speak the language	Value of its contribution
1. Previously written materials alone	1a. deliberate memoriza- of words, paradigms, and sentences	low
	1b. filing, alphabetiz- ing, copying, typing	low
	1c. analyzing, describ- ing, translating	low
2. Previously tape-recorded materials	2a. passive listening to drills and text	low
	2b. silent continuous mimicking (tracking)	low
	2c. active mimicking of drills and text	medium
	2d. responding to drills and model conversa- tion	medium
3. A speaker of the language alone	3a. passive listening to people talking	low
	3b. silent continuous mim- icking (tracking) of people talking	low
	3c. mimicking a language helper sometimes	low

Source of language information for the learner	Technique that contributes to learning to hear and speak the language	Value of its contribution
	3d. eliciting, writing, and checking the meaning of words and sentences bilingually	low
	3e. eliciting, writing, and checking the meanings of words and sentences monolingually	medium
	3f. using parts of model conversation that have been learnt	medium
	3g. casual conversation	medium
	3h. purposeful conversation	high
	3i. conversing during and about some cooperative activity	high
4. Written materials plus a speaker	4a. translating in either direction and checking the meaning or accuracy of the translation bilingually	low
	4b. translating in either direction and checking the meaning or accuracy of the translation monolingually	medium
	4c. designing, checking, and tape-recording structural drills	medium
5. Tape-recorded materials plus a speaker	5a. transcribing recorded text and obtaining literal and free meanings	low
	5b. mimicking drills and text with speaker correcting until adequate	high
	5c. responding to drills and model conversation with speaker correcting until adequate	high

Progress in Language Learning

Intensive language teaching programs developed during

and since World War II usually involved the learner for six
to nine hours per day for a period of six to nine months. A
self-designed and self-administered learning program in the
field is rarely as intensive or as carefully designed as
these. Nevertheless, the learner should give all of his time
and energy to language learning for the first twelve months
of residence in the language area. Only then can he afford
to change over to activities related to the long-term goals
of his field work. At the same time he should maintain a
small-scale and relaxed program of continuing learning;
there is no end to what we can learn and to how it will
benefit our long-term goals.

During a language-learning program the learner may several
times be discouraged by an apparent lack of progress. Such
learning plateaus may result from several causes.

(a) Boredom. Try more variety and novelty in learning
     techniques and situations.

(b) Reduced exposure to the spoken language. Revise your
     schedule to spend more time with people and discipline
     yourself to converse with people more often.

(c) A mind overloaded with too much new language material
     each day. Revise your schedule to spend less time on
     the formal practicing of new material, a little more
     time on consolidating partly learnt materials, and a
     little more time on informal conversation-plus-activi-
     ties where new materials are learned with less psycho-
     logical strain.

(d) The supply of readily available new material to be
     learnt is nearly exhausted. This happens first with
     pronunciation, then with grammatical patterns, and
     very much later with vocabulary. In most instances
     the learner never reaches a plateau in his learning of
     idioms, the possible collocations of words, and the
     areas of meanings of words.

It is occasionally helpful to evaluate how far the learner
has progressed through the following successive stages of
proficiency in his second language. The achievements listed
in each stage are appropriate to a balanced program of language learning.

(1) He recognizes and attempts to use greetings, leave-
     takings, and courtesies.

(2) He recognizes a few words and phrases and can barely
     make known his very elemental needs. He usually

cannot express anything new that he really wants to say. As a consequence he feels very discouraged and helpless because he is unable to communicate.

(3) He can understand and use most of the basic expressions needed in his daily contacts with familiar people in the home, market, and place of work. Outside of these three environments he attempts simple conversations but usually he understands little of what the other person says unless it is a person who knows the learner's limitations and carefully controls what he says to him. Consequently he is alternately excited and discouraged in his attempts at conversation. He attempts to use the vernacular to elicit language information, but is often very frustrated with his minimal success.

(4) He feels comfortable and can communicate well in the home, at market, and at work. He attempts conversations in all other situations and has moderate success in conveying his messages, but still finds it difficult to understand much of what is said to him if the other person is a stranger. While he is talking he is constantly groping for words and grammatical constructions, and is mentally matching vernacular forms with their English (mother-tongue) equivalents as he consciously translates what he wants to say. He understands the gist of speeches or sermons on familiar topics.

(5) He is comfortable in conversations with strangers on familiar topics. When he hears a word or an idiom that he does not know, he freely elicits an explanation from the vernacular speaker. He still sometimes gropes for words or constructions, but his use of them is quite accurate. He is aware of the different modes of expression of the two languages and attempts to use the appropriate vernacular expressions and idioms in most situations rather than always laboriously translating from English. He uses the vernacular in almost all of his work and elicitation with language helpers.

(6) He can converse comfortably on any topic. He no longer gropes for words and constructions and for all practical purposes is fluent in the language, though not necessarily expert. He can understand reasonably well any speech or sermon.

(7) He can understand and participate in rapid conversation on any topic, and speaks without hesitation. He is aware of the meaning of what is said to him but not conscious of the language it is said in. He thinks and dreams in the second language quite often.

(8)   He has complete facility in the language including the
      ability to joke, pun, use double meanings, and use pro-
      verbs and rarer idioms in the proper contexts.

      The rate at which a learner progresses through these
stages depends on his degree of exposure to the language.
In a typical field situation where the learner has to design
and administer his own program, he might expect to see the
following rates of progress if he gives language learning
his full time and enthusiasm.

         stage 3   2 - 4 months in the language area
         stage 4   4 - 8 months in the language area
         stage 5   9 - 18 months in the language area
         stage 6   18 - 36 months in the language area

Assignments

      If you are preparing to learn a language as a part of
field work, you should do the following four assignments.

(a)   Visit a home of your own culture in which a small child
      12 to 24 months old lives. Observe how he goes about
      learning to speak--both the way he accepts and uses in-
      struction from his parents and especially the things he
      does at his own initiative to investigate and practice
      new expressions.

(b)   Try to find some adult who is in the process of learning
      a second language (preferably in circumstances similar
      to your future situation). Visit him and watch the
      various methods he uses. After each visit make notes of
      the methods used for language learning.

(c)   Interview three people who learned a second language
      as adults. Ask them to tell you how they went about
      it, which methods and circumstances they found especial-
      ly helpful and which ones they found to be a hindrance.
      If any of the basic goals and methods described above
      seem (in prospect) to be impossible to you, then ask
      these three people how they used this method or achieved
      this goal.

(d)   Read carefully through Unit 10 of this *Guide* and then
      make a list of all the ways it follows the methods
      described above. Also list the ways in which Unit 10
      departs from these methods, and suggest how the unit
      could be improved.

Bibliography on Language Learning

If you are teaching or studying a course on the theory
and practice of language learning, the following additional
reading is recommended.

Nelson Brooks, 1964. *Language and Language Learning.*
Second Edition. Harcourt, Brace and World: New York.
[This book describes the Audio-lingual Method. Pages 45-
59 discuss language learning.]

P. J. T. Glendening, 1965. *Teach Yourself to Learn a Language.* The English Universities Press: London. [Especial-
ly pages v-23; also pages 24-113, 243-280.]

Robert Lado, 1957. *Linguistics across Culture: Applied
Linguistics for Language Teachers.* The University of
Michigan Press: Ann Arbor. [This book shows how a contrastive study of two languages can predict the kinds of
difficulty a speaker of the one will have in learning
the other.]

Robert Lado, 1964. *Language Teaching: A Scientific Approach.* McGraw-Hill: New York. [Pages 32-45 present a
theory of second-language learning.]

Donald N. Larson and William A. Smalley, 1972. *Becoming
Bilingual: A Guide to Language Learning.* Pre-publication
Edition. Practical Anthropology: New Canaan, Conn.
[This book is excellent, and is worth reading right
through. It is by far the most comprehensive one on this
subject as it relates to learning in a field situation.
It has an excellent bibliography which includes older
books by Cummings, Sweet, Palmer, Bloomfield, etc.]

Edward W. Najam, editor, 1966. *Language Learning: The
Individual and the Process.* (= IJAL Publication 40).
Indiana University: Bloomington. [Especially
pages 15-23, 108-146.]

Eugene A. Nida, 1957. *Learning a Foreign Language.* Revised Edition. Friendship Press: Cincinnati, Ohio.
[Pages 1-85 give a lot of sound advice without jargon.]

Wilga M. Rivers, 1964. *The Psychologist and the Foreign-
Language Teacher.* University of Chicago Press: Chicago.
[This book presents the assumptions about learning that
are basic to the Audio-lingual Method of language teaching.]

Earl W. Stevick, 1971. *Adapting and Writing Language Lessons*. Foreign Service Institute: Washington, D. C. [Especially pages 1-65, 136-7.]

Thomas Rhys Williams, 1967. *Field Methods in the Study of Culture*. Holt, Rinehart and Winston: New York.

In addition, read the articles in the Appendix of this *Guide*.

Language Learning in Relation to Focus

Eunice V. Pike

1. Introduction. Part of learning to talk a second language is a sociological problem. In order to learn, you must be among those whom the people of that culture select for attention; that is, you have to be in focus. It has been observed that when for some reason someone (e.g. a Peace Corps volunteer, or a missionary) goes as a replacement worker to some exotic place, he frequently has trouble learning the language of the primitive community there. Focus is almost certainly involved in the problem.

Since people are apt to put outsiders in a senior versus junior category, the problem applies to others in addition to the one who most recently arrived in the new language area. Sometimes the dividing factor is age, sometimes experience; it might be husband versus wife, fast learner versus slow learner, one with outgoing personality versus one with a retiring personality. I will use the term "junior" worker and by it I mean anyone who has not been put in the role of seniority by the people of the region.

The advantage of being in the senior role is that people talk to you; the disadvantage of being in the junior role is that for cultural reasons people talk to your companion instead of to you.

The one in the senior role[1] may be aware of the problem but there are certain responsibilities involving talking

---

[1] For a theoretical discussion of focus, see Kenneth L. Pike, *Language in Relation to a Unified Theory of the Structure of Human Behavior*, (2nd ed.) The Hague: Mouton, 1967, (1st. ed. Vol. I, 1954; Vol. II, 1955; Vol. III, Santa Ana, Calif. 1960) pp. 98-110. For a discussion of role with bibliographical comments on other people's view of role, see pp. 670-74.

Reprinted from *Language Learning: A Journal of Applied Linguistics*, Volume 19, Numbers 1 and 2, pages 107-115 (June 1969) by permission of the publisher and author.

that cannot be put aside. Business matters must be carried on; information must be exchanged; social relationships must continue. The most troublesome bit is that in many cultures the senior must greet people, must chitchat, because a person who is able to talk but does not is considered to be impolite or angry. She cannot, therefore, remain silent, even though she would like to give her junior companion an opportunity to talk.

(Throughout the paper I speak of a worker as "she" because within my own experience most workers have been women, but men may also fill either role. The paper is colored by my experience which was in a community where we were translating the New Testament, preparing literature for the people, and helping them with minor medical needs and in other practical ways.)

Sometimes the cultural situation may require that the younger worker, or the wife, be kept out of focus. In the article "Mazatec Focus"[2] I mentioned that a teenage girl must be kept out of focus except under special circumstances. The result is that frequently the junior worker does not talk well because she has not found a way to be in focus. The solution to the problem, then, is to FIND A WAY TO PUT THE JUNIOR WORKER IN FOCUS IN A SOCIALLY ACCEPTABLE SITUATION, but at the same time in a situation in which she can handle the conversation.

The value of being in focus is more than that it provides practice in hearing and responding, however. Part of the value is that by interacting with people, the vocabulary and the grammatical constructions are more easily remembered because they are associated with people and with the behavior of people rather than with a mere language lesson.

Focus is so important that a junior worker whose time in focus has (for any reason) been very limited may take longer than the first worker did to acquire the ability to carry on a simple conversation on various topics. This is true even though the first worker had to do the language analysis and prepare dictionary and grammatical materials, whereas for the junior worker such materials were by then available. After that initial stage, however, the junior

---

[2] *Practical Anthropology* 9:27-28, 48 (1962).

worker, because of available materials, frequently makes
faster progress than the senior did.

2. <u>Exploiting the time when out of focus</u>. The first
days in a region can be advantageously spent even before
the junior can be expected to take part in a conversation.
At that time she has hours when out of focus and she should
exploit this nonfocus situation by mentally mimicking the
conversation around her. Before she knows enough to pick
out words and attach meanings to them, she should pay
particular attention to the general flow of the voice.
That is the time when she may best be able to pick out into-
national-like features.

She should select one specific thing to listen for at
a time: (1)   What pitch contours are used just before
pause?   (2)   Do the vowels of some words stand out as longer
than the vowels of others?   When?   When they are angry?
When they are emphasizing something?   (3)   Do the consonants
of some words stand out as longer than others?   (4)   What
kind of rhythm does the language have?   Is stress identifiable?   (5)   When people talk at a distance, how can the language be identified?   By rhythm?   By vowel quality?   By
sentence tunes?

Language consists of more than words, and languages differ in more ways than in words.   Many of these differences
are more easily picked up when a person is not actively
taking part in the conversation.   (1)   How do people get
the attention of the senior worker?   By a cough?   By sniffing?
By knocking?   By calling out?   (2)   What noises do they make
when comforting a baby?   When they hurt themselves?   When
they are cold?   (3)   How do they signal to animals?   How do
they call chickens?   pigs?   dogs?   How do they chase chickens?   How do they send a dog out of the house?   (4)   How do
they show anger?   By raising the pitch of their voice?   By
lowering their voice to a mumble?   By pouting?   By lengthen-
ing the vowels?   (5)   What is characteristic of the voice of
a drunk man?   Of a person with deep sorrow?   (6)   What facial
gestures are characteristic of that cultural group?   Are the
lip movements restrained or vigorous?   When do they pout?
Do they pout when showing cordiality?   When petulant?
When puzzled?   How and when do they use eye movement as a
gesture for communication?   (7)   What is characteristic of
their posture?   Do the women cross their knees?   Always
have both feet flat on the floor?   Sit on their feet?
How does their walk differ from that of the average American?

In some cultures, even when children know that a person can't yet understand their words, they call her name, just for the fun of seeing her look up. It is good practice to try to identify and to mentally mimic the different intonation patterns with which a name is called. For example, in Mazatec if the name Victoria has an upglide on the last syllable it signals affection, with a final h it signals urgency; when the last syllable is long and intense, it signals irritation.[3]

3. <u>Acceptable focus</u>. The junior worker needs at least occasionally to be in a situation in which she can practice the words she knows without the embarrassment of talking in front of the senior worker, and also in which the senior is not culturally required to participate.

An ideal situation is one in which the junior can misunderstand or be misunderstood without jeopardizing plans or relationships. This security is helpful since some senior workers tend to interrupt a conversation to correct the junior's language errors, and some juniors interrupt their own conversation to request a translation. Both actions are a hindrance to language learning since they divert the focus from the junior to the senior and emphasize the junior-senior relationship. Many times when the conversation resumes after such an interruption, it is the senior, not the junior, who is participating.

Among the Mazatecs of Mexico we created one "ideal situation" by making a series of scrapbooks with simple pictures; for example a banana, a pair of scissors, a chicken, a pig, etc. When the junior was in the beginning stages of learning, the name of the object was written lightly in fine print beside each picture.

Armed with the scrapbook, the junior could sit beside a child and "carry on a conversation." At first it consisted in pointing to the picture and reading off the name beside it. Simple as the conversation was, most children enjoyed the attention, and the fun of hearing a stranger trying to talk.

---

[3] For a technical description of Mazatec intonational features, see pp. 314-5 in Eunice V. Pike, Huautla de Jimenez Mazatec, *Linguistics*, Vol. V.   Norman A. McQuown Vol. Ed. *Handbook of Middle American Indians*, Austin: Univ. of Texas Press, 1967, pp. 311-30.

The next step was to erase the penciled translation, and go through the book[4] with a series of children. A further step was to add question-answer drills. The junior would ask, "What is that?" and usually got the answer, "A chicken." If instead the child answered, "It looks like a chicken, but its feet are different," she would not have understood, but it was socially acceptable to ignore the answer.

Soon the junior could ask, "Is that a chicken?" and hear, "Probably," or "I don't know." The junior could point to a pig and ask, "Is that a chicken?" and hear, "No! That's not a chicken; that's a pig!" The possible addition, "Don't you know what a pig is?" could be ignored.

Thus the junior had a situation within a controlled context in which she could talk to the limit of her ability. In that situation there was a built-in redundancy and she could talk to children, who like redundancy, and to a series of different children. By using the books she was in focus, but she was on a lower level in a kind of hierarchy of focus. The senior could be talking business with the adults in one part of the room while the junior and children were talking a short distance away. She was in focus from the children's point of view, out of focus as far as the situation as a whole was concerned.

As the junior mastered one book, she graduated to another with a different vocabulary, or to a book with more complicated pictures. As she started using the pictures she might have a question written beside each one. For example, "How many little pigs are there? Count them." or, "What

---

[4] While still in the States, we bought a number of animal and story books for children. The most easily obtained were *Little Golden Books*. (One of my favorites is by Selma Lola Chambers, *Words*, New York: Golden Press, 1948). If chosen carefully, they served as well as scrapbooks, and because they were already made, they were a great time-saver. The books we rejected were those in which the animals were clothed and acting like human beings instead of like animals. Although that type of book fits well into the culture of English-speaking people, we found it puzzled the tribes-people of Mexico.

color is the little girl's dress?" or, "What is the little boy doing?" With bashful children statements sometimes worked better. For example, "There are four little pigs. Look! Let's count them." or, "The little girl's dress is blue; her mother's dress is green."

As the junior developed efficiency, she graduated to something with the complexity of the *National Geographic*, explaining the pictures, or asking questions about them as best she could. Even adults, especially those who have limited access to books, enjoy a guided tour through a picture book.

4. <u>Excuses for conversation</u>. Talking is a skill like playing the piano--you have to practice. Most of us are uncomfortable if we think we are forcing ourselves on people, so we need to find activities involving talking which we know the people welcome.

We found that helping children put together jigsaw puzzles was a good excuse for conversation. The topic might not be about the puzzle, but it gave the children opportunity to ask, "How much did your shoes cost?" and stimulated the junior to figure out a way to answer.

Such unanticipated conversation is good since (if the language learner manages to understand and respond) it provides the thrill-of-discovery which helps a person to associate idioms and grammatical constructions with the situation in which they were "first heard." When a similar situation arises, she may remember to use the item more easily than she remembers to use one which has a dictionary association only.

Adults were glad to talk when we joined them in such activities as shelling corn, and they would sit with the language learner by the hour if she would teach them how to crochet, to tat, or to knit. (No, you do not need to say much to teach those things--mostly you demonstrate and say encouraging phrases like, "That's good.")

It is socially acceptable for the junior to do the shopping. Being desirous of making a sale, the storekeepers take time to listen to her jumbled-up sentences. We deliberately broke our USA habit of buying a whole week's supply of groceries at one time, and all in one big supermarket. We bought a box of matches one day, and a bar of soap the next--that gave us two opportunities to talk

instead of one. In villages where there were several stores,
we would buy rice in one store, and sugar in the next--
that gave us the opportunity of talking to two people instead of with only one.

5. Making conversation. All of us know when we talk
about the weather in English, that our main purpose is seldom
to convey information about the weather. Usually our main
purpose is to show that we have a friendly attitude toward
the person to whom we are speaking. Other cultures have
ways of conveying that information too, but it may not be by
talking about the weather.

Several tribes in Mexico use an echo-type conversation.
The technique is for the one who initiates the conversation
to say the obvious; then the one spoken to echoes back the
sentence, sometimes with no change, and sometimes with a
necessary change of pronouns. For example, a passer-by
sees someone washing. She says, "You're washing." The other
echoes back, "I'm washing." That may be the whole conversation, or there may be another round. "Clothes get dirty
quickly." Answer, "Clothes get dirty very quickly."

As an initiator of the echo-type conversation, the language learner does not have to think up something new or
interesting to say. She can use a few sentences over and
over. "You're going to market," or, "You got caught in the
rain," or, "You're on your way to school."

As one who responds in such a conversation, the language learner gets good practice in substituting pronouns.
If no pronouns are used, she can fulfill her social obligations by quickly mimicking the sentence she has just heard.
Some common ones in our area are, "It's tiresome to walk up
hill," or, "The road is muddy"--in wet season, or "Water
is scarce"--in dry season.

The echo-type conversation is so helpful to beginners
that they should make an effort to find out if it is the
custom in the language which they are studying.

6. Deliberately shifting the focus. When people came
to our house to sell eggs, for medical help, or to borrow
the hammer, because of habit or courtesy, they usually approached the senior worker. Many times the junior worker
could have taken care of their need just as well as the
senior and she would have benefited from the language

practice, whereas to the senior it was an unwelcome interruption.

With a bit of teamwork, the junior and senior worker
can teach the people the type of activity that is in the
domain of the junior worker. For example, buying eggs.
When, as senior worker, someone approached me and asked,
"Will you buy eggs?", even when I knew that we had plenty
on hand, I'd answer, "Ask Mary." It gave the junior opportunity to say, "No, thank you. We'll buy another day."

Insisting that the woman ask the newly arrived worker
about our need for eggs served an additional purpose. It
taught the people her name and helped them to become aware
of her as a person. (People are not "introduced" in that
culture; they become acquainted in some oblique way.)

Living in an area where the school, the townhall, our
house and a few others, were the only places with clocks, we
were asked ten or more times a day, "What time is it?"
To give the junior worker language practice, we agreed that
I would not answer that question. When the rule first went
into effect, she sometimes did not recognize the question, so
I'd say softly in English, "They are asking you the time."
When she had the time-telling lesson well learned, I again
took a turn at answering, but by then the children were
accustomed to speaking to her and getting a response.

Medical work--the kind that could be done without words--
was another device we used to bring the junior worker into
focus. Children who came with a small infection, a stubbed
toe, etc., from habit asked the senior worker for medicine.
To break them of the habit I would say, "Ask Mary." Her
eyes alone told her what was needed, but she could practice,
"Does it hurt?" and "What happened to you?" If she didn't
understand the answer, it seldom mattered. The children
soon discovered who it was who would fix up their little
wounds, and after a bit they by-passed the senior worker
without a glance.

Deliberately, by language areas, the junior should be
brought into focus and given responsibilities that she can
handle both according to her own and to the people's satisfaction. When she has mastered the typical conversation
required in one area, the people should be encouraged to
accept her in another. It is to be hoped, of course,
that eventually the junior and senior workers can substitute
for each other in any area.

7. A yen to be out of focus. In the other sections,
we have been suggesting ways in which the junior worker
could be brought into focus so that she could learn to talk.
Sometimes, however, she thinks she is too much in focus,
and she would like to be out. Of course people laugh when
she talks, but many times it is a laugh of appreciation. In
the USA we have heard hundreds of foreigners stumble along
in English, and we are no longer interested in the way they
sound. But people of the little-known languages have seldom,
or never, heard an outsider try to pronounce their language.
The first time they hear someone make the effort, they are
fascinated.

People may try to get you to talk in front of their
friends--and then everybody laughs. It is not a mean
laugh; rather it is like a grandmother's satisfied clucking
as she shows off her grandchildren. Until you can talk,
you are of necessity filling the role of a minor, and as
such you have to put up with the friendly (and unfriendly)
attitudes of the people around you.

8. More than focus is needed. I do not want to give
the impression that, if the junior worker manages to get in
focus, her language-learning problems are automatically
over. I know of no alternative for the drudgery of memorization of words, of verb paradigms, of idiomatic expressions,
of whole sentences, of a story or two.

It is also good to remember that a concert pianist
practices before the audience arrives.

Several have found that it is helpful for co-workers to
talk to each other for half an hour a day in the language
that one, or both of them, are learning. To assign a time
for the language practice is better than saying, "We won't
speak English to each other any more," because no one ever
keeps that resolution, and because the things co-workers
need to say to each other are not the same as the things
they would say to the people of the new culture.

There needs to be an understanding about the half-
hour conversation. It should center about the language
area that the junior worker is in the process of mastering, or has already mastered. For example, if she is about
to take over the responsibility for buying eggs, the
conversation could be:

"Will you buy eggs?"
"How much are they?"
"They are 50¢ each."
"How many do you have?"

The same questions and answers could be repeated, with or without variation, until the junior worker can respond smoothly.

After the junior worker is more proficient, the limits of, or topic of, the conversation need not be defined, but it should be understood that the conversation is make-believe. That is, neither is limited to the truth. If one asks, pretending that the other is a carpenter, "Do you know how to make a chair?" the other should be able to answer, "I'm the best chair-maker in town" even though she may never have sawed even one board successfully.

Grammatical Drills

Amy Chipping

The purpose of grammatical drills is to help the learner gain automatic control of structure, of function morphemes or words, of intonation and rhythm, and of common
stimulus-response sequences in the new language he is seeking to master.

In designing drills, the learner should always use complete sentences. Changes within a drill should always be
introduced gradually, so that the difficulty of response is
carefully controlled. Thus, each new drill should contain
a minimum of new grammatical features or function morphemes
to be learnt——if possible, only one. Well known, previously drilled grammar and vocabulary material should be
used to complete the drill, until the new feature is mastered.

New drills should have only one major change in each
sentence (or, in transform drills, one major change in each
sentence pair) when compared with the previous sentence.
That is, as the learner works through a drill, he should
attempt only one change of vocabulary (noun, verb, or
adjective, etc.) in each sentence or sentence pair. In
addition, this change should at first be restricted to the
same slot. In this way the learner is not prevented from
achieving automatic control of the grammar by wrestling
with large amounts of poorly memorized vocabulary. It is
the items which remain constant that are learned; the items
which are changed should be well-known ones.

Any one drill should aim at mastering only one feature
at a time. It should concentrate on a new structure or a
new function morpheme or new vocabulary, but not two of
these types of material at once. Only when all the component
structures and vocabulary have been well drilled and learnt
should more complex drills be used, in which two changes are
introduced (either simultaneously or alternately), or in
which two types of drill are combined.

The learner may participate in drills in two different
ways--by mimicking and by responding. New material should
always be presented in a way which enables the learner to
mimic it. Drills that require the learner to respond should
contain only material which is already familiar to him; and

when he has responded he should immediately be given the correct response to mimic.

Drill activities should be varied and briskly conducted to avoid monotony and boredom. As you practice, keep changing from one type of drill to another. Sometimes plan a series of drills which progressively teach the same structure. Vary the kind of participation that is involved and the kind of cues that are given. Use more than one method of drilling, sometimes using a tape recorder, sometimes your partner with a vernacular speaker, sometimes a willing villager, or children who will regard drilling as a game. Drill by yourself too. Try greeting every new tree along the road! (e.g. the child repeating his multiplication tables as he jumps from square to square along a sidewalk.) Use your drills in as many imaginatively varied ways as you can.

If you do not make your drills so easy that they bore you, nor so challenging that they discourage you, you will find you learn most quickly. Remember too to base your drills on vocabulary that is generally useful, so that you have the added encouragement of being able to make good use of all you have learnt. ALL LEARNT DRILLS SHOULD BE USED IN CONVERSATION.

Frame drills (substitution drills) are the simplest type of drills. They are used when there is a difference in structure between the learner's own language and the new language he is learning (e.g. word order). In frame drills a constant frame should be used to form a simple utterance, and substitution items should be inserted at or near the trouble spot. The learner should drill by practicing the set of sentences consisting of the frame with each substitution item in turn. In the following example the trouble spot being drilled is underlined.

DUSUN example:

Frame:				Substitute:
Verb	Subject	Location Referent	Directional	Place
mongoi	*o tanak*	*hilo*	*id*	*kadai.* *kampung.* *kabun.* *tumo.*

ENGLISH translation of the DUSUN drill:

Frame:			Substitute:
Subject	Verb	Directional	Place
The child	is going	to	the shops. the village. the garden. the farm.

NOTE: This particular drill is not aimed primarily at drilling the difference in word order between the English and Dusun subject and verb, but the locational referent *hilo* which has no English equivalent. Since this cannot be substituted by other items, some place items are substituted within the locative phrase instead.

More difficult types of substitution drills can be used for variety once the frame of the simple drill is fully mastered. For example, there is the <u>multiple substitution drill</u> in which two vocabulary items are changed at once throughout the drill. There is also the <u>progressive substitution drill</u> (or <u>selection drill</u>). In this type of drill a change may be made in any one of two (or more) different slots. The learner puts the new item in whichever slot he considers to be the most appropriate.

ENGLISH example:

Prompter says:	Learner says:
mango *green* *John*	*He has a ripe banana.* *He has a ripe mango.* *He has a green mango.* *John has a green mango.*

A <u>system drill</u> is one which is set up to master classes of function morphemes——either a small class of words such as pronouns, or a set of affixes that mark various categories such as tense. Such a drill is like a frame drill except that the substitution items are a closed minor class, not an open major class. It is important that affixes should be drilled in a complete sentence frame, not merely in a word paradigm that is less than a sentence.

Example from LATIN:

Frame: Object: 'girl'	Substitute: Verb: 'love'	
puellam	*amo.* *amas.* *amat.*	I love the girl. You (sg.) love the girl. He loves the girl.

A <u>multiple system drill</u> involves changing two separate
sets of such function morphemes simultaneously within a
sentence. Each of these two categories should be separately
practiced as a simple system drill first, before using the
multiple system drill. Use multiple system drills when two
sets of affixes co-occur in the same word and especially
when morphophonemic changes are involved.

<u>Transform drills (transformation drills)</u> are used
when there are clearly related structures to be learnt,
for example:
(a)   continuative/punctiliar aspect
(b)   active/passive voice
(c)   positive/negative mood
(d)   dependent/independent clauses

<u>Question and answer drills</u> are another kind of transforma-
tion.

In setting up such drills the related utterances are
put side by side:
(a)   *She was eating a banana./She ate a banana.*
(b)   *Mary ate the banana./The banana was eaten by Mary.*
(c)   *She was eating a banana./She was not eating a banana.*
(d)   *After she had eaten the banana, she went home./She ate
       the banana and went home.*
(e)   *She was eating a banana./What was she eating?*

In the simplest kind of transform drill each utterance of such a pair is developed into a frame drill,
with new items being substituted at or near the trouble
spot in the structure. In the examples below the trouble
spots are underlined.

Two ENGLISH examples follow:

Frame: Subject	Substitute: Verb	Frame: Object
She	ate cut peeled cooked	a banana.

	Frame: Subject	Substitute: Verb	Frame: Object
	She	was eating was cutting was peeling was cooking	a banana.

Substitute: Subject	Frame: Verb Object
Mary Peter You	ate the banana.

	Frame: Subject Verb	Substitute: Agent
	The banana was eaten	by Mary. by Peter. by you.

The learner should drill by having a vernacular speaker or a tape recorder give the first utterance on the left hand side, and he should respond promptly with its transform found on the right hand side. Then the speaker or tape recorder should give the transformed utterance, to correct or reinforce his attempt. The process should be repeated for each succeeding pair of utterances in turn. The next time the transform drill is used, commence with utterances on the right hand side and transform to utterances on the left hand side. In addition either or both of the sides may be used as a frame drill. Note: Remember to drill changing only ONE item at a time.

A more difficult kind of transform drill may be con-structed by putting down on the two sides utterances which

are of the same general structure but which do not necessarily have any vocabulary items in common, that is, they
do not constitute a frame drill.

ENGLISH example:

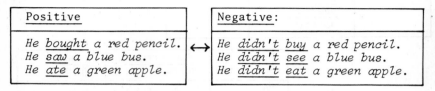

Positive	Negative:
He _bought_ a red pencil. He _saw_ a blue bus. He _ate_ a green apple.	He _didn't buy_ a red pencil. He _didn't see_ a blue bus. He _didn't eat_ a green apple.

NOTE: Use only familiar vocabulary.

     Context forcing drills (correlation drills) are used
when a given context forces a choice between two or more
alternatives (alternative categories or alternative allomorphs) in a grammatical system (e.g. where there is some
sort of agreement or concord in the language). To practice
this sort of drill a prompter (or tape recorder) is essential to help the learner. The prompter says one item of
the phrase or clause which forces the choice of category of
a second item. For example, English agreement between time
phrase and verb (the trouble spot for agreement is underlined):

Prompter says: Time word	Learner says: '... I go to town.'
Yesterday _Now_ _Tomorrow_	_Yesterday I went to town._ _Now I'm going to town._ _Tomorrow I'll go to town._

     Context forcing drills can be used where two (or more)
systems operate simultaneously. In such a multiple context
forcing drill, the learner should first drill by changing
only one of the two items at a time. Nevertheless, the
prompter should actually say both items. Thus, to drill
agreement in English between both time word and pronoun,
and the verb:

(a) Drill the person distinctions in the present tense.

Prompter says: Time word + pronoun	Learner says: '... go to town.'
now I *now you* *now he*	*Now I'm going to town.* *Now you're going to town.* *Now he's going to town.*

(b) Drill the person distinctions in the other tenses similarly.

(c) Then in the multiple context forcing drill the prompter gives any combination of two items which forces the learner's choice of the third one.

Prompter says: Time word + pronoun	Learner says: '... go to town.'
now I *yesterday you* *yesterday he* *now he* *tomorrow I*	*Now I'm going to town.* *Yesterday you went to town.* *Yesterday he went to town.* *Now he's going to town.* *Tomorrow I'll go to town*

Context forcing drills can also be used for practicing both phonologically determined and morphologically determined allomorphs.

Example:

Prompter says: Adjective	Learner says: Frame Negated adjective
capable *practical* *logical*	*He is incapable.* *He is impractical.* *He is illogical.*

Expansion drills. This kind of drill is used to develop mastery of longer utterances, at the correct speed and with correct intonation. In these drills a clause or phrase is taken and expanded by one item or slot at a time until the maximum useful construction that would normally be used is built up.

Example:

Sentence Frame	Expansion:
I went to the garden.	
I went to the garden	*yesterday.*
I went to the garden	*yesterday morning.*
I went to the garden	*yesterday morning to dig.*
I went to the garden	*yesterday morning to dig yams.*

Contraction drills (reduction or deletion drills) are
used when a word or phrase can be replaced by a shorter
form, such as an adverb for an adverbial phrase.

Example:

He went to the village.	*He went there.*
He went out to the garden.	*He went out there.*

⟷

Or it may substitute a pronoun for a noun or noun phrase.

He saw the little boy.	*He saw him.*
He saw a black cat.	*He saw it.*

⟷

Longer sentences can also be contracted progressively.

Example:

The boy	*did not see*	*the old woman*	*at the market.*
The boy	*did not see*	*the old woman*	*there.*
The boy	*did not see*	*her*	*there.*
The boy	*didn't see*	*her*	*there.*
He	*didn't see*	*her*	*there.*

Full and elliptical answers to questions can be drilled
similarly.

Examples:

Question:	Full answer:	Elliptical answer:
Where's the book?	*It's on the table.*	*On the table.*
	It's on the floor.	*On the floor.*

What are you doing	I'm chopping wood.	→	Chopping wood.
	I'm carrying wood.		Carrying wood.

Tail-head linking drills (a progressive drill).   When
a sentence describing a sequence of several actions would
normally use two different kinds of verbs e.g. subordinate
and main (dependent and independent), then this kind of
progressive drill may usefully be prepared.   In this drill
each utterance is a sentence of 2 or 3 clauses.   The sentences are so chosen and arranged that one clause (usually
the first) recapitulates the content of a clause (usually
the last) in the previous sentence.

Example:

Transformed Clause:	New Clause:
After she had swept the room,	she washed the floor.
After she had washed the floor,	she lit the oven.
After she had lit the oven,	she cooked the meal.
After she had cooked the meal,	she ate it.

To use this drill, write out on a page in logical
order, one under another, all of the individual clauses
describing the series of actions.   These clauses should be
in the form of single clause sentences.   Look down the
list, taking the clauses two at a time, and join them by
transforming them into the appropriate two-clause sentence.
Have a vernacular speaker correct you and you mimic him.

Other multi-clause sentence drills also involve a combination of substitution and transformation.   Simpler than
the tail-head linking drill above is the drill below in
which only the dependent clause is varied.   In this drill
the prompter gives the learner a simple sentence which he
transforms into a dependent clause and drills in a frame.

Example:

Prompter says: Sentence	Learner says: Transformed clause	Frame clause
She swept the room.	_After_ she _had_ _swept_ the room,	she sat down.
She washed the floor.	_After_ she _had_ _washed_ the floor,	she sat down.
She lit the fire.	_After_ she _had_ _lit_ the fire,	she sat down.
She cooked the meal.	_After_ she _had_ _cooked_ the meal,	she sat down.

Integration drills are another type of drill for multi-clause sentences. This kind of drill involves using two simple sentences as frame items, e.g. _She swept the room. She sat down._ The prompter suggests different linking devices, each of which has been previously drilled. The learner then uses these to join the frame clauses together.

Example:

Prompter says:	Learner says:
After	_After_ she _had_ _swept_ the room, she sat down.
and	She swept the room _and_ sat down.
but...not	She swept the room _but_ she didn't _sit_ down.
if	_If_ she _had_ _swept_ the room she _would_ _have_ _sat_ down.

In addition to all these drills, it may also be profit-able for the learner to set up stimulus-response sequence drills. If there are situations and utterances in the lan-guage which call for a response that is either partly or fully stereotyped, stimulus-response drills can be used to drill them until the patterned responses become automatic. Greetings and leavetakings usually fall into this category, and so may some conventional conversation-making sequences (e.g. English: _"It's cold today, isn't it?"_ _"Yes, very.")_

Also, if there are question-and-answer patterns in
which elliptical answers are commonly given in preference
to a full statement, the learner may prefer to drill them
by this method instead of in a contraction or a transform
drill. E.g. *Where is it? Here.*
Do you like it? No, I don't.

Wherever the language learner is aware of a difference
which he needs to control between his own language and the
new language to be learnt, he should set up suitable drills
to master it. Properly planned drilling, cheerfully tackled,
is invaluable in a successful language learning program.

For further information on grammatical drills see:

British School of the Summer Institute of Linguistics,
    Language Learning, (mimeographed 1969). (Especially
    chapter 3.)

Nelson Brooks, 1964. *Language and Language Learning: Theory
    and Practice,* Second Edition. Harcourt, Brace and World,
    New York. (Especially pages 152-163.)

Mary Finocchiaro, 1964. *English as a Second Language: From
    Theory to Practice.* Regents Publishing Co., New York.
    (Especially pages 60-68.)

Francis W. Gravit and Albert Valdman, 1963. *Structural Drill
    and Language Laboratory,* Publication 27 of I.U.R.C.A.F.L.
    Supplement to I.J.A.L. Vol. 29, No. 2. (Especially
    pages 3-51.)

Donald N. Larson and William A. Smalley, 1972. *Becoming
    Bilingual: A Guide to Language Learning,* Pre-Publica-
    tion Edition. Practical Anthropology, New Canaan,
    Connecticut. (Especially pages 141-157, 190-290.)

Earl W. Stevick, 1971. *Adapting and Writing Language Les-
    sons.* Foreign Service Institute, Department of State,
    Washington. (Especially pages 310-364, 391-430.)

Programed Review Cards

J. E. Henderson

I find drills very helpful in language learning. At first, when I made a new drill I would review it every day for a few days, then I would ignore it for a few weeks. Later, when I had some time, I would listen to all the drills I had made to date. I found, though, that I didn't gain much from these long sessions.

Then I remembered a suggestion from a course in study methods, that each time we review something we remember it for twice as long. I devised a system of cards for programming review based on this idea, which I have found quite a bit more effective than my earlier practice.

Experimental Basis

Research into memory and forgetting shows the following.

(1) Repetitions of the material to be learned are more effective if they are distributed over a number of short sessions instead of being massed together in one long session (Lorge, 1930, quoted in Berelson et al. 1964, p. 159).

(2) We remember 2 or 3 times as much if we say the material out loud rather than just reading it (Gates, 1917 in Berelson et al. 1964, p. 166).

(3) When learning is followed immediately by sleep retention is high (82 - 86%), but when learning is followed by waking activity retention is less (59 - 64%). (McGaugh and Hostetter, 1961 in Berelson et al. 1964, p. 65).

(4) "Mastery of subject matter becomes more stable the longer it is maintained, requiring less and less review." (Woodworth and Schlosberg, 1954; Youtz 1941 in Ruch 1958, p. 343).

How to Use the Cards

When you make a drill, prepare a review card for it. Lay a blank 3 x 5 card over the master on p. 319 and fill in the topic and reference lines on it. Then write the date in the box labeled "tonight", tomorrow's date in the next box and so on until all the boxes have dates. These are the occasions on which you should review this particular

to-night	to-morrow	+2 days	+4 days	+1 week	+2 weeks	+1 month	+2 months	+4 months

Topic →

Filing ref. →

Tape ref. →

Lay a 3 x 5 card over this master, and fill in the dates across its top. Draw a box around the "+ 4 months" date for annual review as well.

drill. The finished cards should look like those illustrated below.

Just before you go to bed, review the drill, repeating the utterances out loud and then cross out the "tonight" box. Next day, review the drill again and cross out the tomorrow box. Repeat this procedure as you make more drills, keeping the cards filed in the order of the left-most date that is not crossed out. Every day just check the front card in the stack to see if there are any drills to review that day.

The diagram shows what the stack of cards would look like on the afternoon of 8th March if a drill had been made on each of the 1st, 4th, 5th, 7th, and 8th of March. The drills labeled a, c, d and e need to be reviewed on the 8th.

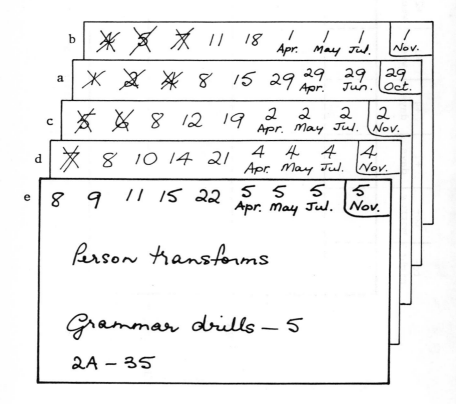

It is good to keep drills shorter than 5 minutes and not to enter more than one new drill each day. If you get a few days behind, it is better to do two dates per day until you catch up, rather than doing a lot of drills at once. When you have reviewed a drill on all the dates listed on the review card, do not cross off the "+ 4 months" box, but keep the card in the stack for annual review on that date.

Modify the system to suit your own needs and temperament, keeping the basic principles in mind.

References

Bernard Berelson and Gary A. Steiner, 1964. *Human Behavior: An Inventory of Scientific Findings*. Harcourt, Brace & World, New York.

Arthur I. Gates, 1917. "Recitation as a Function in Memorizing." *Arch. Psychol.* 6, No. 40.

Irving Lorge, 1930. *Influence of Regularly Interpolated Time Intervals on Subsequent Learning.* Teachers College, Columbia University.

J. L. McGaugh and R. C. Hostetter, 1961. *Retention as a Function of the Temporal Position of Sleep and Activity Following Waking*, unpublished ms.

Floyd L. Ruch, 1958. *Psychology and Life*, fifth edition. Scott, Foresman and Co., Chicago.

R. S. Woodworth and H. Schlosberg, 1954. *Experimental Psychology*, Henry Holt & Co., New York.

A. C. Youtz, 1941. "An Experimental Evaluation of Jost's Laws." *Psych. Mono.* 53, No. 1.

Language Learning without Tears

Alan Healey

At some time or another most of us despair of ever becoming fluent in the unwritten language we are trying to learn. Our tongues are too slow, our memories like sieves, and our grammar atrocious. But even in our darkest moments there are things we can do to encourage ourselves.[1]

If we are to have the deep satisfaction of success in language learning it is important that we should set goals for ourselves and that we should reach them. Most goals should be short-term ones that apply for a week or a month. They must be realistic goals--ones that we have a good prospect of achieving in the set time. On the other hand they should not be too easy; they should contain some element that challenges us.

Set very specific goals——a definite number of hours per day in each kind of learning activity; a definite number of useful expressions to be over-learnt each week; a specific number of words or stems to be memorized, practiced, and entered in the dictionary file each week; a specific number of grammatical constructions to be drilled each week until they can be used automatically; a minimum number of people separately conversed with each day.

In addition, it is wise to assign priorities to all of our goals so that we will give the more important goals our best hours and main effort each day. Then if we should be unable to achieve all of our goals by a particular deadline, we will know which one to postpone until next month.

Once we have set our goals, we must work at them regularly and systematically. It is good at the end of the day or week to know that we have achieved what we aimed at; the desire accomplished is sweet to the soul (Prov. 13: 19). If we consistently meet our goals over a period of many months, we will be surprised at our progress in conversational ability.

In the first few weeks we may well find our inability to communicate with people very frustrating. Several steps can be taken to avoid this problem.

(a) Insist that whoever helps you settle into the village
where you are to live uses part of his time to elicit some
expressions that will be useful to you in daily living.

(b) He should be sure to also elicit some of the commonly
useful information questions of the Who? What? Which?
How many? Where? How? Why? type.

(c) Important for him to elicit are the commonly used
greetings and especially the leave takings. You need to
know how to back out of various kinds of social situations
politely.

(d) He should also elicit several expressions that would
be useful as replies in a wide variety of circumstances.
You should aim to learn ten of these thoroughly in the
first week you are in the village.

(e) Spend a lot of your time with people, listening to
what they say and tracking (silently mimicking) when you
are not involved in trying to converse.

(f) Especially try to be with people when they are doing
things (rather than just talking) as this is the most
opportune time, both for joining in the conversation
(with an occasional brief question, for instance) and for
guessing at the meaning of some of the things that you
hear said.

On one or more occasions later on, you are likely to
reach a learning plateau when you seem to be making no
noticeable progress in your understanding or speaking of
the language. Sometimes this is more apparent than real,
and at other times it is a natural stage at which the mind
needs to systematize, consolidate and reinforce all that
it has absorbed. If this situation depresses you, then
go back a little to what you know and understand well, and
start building on that again but with a change in focus.
Drop any recent materials that have discouraged you and
start with different materials that seem fairly easy.

Are you at a standstill because of some specific
problem in the language that you can't solve? Stop trying
to solve it. Put the problem aside and concentrate on
some completely different facet of the language that is
unrelated to the problem area. That is, find a path around
the road-block instead of smashing yourself to pulp trying
to drive through it. When you come back to the problem in
a few months, it may well have already resolved itself
through your increased familiarity with the language. If

not, arrange for some colleague to look at the problem
with you and give you some help.

Many of us feel that we are not born conversational-
ists, and we cringe at the thought of spending an hour each
day conversing with our fellow villagers. Except perhaps
at times of bereavement, it is fruitless to sit with someone
for long periods of uncomfortable silence, trying to think
of something we are capable of saying that might be interesting. As you approach each new conversation, arm yourself
with a couple of topics or questions that you would like to
raise if there is opportunity. (Keep an up-to-date list of
topics and specific questions pinned up in a prominent place
in your house ready for each new opportunity for conversation.) Plan beforehand, if possible, the actual wording of
what you want to say or ask, so that when the opportunity
offers you need not be tongue-tied. Once your topic has
been completed and before either of you run out of things to
say, excuse yourself with the appropriate leave-taking formula, and part as friends who enjoyed the brief conversation.

Are there times when someone is talking to you and
you feel swamped? The topic or the language or the personality of the speaker seems to overwhelm you and you cannot
think of a thing to say? Then listen carefully to what your
friend is saying and ask him an appropriate question. If
you cannot understand what he is talking about choose out
one frequently occurring word and ask its meaning. If you
understand some of what he is saying, then perhaps you could
ask the reason for some particular event that he is describing. Then follow this up with more questions. Take the initiative and change the monologue into a dialogue. Then before you run out of ideas find an opportunity to take leave
of your friend.

Many brief conversations with many different people
are much less strain and teach you more than a few long
near-monologues with a handful of faithful friends who
find it as much of a drag as you do. Try and avoid doing
anything that would give people the impression that you
are merely using them as an unpaid source of language information and practice. Take a genuine interest in people
and their way of life and see that the friendships you form
are as reciprocal as possible in every way.

When there are several bilinguals living in the village they are often inclined to talk to us in the lingua

franca. If we are always careful to talk to them in the
vernacular--whether we start the conversation or they do--
they will usually use the vernacular to help us to learn
it. Provided that the bilinguals see that we are genuine
in our desire to learn the language and that we discipline
ourselves to use it all the time, they will almost always
come around to using the vernacular with us. It is true
that in a village with a lot of bilingualism, there may be
certain social situations in which everybody uses the lingua
franca. Yet even on these occasions it is advisable to per-
sist in using only the vernacular, except where it involves
visitors from another language group.

Rote memorization, drilling, and several other aspects
of language learning can become very boring and tiring. To
avoid this we should select materials that are both interesting and useful. In planning our learning we need to keep the
program as varied as possible, so that monotony will not
slow us down and discourage us.

Regular relaxation is almost as important as regular work
if we are to achieve our learning goals. A five minute
break every hour works wonders, as long as we go back to work
immediately. Each one of us needs to find some way of relaxing at the end of the day--a swim, a hobby, a game with some
young people. Occasionally, we may feel the need to escape
from the pressures of the learning program and village life.
A day's trip away from it all can be tremendously refreshing--
a trip hunting or fishing, collecting bugs or orchids, visiting a potential tourist attraction or another village. Or
perhaps your friends in the village have some other method
of escape that you would like to try. Other factors such
as a good diet, comfortable chairs and tables for written
work, and regular sleep also play an important part in how
efficiently we work.

Each month, before you set your new goals for the
next month, it is essential to evaluate how well you
achieved the goals you set for the previous month. You
have every reason to feel encouraged about those that were
fully reached. If you didn't reach some goals, assess
the reasons carefully. Was the goal unrealistically high?
Then set a somewhat lower target for next month. Was there
some specific circumstance that hindered you in this part
of your learning? Discuss with your partner how to remove
or avoid this hindrance in future. Perhaps you feel de-
spondent about your slow progress despite achieving last
month's goals. Then go back to a tape, vocabulary items,

useful expressions, or grammatical constructions you began
studying several months ago and notice how much easier
they are than the things you are struggling with at present.
You really ARE learning!

It is important to start the new month with a clean
sheet and no further self-recrimination about past "failures".
The goals should be a new set, and rather different from
those of the past month, and you should attack them with a
new vigor. You may find that, combined with this monthly
time of self-evaluation and goal-setting, a morning of prayer
will give you the kind of encouragement you need to make a
fresh start.

NOTE

[1] I am indebted to Felicia Brichoux for several of the
ideas presented in this paper.

Stress-Producing Factors in Cultural Adjustment

T. WAYNE DYE

I did not expect to be experiencing culture shock still after several years of living among the Bahinemo, but I was. Furthermore, I was not alone. In anthropology seminars it became apparent that quite a number of field-workers continue to experience stress after many years of living in a village. From reading the early literature, we consultants had expected that the shock would be over in a couple of years: the very term "shock" implies something that is severe but brief. According to Oberg's original description (1960:177), culture shock is caused by ". . . the anxiety that results from losing all our familiar signs and symbols of social intercourse." These field-workers, however, already knew a variety of cultural cues and used them in communication with the villagers. Yet they were still under strain. Even field-workers with considerable education and preparation experienced these problems.

When Does Cultural Adjustment Occur?

In an effort to understand the source of the problem, I re-examined Oberg's article. He postulated four stages of culture shock and described the fourth as follows:

In the fourth stage your adjustment is about as complete as it can be. The visitor now accepts the customs of the country as just another way of living. You operate within the new milieu without a feeling of anxiety, although there are moments of strain. Only with the complete grasp of all the cues of social intercourse will this strain disappear. For a long time the individual will understand what the national is saying, but he is not always sure what the national means. With complete adjustment you not only accept the foods, drinks, habits and customs, but you begin to enjoy them. When you go home on leave you may even take things back with you, and if you leave for good, you generally miss the country and the people to whom you have become accustomed (Oberg, 1960:177).

This paragraph gave us the clue that we needed to understand what was happening to us and our colleagues. Though we

Reprinted from *Missiology: An International Review*, Volume 2, Number 1, pages 61-77 (January, 1974) by permission of the publisher and author.

understood the Papua New Guinean's cultures fairly well, we could never reach the place of accepting their customs for ourselves or enjoying them.

This helped me to see that two distinct kinds of stress were involved in culture shock. One was the confusion and helplessness that arose from "complete loss of cultural cues." The other was the stress which came from change to a new way of living. I prefer to call the first *culture confusion* and the second *culture stress*. Culture confusion is soon over but culture stress can continue for many years. Let us take a close look at the causes of culture stress:

Formula for Culture Stress

Several factors seem to affect directly the degree of culture stress one will experience. These factors are expressed in the following formula.

$$\frac{\text{Involvement} \times \text{Value Difference} \times \text{Frustration} \times \text{Temperament Difference}}{\text{Acceptance} \times \text{Communication} \times \text{Emotional Security} \times \text{Inner Spiritual Resources}} \times \text{Unknown Factors} = \text{Amount of Culture Stress}$$

Increasing the value of a factor above the line will increase the stress. Increasing a factor below the line will reduce the stress. No numerical values can be assigned, however, so the "formula" should not be interpreted in a true mathematical sense. The relative importance of these factors varies with the individual.

Factors Which Increase Stress

1. Involvement

Involvement is here defined as psychological presence in a cross-cultural situation. It can mean any interpersonal relationship, whether learning a language or teaching by discussion or trying to help materially, or working with nationals in business or research. Not only anthropologists, linguists and missionaries, but expatriate public health workers, agricultural extension agents, school teachers, magistrates trying to apply national law in a local culture, and businessmen employing many local workers, can all be extensively involved with nationals. Such involvement with one's hosts in their own cultural environment leads to a proportional amount of culture stress.

Because involvement with a foreign community increases

stress, people instinctively avoid it. A person beginning work in a foreign culture may recognize the importance of involvement in bringing beneficial change and may have every intention of interacting with his hosts as much as possible. But as stress builds up, he feels forced to withdraw enough to be able to function. Usually his unconscious defense mechanisms provide good "reasons" for limiting his interaction with nationals. I believe this is the principal cause for "missionary ghettoes" (Taber, 1971:193), and for the rationalizations which keep ethnic groups separate from each other all over the world.

But for the field-worker, involvement is absolutely necessary for effective communication and for constructively influencing change. It cannot simply be avoided without serious loss of effectiveness. When one is already living in an alien environment and committed to learning or teaching, or helping in some way, then keeping away from people can be worse than mixing with them. In spite of the relationship between involvement and stress, the best advice for this situation is to "get involved," to get out and get to know people. Purposeful interaction with people can minimize one's frustration by helping one meet goals; it can aid communication and acceptance. As a consequence, such involvement actually operates to decrease the net stress.

2. Value Difference

The greater the *difference* in *values* between one's home culture and the host culture, the greater the stress. For missionaries it is not the central Christian values which cause the most difficulty, but cultural values such as cleanliness, sense of responsibility, and use of time. For example, the Bahinemo viewpoint on caring for dogs was a source of resentment to me for years. They will not kill any dogs because of their belief in a dog's afterlife. As a result, the dogs multiply until there are more than can be fed in their subsistence economy. Only puppies and good hunting dogs are fed. The others are kept away from the family's food by frequent kicking and clubbing. Some dogs slowly starve. I hold an opposite value: a dog should either be fed and cared for or put out of its misery.

Other values that are often in conflict between Westerners and Papua New Guineans include disciplining of children, patterns of giving, when to ask for things, clan centeredness, and how much to do for the sick. These value conflicts seem to be particular aspects of cultural differences which keep us from ever completely accepting ". . . the customs of the country as just another way of living" (Oberg, 1960:179).

Frequently, cultures which are similar in outward form have very different values. Individuals will plunge into the outwardly similar culture expecting the values also to be the same, but they are not. I believe this may explain Guthrie's observations (as cited by Brewster, 1972:41), that Americans suffer more culture stress in the Philippines than in Thailand. I propose that the crucial factors here are value difference and involvement, not the superficial similarity. Noticing cultural similarities because of Westernization in the Philippines, Americans are likely to interact much more with the local people than would Americans in Thailand, who naturally expect to stay in separate housing, eat different foods, and use go-betweens. A more detailed look at the actual conflicting values in the Philippine cross-cultural situation would clarify the reasons for this unexpected stress.

In Papua New Guinea, Westerners from many countries work together in a common effort. In their way of life they seem to be alike; but different values, particularly in use of money, child rearing, housekeeping, and hospitality, cause unexpected stress. For instance, most Australians highly value carefulness with money. Good use of resources requires that time be taken to find and use the least expensive way in each situation. Convenience foods, ready-made women's clothing, and automatic transmissions on cars are examples of items which are considered "wasteful" and do not sell well, even to people who "can afford" them. Because purchases on credit waste interest money and encourage spending beyond one's means, they are voided, even when the consequent delay in purchasing results in more time spent maintaining wornout equipment or doing without.

In comparison, Americans generally are extremely casual about money. If one "can afford" a comfort or convenience, he should have it. To them the commodity to be guarded is time. Good use of resources requires spending money whenever needed to save "valuable time." It seems petty to use time to keep track of small expenditures and shortsighted not to "invest" in extra equipment to save time.

The difference is a matter of degree and neither group seems consciously aware of the value differences. As a result, both nationalities have frequent cause for making allowances for the other's "poor stewardship" (missionaries) or "lack of business sense" (others).

There is evidence that adjustment is more difficult for a value which is held strongly in one's own culture but held weakly in the host culture. Spradley and Phillips (1972:526) found that a sample of 83 American Peace Corps veterans considered adjustment in the areas of punctuality, personal cleanliness, and privacy to be much more stressful than adjustments to differences in family closeness and parental obligations to children. A sample of Chinese students in America gave the opposite ranking. In American culture punctuality, personal cleanliness and privacy are strongly-held values. Chinese see family closeness and parental obligations to children as much more important. ". . . it would appear that difficulties in cultural readjustment often arise from the feeling that individuals in the new culture are violating norms [values] learned in one's native land."

3. Frustration

A great deal of *frustration* arises from dealing with the people of the new culture over and above the actual process of adapting to their culture. Life in a village can be very trying for an outsider. He arrives with various goals in mind, such as language learning, academic research, literacy, evangelism, improved hygiene, economic development, and Bible translation. But he soon finds that interruptions are normal and misunderstandings frequent. Cultural differences, the demands of the people, and the lack of the usual amenities cause a thousand little frustrating hindrances to his work. His goals for his hosts and their own goals may be utterly different. The process of discovering the underlying value differences by trial and error brings frequent conflict and frustration.

Besides being a basic component of culture stress, all of this frustration builds negative attitudes toward the new culture, and increases inner resistance to acculturation. This uncomfortable situation sets into motion the mind's automatic censoring system which attempts to shield the conscious mind from unpleasant thoughts or actions through fairly predictable defense mechanisms or reactions.

4. Temperament Difference

Individual *differences* in *temperament* and personality cause each individual to be affected differently by the same cross-cultural situation. In general, the more differences there are between the field-worker's own temperament and the "modal personality" (Honigmann, 1967:118-122) of the host community, the more difficult adjustment will be. For instance, shy, reserved people find it hard to adjust to the boisterous and affectionate New Guinea Highlanders. Decisive government officers are often frustrated by the indirectness and traditional orientation of many peasant peoples.

In a few month's visit, people who thrive on variety adjust to a new culture better than those who depend on regular habits and customs for their emotional stability. But the long term situation may be quite the opposite. One American couple found the "dull gray sameness" of village life, where nothing new or different seemed to happen, to be the most difficult adjustment of all.

Factors Which Decrease Stress

1. Acceptance

Acceptance of the host culture as a valid way of life decreases stress. Conversely, if a missionary cannot see how the host culture can become a valid vehicle for Christianity, he cannot adjust to it.

Acceptance has both an intellectual and a non-intellectual, component. The intellectual component is the extent to which one accepts other customs and values as being equally "right" as one's own, and how much one understands the host culture. This understanding can be taught (Brewster, 1972:31). The non-intellectual component is a product of moral and value training in childhood and individual character. This is much more difficult to change.

It is easier intellectually to consider a custom to be valid for others than to become so convinced of its worth that one can live comfortably with those who follow it. It is still more difficult to make a formerly repugnant custom one's own.

In rural Papua New Guinea a measure of accommodation is all that most Westerners aim for. They never really come to prefer local customs for themselves. For this reason acceptance is much more difficult when one's children live in the village. A mother may be able to accommodate herself to a new culture, but when she sees her children genuinely adapting to it, she feels threatened. She fears they will lose their own cultural heritage, and that they will not fit into their home country after growing up in the village. One linguist and his wife forbade their children to learn any more words of the new language that they were picking up so readily.

In this cross-cultural environment a mother is torn between two natural desires. She wants to have her children with her in the village but that means they will absorb much of the new culture. She wants them to grow up in her own Western culture and fit into it as adults, but that often necessitates their living away from her in a European enclave or in the homeland.

2. Communication

Communication reduces stress in several ways. Most people inherently need to communicate and interact with others. Loneliness and a sense of isolation from one's own kind is very difficult. Many people, in talking about culture stress, have focused on the difficulty of isolation. But further questioning nearly always shows that they are not isolated from all people. Usually they are in daily contact with dozens of people. They are isolated from others with whom they can relax and be themselves, that is, from people with whom they share common language, viewpoints, and interests that allow them to really communicate.

One expatriate in Papua New Guinea said to a visitor, "You are most welcome, as you are the first human being I've talked to in months." At that time he was living within a mile of 10 other Westerners and taught dozens of nationals each day in school. But none had exactly the same cultural and religious background.

A Westerner living in rural parts of an underdeveloped country often lives on an isolated government or mission station rather than within a local community, partly so that he can maintain his own cultural heritage. Learning the local language may seem too difficult and time consuming, and the local culture may offend him. As a result he cannot really communicate with anyone and the sense of isolation is almost unbearable.

At one small government station, a day's travel from the nearest other expatriates, at least five people have had to leave in the last decade because of aberrant emotional behavior. Many others showed signs of stress after their term of service. The stress of isolation is so severe that the government allows its officers only six months non-renewable tours of duty there. Hundreds of nationals live near this post but the cross-cultural situation is such that communication is minimal.

Communication also builds mutual understanding with one's hosts and so aids acceptance and minimizes frustration, anxiety and resentment.

Communication also helps to bring value differences into conscious focus so that one can adjust one's behavior to cope. When one of my friends in the village capsized my motor canoe after not following instructions, I insisted that he pay for someone else's axe lost in the accident. Only after the village leader complained to me of my unfair attitude did I learn that in Bahinemo culture borrowed items are used at the lender's risk, not the borrower's. Now, what used to be seen as irresponsibility can be recognized as a different rule for behavior, and I have adjusted my own behavior accordingly.

3. Emotional Security

Emotional Security is an important factor because acculturation inherently involves a change in one's personality. Our culture is the part of ourselves that we hang on to most strongly. When we change our customs we are changing part of our very selves. While one's conscious mind is keeping to the task of learning the new culture, the inner self that has been shaped by all our previous childhood experiences is resisting acculturation.

Dr. Kenneth Pike suggests that learning a language can also threaten the self:

Our language is a system of cast iron units, patterns, rules. So precisely is the language of, say, Timbuktu. The clash between them draws psychological sparks when I try to shift from one set of whirling gears to another . . . It hurts (Pike, 1967:109).

Because acculturation often appears as an attack on the self, it will cause more stress on those with inferiority feelings or who are unsure of themselves. For them, change becomes a greater threat to the self. For this reason, the kind of acculturative changes which damage one's self-image are more difficult to make than those which are neutral.

For example, it has long been recognized that culture shock often affects western wives more than their husbands (Oberg, 1960:180). A man's self-image is largely derived from his success in his occupation. His surroundings do not affect his psychological well-being very much. A wife's principal work is the maintenance of a home, making it a worthwhile place to be. The kind of food she serves, the standard of cleanliness, and the general quality of the home are what affect her image of herself. Because her own domestic standards are difficult to maintain in a cross-cultural situation, a woman is often unable to do her work effectively enough to feel successful. Consequently, difficult living conditions are not only uncomfortable, but they attack her sense of self-esteem.

In contrast, difficult living conditions are not as often a threat to her husband. Adjusting to the host culture can ultimately produce satisfaction for him because it helps his work. But if the wife becomes like the local people, she is thereby failing to maintain the standard trained into her by her home country.

On the other hand, a missionary wife's personal goals may enable her to have more "success" in the long run than her husband. Because maintaining the home and caring for and sometimes educating the child take so much time, she may limit herself to such additional tasks as sewing classes, dispensary or local public health programs, and small scale literacy instruction. These are much more likely to be accomplished successfully than her husband's goals of making converts, developing an indigenous church, or training effective Christian leaders, which are more subject to factors outside his control.

4. Inner Spiritual Resources

One's *inner spiritual resources,* including the power of Christ and His Spirit, constitute an important factor in reducing stress (II Pet 1:3,4; Philem 4:13). But, however available these are by faith, they don't really help until the benefits and power of these resources become a reality in the life of that individual. This may require spiritual renewal.

It is recognized that this analysis is tentative. There may be *unknown factors* that have not been mentioned that could be most important of all in producing or reducing culture stress.

Other Stresses Add to Culture Stress

There are other kinds of stress present in a village situation which add to the stress of acculturation. Oberg (1960:179) mentioned some of these. The most important in the first year or so is *culture confusion,* the disorientation from loss of cultural cues mentioned above. Adjustments to tropical heat, new health hazards and danger from animals are stressful, especially to parents of small children. Such things as using pressure lamps instead of unlimited electric lighting, having woven or mud walls instead of painted ones, shortages of water, and the presence of cockroaches, scorpions, rats or snakes in the house can cause stress. New roles, loneliness, a new work load and new responsibilities, problems in travel, and supply difficulties are all stressful.

Children's health is the most frequently expressed fear of a western mother. Child molesting is another great fear.

Single women linguists in an isolated village find role conflicts a special problem. In the first place, they must be very self-reliant, often doing tasks such as plumbing, carpentry, and generator repairs that would be a man's job in the home country. Women liberationists might like this, but most women are not prepared for it.

Much more serious is the conflict between the requirements of their work and the role of a woman in village cultures. In Papua New Guinea, women are expected to keep busy gardening and raising pigs and are under the authority of their brothers or husbands. They do not teach men, supervise their work, talk as equals with community leaders, or know religious secrets. Only bad girls remain single and talk frequently with men. But the linguist's work requires them to teach literacy to men, to do desk work instead of gardening, and to be somewhat independent of community leaders. The language helpers they employ usually must be men, for women are too busy with gardening for consistent employment and too low in prestige to introduce translated Scripture effectively.

The only solution seems to be to avoid fitting completely into a woman's role in the host culture. Instead, a woman must establish a new role which, in terms of local role expectations, is neutral or even somewhat masculine. This facilitates the work but may result in internal conflicts in the single woman.

Added to the cultural and environmental stresses might be any of the normal life stresses which are experienced by people anywhere, such as emotional problems from childhood frustrations, marriage, problem children, and living and working with colleagues from different backgrounds and with different personalities. It has been demonstrated that any change, even a beneficial one, causes its measure of stress *(Time* March 1, 1971:43).

Since the emotional loading of culture stress is essentially no different from any other kind of stress, all of these add together to produce the resulting load on the individual. A formula for this might be:

$$\begin{array}{ccccccc} \text{Culture} & & \text{Culture} & & \text{Other} & & \text{Total} \\ \text{Stress} & + & \text{Confusion} & + & \text{Stresses} & = & \text{Stress} \end{array}$$

An individual can easily cope with a certain amount of stress. In fact, some psychologists hold that man needs a moderate amount of tension to work productively (Spradley and Phillips, 1972:520). But as stress increases, more and more creative energy must be used to handle it.

Most long-term workers in foreign countries have been screened by some sending organization and are able to cope with a large amount of stress. Nevertheless, culture stress remains a significant problem. Of over two hundred Westerners we have known who have lived in Papua New Guinea villages for long periods of time, about 10% have suffered reactions from stress which have seriously hindered their work and even the work of some of their co-workers. In most instances cultural stress seems to have been the main cause. These reactions included incapacitating fatigue, physical illness, emotional symptoms, and work and living habits which prevented them working with reasonable productivity. Another 15% were seriously hindered by these same symptoms, but the extent to which stress was a precipitating factor is uncertain. Another 70% seem to have experienced varying degrees of stress, but have found solutions without extensive hindrance to their work. The remaining 5% do not appear to have been affected by culture stress.

These variations underscore the fact that individual reactions to stress vary widely. Individuals vary in temperament and emotional security and in patterns of operation of psychological defense mechanisms. If one perceives difficulties as a personal threat, his reaction will be more severe than if he perceives them merely as obstacles to be overcome (Lehner and Kube, 1955:102, 104).

When stress overloads the individual's psychological defense system, he can go into a state of emotional shock or even breakdown. (This process is explained in S.Dye, 1974). The state of emotional shock resulting from culture stress could logically be called "culture shock," except that "culture shock" is widely used as a cover term for all of "the difficulties and frustrations of living in a foreign culture" (Spradley and Phillips, 1972:520). Confusion between these two senses of the term is one reason that very few people ever admit to experiencing culture shock.

Ways to Decrease Culture Stress

The following suggestions, based on factors in the formula, are not necessarily new but provide ways for an individual to decrease stress in a contact situation.

1. Recognize the Culture Stress

Recognize that culture stress is inevitable in cross-cultural contact. Everyone experiences it to some degree depending upon the intensity of the contact. When stress occurs, it must be recognized for what it is — ordinary stress. If one's father has just died, his wife is in the hospital, and he is left with the four children, and on that day he has a minor collision, he should not be surprised at being a bit irritable and overly tired and unable to work at full efficiency. Under these conditions one has been taught to say, "That's understandable. I'm under stress. I'll have to make allowances for myself for awhile." All his friends recognize his situation and make allowances for him, too.

But when one is suffering from culture stress, he may simply push on as if nothing happened, leaving his mind's censoring system to make all the adjustments. The consequence is a psychological chain reaction which eventually results in culture fatigue, illness, or emotional symptoms. Most of this chain reaction can be avoided by conscious recognition of the fact that one is facing stress.

To look for stress one might ask himself questions like these: Have a lot of irritating things happened lately? Have the local people been doing unusually inexplicable things? Does the work load seem mountainous? Have I become indignant more frequently? Are there more problems than usual? Have certain colleagues become especially unpleasant or unfair? Would a vacation really be nice, though out of the question with my work load? Do I seem nervous? Is it unusually hard to sleep? Have headaches or backaches or indigestion been more frequent? Each person must recognize his or her own characteristic stress symptoms and look for the cause.

This is usually more difficult for men in western culture than for women. A man is trained to ignore difficulties and never to complain about stress, even to himself. It is acceptable for a woman to admit discomfort and difficulty, so women are more often aware of stress and can do something about it. Men suffer also but bottle it up to react in more indirect ways.

2. Escape

Since involvement is a key factor in culture stress, temporary escape is an effective remedy. One can escape from an alien culture and a difficult living situation at the same time. Temporary escape in light reading, music, or sports is not a new idea. We and our colleagues have often proven its effectiveness.

During our first two years in a village, my wife and I never seemed to complete enough work during a week to "justify" taking time off on Saturdays. The work was burdensome and progress was poor. Finally we decided to take hikes in the forest every Saturday "for the children's sake," even though our week's work was not complete. We soon found that significantly more work was getting done in five days than we had been doing in six.

More complete escape is also important. One should be disciplined to take vacations and make them as much a relaxing escape as possible. Time and money spent on getting completely away from our normal surroundings, or even from the host culture, and in doing something really enjoyable is actually a far-sighted investment in the work.

Many people feel guilty about rest times but a pattern of life that includes daily, weekly, and annual relaxation usually results in diminished stress and, therefore, much greater effectiveness during work periods. This is particularly true with missionaries for whom success is more a result of love and joy manifested to one's neighbors than it is to getting a certain amount of work done.

3. Decrease Frustration

The frustration factor can be decreased by increasing one's sense of accomplishment. The most effective way to do this is to set realistic goals that can be achieved. Missionaries and academic researchers in particular frequently come to the field with great ideals and ambitious goals. Goals must be based upon the real situation or the continuous frustration of these unattainable goals will greatly increase the emotional conflict.

Since success will decrease stress, one should divide the work into short term (weekly and monthly) goals that are realistic and can be achieved, as well as keeping reasonable yearly goals and flexible long-term goals. Accomplishing these goals will increase the satisfaction in the work and decrease the sense of frustration and failure.

When one organization began encouraging its translators to count Bible verses completed instead of books, many of them were much encouraged. A printed chart was distributed which showed exactly how many verses are in each New Testament book and that book's percentage of the whole. Formerly, only a few people took the trouble to measure their progress toward a translated New Testament. Now everyone's progress is measurable, realistic goals can be set and achieved, and the New Testament no longer seems like a lifetime job.

One must also be aware of how often the "interruptions" are more important to long-term goals than "the work." This is often the case when a teacher is approached by a student while preparing a lecture, or when a government officer is visited by a village leader, or when an agriculturalist is interrupted to explain about a crop which he is not planning to introduce. Missionaries especially need to be sensitive to the opportunities presented by such "interruptions".

4. Build Acceptance

One must recognize that most of his own cultural values are not absolute. A missionary must, in addition, carefully identify which of his long-held "Christian" values are really just values of his own culture; as a Christian he can only justify holding tightly to those values that are specifically commanded in the Bible. Since the tremendous variety of peoples and cultures around the world are all equally a part of God's creation, one must learn to accept and appreciate another people's set of values as valid for their lives, just as my American values are largely valid for my life in the United States. Learning as much as possible about the host culture builds understanding and appreciation of the reasons for their customs. Reading about many other cultures in books or magazines can help condition one to accept the specific culture where one is a guest.

5. Improve Communication

Larson and Smalley have shown (1971:43) how the ability to communicate meaningfully with one's hosts decreases stress. For this reason, it may be less stressful in the long run to plunge in and learn the language, even though language learning itself causes stress. In a recent survey (Spradley and Phillips, 1972:524), 83 Peace Corps veterans rated language difference as almost twice as serious as any other cause of culture stress.

Language learning is only a part of communication, however. As is true in one's own culture, one can know the language perfectly but be unable to communicate genuinely with others. This is related to attitudes of respect and eagerness to listen to others. It requires learning the host culture's system of gestures and facial expressions, their rules of conduct and etiquette, and what all kinds of life experiences mean to them (Hesselgrave, 1972:9).

6. Strengthen Emotional Security

Emotional security requires self-acceptance and self-forgiveness. But both of these must begin with self-awareness, because one's unconscious mind is constantly reacting to one's limitations and past failures (Smalley, 1963:55). Genuine self-acceptance recognizes and finds a way to live with these limitations. Self-forgiveness deliberately quits accusing or punishing oneself for these failures. For Christians this can be achieved by a deep awareness of God's forgiveness. Participating in sharing groups with these purposes and confession have both helped many people become emotionally secure.

One can also be strengthened by encouragement and other supportive measures from one's colleagues. Receiving understanding and love are especially valuable when one's inner self seems to be under attack, as it does during adjustment to a new culture.

Several excellent books on this topic have appeared recently. I found *I'm O.K. You're O.K.* (Harris, 1967) and *The Art of Understanding Yourself* (Osborne, 1967) especially helpful.

For many anthropologists the process of learning the new culture builds up their self-confidence, instead of threatening their emotional security. The same is true of linguists who make good progress in learning and analyzing the language of the host culture. This seems to happen unconsciously. For anthropologists this is a result not only of their achieving specific research goals, but also of their growth in "objectivity" and cross-cultural understanding.

But one can do this consciously by realizing that he is really a kind of bi-cultural or multi-cultural person, capable of operating within more than one cultural milieu and playing more than one role. When in the home country he is able to live as its citizens live. When in a village of the host culture, he can live like the people in that village and play the appropriate role while in that environment. When among colleagues in the city or on a mission compound, he can change roles again and live like those in that community.

For example, when in the village, my wife is accepted as an equal with the women. She dresses similarly to them and is called by the appropriate name, though she is respected for her teaching and her western medical knowledge. They relate to her in this role. But in the European town where our children attend school, she is a mother and refers all medical problems to the medical doctor. She is one of the Bible translators. All her daily routines, living style and relationships are different. When in the home country on furlough, she has yet another role vis-à-vis our home constituency. Each of these roles is a part of her personality, but not one of them is the total.

You may be a missionary, a parent, a husband, a teacher and an employer. You do not have a split personality. You can shift from one role to another without difficulty because each is part of you.

As acculturation is faced in these ways, one can become such a versatile person that he can adjust to any of the two or more cultures he has learned to live in. So the sum of his personality is more than any one of these alone. Instead of becoming a less proper American (or Englishman or whatever), he is actually becoming a kind of world citizen, a more capable human being. If he is a missionary, he can say, "So I become all things to all men, that I may save some by any means possible" (I Cor 9:22 TEV).

References Cited

Brewster, E. Thomas and Elizabeth S.
1972   "Involvement as a Means of Second Culture Learning" *Practical Anthropology* 19, 1:27-44

Dye, Sally Folger
1974   "Decreasing Fatigue and Illness in Field-Work" *Missiology* Vol. II, 1

Harris, Thomas A.
1967   *I'm O.K. – You're O.K.* New York, Harper & Row

Hesselgrave, David J.
1972   "Dimensions of Cross-Cultural Community" *Practical Anthropology* 19, 1:1-12

Honigmann, John J.
1967   *Personality in Culture* New York, Harper & Row Publishers

Larson, Donald N. and William A. Smalley
1972   *Becoming Bilingual: A Guide to Language Learning* Ann Arbor, Cushing — Malloy, Inc.

Lehner, George F.J. and Ella Kube
1955   *The Dynamics of Personal Adjustment* Englewood Cliffs, Prentice-Hall, Inc.

Oberg, Kalervo
1960   "Cultural Shock: Adjustment to New Cultural Environments" *Practical Anthropology* 7, 4:177-182

Osborne, Cecil
1967   *The Art of Understanding Yourself* Grand Rapids, Zondervan Publishing House

Pike, Kenneth
1967   *Stir, Change, Create* Grand Rapids, William B. Eerdmans Publishing Co.

Smalley, William A.
1963   "Culture Shock, Language Shock, and the Shock of Self-Discovery" *Practical Anthropology* 10, 2:49-56

Spradley, James P. and Mark Phillips
1972   "Culture and Stress: A Quantitative Analysis" *American Anthropologist* 74, 3:518-529

Taber, Charles R.
1971   "The Missionary Ghetto" *Practical Anthropology* 18, 5:193-196

[Another relevant book is:
Henry, Frances and Satish Saberwal, editors
1969   *Stress and Response in Fieldwork* New York, Holt, Rinehart and Winston -- Ed.]

Obtaining Linguistic Data

Alan Healey

When undertaking the study of a previously unwritten language it is vital to start off on the right footing with the people who speak that language. Care must be given to foster and maintain good relations with them.

An early and vigorous attempt to learn and speak the vernacular is the best demonstration of the sincerity of one's interest in the vernacular. In fact, if one's study of the vernacular is to extend more than a few weeks, then conversational fluency in the vernacular is invaluable to grammatical investigations and worthy of top priority for the first few months of field work. An important condition for conversational fluency is adequate opportunity to hear and participate in conversations with as many different people as possible. This may best be achieved by living in a village, or right beside the largest hamlet in an area, or on the busiest road in an area at a place where people stop for water or shade, or close to a place where people gather daily. Alternatively, conversational practice may be gained by daily visiting places where there are lots of people, taking short trips with people, or sharing in people's various tasks——in such a way as not to hinder their work for an employer or for subsistence.

Particularly in the early stages of language learning and data collecting, it is important not to rely on a single paid helper, but to work with many different people on an informal basis. This will allow you to give your main attention to language learning rather than being committed to several hours of desk work each day with a paid assistant. It will also allow you to get to know many different people and their particular linguistic abilities as they try to help you learn their language. Then by the time you are ready to settle down to regular formal language research, you have a much better idea of which people are potential research assistants. During this informal stage it is unwise to pay cash for help given with language learning. However, it is good to let people know that you appreciate the trouble they are going to to teach you, by giving them appropriate non-cash gifts from time to time.

Later on, when you have regular paid assistants, it is still good to spend a proportion of your time collecting linguistic data from a wide variety of people by informal means. You will get spontaneous data of a kind that often cannot be elicited in a formal session, and it will constitute an independent check on the reliability and naturalness of what you have elicited.

Employing Research Assistants

Normally, a research assistant should be over 15 (preferably 20) years of age and of the same sex as the field worker. In some areas it is socially acceptable for a single woman field worker to employ a male assistant, but in other areas it is not.

When you look for assistants, choose those who are patient with your slow progress, who always correct your errors, who stick at a tiring job until it is done, who are alert and imaginative, who are generally intelligent, and whose temperaments are compatible with your own. As you work with them and as you train them you will come to value the particular abilities and contribution of each one.

Language research is usually a many-faceted project involving several different kinds of activity. If you employ several different assistants, each for one day per week, then you stand to benefit from the variety of skills they have to offer you. One may be patient at helping transcribe texts, another may be adept at explaining meanings, a third may be untiring and accurate in checking tonal contrasts, and a fourth may take a keen interest in checking out the transformation possibilities of grammatical constructions. Few people have all of these skills, so build up a team to do the total job.

The wages for a research assistant should be consistent with the locally accepted rate for a person of his age and education. If he has not been to school, the rate should be somewhat higher than for a laborer because of the greater prestige involved and because rural peoples often consider sitting down answering questions harder work than physical labor. The assistant deserves payment, not for the hours he spends with you, but rather for the hours he spends away from his means of livelihood. For instance, if a man spends only the mornings doing language work with me, but is away from his agriculture for a whole day because his gardens are a considerable distance from the village and

because rain regularly prevents him from gardening in the
afternoons, then I feel responsible for a whole day's wages.
Some anthropologists warn against paying directly for the
quantity of information or texts that an assistant supplies,
and against paying such a high wage as to embarrass other
employers in the area.

Even though you may have several different assistants,
it is usually best to work with just one of them at a time.
When two assistants are used simultaneously, any friction
between them is likely to detract from the linguistic value
of the session. To avoid friction it is important to use
assistants from the same village or clan to ensure their
dialectal uniformity, and it is advisable to interrogate
them with meticulous alternation. In some social situations, however, it may prove necessary to have two assistants——an intelligent young man acting as spokesman and an
old man of some status and experience acting as censor and
consultant.

Employing the one person for both household service and
regular language work may not be very satisfactory. He is
often needed for both tasks at the same time. He tends to
get tired, and a sleepy research assistant is completely
unreliable. The linguist finds it very difficult to maintain
two kinds of inter-personal relationship to the same person
simultaneously——a distant disciplinarian and a friendly co-
worker.

Work sessions should be arranged to suit your assistant's
daily routine. You should be punctual, lest you give the
impression that you don't really value his help and you consider yourself superior to him. Avoid keeping him waiting
while you trivialize. Work sessions should not be longer
than one hour, and a break of 15 minutes between sessions is
advisable. A person who has not been to school and who has
not done language work before may find that one half-hour
session is all that he can bear at first.

You should explain to each new helper, especially casual
ones, what you are doing and why. If a tape recorder is used
it is essential to demonstrate it first with your own voice
or that of a local person familiar with it. Someone who has
not seen or heard a recorder before is likely to be scared
of it, supposing that it will steal his soul or that it contains the voice of his ancestors. Sometimes linguists have
even found it necessary to explain the process of writing
and the purpose of their note-taking.

You should be sensitive to the feelings of your research assistant. When he makes a complaint or offers a suggestion, listen carefully and act upon it in some positive way. When he gives you data which you suspect is "wrong", accept it and use it. It will usually turn out to be more correct than you thought, especially from the assistant's point of view. When he seems hesitant in giving a response to your linguistic inquiry, do not press him to say something for the sake of getting data. His very hesitation is significant. If you are asking him to confirm or choose between forms that you have presented to him, do not browbeat him into agreeing with your opinion. It is HIS language, HE is the authority, so keep silent and wait for him to say whatever he wishes. THE VERNACULAR SPEAKER IS ALWAYS RIGHT. Respect his knowledge, opinions, beliefs, customs, and dignity.

Training Research Assistants

Although there are differences of aptitude from helper to helper, it is nevertheless true that good research assistants are not born, they are trained. And giving this training is one of the major responsibilities of the field worker. Developing countries are no longer willing to allow Western scholars to run a one-man research project, take the data back home, write a dissertation, and receive all the honor and salary increases. Not only do they insist that copies of the data and dissertation must be given to the government, but that the field worker must train some nationals in at least some facets of his discipline and research methods.

To train an assistant in a new task, first show him how to perform the operation on straightforward materials, and give him practice until he has mastered the basic procedure. Then gradually introduce him to materials of increasing complexity and the more elaborate procedures required to handle them. Eventually, he should not only be able to perform the particular task without any guidance from you, but he should be able to do the task better than you can (with more speed, accuracy, or insight).

There is a wide variety of tasks that research assistants can be trained to do, depending on their abilities and interests. The training program should continue until an assistant has gained several skills. These should include, if possible, one skill that he can use in other employment once your research project has finished. For example, typing or editing.

Tasks for Research Assistants

The tasks listed below have all been taught to research assistants from time to time. They are presented in an approximate order of increasing difficulty.

(1) Giving narrative, procedural, descriptive, expository, and hortatory texts to a tape recorder.

(2) Listening to a tape-recorded text then re-telling it to a tape recorder.

(3) Giving both sides of an imaginary conversation to a tape recorder.

(4) Using a tape recorder to interview significant people in the community and to record their legends, autobiographies, opinions, cultural expositions, etc.

(5) Producing natural utterances to correct the field worker's stumbling attempts in the vernacular, and then explain their meanings to him.

(6) Listing all the words and idioms he can think of in a given semantic domain and explaining the meaning of each one.

(7) Providing sentences which exemplify the various uses of a particular word or grammatical construction.

(8) Translating the lingua franca in response to questions of the type "How do you say, 'John went to the market yesterday'?"

(9) Reading and writing. This is a prerequisite to some of the other tasks below.

(10) Typing. If this is adopted as a substitute for writing, then it saves someone on the research team one extra step.

(11) Transcribing text onto paper (in handwriting or typescript) from a tape recording.

(12) Testing words to determine their pitch or stress pattern or their morphophonemic sub-class.

(13) Listing words that contain a particular phoneme, sequence, or contrast.

(14) Testing the acceptable permutations of a sentence.

(15) Testing the acceptable paraphrases of a sentence.

(16) Editing texts that are either poorly composed or that have been transcribed exactly as spoken.

(17) Understanding linguistic concepts and theory. Though this can be taught day-by-day as he is working on research in his own language, there may be some psychological advantage in presenting a more traditional course in introductory linguistics with assignment problems to solve from a variety of languages.

(18) Testing the acceptable fillers in the slots of a construction.

(19) Sorting out forms (inflected words, phrases, clauses, or sentences) according to their grammatical structure.

(20) Conjoining two clauses.

(21) Embedding one clause within another.

(22) Analyzing a sentence into its underlying clauses.

(23) Identifying the semantic roles of the grammatical slots in a particular clause.

(24) Writing a description of a particular morphophonemic rule.

(25) Writing semantic definitions of words for a dictionary.

(26) Writing self-clarifying sentences to illustrate words in a dictionary.

(27) Describing a phoneme system.

(28) Describing a system of affixes.

(29) Describing a construction in terms of its slots, fillers, permutations, and structural meaning.

(30) Describing a small set of grammatical rules in the TG model.

(31) Identify and describe the ambiguity in an utterance, and the corresponding underlying structures.

(32) Identify and describe the several different meanings of a word and for each one indicate its synonyms and collocations.

   As a research assistant shows ability and is trained to do more and more of the above tasks, his role is gradually changing from that of an assistant to that of an independent researcher. He began as your employee but is fast becoming your colleague. Recognize this fact and make sure that you publicly acknowledge his major contribution to the research project. If the results are published he should probably be named as a co-author with you.

Investigating Phonology

It has been found best to limit the number of repetitions of an utterance to three or four. Most people quickly
tire of multiple repetitions and get bored with the work
session; some are inclined to lose interest in linguistic
work altogether because of the field worker's apparent dull-
ness of hearing. Furthermore, continued repetitions of an
utterance rapidly decrease in linguistic value because of
the appearance of tired allophones and intonation patterns,
and because in such artificial circumstances the speaker's
acoustic image of the utterance becomes disassociated from
his semantic image of it, with a consequent uncontrolled
drift in pronunciation that may involve changes of phonemes.
It is no longer a meaningful utterance, but a string of
nonsense syllables. This phenomenon is one reason why you
should make some positive identification of the meaning of
each utterance, rather than rely solely upon the sameness
or difference of their meanings.

When phonological details and contrasts tax your abilities (which happens more often than most of us care to admit)
further repetitions of the crucial utterances can be obtained on several different days. It is wise to put the material
being studied into different contexts so that you won't be
so biased by your memory of a previous session, and so that
your assistant won't take these repeated inquiries as an
insult to his consistency or correctness in speaking his
own language. If you tape-record all that he gives you,
you can then have endless repetitions without tiring him.
Often, when working with difficult phonetics, your brain
will tire and refuse to register previously-identified items
consistently, or refuse to hear the contrast at all. At
this point, or preferably before it is reached, it is expedi-
ent to quit. The matter may be returned to later at another
time.

When eliciting material for a problematic contrast it
is best to establish the contrast with sub-minimal pairs of
utterances, and especially so in the case of prosodic contrasts. Minimal pairs are excellent for demonstrating the
contrast once it has been convincingly established without
them. If minimal pairs that you can barely distinguish are
used at the beginning of the investigation, then it is essential to be meticulous in specifying or requesting the meaning
of every utterance. If you use the utterance in the vernacular to tell your assistant what to say, then it is easy for
him to misunderstand your poor pronunciation and to give the

other utterance instead of the one you intended. This confusion can be avoided by using synonyms of the minimally
contrasting utterances when giving vernacular instructions,
or by using non-linguistic stimuli such as actions or objects,
or sketches of actions or objects, in a way pre-arranged
with your assistant. If he is bilingual, instructions for
uttering minimal pairs can be given in the second language
to avoid confusion. When minimal pairs are difficult for
you to hear, the speaker will often give two or more utterances in close succession——either two the same in an attempt
to help you hear it correctly, or two contrasting utterances
to help you hear the difference between them. Until you
have "tuned in" to the particular contrast, you are just as
likely to assume that two contrasting utterances were the
same or that two identical utterances were different, unless
you take care always to ask your assistant to identify the
meaning of each utterance.

A lot of confusion can be avoided in phonemic analysis
if a complete phonemicization is made for the speech of
just one speaker of the language, especially for phonemic
systems with several hard-to-hear sounds or systems involving
complex interrelated decisions. The speech of other people,
with its variant allophones and allophonic distribution,
may then be compared with this and a fuller picture of the
phonology of the language be gained. All phonological data
needs to be clearly labeled with the name and dialect of
the speaker.

As an aid in hearing pitch, some linguists have suggested teaching one's assistant to hum or whistle the tonal pattern of each utterance. However, I have found this of limited value. When the field worker finds pitch difficult to
hear in utterances, he resorts to this method because he
finds it rather easier to hear with humming or whistling.
However, the very difficulties he experiences in hearing the
tonal patterns of utterances will also prevent him from determining how these hard-to-hear utterance patterns correspond with the easier-to-hear humming or whistling patterns.
Without an understanding of this correspondence, the humming
or whistling patterns are of little value for analysis.
Their main usefulness is to confirm patterns which the field
worker has already tentatively identified in utterances,
to clarify his occasional hearing problems, and to identify
tonal morphophonemics and intonation.

For conversational fluency, you have to learn to recognize and reproduce all of the phonemic distinctions of the

language including those which you find difficult to hear.
Tape-recordings, spectrograms, tone analyzers, humming and
whistling, or any other techniques only give temporary help
in recognizing or demonstrating particular contrasts and
features. Ultimately, you have to teach yourself to hear
and make such distinctions unaided. Linguistics provides no
magic carpet to conversational fluency, but rather a map of
the best routes one can walk over a difficult terrain.

Investigating Grammar Monolingually

In a monolingual situation you are cast very much upon
your own resourcefulness and powers of observation. At the
beginning you can use pointing and miming extensively, and
in fact these devices can be used for years as a method of
checking data obtained in other ways. Some linguists make
considerable use of pictures, especially series of related
pictures that tell some kind of story or that may be described by some kind of grammatical paradigm. I have found
pictures fairly satisfactory the few times I have used them
with sophisticated people. However, those who have had
little or no contact with education often fail to recognize
the type of line drawings I present to them. In particular,
sketches of natural species tend not to be recognized unless
they are exact in much more detail than most of us see, and
unless they are life size.

The most vital element of linguistic field work is constant observation, and in a monolingual situation this is
doubly true. If each new kind of utterance heard is noted
down, further inquiry can be made later concerning its meaning and more examples of its structure can be elicited.
Only by being constantly alert to hear what people actually
say to each other can you have an early way of checking the
accuracy of what people say to you. Some field workers have
had the experience of a whole community trying to make
language-learning easier for them by talking to them in a
trade-pidgin or otherwise simplified version of their language. The sooner such a deception is discovered and corrected the better. It has been suggested that one should
deliberately check for this situation in the early days of
field work by having a young man repeat some of his utterances to an old man and watch for the old man's expressions
of approval or disapproval or for any changes he might suggest. An old man is likely to be insulted if a young man
addresses him in the trade-pidgin.

The elicitation of grammatically relevant data by monolingual means is not easy. In fact, at times it seems to be

more efficient to observe than to elicit. That is, it is
relatively easy to be always alert for new grammatical
features and examples of features that are not fully understood. Starting from such data, you are able to inquire
about the meanings of utterances containing such features
and obtain more examples of their occurance. On the other
hand, monolingual eliciting for the vernacular equivalent
of a particular grammatical feature of English can be much
more difficult.

     As you attempt to elicit specific grammatical features
(or vocabulary) you will be using all of your ingenuity to
convey to your assistant what you are searching for. He
on his part will often be puzzled by your efforts and will
be trying to guess at what you want. When he does respond
you must be careful to show appreciation, mimic what he has
said, and write it down. Even if you are certain that it is
not the thing you are searching for, it is nevertheless a
valid piece of the language and your assistant worked hard
to produce it. On no account should you show disappointment
in your facial expression, tone of voice, or subsequent neglect of that piece of data.

     If you find a particular grammatical feature difficult
to control while eliciting any kind of paradigm, then you
are well advised to use some vernacular free word as a
collocational control. For instance, in studying Telefol I
used _amsin sin ilo_ 'the day before yesterday' in eliciting
to make sure that verbs were given in the near past tense
rather than in any of the other four past tenses. In bilingual elicitation either vernacular or trade-language words
can be used as controls.

     Another technique for investigating the meaning and
usage of a function morpheme is that of contrastive elicitation. In this method you ask your assistant to compare the
meanings of two utterances (either previously observed, or
manufactured by you on the spot), one of which contains the
function morpheme under investigation and the other differs
only by the lack of that morpheme or by its substitution by
another similar morpheme of slightly different meaning.
Contrastive elicitation can also be used with features of
syntactic order.·

     Exploratory eliciting involves setting as clear a cul-
tural context as possible and then saying some utterance
based on inadequately understood grammar. Many assistants
will correlate the context and your attempt to say something,

deduce what you are wanting to say, and tell you how one
says such a thing. Utterances elicited in this way need to
be compared with several other such utterances (elicited in
this or other ways) to detect any distortions arising from
your "errors" in the stimulus utterance. The meanings of
such utterances need to be elicited separately. Whenever
exploratory eliciting is used, it is best to note down the
fact that the assistant considered a particular attempted
utterance to be incorrect, partly as a record of the direction in which the "correct" utterance he gave you may be
biased, and partly as a source of negative clues to grammatical structure.

Situational elicitation involves describing a physical
or social situation in some detail and then asking what a
particular participant or observer would be likely to say
in such a situation. Of course, your description needs to
be true to the culture. Often, utterances obtained in this
way will not have the meanings you were attempting to elicit,
so need to be checked, both then and later, for their meanings. When using situational elicitation with someone who
is bilingual, I have often found it helpful to precede the
description of the situation by a trade-language statement
of the utterance I am trying to elicit. The description of
the situation, because it is the longer and later element
in the elicitation process, tends to remain the main stimulus. The trade-language statement prefaced to it merely
helps to narrow down the helper's choice between the hundreds
of different utterances possible in most situations.

Pronouns are best obtained by careful observation. If
the language contains several series of pronouns, once the
commonest series is known in full this may be used as a basis
for eliciting another full series whenever a pronoun of some
new series is observed. In this way I eventually elicited
some 17 series of Telefol pronouns, even though only a few
of the individual pronouns in the later series were ever
observed in text. When eliciting pronouns through the trade
language, you can assume that the average person will not
actually translate all the pronouns, but will interchange
second and first person. The second person can usually be
identified with certainty if you and your helper both address your remarks to another person. The person of possessive pronouns can usually be identified with certainty
by asking who is the owner of some real thing that belongs
to your assistant, something of yours, and so on through
all the possible persons and numbers.

   Questions are the single most useful items in gaining
conversational fluency and in eliciting grammatical material
from monolingual speakers, as well as constituting a major
section of the grammar of a language. Often, the features
that signal interrogation differ from one question to the
next so that your knowledge of the syntax of statements does
not always permit you to form the corresponding questions by
analogy. In a monolingual situation several questions may
be obtained quite early in field work by careful observation.
Monolingual elicitation is also possible. The presentation
of hidden objects or persons and the performing of hidden
actions may stimulate people to ask "What is it?" "Who is
it?" "What are you doing?". Miming a losing-and-searching
situation often evokes "Where is it?", and setting out on
some unusual route will prompt people to ask "Where are you
going?". "Why" and "when" questions require rather more
ingenuity for monolingual elicitation. Once a few questions
have been learned other questions may be obtained either by
exploratory eliciting or situational eliciting. When you
ask someone who is bilingual to give the translation in
the vernacular of a particular trade-language question, he
may answer the question instead of translating it. This
situation can be avoided by formulating the inquiry so that
the bilingual imagines he is asking the linguist or a third
person the question, rather than himself being asked the
question.

   To ensure that one's data include several examples of
each grammatical feature, systematic elicitation of grammatical material is necessary. One way of doing this is to
take a text and go through it word by word, and for each new
morpheme or construction discovered in it, to elicit several
(5 to 20 say) more utterances containing the particular feature. It is good if your assistant can see the systematic
nature of the elicitation, for his intelligent cooperation
can cut the time and frustration involved in early monolingual elicitation to a fraction. When a new feature is discovered it is good to follow it up immediately, while the
semantic or grammatical context appropriate to it is still
fresh in your assistant's mind. Doing so also helps fix the
discovery in your mind for further reference. This means
that work sessions may at times appear rather disorganized
by digressions, but in this way you can get a more balanced
collection of data than if you rigidly follow through your
prepared elicitation program. If your assistant can see
that you are alert he will do his best work.

Paradigmatic elicitation is commonly used for the systematic investigation of grammatical features. In this
method you attempt to elicit a series of utterances which
are identical except for one point in their structure where
a class of morphemes are interchanged. If picture series or
situational eliciting are used the paradigms can be expected
to be fairly reliable, but if exploratory eliciting or bilingual eliciting are used there is a considerable likeli-
hood that a few false forms may be given. You need to be
alert for any hesitancy or facial expression as a clue to
false forms. If you ask whether a particular form is used
in the vernacular, some people will say "yes" just to please
you, even though the purported form be a false one. Any
assistant is likely to be somewhat influenced by hearing
the utterance from your mouth, and from time to time he
may suggest that such an utterance may be used. Some linguists feel that one can never be sure how much the assistant has been influenced by the forms used in the process
of exploratory or bilingual eliciting, and wish to avoid
these methods of eliciting. However, such types of paradigmatic eliciting do speed up the understanding of the
rarer features of the grammar which are just as much a part
of the language's system as are those which occur more frequently. Most of the biased responses can be detected as
inconsistencies if you elicit the same material on several
different occasions and in several different settings.
These false forms can be identified by further checking;
when you inquire into their meaning or usage your assistant
may insist that they are wrong or he may cast doubt on their
acceptability by "You can say that if you like but I've
never heard people say it." or "Only children talk that way."

The main emphasis here has been upon methods of investigating grammar in a monolingual situation because these
methods are applicable far beyond the bounds of these situations. Many a linguist working bilingually finds, at some
point in his grammatical inquiries, that either he or his
assistant has an inadequate grasp of the trade-language for
such detailed investigations. At this point monolingual
methods have to be resorted to.

Determining Meanings

Perhaps the commonest weakness in bilingual translation
elicitation of the "How do you say" type is that, when
either the field worker or his assistant have an inadequate
knowledge of the trade language, the vernacular utterance
is not necessarily an accurate translation of the English

utterance that the field worker had in mind when he began
eliciting. The best remedy is always to ask your assistant
to translate his vernacular utterance back into the trade-
language. Write this trade-language form down as the
"meaning" of the vernacular rather than the original English
utterance that you started with. As you gain a better understanding of your assistant's idiolect of the trade-language
you are in a better position to translate such "meanings"
into English. Thus back-translation can be used not merely
as a checking device, but as the primary technique for determining meaning.

Several observations or occurrences of a grammatical
feature are of more value than a single observation or occurrence. Usually a single occurrence of an item provides
only very ambiguous information about the meaning or grammatical behavior of that item. To ascertain the meaning
of a stem often requires 10 or 20 occurrences of it and a
good deal of explanation of the cultural contexts of its
usage. To ascertain the meaning of a function morpheme
often requires 50 or 100 occurrences of it and considerable
investigation into which grammatical features co-occur with
it. You should expect that some of the function morphemes
of the vernacular will have no translation equivalent in
English, and that some will have several disparate translation equivalents. When working with a bilingual helper
you need to be patient when he is unable to explain the meaning or usage of a function morpheme. Do not press him to do
so. In these circumstances you need a large number of examples of the morpheme in a wide range of occurrences, and
it is your analysis of these that will provide a basis for
guessing at the meaning and making further inquiry. (A con-
cordance of texts is very valuable for this purpose, if you
have one.)

When noting questions that have been observed, it is
important to note also their replies if possible. Once you
understand the paradigmatic variations of a question, you
are then in a position to use this type of question in conversation and to note down the responses. You may also ask
your assistant to give you several typical replies to each
question. The meanings of these responses and replies will
provide the clearest picture of the meaning of the question
which stimulated them.

It is good to note down new words that are heard, even
when there is no indication of their meanings. It is far
easier to elicit examples and the meaning of a word that has

been observed than to elicit the word for a particular meaning that interests you. When inquiring about the area of
meaning of a word or checking on its collocations, it has
been found of only limited usefulness to ask whether or not
that word can be used in a given situation, since every now
and then your helper will say "Yes" when he should have said
"No"—either to please you or to hasten the end of a session
that involves too much hard thinking for him. It seems
preferable to ask him in what situations the particular word
can be used and to request illustrations.

When investigating the meanings of a set of near synonyms I have found the following procedure useful. Taking
each word in turn, inquiry is made as to the situations in
which it is used. Next, a composite list is made of all the
situations mentioned for all the words in the set. Then,
for each situation in turn, I ask which words of the set can
be used in that particular situation, then I inquire whether
their meanings are the same or different in that situation.

When testing for collocations it is good to get several
typical utterances on several occasions to insure a good
spread of meaning variants and usage. For each verb it is
necessary to inquire about its typical subjects, typical
objects (if transitive), its typical beneficiaries or indirect objects, and any other clause-level category that is
closely related to the verb stem. For example, for Telefol
I found it necessary to inquire for each verb whether it
took all persons as subject, or only plural persons, or
only the third person feminine singular (sometimes with an
impersonal meaning). When each new grammatical feature is
discovered, it is economical to examine first just a sample
of the appropriate word class (50 verbs, say) to see how
this feature applies to them. If it is seen to be systematic and predictable in some way, then no further research
is needed. But if there is evidence to the contrary, then
all the words of that class in the lexicon will need to be
examined for this feature, as well as each new word as it is
discovered. For instance, when I was examining a sample of
verbs for their tonal patterns, I noticed that the punctiliar
benefactive forms seemed to have unpredictable tonal patterns. So I then examined some 400 verbs and was able to
confirm the existence of tonal classes among the verbs.

Bibliography

Albert Alvarez and Kenneth Hale, 1970. "Towards a Manual of Papago Grammar: Some Phonological Terms", *International Journal of American Linguistics* 36:83-97.

Paul L. Garvin, 1958. "A Descriptive Technique for the Treatment of Meaning", *Language* 34:1-32.

Zellig S. Harris and Carl F. Voegelin, 1953. "Eliciting in Linguistics", *Southwestern Journal of Anthropology* 9:59-75.

Kenneth Hale, 1965. "On the Use of Informants in Field-work", *Canadian Journal of Linguistics* 10:108-119.

Alfred S. Hayes, 1954. "Field Procedures While Working with Diegueño", *International Journal of American Linguistics* 20:185-194.

Alan Healey, 1964. "Handling Unsophisticated Linguistic Informants", *Linguistic Circle of Canberra Publications* (now *Pacific Linguistics*) Series A, No. 2. [A revision of sections 3, 5, and 6 comprise the second half of this present paper.]

Jules Henry, 1940. "A Method for Learning to Talk Primitive Languages", *American Anthropologist* 42:635-641.

T. J. Klokeid and G. N. O'Grady, 1972. "The Linguist and His Informant", *Australian Institute of Aboriginal Affairs Newsletter* 3(4):30-31.

Eugene A. Nida, 1949. *Morphology: The Descriptive Analysis of Words*. University of Michigan Press, Ann Arbor. (Especially "Field Techniques" on pp. 175-191.)

Herbert P. Phillips, 1960. "Problems of Translation and Meaning in Field Work", *Human Organization* 18:184-192.

William J. Samarin, 1967. *Field Linguistics*, Holt, Rinehart and Winston, New York.

C. F. Voegelin and Florence M. Robinett, 1954. "Obtaining a Linguistic Sample", *International Journal of American Linguistics* 20:89-100.

Charles F. Voegelin and Florence M. Voegelin, 1957. *Hopi*

Domains Indiana University Publications in Anthropology and Linguistics, Memoir 14. (Especially pp. 1-6.)

....., 1970. "Our Knowledge of Semantics and How it is Obtained", *International Journal of American Linguistics* 36:241-246.

S. A. Wurm, manuscript. *A Manual for Eliciting and Recording New Guinea Linguistic Materials.*

Eliciting Vocabulary, Meaning, and Collocations

John Beekman

0. Introduction
1. To discover new words
    1.1 To discover the names of objects
    1.2 To discover the names of events
    1.3 To discover the names of abstracts
    1.4 To discover relationals

2. To discover the meaning of words
    2.1 To discover the meaning of object words
    2.2 To discover the meaning of event words
    2.3 To discover the meaning of abstracts
    2.4 To discover the meaning or function of relationals

3. To check on meaning

0. Introduction

This paper presents a procedure by which one may discover new words along with their usage and meaning, discover equivalents for specific concepts needed, and check on the meaning of words or paragraphs. All of the procedures suggested in this paper involve the assistance of a native speaker.

Most of us have played the game of twenty questions. The object of this game is to discover the name of an object which has been chosen by another individual. One begins with a question which makes use of a very generic classifier such as inanimate or animate. Is it animate? Such a question immediately removes from consideration a large bulk of the material world. The questions which follow use less generic terms until one can name the specific object which the other person has selected. When traveling by car, our family sometimes plays a more complicated version of this game in which the questioner is expected to discover a whole sentence which has been formed by another. Of course,

Reprinted from *Notes on Translation* 29 (1968):1-11, with the permission of the author and editor.

this involves more than a series of twenty questions and
includes questions relating to grammar.

The game of twenty questions suggests that by using
questions it is possible to discover words and concepts
which are hidden in the mind of another. Of course, the
procedure that one follows when using a language known to
both individuals is quite different from the procedure
used when one enters a situation as a foreigner and asks
questions of a person whose language is different from his
own. In the game of twenty questions all of the questions
are answered with a simple yes or no. In eliciting information from helpers the questions should almost always be content questions. In playing the game of twenty questions one
begins with the use of generic classifiers which divide the
world into certain categories. In asking questions of a
native speaker whose language and cultural background is
unknown to us, we begin with questions about specific objects, events or abstractions. These procedural differences,
while of interest, in no way reflect on the usefulness of
questions in gaining information which is hidden in the
mind of another.

Elicitation of desired information may occur in a real
situation or in a displaced or assumed situation. In the
first, what is talked about is present and forms part of
one's immediate environment or experience. This method
is the most direct manner of elicitation and one which mis-
sionary-translators use freely and frequently. Questions
and commands as those which follow are typical in a real
situation: What is this? What is he doing? Where is the
book? Tell me about that object; Jump; Scratch something;
and, Show me what is wet. The advantage of this kind of
elicitation is obvious since the conclusions reached concerning the meaning of words are based upon empirical
evidence. The procedure followed in a real situation overlaps with but is not so inclusive as that used in assumed
situations. For this reason, it is expected that while this
paper does not give procedural hints to be asked in real
situations, nevertheless, anyone who benefits from the procedures suggested here, will be able to effectively apply
that which is relevant to real situations.

One of the earliest sentence types one learns is that
of the question. As the translator unpacks his belongings
these questions will be asked again and again: What is this?
What is this for? It is not expected that one will be able
to apply the question procedure as thoroughly in his earlier

experience in the language as at a later period. However,
questions learned early should be used freely so that while
one is analyzing the grammar he can at the same time be
building his vocabulary.

As one looks over the various items in the outline, he
may wonder whether he will ever be able to transform all of
these into questions. It is quite likely that words for
some of the generic classifications will not even exist in
many languages. This, however, should not be a disadvantage
to the imaginative investigator. Let us suppose, for example, that one finds no word for shape. In asking for the
features of a certain object, one might therefore feel that
he cannot ask the question: What is its shape? By this time,
one may have discovered that a ball is round and that the
baby's blocks are square. With these two examples one need
merely set up a pattern as follows: This ball is round.
This block is square. What is so and so like? In this manner one has asked for the shape by giving two examples in
which words describing shape are used. The same can be
done for any of the other categories listed in the outline.

One should not be afraid to make use of the question
'why?'. It is true, that when we are dealing with phonetics
or morphology it would be wrong to ask: Why do you pronounce
it that way? Or: Why don't you put a k suffix here? This
is asking for structural information which the language
helper is not generally in a position to give. However,
when we are dealing with the lexicon, the question 'why?' is
not only legitimate but one of the most useful. For example,
in checking one of the gospels the question was asked as to
why Jesus called himself the 'Son cf Man'. The reply was
unexpected. "Jesus was ashamed of his poverty and didn't
want people to know that he was speaking about himself."
The reply had its basis in their own use of third person
forms when speaking about themselves.

A precaution should be mentioned in connection with the
application of these procedures. Although the outline moves
sequentially from the discovery of names for objects, events,
abstracts, and relationals, and to checking for meaning, it
is not intended that the study of vocabulary follow this
order. It would be a mistake for example, to first of all
study only objects and then later study events, etc. One
should rather be studying whatever word comes to his attention which he does not fully control. In asking for the
function of a specific object there may be an event word
or another object word included in the answer which is not

understood. At this point, the investigator should apply the
question technique to those words as well.

The learning process is fastest when the various senses
are involved. The question technique properly applied makes
continuous use of most of the senses. When a question is
asked, this involves practice in pronunciation, practice
in using the proper form of the word, practice in placing
them in their proper syntactic arrangement, practice in combining words according to their co-occurrence or collocational restrictions. When the response is received, the
ear must hear and the mind must decode. Moreover, the response should be repeated orally and written down to further
impress upon the mind the various grammatical and lexical
features of the sentence. The full reply to the question
should be written, not a one-word definition or clue to the
response received. If the reply consists of various sentences, never should one record less than a full sentence.
At the end of a session the words learned should be used
preferably with a different helper. Using the technique
outlined in this paper, one should never need to memorize
vocabulary lists. When there are memory lapses, one need
only review the questions asked and the written responses
made by the language helper. The author and his wife used
the essentials of the procedure suggested in this paper in
learning the lexicon and culture of the Chols. Our experience and that of others suggests that this is one of the
easiest ways of internalizing the lexicon of a language
without any necessity to resort to heavy rote memory.

Lest the impression be given that the learning of a
language consists exclusively of the application of these
techniques, let me sketch another aspect of language learning applied among the Chols. We began first of all by
analyzing and studying simple construction types. Frames
were constructed of possessive constructions, passive constructions, stative constructions, transitive and intransitive constructions. Probably the earliest sentence types
learned were the question and imperative sentences. Later
followed purpose, negative and conditional sentences.
Eventually we had a list of about sixty basic construction
types set up in the form of frames with emphasis upon the
verb and pronominal system. Elaine and I spent a period of
three months in a small-town hotel to avoid becoming
swamped with data. During this time we memorized cold the
construction types. Vocabulary substitutions were made as
frequently as possible. We never memorized grammar rules
but rather drilled each other on actual examples until the

various structural patterns became so fixed that they were
used hardly without conscious thought. From that point on,
our study of the language turned almost exclusively to the
use of the procedures outlined here.

It is a curious fact that some translators feel that
the analysis of a grammar can be done at a desk but that an
understanding of lexical content and usage can only be acquired by joining the people in their daily activities, even
traveling from village to village. This is not the case.
The lexicon can be studied and mastered at one's desk. This
is not intended to say that most translators do not need to
spend as much time as possible with their people both for
conversational practice and to identify themselves with them.
Since we learned our own language by direct involvement in
the activities of our own culture, it might seem to follow
that the most efficient way in which to learn vocabulary content and appropriate usage would be by direct involvement in
various situations of the adopted culture. However, just
as we do not attempt to internalize the grammatical structure
of a language as a child does, but apply certain linguistic
techniques by which we can shorten the time that it takes to
understand and use the acceptable grammatical structure, just
so it is preferable to apply a technique which will shorten
the time to grasp and master the situations represented by
a word or expression. Any adult representative of the language to be learned has an accumulation of experience and
understanding concerning his culture and his environment
which he can convert into speech. All of this experience
and understanding hidden away in his mind can be made available to us in small digestible pieces through the use of
questions. The proper questions will disclose much of the
lexical structure along with the situations when it is appropriate for such words and expressions to be used. A question
technique rapidly increases one's vocabulary; it shows the
range of usual collocations; it catches inherent but relevant
components of meaning which otherwise might be overlooked;
it gives rich insights into the patterns of thought, the
value system, and the world view of the people; and it is
pedagogically sound.

1.   To discover new words

One of the purposes of a question technique is to discover new words. Semantically there are four classes of
words, namely, objects, events, abstracts and relationals.
Object words as used in this paper refer to identifiable
entities of all kinds. This includes tangible (man) and

intangible (God) objects, and animate (horse) as well as
inanimate (rock) objects. Event words refer to actions and
processes. Anything that happens or takes place is an
event. Abstracts refer to qualities or attributes of all
kinds. The term is not to be confused with abstract nouns
many of which represent events. Relationals refer to words
or affixes which relate two or more distinct elements within
a sentence. They are generally prepositions, conjunctions
or case markers. Of these four lexical classes the first
three can easily be elicited through a question technique.

     It is characteristic of all languages that objects,
events, and abstracts are used in certain relationships one
to the other. Some of these relationships are without doubt
universals of all languages. That is, the fact of the relationship not the manner in which the relationship is shown,
is a characteristic of all languages. In eliciting new
vocabulary items it is helpful to make use of these basic
recurring relationships which uncover meaning and show the
acceptable collocations.

1.1 <u>To discover the names of objects</u>

     Let us first of all consider the discovery of new
words representing objects. As pointed out in the introduction, these are the easiest to obtain. The relationship of
objects to events, to abstractions, and to other objects
which may be the basis for questions to be asked follow:

1.1.1 An object is related to other objects. One may discover new objects by asking questions suggested by the following relationships.

1.1.1.1 Generic terms refer to various objects which are
different but related. One may want to elicit generic
terms or the membership of a generic term. Since the
grouping of objects into classes covered by generic terms
will differ from one language to another, we cannot assume
that the divisions into groupings made in English or any
other languages will apply to the language under investigation. Therefore, in presenting an elicitation pattern we
should use only generic terms already known. While the examples below are taken from English, it must be kept in mind,
that these would be substituted with generic terms already
known in the indigenous language. An example of a pattern
to elicit generic terms follows. The blank spaces are
already known to the investigator but permit his helper to
gain confidence to do others and affords a method by which

one can determine if the pattern has been understood.

      a chair is a piece of furniture
      a dog is an animal
      a cup is _____
      a machete is _____
      a shovel is _____

    In discovering new objects, one can elicit the class membership of a generic term. For example, if one knows that the word for furniture is generic, the question may be asked: What else is furniture? Or when one has found the word which is thought to mean animal, the question may be asked: What is an animal? What else? This type of question may be continued until the whole class belonging to the term animal has been discovered.

1.1.1.2 Objects have parts which are also objects. For example, a tree has roots, a trunk, branches, leaves, bark, sap, etc. The question may be asked concerning the parts which make up a whole. If one is at a loss in his early language experience to phrase a question such as is suggested, one can use the patterning device introduced earlier. By explaining that a pencil has an eraser, a shaft, lead and a point, and that a chicken has legs, wings, head and so forth, one may then simply ask: What does a tree have? The examples give specificity to the rather general question that one in his early stage of language learning may be able to ask.

1.1.1.3 Groups of near identical objects are referred to with collective terms (forest). In attempting to elicit collective terms it is best to present a series already known asking the language helper to add additional pairs. The following series presents four pairs in which the last, although already known to the investigator, may be left blank. This not only prepares the helper to look for additional items to continue the series, but confirms whether he understands what is desired of him.

        many trees - a forest
        many dogs   - a pack
        many people - a crowd
        many birds - _____

1.1.1.4 Some objects have "opposites". We do not usually consider objects to have antonyms or opposites. Sometimes however, a significant abstract component is part of the meaning carried by an object term. In these instances, it

is possible to set up a pattern by which the language helper
can proceed on his own to add additional pairs. The component of sex is often the basis for different object terms
as seen in the following example:

> cow   - bull
> girl   - boy
> queen - king
> mare   - _____

1.1.1.5 Objects resemble others. The resemblance may be
behavioral, functional, or attributive (cf. 2.1.2 and
2.1.3). For example, a stool may suggest a chair, a bench,
and a sofa, because each serves the same function.

1.1.1.6 Objects have causal agents. Man's mind is so con-
stituted that he posits a cause to all effects which he ob-
serves. This applies to all objects. A causative agent
(animate or inanimate) can be elicited by asking: Who made
it? How did it come to be? The last question often elicits
interesting origin stories.

1.1.1.7 Objects suggest others which are generally together
in space. Again we make use of an illustrative pattern
from English.

> hammer and _____
> table and   _____
> socks and   _____

Most people can follow a pattern of this type and list additional pairs without the need of the translator's direct
interrogation.

1.1.2 An event is related to participants which are objects.
These participants may be actors, goals, or instruments.
Let us suppose that the investigator has elicited the word
'to give'. He may then discover new objects by asking:
Who gives? Who else gives? What is given? What else is
given? To whom is it given? To whom else is it given?
Or he may know the word 'to sew'. He may ask: Who sews?
Who else? What is sewn? What else is sewn? With what does
one sew? With what else does one sew? For whom does one
sew? For whom else does one sew?

1.1.3 An abstract quality relates to various objects. One
may therefore elicit new object words by asking what objects have a certain attribute. What is red? What else is
red? What is tall? What else is tall?

1.2 To discover the names of events

In eliciting words for events not yet known, questions
are based upon the relationship which events have to other
events, to objects, and to abstracts.

1.2.1   An object is related to events. All objects have
behavioral characteristics, i.e., what the object does and
what can be done to it. All objects which are useful to
man possess function, i.e., use, purpose. One may learn
additional event terms by asking for the behavior and the
function of objects already known.

1.2.2 An event is related to other events. The following
relations serve as a basis for the formulation of questions
which will elicit the names of new events.

1.2.2.1 Generic terms refer to various events. When one
suspects that an event word is generic, he may then ask for
the different events which may be classed under the term
under study. For example, one may want to ask: What is
sin? What else is sin? Such a series of questions will
elicit a number of different acts which are considered sin-
ful.

The more difficult situation that often faces a translator is the discovery of a generic term to represent
various different but related events. One procedure which
has been used successfully involves presenting various
hypothetical situations. This procedure is not always
effective inasmuch as a comparison of the generic vocabulary of one language with another shows that they are never
identical. Failure to find a term or idiom to cover the
concept for which one is searching does, however, give useful information since one is then justified to assume, for
the time being at least, that no generic term exists for
that concept and he may then proceed to translate the concept with a descriptive equivalent.

Let's look at the word 'disobey'. First of all we
look for the situational components which should be represented in the hypothetical examples. We know that there is
a value component involved namely, badness. This is a
generic abstract which has caused translators no problems.
It is easy, therefore, to elicit a number of examples in
which an individual has done something which is bad. There
is a further component of command. Someone must make some
type of injunction before there can be any disobedience.

After accumulating a list of bad deeds which a boy might do
in a particular culture, choose those which a father is
likely to instruct his son to do or not to do. Since one
can suppose that there might be a distinction between disobedience to negative commands (prohibitions) in contrast
to disobedience to positive commands, it would be well to
set up the hypothetical situations choosing only one type.
Then after listing a number of commands by the father, one
can conclude each by saying that the boy did not do what
his father told him to do. Then a generic question: "What
would you say about a boy like this?" Answer: "He is a
bad boy." "Why do you say he is bad? How is he bad?"
"What else would you say about him?" You may get a word
which is an equivalent to 'disobey'. On the other hand, you
may find that the equivalent to disobedience is a clause
such as: Not to do what is commanded.

     The approach illustrated above attempts to find a
word which represents a negative notion. Sometimes it is
more useful to set up situations which will elicit the term
representing the positive. In this instance 'obey' is the
positive, 'disobey' the negative. Some languages express
negative concepts by negating the positive. In these
cases, the language helper may have less difficulty in
producing the positive. In most instances, it is good to
make use of both the negative and the positive approach.
One serves as a check on the other.

     Hypothetical situations have been used again and
again by translators in looking for an equivalent for
'salvation'. Again, let us underscore the need to first of
all select the situational components which should be high-
lighted in developing the hypothetical examples. In
'salvation' there is (1) personal danger to life or well-
being, and (2) the beneficial help of someone involving
personal risk. Do not stop with one example such as that
of a drowning person. Rather, give several examples which
make use of the situational components. Then after one has
given a whole series, one may conclude by asking the question: "When the man did this and the other thing, etc.,
what did he do?" It is very unlikely that he will respond
with a specific answer for each different example given.
He has been led by the procedure to look for some generic
term which will cover all or most of the varied examples.
If there is a generic term, it is likely that he will produce it. In many Mayan languages the above procedure
would elicit the word 'help', which although the component

of personal risk is not necessarily involved, still is the best equivalent for salvation.

1.2.2.2 Events have antecedent events. These may be the motive, purpose, cause or reason for an action.

The following is what was found in working with a Chol language helper in searching for a term for discipline. A boy was disobedient and his father spanked him with the leather case of his machete. "Why did he do it?" The answer: "Because he was bad." The question was then re-phrased: "Why does the father spank the boy when he is bad?" The answer: "So he will be good." The question was again rephrased: "Why does the father spank the boy when he is bad in order that he'll be good?" The answer: "In order to put his heart down." Further checks confirmed that we had found a word which is a very close equivalent to 'discipline'. The means by which one disciplines another is not limited to spanking. If there had been no word for this concept, the last question would have drawn a complete blank. It would be a false assumption to expect that every language will have a word or idiom which means to discipline another. In some languages, it will be necessary to spell out the specific components to form a descriptive equiva-lent. In some contexts it may be rendered: 'to punish so that the person will do good'. In other contexts it may be: 'to reprove so that the person will not do bad'.

One final illustration. In searching for the word 'believe' we note that there is first of all a state of mind which relates to what another individual has said. If we are not able to find a term to express the word 'believe', we might use the following illustration: A rancher visited one of the colonies telling the Indians that the world was going to come to an end. All the Indians laughed except one. That one had been told that by going to Tumbalá, the navel of the world, he would escape destruction when the world came to an end. The fellow went to Tumbalá. The rancher told him that the world was going to come to an end. The Indian went to Tumbalá because he did not want to die. "Why did he go to Tumbalá?" Answer: "Because he was afraid." "Why did the other men not go?" Answer: "They were not afraid." "Why did they laugh when the man told them that the world was coming to an end?" Answer: "Be-cause they did not believe the world was going to come to an end."

Other examples:

```
The man kicked the dog.  Why?
The tree fell down.  Why?
The boy died in the water.  Why?
The man chopped wood.  Why?
The man went to town.  Why?
```

1.2.2.3 Pairs of events have intermediate events. These
may be cause, reason for, or means.

```
My clothes were dirty now they are clean.  Why?
I did know Bill's name.  Now I don't.  Why?
I saw a man on the ground.  Now he's up in the tree.
  What did he do?  How did he get there?
My pencil was in my pocket.  Now it's on the ground.
  What happened?  How did it get there?
```

Perhaps at this point it might be good to point out
that one can make use of stick figures, maps and sketches
in order to talk about items which are not in the immediate
environment. Although it is a somewhat sophisticated system of symbolization, when accompanied with verbal explanations, many translators have used rough sketches successfully. It has been used in eliciting relations such as
those which exist in a kinship system. Its use is not limited to kinship or geographical relations. Another use is
illustrated in the following: Let's suppose one makes a
hasty sketch of a brook with a man on one side. The next
time, one explains, the man is on the other side and his
feet were not wet. How did he get there?

1.2.2.4 Events have subsequent events. Subsequent events
are effects, results, or consequences.

```
The corn was this high.  It did not rain.  Then
  what?
The baby would not nurse.  Then what?
The husband came home to eat.  The wife had prepared
  no food.  Then what?
```

1.2.2.5 Some events have synonymous events. Since synonyms
are heavily dependent upon context, any patterns which are
given to a language helper should consist of full sentences.
Examples may be given as follows:

```
He will speak to me tomorrow.  He will talk to me
  tomorrow.
He spanked me last night.  He whipped me last night.
  He beat me last night.
```

Some synonyms which are quite similar in meaning have
a distinctive distribution. This distributional difference may represent a semantic restriction, as e.g. when a
different class of objects serves as the agent of each word.
The following pattern making use of known collocations has
been found useful. Let us suppose that in eliciting the
agent for the word 'love' and for the word 'forgive' the
language helper never made mention of God. This is significant since the word used with man need not be identical with
that used for God. The following pattern making use of
event words where man and God appropriately serve as the
agent sets up a pattern from which the language helper can
give the appropriate term to cover the synonymous concept.

    man watches man--God watches man
    man punishes man--God punishes man
    man helps man--God helps man
    man loves man--What does God do?
    man forgives man--What does God do?

1.2.2.6 Some events have antonymous events. Those events
which carry an implicit abstract component have antonyms.
A pattern of known opposites may be presented to the language
helper with the request that he continue it:

    blow--suck
    walk--run
    to freeze--to melt
    to hide--to reveal

One may find specific concepts by presenting two contrasting hypothetical examples giving the word which sym-
bolizes the one and asking for its antonym. Let us suppose
we are in search for the word 'love'. We already know the
word 'hate'. A situation is presented which illustrates
the word 'hate'. Then a situation is given which is intended to illustrate the word 'love'. After these two illustrations have been given, one may refer back to the first
indicating that this shows how one man hated another. Then
in contrast the second illustration is referred to with the
question: What would you say about the man who did such and
such? The contrasting illustrations with a term known to
represent the one, is likely to focus the attention of the
helper sufficiently on the desired concept, so that even if
the illustration is not one of the best, he will be led to
give the desired term or a statement representing its
equivalent.

1.2.3 An abstract relates to various events. What can be done fast? What else? Additional qualities which one has found applying to an event may be used in similar questions to elicit additional event words.

1.3 To discover the names of abstracts

In discovering new words for abstracts the following relations may be exploited:

1.3.1 An object has various abstract attributes.

What is a pencil like, i.e., what are its characteristics? See 2.1.3 for ideas in forming additional questions.
What is the appearance of a ball?

1.3.2 An event has various abstract attributes.

We can walk slowly. How else can we walk?
We can talk straight. How else can we talk?
   or:
How does a mother carrying a load of firewood walk?
How does a mother carrying a baby walk?
How does a drunkard walk?
How does a man going to work walk?
How does a man returning from work walk?

1.3.3 An abstract is related to other abstracts. There are three relations which may serve as the basis for questions.

1.3.3.1 Abstracts have antonyms or scaled opposites in a continuum. This time we make use of a pattern of known antonyms or scaled opposites.

big--small
soft--hard
high--low
back-- _____
wet-- _____

cold - cool - warm - hot

solid - mass - liquid - gas

1.3.3.2 Generic terms refer to various abstracts which are related but different. Thus, the abstract 'location' includes antonyms as well as synonyms. This concept includes such words as: up, down, far, distant, near, here, there high, low, etc. The concept of 'size' includes: big, large,

small, little, and medium. The concept of 'temperature'
includes: cold, cool, warm, hot, etc.

1.3.3.3 Abstracts have synonyms.

He nearly died. He almost died.
The field is far. The field is distant.
An elicitation pattern may be utilized for this kind of
synonym similar to the example given in 1.2.2.5.

1.4 To discover relationals

Objects, events, and abstracts are related to other
objects, events, and abstracts and to one another. The
relation may be implicit or explicit. Explicit relations
are signaled by order or some linguistic marker. The latter
are discovered in sentences elicited from the procedures
outlined in this paper and from native texts. In eliciting
objects, events, and abstracts the response to questions
asked will not consist of isolated words but rather of full
sentences which combine objects, events and abstracts.
Explicit relationals will occur in these sentences so that
the discovery of relationals is a by-product of the elicitation questions and patterns used for objects, events, and
abstracts.

2.   To discover the meaning of words

The second purpose of this procedure is to discover
the meaning of words. This section overlaps with the outline given for section 1. One really cannot apply the technique for the discovery of new words without at the same time
learning much about the meaning of those words. The distinction between the approach to the discovery of new words
and to learning their meaning appears to be an arbitrary
one. One does not come upon new words in isolation; they
are always connected with some context or situation. And it
is the context or situation which reveals the meaning of a
word. However, in spite of the heavy overlap that will be
noticed, the division may help to show how the same characteristics of lexical structure serve both to discover new words
and to focus upon the meaning and usage of those already discovered. Comparing the outline for purpose 1. with that of
purpose 2. shows that the same questions are suggested somewhere in each section but with a different purpose in focus.
For example in 1.1.3 one would ask: What is red? What
else? in order to elicit new objects. In 2.3.1 the same
questions are asked to determine the objects which collo-
cate properly with abstract and at the same time give part

of the real-world meaning of the abstract under study. The
same overlap occurs elsewhere as indicated by the cross-
reference use of cf.

  This section may also bring into clearer perspective
that (1) a word which is basically of one semantic class
implicitly carries components from other classes and (2) a
word of one class is closely related to words of the other
classes.

2.1 To discover the meaning of object words

  It is always best to begin with a very generic question
or request. Tell me about this object, is better than more
specific questions which can be formed from items in the
outline already given and which follow. In many instances
the generic question or request will elicit sufficient information about the object under study. Not every object
word will be investigated with the same thoroughness as
others. Their relative value for the purpose of the translator and their degree of complexity will determine the
depth to which one investigates each term. When investigating the meaning of the word 'spirit', one would want to ask
all of the questions which the list suggests. Additional
questions to learn the full meaning of this term would also
suggest themselves as responses are received from the language helper.

  In order to properly understand the meaning of an object word, one needs to know its relation to events, to
abstracts and to other objects. In many instances, event,
abstract, or relational components of meaning have been
fused into the term representing the object. They combine
to form the meaning of what is basically an object word.
For example, the word 'martyr' is basically an object word
referring to a person. The term however, is related to an
event, namely, that of having been killed. The event in
turn carries with it a reason component, namely for not
denying his beliefs. Thus the word 'martyr' while basically
an object word has various implied components. One should
keep in mind, therefore, that the following outline represents information which may be explicitly stated about the
object or represents information carried implicitly as one
of the components of meaning of the object word.

2.1.1 Ask for objects to which the object is related
(cf. 1.1.1).

2.1.1.1 By kinship. The word 'son' is not understood
fully until one knows the implied objects, namely, father
and mother to which a son is related. Who calls the boy
'son'? Who else?

2.1.1.2 By role. A husband has a role which represents an
event attribute but this role is directed toward a certain
person called 'wife'. It is important to know the recipient
of all role relationships in order to properly understand
the term under study. Boss versus employee; king versus
subject are further illustrations.

2.1.1.3 As a generic classifier or by class membership
(cf. 1.1.1.1). An object is related to another object by
virtue of belonging to the same class. Thus an object word
may relate to a generic classifier as well as to the other
objects in that class. When one knows or suspects that an
object word is generic he may ask such questions as: What
else is a plant? What is a grass? What other kinds of
grasses are there?

2.1.1.4 By part-whole relations (cf. 1.1.1.2). Objects
have parts. In order to understand fully the meaning of a
branch one must know that it is a part of a tree. What are
its parts?

2.1.1.5 By spatial relations. Spatial relations are to be
distinguished from spatial attributes. The latter refers
only to an object under attribution; the former relates two
distinct objects in space, e.g. boy and tree as in: The
boy in the tree. An island is land surrounded by water.
Here we have an object word (island) which upon analysis
consists of two objects (land and water) related spatially
with the words 'surrounded by'. For another kind of spatial
relation (cf. 1.1.1.7).

2.1.1.6 By resemblance (cf. 1.1.1.5). What other object
is this like? See 2.1.2 and 2.1.3 for specific kinds of
resemblance.

2.1.1.7 By opposition (cf. 1.1.1.4). When an object has
an implicit abstract component, it will likely have an
opposite. Thus, the question: What is the opposite of a
boy? may receive two answers, i.e., a girl or a man.
Either is correct since the word 'boy' carries both an
abstract of sex as well as age.

2.1.1.8 By causal agency. All objects have an origin or

cause which may be animate or inanimate. The man made the
table. The river formed a cave. Origin is an important
component of meaning in understanding objects.

2.1.2 Ask for the event attributes of an object (cf. 1.1.2
and 1.2.1). These may be divided between behavioral and
functional attributes.

2.1.2.1 Behavioral attributes. Behavior is used in a sense
which refers not only to social conduct but includes anything that can be done by the object or to the object
whether that object is animate or inanimate. The only
exceptions to this statement are the functions of an object
treated in the next section. What does the object do? A
ball bounces. A dog barks. A man sleeps. How does the
object act? Fiercely, friendly, wild, are some terms which
would answer this question. What can be done to the object?
It can be bent. What happens to it? It dies. It wears
out. Where does it come from? or What is its destiny or
end?

2.1.2.2 Functional attributes. Ask for the functions of
the object. This may be the purpose, the use, the function, the role or duty of the object. It will be noted
that two of the questions suggested above also apply here:
What can be done with the object? What does the object do?
However, behavioral attributes do not include functional
attributes as defined in this paper.

     Function can be distinguished from behavioral events
in that the former always has reference to its usefulness
or value to man. Some objects will therefore have no function. A splinter and weeds are two examples. The very con-
notation of the word 'function', is that it has some useful
purpose. Weeds and splinters cannot be said to possess
function unless in some special situation they can fulfill
some value for man.

     Function may be looked at from the normal cultural
function or from a special situational function. A meat
cleaver is used by the butcher to cut through chunks of
meat. It may also be used to kill an enemy.

2.1.3 Ask for the abstract attributes of objects (cf.
1.1.3 and 1.3.1).

2.1.3.1 Spatial attributes. Tell me about its appearance.

What size is it? Notice that in asking for the size of a house we are dealing with an attribution which must be stated explicitly. But when asking concerning the size of a splinter while it can also be modified as to whether it is small or large, it possesses an implicit component of meaning concerning its size. If a splinter is contrasted with a stick, this becomes clear.

What shape is it? A bench, a stool, a chair while they have a common function differ in shape. The difference in name is based upon this implicit component of shape.

What position is it in? In asking for the position of a dog we are asking for a variable. In asking for the position of a wall, fence or floor we are dealing with something more constant and in this case carried implicitly by the term.

Where is it? The location of an object may be important in understanding its meaning. One may ask for the location of the sun, the clouds, God, and spirits. The location of a nest may be the basis for a different term depending on whether the bird makes its nest on the ground or in a tree.

2.1.3.2 Temporal attributes. What age is it? The distinction in meaning between child, youth, adult is based upon this component. What is its stage of growth or development? The difference between corn in its various stages of growth as well as fruit in its stages of maturity depends upon this component in some languages.

2.1.3.3 Tactile attributes. What does it feel like? This may involve temperature for such items as ice, water, etc. It may involve moisture. Whether the object is wet, moist, etc., may be significant. It may involve the texture scale. Is it smooth, rough, sticky, hard, soft, etc.?

2.1.3.4 Visual attributes. What color is it? What are its transparency characteristics? It may be clear, opaque, etc.

2.1.3.5 Audio attributes. What sound does it make?

2.1.3.6 Olfactory attributes. What kind of a smell does it emit?

2.1.3.7 Gustatory attributes. What taste does it have?

2.1.3.8 Quantitative attributes. How many are there?
This is significant in knowing the meaning of such terms
as flock, herd, crowd, trio, etc.

2.1.3.9 Qualitative or Connotative. What do you say
about a thief? What do you say about a mother? The thief
may suggest a bad person or evil deeds; mother may suggest
kindness; a home, security and kindness; a hammer may suggest noise; a girl, beauty; an invalid, sickness.

2.1.3.10 Sex attributes. What sex is it? Does a spirit
have sex? The terms for boy, girl, king, queen, bull, cow
are based at least partially upon a distinction in sex.

2.1.3.11 Substance attributes. What is it made of?

2.2 To discover the meaning of event words

Again, we begin with a very generic request which is
repeated to obtain as many sentences as possible in which
the word is used. Use this word in a sentence. Another
sentence. Such a request gives the basis to discriminate
between various senses which the word may have and at the
same time makes it possible to learn how the event is related to abstracts, objects, and other events. The same
phenomenon true of objects is found to occur also with
verbs. As nouns have both implicit relations to other semantic classes, so also verbs; in addition to explicitly stated
relations, they have implicit relations. Thus, in order to
really know and understand the meaning of an event one must
know the objects, abstracts, and other events to which it
is related. These as already indicated may be explicitly
stated in the sentence or carried implicitly by the event
word itself.

2.2.1 Ask for the object participants of an event (cf.
1.2.1).

2.2.1.1 Events have agents or actors. Who, what does it?
Who else?

2.2.1.2 Events have goals known grammatically as direct
objects. To what is this done? To what else? To whom
is this done? In 'he nodded', head is an implicit goal.

2.2.1.3 Events have benefactives known grammatically as
indirect objects. For whom is it done? To whom is it
done?

2.2.1.4 Events have instruments by which the event is carried out. With what is it done? What else? The following event words carry implicitly a reference to the instrument used in accomplishing the event. Kick (foot), punch (fist), slap (open hand).

2.2.2 Ask for events to which an event is related (cf. 1.2.2). All events have a basic event component. Most events are complex and take in other components to form a composite conveying what seems to be one single idea. Some of the object and abstract components which may be implied in an event may be seen in 2.2.1 and 2.2.3. In addition to these, event words are related to other events either implicitly or explicitly.

2.2.2.1 As a classifier or by class membership (cf. 1.2.2.1).

2.2.2.2 Related to an antecedent event (cf. 1.2.2.2). The antecedent event may be purpose, motive, intention, reason for, occasion of, grounds, cause, or condition of. All events have their antecedents. 'Discipline' has an implicit purpose component. One may paraphrase as: 'to punish in order to correct.' 'To martyr', has a reason component: 'to kill for adhering to one's beliefs'. Ask: What causes this event? Why does it happen? Why is it done? Why does he do it? When is it done? When will it be done?

2.2.2.3 Related to a simultaneous event. A simultaneous event is often the means, manner or the occasion. For example, when the moon is full in a certain month, the idol is washed. The word 'discipline' noted above contains a component of means and of purpose. The means--to punish; the purpose--to correct. I wash my face by moving a face cloth all over it. I run by moving my legs quickly. How does one run? What does one do at the same time? What happens at the same time?

2.2.2.4 Related to a subsequent event (cf. 1.2.2.4). A subsequent event may be effect, result, or consequence. 'Swallow' not only involves the action within the throat, but also the result of the food entering the stomach. If someone jumps in the water, then what? What will happen if this event is done? What will happen after this event is done?

2.2.2.5 Some events have synonyms which may be elicited as described in 1.2.2.5.

2.2.2.6 Some events have antonyms as described in 1.2.2.6. Their meaning is at least in part discovered by noting the abstract quality which is in contrast.

2.2.3 Ask for the abstracts to which an event is related (cf. 1.2.3).

2.2.3.1 Temporal modifications. (1) Duration of the event: How long is it done? Note the implicit reference to duration in wink, glance, stare. (2) Frequency, intermittancy, or repetition of the event: How often is it done? Stammer, pound, interrogate. (3) Speed of the event: How fast is it done? Walk, run, turn, spin. (4) The time of the event: When was. it done? When is it done? When will it be done?

2.2.3.2 Spatial modifications. (1) Direction of the event: What direction/s does the object move? Note the implicit direction component in the following events: sway fall, climb, come, go. (2) Position of the object involved in the event: What position does the object take? Dive, jump, roll, slide, lie, sit. (3) Location of the event: Where is the event done? Note again the implied location component in: swim, lie, skate, dig. (4) Distance of the event: How far does the object move? Walk, hike.

2.2.3.3 Intensity modification. Ask for the intensity of the event.

2.2.3.4 Appraisive or Evaluative modifications: What do you think of someone who does that? What do you think of a person who says that? What will people say about that?

2.2.3.5 Manner modifications. Ask how the action is done. This will overlap with temporal and spatial modification. There may be some manner modifications not included in the above list, however, which may be significant.

2.3 To discover the meaning of abstracts

      Use this word in a sentence. Another sentence. Since abstracts have already been treated in their relationship to objects and events, the following treatment does not include any complex types of that kind. Abstracts may be classified according to their semantic reference. Such a list will be seen under 2.1.3 and 2.2.3.

2.3.1 Ask for the objects to which an abstract is related (cf. 1.3.1). Unless one knows with what objects the

abstract combines in a modifying relationship, he really
does not control or fully understand the meaning and use
of such abstracts. What is green? What else is green?
This type of question will discover this information.

2.3.2 Ask for the events to which an abstract is related
(cf. 1.3.2). What has been said in 2.3.1 applies here as
well. What is done fast? What else is done fast?

2.3.3 Ask for the abstracts to which the abstract is related (cf. 1.3.3). Abstracts have antonyms, scaled opposites, synonyms and generic classifiers. An abstract is
really not understood until one knows as much of this
information as is easily elicited. In the case of scaled
opposites it is important to know when one term blends into
another in order to use the word correctly.

2.4 To discover the meaning or function of relationals
     (cf. 1.4)

     Use this word in a sentence. Another sentence.
Study relationals as found within sentences and natural
texts. The semantic class known as relationals is not amen-
able to elicitation through questions. It is always preferable to study relationals in native text materials. After
one has discovered explicit relationals from these sources,
one may then ask the helper to use the relational in various
sentences. There is probably one exception to the statement
that relationals cannot be elicited by questions. One can
ask for the location of objects. Where is the book? The
answer will generally always involve a specific relational
word indicating the relationship of the book to another
object in its vicinity. For example, the answer may be:
The book is on the table. Relationals may show objects to
be agent, goal, instrument, a location, a possessor, an
opposite of, the kin of, etc. A relational may show an
event to be antecedent, simultaneous, subsequent, cause,
effect, motive, a reason for, grounds of, manner, means,
purpose, result, consequence, antithetical, adversative,
conditional, etc., in its relationship to another event. A
relational may show an abstract to be the modifier of some
object or event. This list is, of course, not at all
exhaustive but merely suggestive.

3. To check on meaning

     The third purpose of the question technique is to check
on meaning. It is important to know what we communicate
when we speak. It is perhaps even more important to know

exactly what is communicated in materials which we put out
in print. As one gains fluency in the language he will often
use words which are only used passively in his vocabulary,
that is, there is an understanding of the meaning of the word
from having heard instances of its use, but these words have
not yet become part of one's active vocabulary. As a matter
of principle, such words should never enter into printed materials until after they have been fully checked as to their
usage. Moreover, in checking the meaning of materials prepared for printing, one should not only focus upon words and
expressions but also upon full paragraphs.

     In checking the meaning of words and expressions a
useful procedure is to take the word or expression out of
the context in which it has been used. The question technique is then followed in order to elicit contexts and
situations in which the native speakers themselves use the
word. Here again, it is important to continue the questioning
in order to elicit as many different sentences as possible.
Once these have been listed it is a simple matter to note
the situation suggested by the context from which the word
has been lifted and compare this with the situations just
elicited. If these compare favorably with the usage as
seen in one or more of the sentences elicited in the check,
then one can be assured that this usage is natural and the
sense correct.

     A more exact procedure in checking the meanings of
words and expressions is the "cycle check". It has already
been noted that responses to hypothetical situations may be
quite different from the word which one expects and yet the
answer be perfectly legitimate for the question which has
been asked. This often leads one to falsely assume that
the word elicited has the meaning which one was expecting.
Likewise, instances where words have been heard in the conversations of others have been wrongly defined and subse-
quently used innocently in a wrong sense. It is important,
therefore, to check these words with the use of a language
helper other than the one from whom the word was heard or
elicited. For example, if one started with a hypothetical
situation and thereby elicited a new word to which a meaning
has been assigned, then this word should be checked with a
different language helper. The word would be mentioned to
the second language helper apart from the situation used to
elicit it. The sentences of explanation given by the second
language helper will include the situations in which the
word may be correctly used. A comparison of the original

hypothetical situation which elicited the word with the situations elicited by the word itself will determine whether the correct meaning has been assigned. This then completes a full circle in that one begins with a situation to elicit a word, and then goes to a second language helper. Beginning with that word, one should end with the same situation with which one started.

Of course, if the second language helper gives the situation which applies to one sense carried by the word, and the original situation relates only to a second sense, then the meaning assigned may seem to be in error due to incomplete information on the use of the word. It is always important, therefore, to ask for several sentences using the same word.

In checking paragraphs or larger units one may ask for a paraphrased resumé of the meaning. It is important to explain to the language helper that the meaning is to be restated in his own words. If not, he is likely to attempt to memorize the exact words and in frustration claim that he is unable to do what has been requested of him. It should likewise be explained that he should not expect to remember every detail. As he restates a paragraph it should become clear whether or not the proper meaning has been communicated. The translator will also notice omissions which may be due to memory lapse or to a lack of understanding. If the omitted parts were clearly understood but lost in the process of retelling, the information can generally be readily recalled by the helper when one supplies the antecedent information and asks what followed or provides the subsequent information and asks what preceded. Sometimes it may be necessary to provide both the antecedent and the subsequent information asking for the missing intermediate information. When the information cannot be provided, the translator should suspect that the fault lies in the translation rather than in the helper.

At first a helper may have difficulty in giving a resumé of a full paragraph. But even if he gives just one sentence this is a sufficient base from which to begin asking questions which contain no more information than that which he himself has provided. With practice one can blanket every part of a paragraph with questions which do not provide answers to other parts of the paragraph which were also omitted in the resumé made by the helper.

Even after the helper has given a good resumé of a paragraph, it is important to go back and ask for the purpose, motive, or intention of certain events named in the paragraph. One example will suffice. The question was asked as to why John the Baptist said he was not worthy to stoop down and untie the sandals of our Lord. The answer: "He was not sick needing this assistance and, since Jesus was not ill, the only other reason to take off the sandals of another is when in anger one wants to throw them into a thorn bush or into a mud puddle."

Use plenty of questions in the process of learning an aboriginal language and in checking translated materials. Remember that content questions beginning with 'who?', 'what?', 'when?', 'where?', 'how?' are the most effective.

A Method for Eliciting
Paradigmatic Data from Text

R. S. Pittman

The big handicap of text is that it does not give paradigmatic materials, i.e., does not show the substitution
possibilities in the sentences. The big trouble with most
paradigms is that they are highly artificial, and may be
very far from actual usage. Both of these difficulties can
be offset to a remarkable extent by the following procedure:
After a person has gotten some good text (especially ordinary
conversation text--it is much better than folktales), he
should try to get other text on the very same subjects, or a
repetition of the same text from a different point of view
(without letting the speaker see his first text). He should
also try to get, from the same person or others, a great deal
of discussion of the details of the text. This can be
prompted by questions asked by the linguist. These questions
should be recorded, even though they may be in a trade language, or "broken" vernacular, since they provide the context of the answer. The extensive discussion of the text
and repetition of details in it, often in variant phrasing,
will give a great deal of the substitution possibilities
that a person is hunting for, and they will be far more
reliable than a translated paradigm.

Let me give an example. Suppose I am trying to analyze
English, and have a text on Little Red Riding Hood. In
order to get some of the substitution possibilities which do
not appear in the text, I could ask questions such as the
following: "Did LRRH go to her grandmother's every day?
Would she have gone if it had been raining? Did she walk or
run through the forest? Do you think she will go again?
How did the wolf go in the forest? Does a wolf run like a
horse? Like a rabbit?"

I grant that a helper may object to some questions as
being "silly", and simply shrug for an answer. But it should
be possible for the investigator eventually to get across to
the helper that he wants the discussion, even though it is
on an imaginary basis, for the sake of the language forms he
can get and not for the plot of the story. This would be
especially true if the text is a real life conversation
rather than a folktale. I used LRRH only for illustration.

I remember that Bloomfield, in one of his volumes of
text, has seven different versions of one story. I once
thought that a great waste of effort. Now I realize it is
a priceless goldmine of paradigmatic materials, and also of
transforms.

On Eliciting Transformations in Vietnamese

Richard Pittman

I. Methods

1. Battery of sentences model
2. Elicitation of questions from statements
3. Sentences from function words
4. Transforms from text
5. Constructions from text
6. Word-plus-prop situational sentences
7. Equivalent strings
8. Variable word order and answers from questions

II. Notational Devices

9. Option
10. Permutation
11. Substitution
12. Co-occurrence
13. Capability formulas
14. Transformational rules
15. Conclusion

"I don't care HOW you get them," Chomsky is alleged to have said. No doubt he added, under his breath, "But I do care THAT you get them."

Just in case there is one who DOES care HOW, this is a note on my try at eliciting grammatical transformations in the spring of 1965.

My teacher at the time I made this attempt was Mr. Nguyen Van Thuong, of Central Viet Nam. I already knew enough Vietnamese to be able to carry on all discussions of what we were doing in that language, but I did not know in advance the conclusions described on the following pages. Assumptions, deductions and clues I certainly had and fed into the elicitation process. But the conclusions are based on the free initiatives of my Vietnamese guide rather than on my preconceptions.[1]

I. Methods

1. Battery-of-sentences model. Impressed by what Thomas (1964 a,b) and Banker (1964) had achieved in transformational paradigms, I tried them first. My approach

was to show Thuong a set of transformations of an English
kernel sentence, then remove it so he could not translate,
at the same time asking him to build a paradigm of his own
from a Vietnamese core. He could read enough English to
get the idea readily.

An early set I showed him went like this:

> I got sick.
> I got sick with malaria.
> Malaria made me sick.
> Malaria is what made me sick.
> Did you get sick?
> Did you get sick with malaria?
> What made you sick?
> What were you sick with?
> Did malaria make you sick?

One of my reasons for trying this particular paradigm
was to determine the pattern of the unpleasant-passive
construction (which contrasts in Vietnamese with an agree-
able-passive construction).

When I had removed the English examples, Thuong gave
me the following Vietnamese paradigm, which I have angliciz-
ed for English readers: (The unpleasant-passive-particle
will be translated "get").

> You get sick illness which?
> I get sick illness malaria.
> I get sick head.
> I caught sick malaria.
> I get caught sick malaria.
> I get illness malaria.
> I sick stomach.

In eliciting batteries of sentences I did not always
give an English battery as an example. After Thuong caught
on to the battery pattern, which did not take long, all I
had to do was give a sample kernel sentence and ask him to
give me a similar sentence (not a translation) in Vietnamese, then give all variations which he could think of.
The result was a battery.

There was one important condition, however. I had to
make plain to him that the actor-action-goal referents must
be held constant.

Thus: The dog bit the fox.

The fox was bitten by the dog.
The bite which the dog gave the fox...
The bite which the fox got from the dog...
All of these were acceptable, but "the fox bit the dog" was
not acceptable because the referents had changed. Note
that the "referents" in this case refer to the open class
(unlimited membership) word bases, not to the closed-class
(limited membership) morphemes.

Note also that this principle admits "The rat was seen
by the cat" as a transformation of "The cat saw the rat" but
rejects "The cat was seen by the rat".

Other typical paradigm-generating sentences used:

The man made the box for the boy.
This tree is taller than that one.
The friend went away.

2. Elicitation of questions from statements.
Although I mixed questions with statements indiscriminately
in my first examples, most of the paradigms which I got in
return were sets of statements. Since it proved very
natural to ask for a question that would correspond to each
statement, I asked Thuong to give me such, which he readily
did in most cases. Occasionally there was a statement
which did not seem to suggest a corresponding question.

It soon became quite natural to record the battery of
statements down the right side of the page, leaving the
left side blank for corresponding questions.

On one occasion I had asked Thuong to give me some
examples of sentences using a pair of words meaning
"whenever...then...". The result was the following:

Whenever it rains, then everyone is happy.
Whenever that cloud passes,
then the weather will
clear again.
Whenever I get money, then I
will buy a car.
Whenever much is sown, then
much is harvested.

Some time later I asked him to give me questions
which would correspond to those statements. The results
are listed below to show the sequence in which they were

recorded, but in my original notes each question was
written directly to the left of its answer.

    If it rains, we are
        happy, aren't we?
    When will the weather
        clear again?
    If you get money, what
        will you do?
    What do you do in order
        to be able to harvest
        much?

    3.   Sentences from function words. One of the most
rewarding procedures was to scrutinize text for perplexing
function words then ask Thuong to give additional examples
of a given function word in sentences similar to the
original illustration. One such word could be translated
'no-doubt' at the end of a sentence, but something like
'definitely' before a negative. I chose a sentence from
Hoa's _Read Vietnamese_, pg. 30:

    'South Vietnam has boats, definitely not has pack-
elephants.' When I asked Thuong for additional examples,
he gave me:
    Vietnam has rice, definitely not has wheat.
    Let us eat, definitely not drink.
    Work and work, definitely do-not play.

    Given a sentence 'You are person American no-doubt?'
he gave a further example "Tomorrow you go Banmethuot no-
doubt?'

    In Smalley and Van's _Vietnamese for Missionaries_,
section 18.13, I found a pair of words which could be
translated 'all', and which occurred before another which
could be translated 'each'. The sentence was:
        Call all each person.
To this Thuong added
        In Vietnam all each place together has war.
        In Vietnam all each person together fears war.
        All each thing together expensive completely.
        All each thing bought in market together
           expensive completely.
plus a question transform for each statement.

    Though these added examples introduced no new
transformations, they provided a basis for formalizing the
description of an already existing one.

4. Transformations from text. Occasionally I got a windfall: some text would turn up with two or three simple transformations in plain sight. Thus on pages two and five of Hoa's *Read Vietnamese* I found the following, which I have here combined.

The French prime minister has-just changed the cabinet.	The French cabinet changed.
The French president will establish an army.	An army will be established by the French president.
Mr. Daladier organized the French cabinet.	The French cabinet was by Mr. Daladier organized.

Thoung had no problem in lining up additional illustrations of the same transformations on these models.

5. Constructions from text. In addition to choosing function words and transformations from text on which to crystallize other transformations, I often chose "problem" constructions from text and asked Thuong to give me additional examples. The problems, of course, were always due to my inadequate understanding of a pattern. The examples which Thuong gave contained not only identical structures with various options or substitutions, but also occasionally some authentic rearrangements of the same constituents.

A construction 'give finish' in Smalley and Van 19.23 occurred in the following sentence:
I wash always clothing <u>give</u> <u>finish</u> no?
This precipitated the following examples from Thuong:
You must talk <u>give</u> <u>finish</u> then only can go.
I must work <u>give</u> <u>finish</u> have then only go.
We must work <u>give</u> <u>finish</u> this work today.
Any day's work must be done <u>give</u> <u>finish</u> completely that day.
Then he gave a question transform of each:
You must talk how have then only can go?
You must work how have then only go?
Work this much very do when finish?
Work this in-order tomorrow do able not no-doubt?

Another sentence from Smalley and Van 19.22 had an unfamiliar 'not able' construction in it.
I lift up <u>not</u> <u>able</u>.
Thuong added:

You can move able this table no?   I move <u>not able</u>.
You carry-one-end able this drum no?   I carry-one-end
     <u>not able</u>.
Bring <u>not able</u> well don't try.

6.   Word-plus-prop situational sentences. Some usages
are so complicated that I could think of no way but word-
plus-prop (e.g. salt cellars) to show what I meant. Equivalents for 'take' and 'bring' with their prepositions are
examples. No language has exact equivalents for any other
language in its word-contrast patterns.

The procedure requires a minimum of three objects for
the take/bring checkout. Each object should have an imaginary personal name pasted on it, and written labels for
speaker and hearer should also be pasted on. Then, pointing
to the shakers in turn, the questioner says "Hickory tells
Dickory to...the stick to Dock." Hopefully the language
helper will give his proper equivalent of 'take' at that
point. Then "Hickory says to Dickory, '...the stick to me.'"
Hopefully the equivalent of 'bring' is given.

Pieces of paper with appropriate names and roles
written on them can serve as props. The results may give
both syntactic and/or semantic transformations.

7.   Equivalent strings. Synonyms are most commonly
regarded as one-word equivalents. In elicitation a linguist
may become so preoccupied with one-to-one equivalence as
to overlook synonymy of longer strings, particularly when
two strings or a word and a string are not grammatical
sames.

From time to time Thuong would give alternate strings
as "sames" during the course of an eliciting session. If
these "sames" did not appear to have comparable grammatical
structures, there was a temptation to brush them aside as
uninteresting. As phrase or sentence substitutes, however,
they constitute an integral part of the total grammatical
description. Though I was not, therefore, looking for
"long" synonyms, I learned to appreciate and hang on to
them when they did show up. Some will ultimately affect
the transformational rules. Note, for example, the following translations for 'You're welcome':   Not dare sir.
                                          Not be anything.
                                          Not anything at-all.
As negative answers to a question 'What happened?' Thuong
gave:

No matter something at-all.
No how-come at-all.
No happening something turned out at-all.
Thomas has suggested that these could be termed 'lexical
transforms'.

8.   Variable word order and answers from questions.
Quite early in the elicitation I told Thuong I was interested in alternative word order possibilities. He
immediately understood, and gave me:
    (1)   You study Vietnamese language how long?
    (2)   How long you study Vietnamese language?

Without the answers which may be given to these
questions, they would seem to be free variants of each
other. The answers, however, which Thuong proceeded to
give and discuss, indicated that (1) could refer only to
the past, while (2) could mean either past or future.
(3)   replying to (1):   I study Vietnamese language one year
                         already.
(4)   replying to (2):   Two years already I study Vietnamese
                         language.
(5)   replying to (2):   One week more I (will) study
                         Vietnamese language.

Another pair of questions and answers confirmed the
past/future distinction corresponding to final/initial
position in the sentence.
(6)   When you rest?   (7)   Tomorrow I rest.
                       (8)   This morning (past) I rest.
(9)   You rest when?   (10)   I rest this morning (past).

II.   Notational Devices

The notational system, as finally developed, proved
to have virtually no innovations. It is appropriate to
indicate, however, that there may sometimes be a difference
between a notation used during an eliciting session and
that chosen for a final description of the same material.
Also, some of the notations, while very conventional, may
look a bit different when used over a long string or used
in combinations of two or more.

9.   Option. The word 'option' and its representation
—parentheses— are used here for optional presence. They
are not used for optional order (which is discussed under
permutation), nor for an optional choice between two or
more lexical items, which is discussed under substitution.

In the following sentence, each of the parenthetical items may be included or omitted, individually or together.
'I have been (by Grandfather Minister Chief of National Education) invited (to go attend party tea day tomorrow).'

In the next illustration, asterisks have been used to indicate that two optional items may be included or omitted together, but not separately:
(I)* not-yet ever time (been-able-to eat mango special at-all)*.[2]

10. Permutation. The following notation is simply a modification for typewriter of what is already customary in long-hand usage.
'Older-brother have be-able change/thing table this no?'
The invertible components, of course, are 'change' and 'thing table this'.

Compare also:
'By illness which/grandfather got sick?'

11. Substitution. Two or more mutually substitutable words have been written in sequence on the line, but separated by slashes. If the substitution is a phrase for a word, the phrase is underlined. If there is no underlining on one side of a slash, the one word immediately ad--joining that side is the only one included in the substitution.
'Do thus how so/that hear for clarity?' ('that' may be substituted for 'so'.)
'Grandfather got caught/sick from illness which?' ('sick from' may be substituted for 'caught'.)

12. Co-occurrence. Asterisks-plus-parentheses for co-occurrence-plus-option have already been illustrated in paragraph 9. Co-occurrence without option can also be marked by asterisks, but parentheses would be ambiguous. Asterisks-plus-underlining therefore, for more-than-one-word sequences, were elected.
'The-more* you drink the* thirstier* you get.'

13. Capability formulas. My usage in capability formulas follows essentially that of Thomas and Banker--capital letters for open classes, representative morphs for closed. Thus N1 Aj bang N2 is a formula for the comparative which would be read "Noun 1 adjective bang Noun 2":

'Grandmother old as grandfather.'

14.   Transformation rules. I have written these with
a combination of Thomas formulas and Chomsky arrows.

Rule: <u>bao lau S? ⟹ T S</u>   in which S means sentence and T
means time expression.

Translation:	How long S? ⟹	T S.
Example:	How long (yet) ⟹	Two days yet
	you arrive Saigon?	I arrive Saigon.

Rule: <u>S bao lau? ⟹ S T roi.</u>

Translation:	S how long? ⟹	S T already.
Example:	You arrive Saigon ⟹	I arrive Saigon
	how long ago?	one year already.

Rule: <u>G bi V boi ai? ⟹ G bi A V.</u>

Translation:	Goal got Verb by whom? ⟹	Goal got Actor Verb.
Example:	You got punished ⟹	I got (by) parents
	by whom?	mine punished.

15.   Conclusion. In summary, elicitation of transformations is quite a workable and useful technique in
field work. Carefully done it need not violate even Bloomfield's rigorous criteria for avoiding artificiality in
language data recorded from a native speaker.

NOTES

[1] I am indebted to David Thomas for the principal inspiration
for this paper, and for valuable comments on it. Alan
Healey also made helpful suggestions and gave the necessary
stimulus for finalizing it.

[2] David Thomas, in a private communication, has this to say
of optionality,
   "I find the standard optional/obligatory contrast
awkward because usually no distinction is made between
elliptical (informational) optionality and structural
optionality.
   "With informational optionality (ellipsis) an acceptable sentence can be filled out from the context e.g. When
did you go? Yesterday. 'Yesterday' is not structurally
acceptable as a full sentence, but has been shortened in
context from 'I went yesterday'. The missing information
necessary to make an acceptable sentence of it is automatically retrievable from the context.
   "Structural optionality is structurally-permitted

expansions giving further information not deducible from
context. And both the long and short forms are equally
acceptable sentences (but saying different things) (while
the long and short forms in ellipsis say the same thing.)
     "Your first example would seem to be an illustration
of optional structure, the second an example of ellipsis."

References

Banker, John E. 1964. "Transformational paradigms of Bahnar
     clauses." *Mon-Khmer Studies I*, Saigon: Linguistic
     Circle of Saigon and Summer Institute of Linguistics,
     pp. 7-39.

Thomas, David, 1964a. "Transformational paradigms from
     clause roots." *Anthropological Linguistics* 6(1):1-6.

Thomas, David, 1964b (mimeographed - published 1969). "A
     discovery procedure for transformational paradigms."
     Mon-Khmer Studies III, Saigon: Linguistic Circle of
     Saigon and Summer Institute of Linguistics, pp. 37-47.

Testing the Recognition of Utterance Pairs

Alan Healey

As one studies an unwritten language sometimes there is
uncertainty as to whether or not two sounds (or two pitch
patterns, etc.) are phonemically contrastive for the speakers of the language. This is especially a problem if one
has difficulty hearing the difference. Harris (1951:32-41)
has devised a simple test to resolve the matter.

One selects two words or longer utterances which appear
to differ at only one point by these two sounds and which
have two demonstrably different meanings A and B. Each of
the two words are uttered an equal number of times in random
order and a speaker of the language is asked to identify the
meaning of each utterance. If his identifications are approximately 100% accurate then the two words are phonologically contrastive. If his identifications are approximately
50% accurate or if he indicates extreme uncertainty in making
any identification, then the two words are phonologically
identical, they are homophonous.

Before commencing the test itself it is vital to train
the person who is going to identify the utterances. This
training consists of putting him through at least two preliminary tests, first using a pair of words that are known
to contrast phonologically and then a pair that are known to
be homophonous. When he is able to give the kind of responses that are expected (100% and 50% accurate respectively) he is ready to participate in recognition tests.

Ways of Conducting the Test

The pair recognition test may be conducted in any one
of several ways.

(a) Using two people back-to-back. The two people should
be of the same dialect. One person utters the series of
words while the other one hears and identifies them. To
insure that the only communication between the two participants consists of the sound of these utterances, it is
necessary to arrange them so they can't see each other —
seated back-to-back on chairs, for instance. So that the
linguist may know the identity of the speaker's utterances,
he may present some kind of non-verbal stimulus to him.

Once the participants have been made familiar with them, I
have had good success with physical representations of the
two utterances being compared (both objects and sketches
have been used).   To avoid confusion in tabulating the
results of a test, I prefer to arrange the representations
on the floor, one to each side of each person, so that the
linguist may stand in front of the speaker and see both of
the representations of A on his own left and both of those of
B on his right, as shown in Figure 1. Alternatively, the
linguist may have an assistant standing in front of the
hearer-identifier to tabulate his reactions. The linguist
points to each representation in front of the speaker in
slow random succession, and at each pointing the speaker
says the appropriate utterance. The hearer points to the
appropriate representation to identify each utterance he
hears, and the linguist tabulates this response along with
his original stimulus given to the speaker. If the hearer
hesitates appreciably before identifying an utterance,
this should be noted.   (It is important that the hearer
not identify the utterances in any audible way, lest the
speaker decide to adjust his pronunciation in some artificial way part way through the test.) Often I run a test on
a pair of utterances twice, the roles of the two participants being interchanged in the second test as a check on
dialect uniformity.

PLAN OF ARRANGEMENT FOR PAIR TESTING

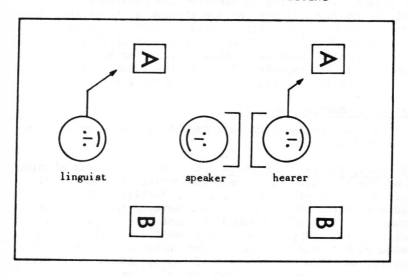

linguist   speaker   hearer

Figure 1.

(b) <u>Using two people and a tape recorder</u>. If a tape recorder with clear reproduction is available, the speaker's
utterances may be recorded on tape. If the second participant is not within earshot at the time, the linguist may
use either verbal or non-verbal stimuli to elicit this
series of utterances, provided that only the utterances
themselves are actually recorded. When the tape is played
back the hearer may respond either verbally by mentioning
agreed synonyms or translations, or by pointing to the
appropriate physical representations. The linguist tabulates these identifications beside the list or original
stimuli, being careful to conceal these from the hearer-
identifier. (It is also important that the linguist not
give any other clues to the hearer-identifier. For instance,
he should always write down the hearer's actual response
rather than √ or X. He should also keep a straight face
throughout the test.)

(c) <u>Using one person and a tape recorder</u>. The same procedure as in (b) may be used when only one person is available for the test. The only difference is that the same
person whose voice is used in the tape recording is also
used to identify the utterances. Precautions should be
taken to make sure that there is no possibility of his repeating from memory the sequence of utterances which he
has recorded on the tape. For instance, a series of
several tests could be recorded on the one occasion or
many more utterances than usual could be recorded for a
test to prevent memorization. Or the listening to the tape
could be delayed a few days to attenuate his memory of the
recording session.

(d) <u>Listening to a tape twice</u>. If at the time the speaker
is uttering the series of words the linguist suspects that
the speaker has become confused and has interpreted one or
more stimuli incorrectly, he should note that fact and later
check to see if these are the utterances where most of the
apparent inaccuracies of identification occur. However,
if the test has been tape recorded, there is another much
more reliable way to detect and eliminate any such confusion in the speaker's interpretation of the stimuli. The
tape can be replayed to the hearer after several days and
a second list of identifications tabulated. If the degree
of matching between the first and second lists of identifications is considerably higher than the degree of matching
of the lists of original stimuli and first identifications,
then we know that the speaker was confused as he interpreted
the stimuli. Furthermore, the degree of matching of the

first and second lists of identifications is a more reliable
indicator of the contrastiveness or otherwise of the two
words. (The reader should not doubt that people can become
confused even when the two words are phonemically contrastive. Tryon (1969:123) tells of one person who so completely
confused the two contrastive words he was listening to that
he gave identifications that were 0% accurate!)

(e) <u>Comparing pairs of utterances.</u> Another form of the
test mentioned by Chomsky (1957:96) does not depend on the
positive identification of each utterance spoken and heard.
Utterances are produced two at a time, and each time both
the speaker and hearer are requested to indicate independent-
ly whether the paired utterances are "same" or "different".
These tabulations are compared, and again, about 100%
matching is interpreted as phonemic contrast and about 50%
matching as homophony. An equal number of actual sames and
differents need to be produced by the speaker. This form of
the test is especially useful if the meanings of the two
utterances cannot easily be represented by physical objects
or sketches--for instance, if one of the contrasting words
is a function word, or if one is trying to contrast intonation patterns on longer utterances.

<u>Designing Tests</u>

     All of the five forms of the test described above are
statistically simpler, more reliable, and easier to interpret if each test involves an equal number of utterances
A and B or an equal number of "same" and "different" pairs
of words. For instance, if A and B should actually be
homophonous, and if the hearer should be inclined to give
80% A and 20% B, say, among his responses (and there is no
basis for assuming he will give 50-50), the degree of matching between his responses and the original stimuli is only
likely to approximate 50% if equal numbers of A and B were
originally included in the test design.

     It is also important in designing both the tests and
the training tests that the utterances A and B, or the
"same" and "different" pairs of words, be presented to the
hearer-identifier in thoroughly random order. The following are some typical random sequences of 10 + 10 = 20 items:

ABBAA-BAAAA-BBBAB-BBBAA
AAABA-BAABA-BBABA-BABBB
ABABB-BAABA-AABBA-BABBA
AABAB-BABBB-AABAB-BAAAB

On more than one occasion when I have presented material
in an alternating or mostly alternating order the hearer
thought that an alternating sequence was an essential
feature of the test. Later during the session he tended
to respond to all homophonous examples by alternating responses. This does no harm, but if one doesn't know the
actual phonological status of the two utterances under
test, then one can't be sure whether an alternating response
is merely a formalized response to homophony or an indication that the hearer-identifier doesn't understand what he
is supposed to be doing in the test.

For recognition tests such as these to have any statistical validity at all, the test must contain at least
20 utterances or same/different word pairs. In fact it is
better to have 40 utterances, but much above this figure
the participants tend to lose their mental image of each
word as a sound-meaning composite and deviant pronunciations and mis-identifications are the result.

Factors which distort the results

(1) As mentioned in procedure (d) above the speaker may
become confused and the apparent accuracy is consequently
lowered. More reliable accuracy figures may be obtained
by comparing two independent identification lists with
each other.

(2) Noise hampers the hearer and reduces the accuracy of
his identifications. For instance, in testing consonants
which contrast, if there is noise as loud as the voice
one cannot expect to get an accuracy higher than about
88%. If the noise is 6 decibels quieter than the voice
then one can expect a maximum accuracy of 95% (based on
Miller & Nicely 1955:347). Tests should be conducted in
circumstances that are as noise-free as possible.

(3) The mediocre frequency-response of inexpensive microphones and small loudspeakers limits the quality of reproduction of tape recorders and this in turn reduces the accuracy of the hearer's identifications. For instance,
when employing a cassette recorder whose response curve
is flat only from 300 to 5,000 cycles per second, one cannot
expect to get an accuracy higher than about 93% for testing consonants which contrast (based on Miller & Nicely
1955:347). The use of better quality microphones and
loudspeakers than are found in most portable tape recorders
will minimize the effect of this factor.

(4) Due to various bodily and mental quirks there is always a small percentage of poorly-formed and mis-heard utterances. My experience is that, even if all other conditions are ideal, this factor results in an average maximum accuracy of about 95%. I know of no way to reduce or eliminate this factor.

Thus, with average human participants, a typical cassette recorder, and noise 6 decibels softer than the voice, one can only expect about 82% accuracy where statistical theory of the ideal case predicts 100% if the two utterances being tested are contrastive in their consonants. The figure may be somewhat higher for vowel contrasts. For two utterances that are homophonous, human error, electronic limitations, and noise masking have a random effect and one can still expect an accuracy of approximately 50% just as predicted by statistical theory.

Interpreting the results

Once we have eliminated the effects of any confused participants we can say that

80% - 100% accuracy indicates phonological contrast, and
40% - 60% accuracy indicates phonological identity
(homophony).

The problem that plagues those who employ the pair recognition test is how to interpret results that fall in the region 60% - 80%.

There are several different things which may produce such a result.

(i) The two words contrast but the speaker and hearer belong to different dialects, or at the least have slightly different norms and ranges of variation for some of their phonemes. If this is the case, a much higher figure in the 80% - 100% range should be obtained by re-running the test with the same person acting as both speaker and hearer (using a tape recorder).

(ii) Word A may have two alternate pronunciations one of which is actually the same as the pronunciation of word B. If the linguist examines his tabulation of the test results and finds that one of the stimuli has about 100% matching with the reactions and the other stimulus has about 50% matching, then this not only confirms that one of the utterances has free variant pronunciations, but it also indicates

which utterance has the free variation should the linguist
find this difficult to detect by ear. In Telefol this kind
of result occurred when the pair test was applied to problematic morphophonemics. Testing àtèém 'frog sp.' and bimor-
phemic àtèém 'hole in tree' (from àt 'tree' and tèém 'hole')
gave about 70% matching, and an examination of the lists of
stimuli and reactions showed that it was àtèém 'hole in tree'
that had two alternative pronunciations that I was finding
difficult to hear. Once the occurrence of free variation
has been established the test can be repeated in a variety
of contexts to see if the free variation is inoperative in
any contexts.

(iii) One of the participants in the test may be almost
equally at home in two dialects or similar languages
(e.g. English and Pidgin English) one of which has the
particular phonological contrast and one of which does
not. It seems that, even in a test situation, such people
sometimes switch back and forth between the two dialects
without realizing it. If this is suspected, then the same
pair of utterances should be tested on a number of different
people (by procedure (c) above) to see whether or not there
are also some people whose responses are about 95% accurate
and others whose responses are approximately 50% accurate.

    This appears to be the situation in Nengone for
aspirated versus unaspirated stops. If one examines the
results tabulated by Tryon (1969:123) for the last four pairs
of words he tested, it can be seen that three people consistently distinguished aspirated and unaspirated stops,
three people consistently did not make the distinction,
five people distinguished them in some words but not in
others, and nine people gave responses almost all of which
were 60%-90% accurate, with an average of 73%.

Other uses of the test

    Determining the phonological status of pairs of utter-
ances with contrastive meanings and with problematic phonetics is the chief usefulness of pair testing in the phonological facet of field work. Pair tests cannot normally be used
for synonymous pairs of utterances, as their meanings or
physical meaning substitutes are unable to identify them
distinctively. However, form (e) of the test could conceiv-
ably (despite elicitation difficulties) be applied to synonyms. Provided that both speaker and hearer are demonstrably
evaluating sounds rather than meaning, 100% matching would
correspond to phonemic contrast with allomorphic (free)

alternation and 50% matching would correspond to complete
phonemic identity. However, if the hearer evaluates meaning
rather than sound, it is to be expected that he will always
respond "same" and the test is incapable of distinguishing
between allomorphic alternation and identity.

To make a detailed study of the free variant ranges
of two contrasting phonemes it would be possible to replay
a tape twenty times, say, and to designate the allophones in
utterances heard most consistently as being typical ones,
and those in utterances heard least consistently as being
allophones at the fringe of the range of free variation.
This suggestion is equivalent to the form of the pair test
given by Halle (1954:200). A similar procedure could be
used to investigate differences between dialects.

It is quite possible to design a test for simultaneously testing three or more utterances (for example, utterances that are suspected to have contrastive pitch patterns)
and the results may be presented in a "confusion matrix" as
done by Miller & Nicely (1955). However, the results of
such a test will not be as reliable as several tests of the
same size comparing the utterances of each pair at a time.

Warning

Pair testing is only an aid in phonological investigations; it does not do away with the linguist's need for
phonetic acuity. The pair test can show that two utterances contrast, but it cannot indicate the nature of the
phonetic difference between them. If the field worker can't
hear any difference, then listening to other contrasting
pairs of utterances may sharpen his hearing in time. Alternatively, a more experienced linguist may be able to listen
to his material and suggest the phonetic nature of the difference. If the field worker can hear several phonetic
differences between two contrasting utterances, then a pair
test cannot indicate which difference is the characteristic
or phonemic one. This is determined by careful phonetic
observation of which difference is subject to the least free
variation and by consideration of symmetry in the process of
phonemic analysis. In Telefol, an early pair test showed a
contrast between [bíl] 'wild banana sp.' and [bĭ·l] 'valley',
but it wasn't until much later that it could be seen that
these words contrasted in vowel length and tone pattern,
but that vowel quality was not significant, being conditioned by length (and by the author's Australian English
vowel bias). The final phonemicizations were /bíl/ and
/bĭíl/ respectively.

Bibliography

A. Noam Chomsky, 1955. "Semantic Consideration in Grammar", *Monograph Series on Languages and Linguistics* 8:141-158.

_____, 1957. *Syntactic Structures*. Mouton: 's-Gravenhage. [See pp. 96-9.]

_____, 1961. "Some Methodological Remarks on Generative Grammar", *Word* 17:219-39. [See p. 226.]

M. Halle, 1954. "The Strategy of Phonemics", *Word* 10:197-209. [See p. 200.]

Zellig S. Harris, 1951. *Methods in Structural Linguistics*. Chicago University Press. [See pp. 32-41.]

Alan Healey, 1964. "Handling Unsophisticated Linguistic Informants", *Pacific Linguistics*, Series A 2:1-30. [See pp. 8-11.]

C. F. Hockett, 1955. *A Manual of Phonology* (= Indiana University Publications in Anthropology and Linguistics, Memoir 11). [See p. 146.]

George A. Miller and Patricia E. Nicely, 1955. "An Analysis of Perceptual Confusion Among Some English Consonants", *The Journal of the Acoustical Society of America* 27:338-52.

D. T. Tryon, 1969. "Another Sound Change in Progress? The Case in Nengone", *Oceanic Linguistics* 8:120-30.

Collecting Genealogies

J. E. Henderson[1]

A genealogy is a list of someone's relatives, arranged to show how they are related to him. It also shows each person's clan membership, totem animal, date of birth, former place of residence, current place of residence, and any other details of interest to the investigator. It is usually displayed in chart form, and is then very useful in revealing actual patterns of marriage, residence, etc.

When collecting someone's genealogy, if you start to draw the chart straight away, you are bound to end up with a confused chart as you try to fit in people's children and siblings' children where there isn't room on the chart. It is much better to collect the details in a notebook first then draw the chart afterwards.

Start with an adult male as "ego" and record his vernacular name, lingua franca name, clan, totem, former residence, present residence, actual or estimated date of birth, and any other details you have decided are important for each person. Then record his first wife's name, and all the same details for her. If he has or has had other wives, record the same details for each of them in order. Record or estimate the dates any marriage(s) of his ended by death or divorce (and state which). Record any extra details he gives you.

Move now to his children by his first marriage, and for each one record the relevant details, plus the child's marital status and present residence. Include ex-nuptial children, and children who have died already. Repeat this for each subsequent marriage.

When all of ego's children have been recorded, focus on each of them in turn, and record the relevant details about his or her spouse and children. Work down in this way until all of ego's descendants have been recorded.

---

[1]These ideas are summarized from J. A. Barnes, 1967 "Genealogies" (in A. L. Epstein, ed., *The Craft of Social Anthropology*, Tavistok: London, pp. 101-127) and modified on the basis of my own experience.

Next, record the details for ego's parents and their descendants in the same way. A complete genealogy requires that these details be recorded for each of ego's ancestors, until people can no longer remember them. The more generations you elicit, the more relationships you can chart and the more useful the genealogy will be in helping you to understand behavior. Note and cross-reference any relationships other than descent between the people you record.

Charting the Details

A chart with descent running horizontally is usually the most useful. The chart starts with the most remote ancestor about whom you have fairly complete details and shows the relevant details against his symbol. His first wife then enters the chart, with her symbols and details below his. To the right of them a vertical line links their children, with the first-born at the top. His or her first spouse appears below, and their children can be listed to the right again. The generations are charted from left to right, and the children of each marriage from top to bottom. Double foolscap paper (43 cm x 34 cm) is convenient for charts, as it can be filed when folded in two. As a chart extends over more than one page, each page should be numbered, and where a line runs off the edge of a page there should be a column and row reference to where the line is continued on another page. Marriages between people listed on the chart should be cross-referenced by a page, column, and row number. It is easy to keep the chart neat if, while making it, you place the page over another page ruled in black ink with a vertical line about every 2-1/2 inches (65 mm) and a horizontal line every 3/8 inch (10 mm). Study the sample chart.

Smaller Genealogies for Language Learning

Complete genealogies such as this are very useful for showing how various people you know are related to each other. Full genealogies involve a lot of work, however, so for language learning purposes smaller genealogies, one for each hamlet or small cluster of families, are more appropriate. They are quicker to collect and chart, and it is easier to find names on them. Each genealogy could cover an adult male and his wives and descendants, and possibly his parents and siblings and their descendants. Later a chart could be constructed for the ancestors, to show how the separate genealogies are related to each other.

410

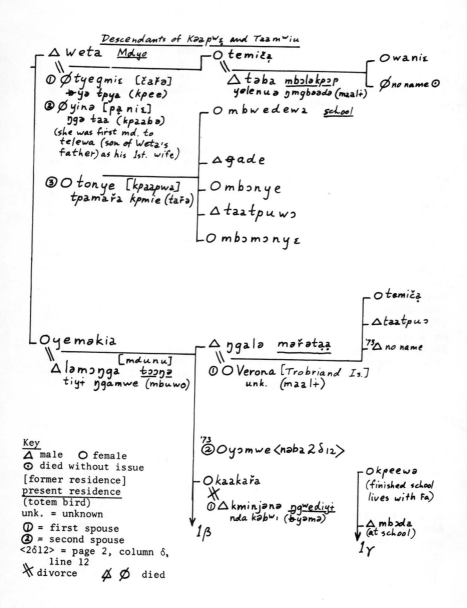

Descendants of Kəəpʷɛ̨ and Tɛɛmʷiu

△ weta _Mdyo_ ── O temičą̈ ── Owaniɛ

① Ø tyeqmiɛ [čařə] → Ø no name ⊙
  → yə tpya (kpee)
② Ø yinə [pą niɛ] △ təba _mbɔləkpɔp_
  ŋgə tɛɛ (kpɛɛbə) yelenuə ŋmgbəədə (mɛɛl+)
  (she was first md. to
  telewa (son of Wetə's ── O mbwedewə _school_
  father) as his 1st. wife)

③ O tonye [kpɛɛpwə] ── △ gade
  tpamařa kpmie (tařə)
  ── O mbɔnye
  ── △ taatpuwɔ
  ── O mbɔmɔnyɛ

── O temičą̈
── △ taatpus
'73 △ no name

L O yeməkiə ── △ ŋgalə _mařətąą_
  △ ləmɔŋga _tɔɔŋə_ [mdunu] ① O Verona [Trobriand Is.]
  tiy+ ŋgamwe (mbuwo) unk. (mɛɛl+)

Key
△ male   O female
⊙ died without issue
[former residence]
present residence
(totem bird)
unk. = unknown
① = first spouse
② = second spouse
<2δ12> = page 2, column δ,
         line 12
X divorce   ⱷ Ø died

'73
② O yɔmwe <nəbə 2 δ 12>

── O kaakařa
   X
   ① △ kminjənə _ŋgʷediy+_
     ndə kəbʷ¹ (byəmə)

↓ 1β

── Okpeewə
   (finished school
   lives with Fa)

── △ mbɔdə
↓ (at school)
1γ

Using Tape Recorders

Alan Healey

The tape recorder has become a vital tool in learning and analyzing a language.

Features of Good Recorders

To be satisfactory for language work in the field recorders must be rugged, portable, battery-operated, and of good fidelity.

(1) The recorder should be able to stand a fair amount of vibration and rough handling during travel, as service facilities are often limited or non-existent in the field.

(2) It should be small enough and light enough (say 5 kilos or less) for a woman to carry considerable distances without discomfort.

(3) Most modern recorders operate on flashlight batteries, but some drain their batteries more rapidly than others. (All recorders use more current when recording than on playback.) It is good to find a reliable source of fresh batteries and to keep a modest supply on hand.

(4) The electronic circuitry of many modern recorders is adequate, but cheap microphones and small loud speakers do not allow good reproduction of the consonants.

There are several other features that are desirable for language work, but it is rare to find them all in any one recorder.

(5) Rewind and pause controls that are easy to operate. "Piano keys" are usually satisfactory if they are not stiff. You need to be able to depress the rewind key briefly without locking it, so as to go back a very short distance (say 2 to 5 seconds) to listen quickly to some expression again. It is especially convenient if the rewind key automatically cancels the "play" mode without using the stop key.

(6) An efficient pause key can be used for listening to a word syllable by syllable. A pause key is invaluable when recording grammatical drills, paradigms, and tonal lists in frames. If your cassette recorder doesn't have a pause button, a pencil or a suitably bent paper clip can be inserted temporarily at the left spindle to prevent tape movement.

(7) Automatic volume control takes much of the strain and error out of recording voices. However it also makes background noise more audible when there is no one talking. Note that certain machines with AVC begin useful recording about one second after the tape starts moving.

(8) If the machine does not have AVC, then it is desirable to be able by depressing or half-depressing the record key, to test voices on the record level meter. This allows you to adjust the record level control before actually setting the tape moving.

Before buying a machine consult with experienced technicians and linguists who are familiar with the field where you plan to work and the availability of parts and service there. Obtain a good microphone, earphones, and a dubbing (copying) cord for your machine.

Reel-to-reel versus Cassette Recorders

Tape recorder technology has improved so much in recent years that good cassette recorders have about the same fidelity as small tape recorders of comparable weight and price. However, it is still true that a good reel-to-reel machine recording on two tracks at 3-3/4 inches per second (9.5 cm/sec) has more fidelity than any cassette machine. On the other hand the cassette machines have the advantage of being very light weight and economical on batteries; and the cassettes are easier to handle and keep clean.

Size of Tapes

For language learning there is the need to be constantly going back to specific drills or other items for practice. A lot of searching time will be saved if such materials are recorded on small 3 inch reels or C-30 cassettes. Larger 5 inch reels and C-60 cassettes will be more useful for recording texts. However, in reels it is not advisable to go beyond a 900 ft. "long play" tape on a 5 inch reel; the "double play" tapes give trouble by stretching unevenly and they may also develop print-through. Similarly, there is a limit for cassettes. C-90 cassettes are satisfactory in some brands, but C-120 cassettes tend to jam up in most brands.

Learning to Operate Your Recorder

Before you begin doing language work in the field you need to be thoroughly familiar with the operation of your tape recorder, to be able to make minor repairs and lubricate it on the field, to carry a small supply of fuses and

commonly needed spare parts, and to carry an adequate supply
of batteries if the recorder is battery operated. You should
have or devise some way of telling when the batteries are
flat and need replacing, and when the tape is slowing down
appreciably. For a reel-to-reel machine you need to practice
threading the tape past the heads so that it always records
without fail. The recording level indicator only shows that
the voice is passing from the microphone to the recording
head; the voice may not be reaching the tape if it has been
incorrectly threaded onto the machine. The only sure way is
to listen to the playback, or to record a few seconds and
then play that back, whenever one changes tapes or sides of
tapes on the machine. It is good to have some idea of the
directional properties of the microphone — how much softer
does the same noise sound on the tape when it is made beside
or behind the microphone (at the same distance) rather than
in front of it?

Before recording language material always record the
date, topic, and speaker's name in your own voice, and then
replay it to ensure that the machine is in fact recording
properly. Whenever possible, run a sample of the intended
speaker to get proper volume and distance of microphone from
speaker. Do it systematically. Keep a record of the different settings of the volume control and choose the best. You
need to know what volume control settings to use under
various conditions in case the recording level indicator
cannot be seen (e.g. in the dark).

It is often advisable to record with the microphone as
far away from the machine as the lead length and other factors will permit. This will minimize the recording of motor
noise and of feedback from the loudspeaker. If the machine
is of the type which operates a loudspeaker while recording,
it is better to switch off the speaker or turn it down low.
Another way to reduce the recording of motor noise is to put
the machine and microphone each on soft pads, on separate
tables if possible.

There is always quite a bit of background noise around,
more especially so in most village situations. You can
minimize a lot of background noise by recording at a low
volume with the microphone close to the speaker. (This is
usually a more culturally acceptable situation than shooing
away excess people.) Early in field work you need to listen
critically to the first few recordings to assess the common
types and levels of noise — pigs, dogs, roosters, children,
walking in the house, shuffling papers, coughing, rain on a

metal roof, blowflies, cicadas, night insects — so as to decide what place, time, and circumstances are the most practicable ones for recording. Wind blowing on the microphone
gives a very noisy recording.

Splicing

An ideal tape join is on a diagonal as in the diagrams.
This may be achieved by overlaying two ends of tape and cutting by a sharp pair of scissors or razor blade. This in-
sures that the two ends are parallel. Or you can use a
special tape splicer. Put the splicing tape onto the shiny
side of the recording tape.

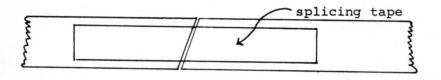

The two ends may then be joined by a narrow strip of
splicing tape as in the diagram above, or by using wide
splicing tape as in the diagram below. The sides then
need trimming: this is most casily achieved by cutting
with scissors.

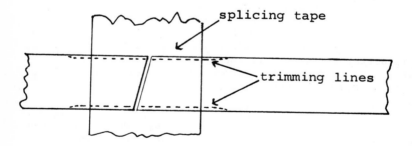

For reference purposes, it is best to mark the top edge of
the splice, by a felt-tip pen. Mark only the shiny side of
the tape. You might want to number it.

NEVER USE ORDINARY "SELLOTAPE" OR "SCOTCHTAPE" for splicing or you will mess up your heads when the Sellotape starts
to ooze a sticky substance. Always use proper splicing tape.

Tape Loops

In language learning and analysis there are occasions
when several repetitions of the same (usually short) stretch
of recorded speech is desirable. One way to achieve this is
with tape loops.

If you have a reel-to-reel recorder you can make loops
of any length you wish by splicing. Playback of loops may
be carried out as for normal tape. Keep the shiny side away
from the playback head on the recorder. Small or long loops
may be used, but remember that there must be some tension on
the loop. Often it is satisfactory to hang the loop over the
edge of the recorder and put a small spool in the bottom of
the loop to provide this tension.

Small tape loops (10" to 20" long) can usually be run
around one or two empty spools in their normal places on the
machine. Medium length loops (up to 6 feet long) can be
played by sitting the recorder up on edge at the edge of
the table, allowing the loop to hang down towards the floor
without touching it, and putting an empty spool into the bottom of the loop so that it can provide tension but yet roll
quite freely. If you need to operate your recorder down
flat on the table, then run the loop horizontally to a free-
spinning empty spool which is set at the right distance to
keep tension in the tape, and at the same height as the
deck of the recorder. The spool may spin on a nail in a
block of wood or a pencil in the mouth of a bottle. Long
tape loops can be run over a set of empty tape spools spinning on nails driven into the wall of the room. Tension may
be maintained either by adjusting the position of one spool
or of the recorder, or by hanging a free-rolling empty spool
in the tape at some suitable part of the loop.

Note that the two essentials for satisfactory operation
of a tape loop are:

(1) That you keep sufficient tension on the loop to keep
the tape from wrapping itself round the capstan. (It can
make an incredible mess in a very short time if it does.)

(2) Keeping the loop itself clean, and especially free from
dust. Otherwise the dust will grind your heads to bits in
no time. Do not let the loop trail on the floor or any

dusty surface while it is playing. When it is not playing
store it in a clean box to keep dust from settling on it.
If in doubt, remove dust from the loop before using by drawing it gently through clean cloth held between your fingers.

     If you have just one reel-to-reel machine, first record
on tape what you want on a loop. Then select the portion of
the recording needed for the loop and cut this piece out,
and make it into a loop. If you want to make small loops of
intonation contours or other items selected from a large tape
without cutting it, these need to be copied onto a second
tape that can be cut. If only one recorder is available,
then have an informant re-record this material, after alternately listening to and mimicking the particular part of the
first tape several times until he seems to be matching the
intonation and rhythm exactly. Alternatively, the loop may
be made first: record on to it later. If you do this make
sure that you stop recording before the loop has made a complete revolution. Otherwise you will automatically erase
the beginning of the recording.

     If you have a cassette recorder it is possible to buy
tape loops in standard cassettes. For instance "TDK" brand
supply endless cassettes of lengths 1/2, 1-1/2, 3, and 6
minutes. In addition, there is one model of cassette recorder (Canon "Repeat-Corder") which contains two cassettes
for language learning. One is a standard cassette which
operates normally; the other is a loop in a small square
cassette which is recording continuously from the standard
cassette and can be replayed at any time. The loops are
available in lengths from 5 to 30 seconds. The learner can
record his own voice on a second parallel track on the loop
and can then listen to both tracks simultaneously. As of
1974 only trial quantities of this model had been manufactured. There is another model of cassette recorder (National
Panasonic Cassette Language Lab 229) which, although it has
no loop, does have a particularly good rewind mechanism
which can be operated to be equivalent to a short loop of
up to 10 seconds.

     It should be noted that tape loops are not the only
way of practicing drills and expressions. Another possibility is to put the material to be practiced onto a tape
three times over with silences in between for mimicking.

Care of Recorder

(a) A plastic bag with silica gel and a humidity indicator

will keep a tape recorder in a dry atmosphere when not in
use. Watch the humidity indicator and rejuvenate the silica
gel when it is over-moist by heating it gently in a frying
pan or oven.

Also guard the machine from dust. Put a cover over
it when not in use. Dust will wear out your heads before
their time and it will not do your motor much good either.
Get yourself a small soft artist's brush and brush away the
dust frequently from near the heads of the machine. Wipe
off other dust with a soft fluffless cloth.

Every once in a while, open the machine up and clean
out all the cobwebs, dead cockroaches, and the like.

(b) Keep a constant watch on the batteries. In general
do not use any other kind of battery in your machine except steel-clad, leak-proof ones and even these have to be
watched in case they leak. Once there is the slightest
sign of leakage throw out the offending battery or you may
finish up throwing out your machine!! Clean off battery
verdigris.

Often poor machine function is due to nothing worse
than weak batteries. Keep a supply of FRESH batteries on
hand (but never stockpile batteries). Buy your batteries
from a reliable shop with a fast turnover; stale batteries
are a waste of money. Watch the battery life indicator on
your machine if you have one and do as it says. If you
have not got a battery life indicator it may pay you to invest in a small cheap voltmeter to test your batteries.

Poor recording is sometimes due to a dirty recording
head. The heads, capstan, and rollers should be cleaned
from time to time with cotton wool dipped in alcohol on
the end of a stick. Do not touch the heads with anything
which is magnetized — consider anything made of steel as
suspect in this regard.

Magnetic Tape

Always buy good quality tape. Cheap tape may be de-
fective in various ways. For instance it may have a hard
coarse coating that abrades the record and playback heads
excessively, or it may be slightly wider than the standard
and squeal as it goes through your recorder.

Magnetic tape is relatively cheap compared with the

price of a recorder. Keep an adequate supply on hand and
be generous in using it. There are many situations where
tape recording is vital — the language helper is available
for only a short time, or he is the last speaker of an otherwise extinct language, or for one reason or another he will
not repeat any utterance — so vital that it may even be
advisable to have a tape recorder running without stop
right through the elicitation session. This provides much
more information than one's written record usually contains.
Also, this is much more economical of time than the method
of just recording the more important items of data. For
instance, in survey work I have found that to alternate
between writing and recording wordlists takes about 50%
more time than does simultaneous writing and recording.

      With a cassette recorder, it is very convenient in lan-
guage learning to take a cassette out of the machine and put
a new one (or one that you had previously left) into the
machine without needing to rewind anything. With a reel-to-
reel recorder a similar convenience can be achieved in
changing tapes without rewinding (e.g. for practicing recorded drills) if you take several spare empty spools with
you and use a new one each time you wish to interrupt his
work on one tape to use another tape. Eventually, this
saves a lot of time that would otherwise be spent in rewinding the tape and finding the right place again.

      In the tropics tape, especially in reels, tends to grow
mould on its edges which may at times lock several layers of
tape together. This gives the tape a jerky motion as these
adhesions are broken, thus producing a poor recording. If
you want to record on a tape that you have not used for a
considerable time, any adhesions can be broken by running
the whole tape through first on fast forward followed by
fast rewind.

Mimicry in Language Learning

      Any kind of material recorded for mimicry should be
recorded with the best equipment available at the time, at
3-3/4 inches per second or faster if using a reel-to-reel
machine, with the quietest background that you can arrange,
and with adequate silences between each recorded utterance
to permit you to mimic it. When you use such tapes for
mimicry practice, it is best if you can have a vernacular
speaker present who can correct you and give you extra
practice on your weak points.

It is best to actually record TWO utterances of the
same sentence, with a silence between. To use it for practice you listen to the first utterance, mimic it in the
silence that follows, then listen to the repeat utterance
to correctly reinforce your attempt to mimic it. Thus the
last impression you hear of any utterance is the correct one.
If you have a machine which will record your mimicking on a
second track, you should do this OCCASIONALLY. Listening to
such double recordings may constitute a form of shock therapy
to spur you on to more frequent and careful mimicry.

You should always include silences right on the tape
for mimicry. If there are no silences you will be constantly stopping the machine to mimic and then restarting
it, which will be hard on both the recorder and you. If
you cannot get two identical utterances from your helper or
if you are wanting to practice sections of a text, then if
you have or are able to borrow a second recorder you could
prepare a practice tape with two utterances of each sentence
with a silence in between by copying from the original tape.

Preparing mimicry drills (and stimulus-response drills)
involves the recording of short portions of speech at close
intervals, and this requires good control of the stop-start
mechanism of the tape recorder. It also requires a considerable degree of cooperation from the helper so that he will
say exactly what is needed when it is needed. A method I
found useful with Telefol was to indicate to my helper in
the trade-language the utterance that I wanted and then wait
until he said it. When he said the vernacular I wanted, I
would switch on the recorder, say something in English to
identify or translate the item, pause, then signal my helper
who would say the vernacular utterance into the microphone.
If my helper didn't say the desired utterance, I would re-
elicit until he did. It is essential to have your helper
actually say the desired utterance before beginning the
recording, otherwise he is likely to hesitate at the crucial moment in the recording or say something else that is
not wanted. In either case you may feel this has spoiled
the recording and take time to erase it, and in the process
perhaps offend your helper.

If you have made a tape loop of material to mimic, for
instance, use it as follows:

(1) Play the loop several times while you LISTEN ONLY.
(Do not mimic at this stage.)

(2) Play the loop again, concentrating on "hearing" the
INTONATION. Once you begin to "hear" the intonation, stop
after each pause on the tape and mimic the intonation by
humming or whistling. Then, mimic the intonation simultaneously with the tape. Also use silent tracking occasionally. (Do not attempt to mimic the segmentals at this stage.)
Repeat this process until the intonation is being heard
clearly and mimicked accurately.

(3) Play the loop again, concentrating on "hearing" the
STRESS pattern. Mimic the stress by tapping, first <u>after</u>
the tape, and then simultaneously with it.

NOTE: Steps (2) and (3) may be reversed if you find the
stress easier to master first. Always begin with what is
easier and progress to the more difficult.

(4) Mimic intonation and stress together, first <u>after</u> the
tape, and then simultaneously with it.

(5) Finally, concentrate on the SEGMENTALS and mimic these,
while keeping the intonation and stress correct also.

     Whenever at any step you find that there is some point
which you are not mastering, play that one stretch of the
tape over and over again, listening and mimicking until you
master it. Then 'fit it in' to the whole, listening first
and then mimicking until the whole thing is mastered.

Listening in Language Learning

     You may listen to both texts and pronunciation drills
on tape as a way of strengthening your auditory image of
rhythm and intonation patterns in general and of the stress,
length, and pitch features of individual words as well.
It will also improve your recognition of function morphemes
and common word combinations. Listening to long loops of
text, especially conversation, while doing some manual
activity can be beneficial without giving much mental strain.

Recording Phonological Data for Analysis

     Whenever phonological contrasts (especially prosody)
present a hearing difficulty liberal use can be made of a
tape recorder to take down all the data that seem to be
crucial to the phonemic analysis. Such tapes can be used
for multiple playback (without tiring as does your language
helper), can be stored for checking later when your hearing has sharpened by practice, or can be submitted to a more
experienced linguist for his evaluation. Or perhaps you
need to have a piece of analysis checked with a consultant,

but circumstances make it difficult for you, your helper,
and a consultant to actually meet and work together. In
such a case, a good recording is of tremendous help to the
consultant. For such a purpose, the recording should be
the highest possible quality, i.e. the fastest speed on your
machine. Do not waste time recording at 1-7/8 or slower
for this sort of material; a low quality recording is not
much use.

    Line up your materials for phonemic contrasts in lists
of "same" or "different". If you want to contrast two
sounds, let the contrasting utterances in which they occur
be recorded next to each other on the tape, and not separated from each other by a couple of minutes of winding
time. Remember that if you have this separating time between the two utterances, the consultant will have forgotten what the first utterance sounds like by the time he is
ready to hear the second. Remember that the consultant does
not speak your language. If you want to make sure of contrasts between two segments occurring in two words, it is
advisable to record the two words first in one order and
then in reverse order. If you are recording in terms of
contrastive lists, first of all make sure that each of your
lists is uniform within itself. Next record each list in
turn. Then, for the lists that contrast against each other,
record the contrasts of pairs of sounds in opposition. Thus
the consultant can hear not only the similarities but also
the contrasts. Make sure that each utterance is recorded at
least three times to give some evidence for its range of
phonetic variation. Tape the entire phonemic system in
this way, if necessary.

    You may wish to record certain kinds of data for your
own careful listening and analysis. Again the fidelity
needs to be the highest you have. Many machines record
well but have a poor playback because of a rather small loudspeaker — in the majority of cases it will be worth your
while to invest in a good pair of earphones. You will
hear things much more clearly, and annoy your neighbors less.

    Such recordings can be of anything such as minimal or
near-minimal pairs, difficult consonant clusters, intonation or tone frames--in short, anything that you need to
listen to intensively to master because you are still not
familiar with it. Often such a recording can really save
the patience of your language helper.

    If you are recording material for testing on one of the

several kinds of speech analyzers, you should take special
precautions in making the recording. Use a high fidelity
microphone and reel-to-reel recorder. Record on one track
only of new tape, at 7-1/2 inches per second preferably or
at 3-3/4 i.p.s. Identify each word or sentence clearly on
the recording and record five utterances of it at a uniform-
ly moderate tempo. Make the recording in a soundproof room
if at all possible.

Recording Text Materials

     With a little imagination and people who are willing to
be recorded, you should be able to record a wide variety of
texts. Ask your language helper who are the best people in
the community to give you texts on various subjects, and get
him to help arrange a recording session. Try to get accounts
of recent events in the community, accounts of famous events
in remembered history, legends, descriptions of everyday life
in the community, procedural accounts of how things are made
and done (hunting trips, house building, etc.), descriptions
of public ceremonies and festivals, explanations of why certain customs are observed, exhortations to the community to
take some course of action, advice to a bride and groom, and
the like. If the language is used in radio broadcasts, this
could provide another source of texts.

     Sometimes it is difficult to get text material. People
who seem uninterested in giving texts may be encouraged to
give an account of some very recent event in which they participated. Some field workers encourage such people to tell
a story in the trade-language and then ask them to say the
same thing in the vernacular. However, it has been my experience that the vernacular version, being a repetition, is
usually much shorter and less interesting than the trade-
language version. Personally I have avoided recording
Telefol legends because they are the property of the initiated men. It was important to avoid accidentally breaking
taboos by playing them back within earshot of women or children.

     Another device for getting text material is to replay
a story or account previously recorded, and then ask someone to tell the same story again in his own words. This
may be done several times over for the one story, either
with different people or with the one person over a period
of months, thereby providing a set of similar texts all
describing the same physical or social situation. These
are a potential source of paradigmatic material and for

USING TAPE RECORDERS   423

material involving grammatical transformations.

     Another way to get text material when language helpers
don't get the idea, is to get a group of people together
when they are relaxed and in a talkative mood (after the
evening meal, say). If one person can be induced to tell
even a short story, the other members of the group are soon
eager to have their turn to record a story and hear the replay. Another way is for you to attempt to tell some short
story, and sometimes stories will come tumbling out in
response. Some linguists first elicit a considerable amount
of vocabulary in a given semantic domain, and then immediately request text material. This vocabulary stimulates people
to give stories or ethnographic accounts, and also prepares
the linguist for transcribing the text.

     In getting text materials, people are often very
dependent on an appropriate situation before they will
talk. For instance, just before, after, or during a festival might be the time they are really in the mood to talk
about this festival. Be ready to record them when they are
in the mood or you may miss a lot. Have your recorder ready
and always a couple of spare tapes at hand. Sometimes it
might be indelicate to ask them to record, they simply want
to talk. Be patient and wait; your time will come when you
have won their trust.

     Conversations recorded on tape are prize material for
the grammarian, but natural conversations are difficult to
record. Those staged in front of a microphone are stiff,
but may become more natural as the participants become more
interested in their topic. (So suggest a "hot" topic.)
It will help if you can forget your tape recorder (or the
direction of the microphone or the level indicator) and take
a genuine but non-vocal interest in the conversation. I record only conversations of a non-personal nature, conversations held in some kind of public situation. It is good to
play back the tape immediately to the participants for their
approval, or if that is not possible, to a trusted friend,
to make sure that no one will be offended by the keeping or
studying of the recording. Conversations between two people
are the best; the more people participating the more likely
it is that several people will talk at once, and this is almost impossible to transcribe from the tape. Linguists have
differing views as to the value of a single person recording imaginary conversations.

Once stories have been recorded, your tape recorder
is likely to become a source of community entertainment.
You will often be pressed to replay various of your tapes
by way of payment for story telling. Whenever I record
text I have found it satisfactory to play back just the
last few minutes of the text. This is still some kind of
reward for the person giving the text, without being boring
or time-consuming, and at the same time serves as a check
that the recording is technically satisfactory.

Because of community interest in your recordings and
because playing them back is likely to be a public affair
at any time (unless you use headphones), it is wise to check
the meaning of what has been recorded as soon as possible,
either with the person who gave the text or with a trusted
friend. If any of the content is offensive in any way, or
involves taboo topics, then this tape must be clearly marked
that it is not for public replaying. I prefer to erase such
material completely so as to avoid any danger or embarrassment or marring of my relationship with the speaker or his
community. One way to avoid recording such material is to
make recordings under circumstances that could be regarded
as public in some way. If both sexes are within earshot at
the time, taboo topics are not likely to be recorded, and
if several people are within earshot insults are not likely
to be used without the linguist knowing. Although taboo
topics are of interest to anthropologists and may even be of
linguistic interest too, the difficulty of finding adequate
privacy for replaying and transcribing it on the field is
considerable, as is the danger of accidentally having the
replay volume too loud, and it seems wise to obtain such
texts without a tape recorder. I know of a field worker who
replayed a tape for entertainment, without realizing that it
contained material highly insulting to one of the audience.
In a flash, the man was brandishing a bush-knife and chas-
ing the speaker and his relatives.

Transcribing Tape-recorded Texts

It is a common practice to record many hours of text
material on magnetic tape, and to bring it back from the
field for transcription and analysis at home. Unless the
linguist knows the language well this is a waste of time
and tape. To transcribe tape without an informant requires
the ability to recognize immediately the elisions and

contractions that occur in speech at normal speed, and the
ability to weigh up the various lexical and syntactic possibilities so as to reconstruct the occasional word obscured
by noise on the tape. Many of us don't know the language
we are studying that well, and need to bring home more than
a text on tape. It is essential to transcribe the tape onto
paper while still in the field. It is best to do this as
soon as possible after recording, using as assistant someone
who was present when the recording was made, if possible the
person whose voice was recorded.

I have found it most satisfactory not to transcribe
directly from the tape, but to use the tape as a prompting
device, and to transcribe from my assistant after he has
heard the tape and repeated it, a few seconds at a time (in
pause groups where possible). Some assistants are good at
this tiring work, but others are quite unsatisfactory because they give the meaning of what they hear from the tape
in different words rather than giving an exact repetition.
Even a good assistant will sometimes say something different
from what the linguist feels he can hear on the tape. It is
best not to argue with him, but to transcribe both versions.
Usually the difference is that between slow and fast forms.
For instance, my Telefol assistant always insisted on the
slow form *kanubeê* 'if' where I often heard *nubeê* on the tape.

After several years' field work I found that every hour
of continuous speech on tape took me about 70 hours (3 hours
per day was about all my helper and I could tolerate) to
transcribe phonemically, to ascertain the meaning of all unfamiliar morphemes and grammatical features, and to obtain
a fairly accurate free translation. Recordings that are too
soft, or have too much noise, or are of speakers who are excessively fast, take about twice as long to transcribe and
usually aren't worth that much field time.

Other Uses for a Tape Recorder

When you are bringing your Dictionary File up to date
and checking the usage of words, a long tape recording of
the discussion can provide you with a record of all the
illustrations that your assistant mentions, many of which
you may not take time to write down during the discussion.
Play back the tape, make a permanent note of all vocabulary
items, meanings, and usages that are new and useful, and
then clean the tape for the next session.

The same procedure can be used for collecting

illustrations of a particular function word or grammatical construction. It can be used for a discussion in preparation for translating some specific passage, or for a discussion of the accuracy and naturalness of a translation once it has been drafted. It has also been used to record the actual drafting of a translation, with the recorder catching the first spontaneous oral draft which is usually fairly good.

Warning

Tape recorders rarely get tired; they do not demand that the speaker slow down to writing speed, and they allow language study when no vernacular speaker is available. But tape recorders are limited. Repetitions by replaying are identical and do not show the range of variations in normal speech. And the recorder abstracts speech from its context in everyday life and from the accompanying gestures.

For these reasons (and others) you must get out amongst people. There is a danger that the learner may prefer to work with the machine even when a native speaker is available, because the machine and solitude are far less demanding. Recordings are an aid, and not a substitute for talking with people.

Bibliography

British School of the Summer Institute of Linguistics, 1970. "The Use of Tape Recorders", and "The Use of Tape Loops" in Alan Healey, ed., *Translator's Field Guide*, Summer Institute of Linguistics, Ukarumpa, pp. 450-463.

Alan Healey, 1964. "Handling Unsophisticated Linguistic Informants", *Linguistic Circle of Canberra Publications* (now *Pacific Linguistics*), Series A, No. 2.

William J. Samarin, 1967. *Field Linguistics*, Holt, Rinehart and Winston, New York.

Plain Card Filing

Alan Healey

Plain filing cards (that is, filing cards that are not
punch cards) come in a variety of sizes. The most popular
sizes are 3 inches by 5 inches and 4 inches by 6 inches.
The cards may be lined or unlined, they may be white or
colored.

The purpose of a card filing system is to put each bit
of information on a separate card so as to be able to collect
in one place in the file all of the cards with similar data.
Any part of the file can be expanded as much as necessary.
When you come to study some particular small topic, the pertinent cards may all be quickly retrieved, spread out, and
consulted. Later on, if your understanding or analysis
changes, you can re-sort the cards into new categories and
file them elsewhere in the system.

The information written or typed on a single card will
normally be an example of some morpheme, word, or grammatical construction. The example should be written in the center of the card and should be accompanied by an English
translation, a guess at the grammatical analysis, a reference
number indicating exactly where in your tape or data file
this example can be found, the name of the speaker, and the
date on which he gave this example. Leave room for rewriting
the example and the heading of the card in any new orthography that you may develop later.

The top edge of the card is reserved for writing an
affix, stem, grammatical label, or symbol that indicates
where this card is to be filed in your system. If a particular word or sentence illustrates three different grammatical features, then make three cards with exactly the same
data on them and head each one appropriately. If a word has
three different English translations make four nearly identical cards for your dictionary file--one headed with the vernacular word and three others, each headed with one of the
English glosses.

In your dictionary file the cards will be kept in alphabetical order. As you write new cards you may file them one
by one. However, if you are writing a considerable number
of new cards it is more efficient to wait until you have a

sizable batch, alphabetize them within the batch, and then
insert them into the file. A grammar file may be partially
in alphabetical order, but much of it is better kept in
some kind of "logical" order that fits your understanding of
the grammar.

The color of the cards may be used as an extra coding
and sorting device, provided that the colors represent some
facet of the data which will not be changed as your analysis
changes.

If you have trouble with constantly dropping cards and
the need to re-sort them, then you may find it profitable to
clip the top right hand corner of all cards.

You may use a Vernacular-English dictionary file for
phonological analysis by sorting through it for all examples
of the particular sound or sequence or syllable pattern you
wish to investigate. Such sorting is more speedily done by
taking a handful of cards out of the file and sorting them
into heaps.

Punch Card Filing

Robert J. Conrad

0. Introduction
1. Equipment
2. Coding
3. Notching
4. Sorting
5. Applications
    5.1 Phonology
    5.2 Grammar
    5.3 Lexicon
    5.4 Anthropology
    5.5 Other
6. Advantages
7. Disadvantages

0. Introduction

Before you begin using a punch card system for linguistic analysis, be sure to weigh the advantages (section 6) against the disadvantages (section 7).

A punch card system is a coding device for indicating occurrence or non-occurrence of certain kinds of information. Data is recorded on cards both by ordinary writing on the center of a card and also by open or closed holes on the edge of the card. By running a long needle through holes representing various kinds of information, the cards which contain a particular item can quite quickly be separated from those which do not.

1. Equipment

The required equipment consists of punched cards, a sorting needle, filing boxes, and a punch to notch the holes. A sorting tray is helpful, but not essential, for keeping sorted cards in order. Alignment blocks are convenient, but again not essential. Cards can be aligned by hitting them against any hard smooth surface. The complete outfit is available at most stationery stores which stock punch cards.[1]

1.1 Cards

Cards are available in sizes ranging from 3 by 5 to 5 by 8 inches. The larger ones are preferable because they have more holes and therefore can store more information.

Prices of cards are variable. Samarin reports some as high as $50.00 per 1000 for 5 by 8 inch cards. However, there are ways of getting much cheaper cards. One may buy plain unpunched 3 by 5 inch cards for as little as $2.00 per 1000 and punch or drill holes along the edges with homemade equipment.[2] The quality of such cards will depend on the quality of the equipment.

Probably a better choice is to use regular IBM cards (3-1/4" by 7-3/8") which have had holes punched all around the edges by a computer. By having every second (or third) column punched on the long edges and every position on the short edges, a card with 100 (or 74) rectangular holes can be obtained. (The larger spacing of holes is advisable if the punch to be used later produces a wide notch.) This type of punch card may be obtained from computer companies for $4.00 to $10.00 per thousand.[3] On IBM cards, one corner is already cut off. This should also be done to other types of cards, as it facilitates straightening out mixed up cards.

1.2 Needle

A metal knitting needle or a piece of STRAIGHT wire that is reasonably rigid will do. A wooden handle can be fitted onto one end of the needle to make it easier to manipulate. For 1/8 inch holes, a U.S Number One or Australian Number Ten knitting needle is needed. For the very small rectangular holes in IBM cards, to get sufficient rigidity, it is advisable to use a special sorting needle that matches the rectangular holes — either an IBM sorting needle or a knitting needle filed flat on two sides.

1.3 Punch

A hand punch is convenient for notching cards in the field situation, but a platform or table punch is faster. If punch cards are going to be used extensively, it is advisable to have a punch which is sufficiently strong to notch several cards at once and which has removable blades. Be sure the punch is appropriate for the particular spacing of holes in your cards. If the punch is too wide, it will weaken the edges of adjacent holes. Errors in notching can be corrected with scotch tape or gummed paper which card manufacturers sell. Success in sorting depends on the cards being accurately notched. The punch should make a V-shaped notch rather than a U-shape, so the cards can fall from the needle easily.

1.4 Filing Box

This is necessary to protect the edges of the cards from being bent. Blank cards should be handled carefully for the same reason.

2. Coding

A field is a set of adjacent holes which are used to indicate one category of information, such as the grammatical class (or the first phoneme) of a word. Suppose there are 11 possible grammatical classes (or 23 phonemes) in the language, then we need 11 (or 23) different ways of notching the field (set of adjacent holes) that has been assigned for recording this information. Our assigning of a certain number of holes as the field for grammatical class (or for first phoneme) and our assigning of various notching patterns to indicate the 11 (or 23) alternative items or possibilities in this category of information is called coding.

There are many different coding systems of varying complexity and economy. Whatever system of coding is used, be sure to make several master cards which show the various fields and their category of information, and write on them the specific information or value assigned to each hole in each field.

2.1 Direct Coding

This is the simplest method, in which one hole stands for one alternative within a category of data. For example, a field may be assigned to represent the first segment of a word, and within that field one hole is assigned to each phoneme or orthographical character. Another field, which would be adjacent to but not overlapping (sharing any holes with) the first field, can be assigned to the second segment of the word, etc., as in Figure 1. See section 5 for further applications.

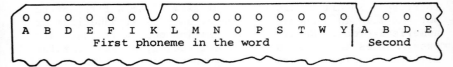

Figure 1 Direct coding of a word commencing with /ka/

2.2   Combination Coding

For many applications the system of direct coding is not satisfactory because it does not allow enough information on a single card. In combination coding, each alternative item within a category of information is assigned a number in order, beginning with 1. (For an example see section 5.1.) One records an item of information on the card by notching its number. This is done by notching a combination of holes, each of which has previously been assigned a special numerical value. There are many systems of combination coding, some quite complex. The more complex the coding becomes, the more time needed for notching and sorting and correction of errors. Very soon one reaches a point of diminishing returns.

The system illustrated in Figure 2 is a practical compromise which has the additional advantage of being based partially on our familiar decimal system of numbers.

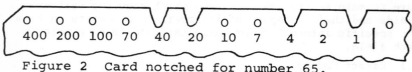

Figure 2   Card notched for number 65.

In Figure 2, notice that holes 40, 20, 4, and 1 are notched, and their sum is 65. This arrangement permits coding of all numbers from 0 (no notches) to 854 (all holes notched). For instance, 19 would be obtained by notching 10, 7, and 2. To notch any number, simply pick the largest numbered hole less than or equal to the number you want to code and then work down to 1.

This type of coding is often used when one desires to retrieve a specific card or set of cards from a file, or to put the file in a special sequence, such as alphabetical or numerical order. Never use combination coding if there are enough holes in the card for direct coding, because the former type requires several sorting operations to retrieve all the cards with a certain type of information, while in the latter this is obtained with one sort only.

For details of the more economical 1-2-4-8-16 numerical

method of coding, and of the less economical but visually
convenient corner and triangle methods, see Day 1964 or
Anon. 1962.

3. Notching

Make sure that the notching is accurate and that the
slot is wide enough to allow the sorting needle to slip out
of it easily, yet not so large that adjacent hole edges are
weakened. Be especially careful not to notch IBM cards too
deeply. See Figure 3.

Notching satisfactory   Notching too deep

Figure 3 How to notch an IBM card.

For rapid notching, superimpose a copy of the master card on
the data card so that the line of holes to be notched is ex-
posed. This eliminates the tedious job of writing the meaning of the holes on each card. Alternatively, mark the holes
for notching with a pencil when the master card is super-
imposed on the data card. This is a slower process unless
you are having an assistant notch cards with a scissors or
punch.

4. Sorting

Do not try to sort too many cards at once. Only about
200 to 300 cards can be comfortably held in the hand.

First align the cards by striking them against a smooth
hard surface. Then insert the needle through the desired
hole at the upper edge of the pack.

Be sure the cards are not tightly packed together. One
way of insuring this is to hold the pack loosely on their
edges with the left hand while inserting the needle with the
right. After inserting the needle, swing it around 20-30
degrees in a horizontal plane, pinch the pack with the left

hand, swing the needle back to the original position, and then release your left hand grip on the pack. This will spread the cards out on the needle if done properly. Then lift the needle so that the notched cards will drop out.

For the procedure for sequence (alphabetical) sorting, see section 5.3.

5. Application

With any type of application, coding should be very carefully planned. FIRST DO A TRIAL RUN OF ABOUT 200 CARDS and experiment in working with these before processing any more. Otherwise you may waste much time and many cards. It is better to re-notch a few hundred cards in favor of a better system than labor with a system that does not show what you need. ALWAYS RESERVE SOME HOLES FOR LATER USE when you will want to add some extra categories of information that you could not envisage at first.

5.1 Phonology

For the Kunimaipa language, whose word patterns can be summarized by the formula $[(C)V]^n(C)$, Pence used the syllable as the basic unit for recording phonetic data as follows:

The first seven fields represent the first six syllables and the final syllable of a word, and each of these fields has four holes to record any one of 15 types of phonetic syllable:

1. bilabial contoid plus front vocoid
2.   "   "   "   central "
3.   "   "   "   back   "
4. alveolar stop or vibrant contoid plus front vocoid
5.   "   "   "   "   "   "   central "
6.   "   "   "   "   "   "   back   "
7. alveolar continuant contoid plus front vocoid
8.   "   "   "   "   central "
9.   "   "   "   "   back   "
10. velar or glottal contoid plus front vocoid
11. "   "   "   "   "   central "
12. "   "   "   "   "   back   "
13. syllable-initial front vocoid
14.   "   "   central "
15.   "   "   back   "

The eighth field has one hole to indicate either of:
un-notched: word has fewer than 8 syllables
notched: word has 8 or more syllables

The ninth field has one hole to indicate either of:

un-notched: word has no syllable final contoids
notched: word has one or more syllable final contoids

A typical notched card is shown in Figure 4.

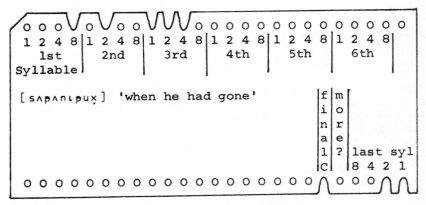

Figure 4. Card notched for syllables

This system utilizes a 1-2-4-8 rather than the 1-2-4-7 coding scheme, in order to code 15 items in a 4-hole field.

It is clear that the particular system used depends on
the language being analyzed and on the state of the analysis.
This particular approach took advantage of the fact that
there seemed to be a fairly small number of phonemes and
syllable types. With a very large number of phonemes, one
might have to abandon this approach in favor of coding distinctive features or individual segments. Pence's approach
has the advantage of rapid notching and sorting, since a
syllable is quicker to encode than individual phones. Of
course, it assumes the working definition of a phonetic
syllable. More complex CV patterns would necessitate each
syllable having a larger field (i.e. more holes). Note
that unused holes are reserved for further distinctions at
a later analytical stage.

An approach using the segment rather than the syllable works for the same data. For each segment, use a
field of 3 holes with numerical values 1, 2, and 4. This
gives a total of 7 distinct items possible for each field,

to be coded as follows: 1. bilabial contoid
                          2. alveolar stop or vibrant
                              contoid
                          3. alveolar continuant contoid
                          4. velar or glottal contoid
                          5. front vocoid
                          6. central vocoid
                          7. back vocoid

A back vocoid, for example, would be coded by notching
holes for 1, 2, and 4. The first 8 segments of a word
could then be recorded on the same size card, in 8 fields
of 3 holes each across the top of the card. Six more
segments could be recorded along the bottom of the card.
A single hole could be used to represent a word of more
than 14 segments. See Figure 5. As before, unused holes
are reserved for future analysis

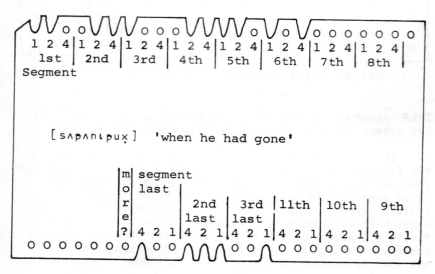

Figure 5. Card notched for segments

     Another approach would be the following (slightly
modified form of the) phonetic coding used by Bee for
Usarufa:

Divide the top of the card into 3 fields of 7, 6, and 7
holes respectively, and on the bottom of the card set off
a field of 9 holes:

Field I: Stops

1. Bilabial
2. Alveolar
3. Velar
4. Glottal
5. Stop Initial
6. Stop Final
7. Length of Stop

Field II: Fricatives

1. Bilabial
2. Alveolar
3. Velar
4. Alveo-palatal
5. Fricative Initial
6. Fricative Final

Field III: Continuants

1. Bilabial Nasal
2. Alveolar Nasal
3. Flap r
4. Flap l
5. Continuant Initial
6. Continuant Final
7. Length of Nasal

Field IV: Vocoids

1. High Front
2. Mid Front
3. Front Semi-vocoid
4. Mid Central
5. Low Central
6. High Back
7. Mid Back
8. Back Semi-vocoid
9. Vocoid Length

These distinctions would then be coded by direct coding into the various fields of the card, as in Figure 6.

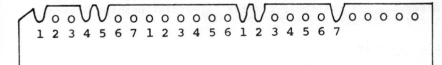

[púyʌmúʔná:m:ʎ] 'a trespass warning'

Figure 6. Card notched for phones

The same information could have been coded by combination coding, using fields of 3 holes each for each of the three sections of contoids, and a field of 4 holes for the

vocoids, with the holes within each field designated
1-2-4(-8). For example, a word-final fricative would be
coded by notching the holes designated 2 and 4. This system would leave more room for added information, such as
the CV pattern, or for adding repeated fields for making
the same distinctions in various specific segments of the
word.

A simpler method for preliminary phonological analysis
is the use of direct coding for all phones occurring in a
word, regardless of position. In this case, one hole
would be assigned to each possible observed phone. Then,
to make check lists and to compare the distribution of
phone [p] with that of [ɓ], for example, only two sortings
would be needed--one pass to sort out the words containing
[p] and a second pass for those containing [ɓ].

At a later stage, all occurrences of each phoneme
could be coded by direct coding. Additional holes could
be used to code CV patterns, stress, etc. The applications,
in phonology as in other areas, are limited only by the
ingenuity of the analyst. For instance, Grimes notched
cards to show the length, stress, tone, and rhythmic status
of each syllable in Huichol words. He then used them to
determine the extremely complex interrelationships between
these factors.

5.2 Grammar

Assuming a gradual build-up of an analytical grammar
file, a general overall plan should be devised first so
that items studied at one level could then be used later to
study other levels. Various tagmemic units or transformations can be coded, depending on which approach is used.

For a tagmemic analysis of the clause level, for
example, fields could be designated to represent such
categories as:

(a) the level (i.e., clause as distinct from phrase or
     sentence)
(b) type of construction within the level
(c) tagmemes occurring in such constructions
(d) classes of fillers which occur in certain tagmemes
(e) type of text from which this example was taken

In the example in Figure 7, direct coding is used for a
clause from May River Iwam.

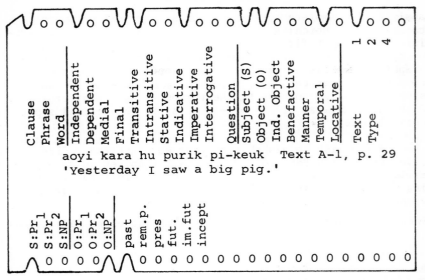

Figure 7. Direct Coding of a Grammatical Construction

As Day has noted, free-order items in a clause can be coded in all of their possible positions of occurrence. The linear order of the holes can be made to match the linear sequence of the elements within the clause, as in the example in Figure 8.

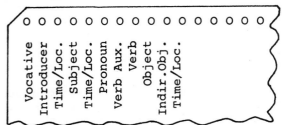

Figure 8 Direct Coding of Tagmemes in Linear Sequence

From such a coding, it is easy to check by sorting whether or not the phrases that occur in these various positions have the same or different structure. From this one can decide whether this is a single tagmeme with variable order or whether there are two or more distinct tagmemes.

5.3 Lexicon

A lexical file can be started even before phonological

analysis is complete by writing words in pencil on punch
cards without notching them. The file can be used as a regular card file at first, and at a later stage the words can
be typed in and the cards notched. Either practical orthographical symbols or phonemes can be coded. If desired,
complex phonemes can be represented by a sequence of two
symbols. Assign numbers to the various single characters,
with the numerical order corresponding to the desired alphabetical order.

If you wish to alphabetize your words by their first
five letters (as Bee did for Usarufa), then set up five
fields on the card, the first field on the left corresponding to the first letter in every word, and so on. For
example:

Phoneme	Number	Combination code (these holes to be notched)
a	1	1
b	2	2
e	3	2 + 1
g	4	4
i	5	4 + 1
k	6	4 + 2
m	7	7
n	8	7 + 1
o	9	7 + 2
p	10	10
q	11	10 + 1
r	12	10 + 2
t	13	10 + 2 + 1
u	14	10 + 4
w	15	10 + 4 + 1
y	16	10 + 4 + 2

If you have no more than 24 letters in the transcription
you are coding onto the cards, then allow 5 holes in each
field and number them 10-7-4-2-1 from left to right. If
you have from 25 to 44 letters to specify, then allow 6
holes in each field and number them 20-10-7-4-2-1. Various
other features such as word class, morphological class,
occurrence with certain affixes, topical category (semantic
domain), number of syllables, and stress or tone pattern
could be added in other holes.

By sequence sorting, a lexical file of the type outlined for Usarufa can be alphabetized to the 5th letter.
The procedure depends on the volume of cards.

Procedure A. For small quantities of data, such that all the cards can be sorted on the needle at one time:

Begin with the hole numbered 1 in the fifth field (i.e., the field corresponding to the fifth character of each form in the file). Separate the file into two piles--those that remain on the needle and those that fall off. Put those that fall off behind those that remain. Follow the same procedure for each successive hole (the hole numbered 2 next, etc.) from right to left, lowest to highest, and in each successive field, from last to first. It is crucial that the cards which have been sorted at any particular step be kept in the same sequence for the rest of the sort. If one or two cards fall out of order in sorting, save them until the end of the process and file by hand.

Procedure B. For large bodies of data, such that the cards cannot be sorted by one pass of the needle, it is advisable to use a breakdown or block sort first. This is to sort the large group into alphabetical order by the first letter only. Note that in the following paragraph all of the sorting procedures are applied to the first field on the left.

First sort all cards on the hole numbered 10, which corresponds to the first segment of a word. This gives two groups: those with their initial segment numbered 10 to 16 (which are those that fell off) and those with their initial segment numbered 1 to 9 (those that did not fall). Sort group 10-16 on the hole numbered 4, and this will result in groups 14-16 and 10-13. Sort the former on the hold numbered 2, separating 16 from 14 and 15. Sort 14 and 15 on the hole numbered 1, separating 14 from 15. Set all these aside, and sort group 10-13 on hole 2, giving two groups: 10-11 and 12-13. Sort each of these groups separately on hole 1. Take group 1-9 and sort on hole 7, giving groups 7-9 and 1-6. Divide group 7-9 into three groups by sorting on hole 2 first and then on hole 1. Group 1-6 should then be sorted on hole 4, separating 4-6 from 1-3. Separate each of these two groups into three groups by sorting on hole 2 first and then on hole 1 in each group. Now there are 16 different groups (blocks) of cards, representing alphabetization to the first letter.

If some of the groups are still too large to sort with one pass of the needle, take each large group and repeat the above procedure completely for the second field from the left, corresponding to alphabetization to the second letter. When

the groups are small enough, then use procedure A above.
When using procedure A following a block sort (procedure B)
it is not necessary to sort the fields already sorted in the
block sort. That is, it will not be necessary to sort the
first field on the left in procedure A if it has already
been done (if procedure B applied first).

If there is room on the card, the first few letters
of the main English meaning can be coded. Double entries
could be used for synonyms. Then sorting according to the
English alphabetical order results in a file from which a
preliminary English-vernacular dictionary can be typed.[4]

5.4 Anthropology

Anthropological data is adaptable to this method of filing by analogy with other applications. The most likely
problems to be handled would be those in which you know some
definite categories and you suspect some complex interrelationships between these.

5.5 Miscellaneous

Punch cards can be used in comparative linguistic analysis. Each card should contain a set of cognate forms. One
field should indicate the dialects or languages represented
in the particular set. Code phonological data so that sound
correspondences can be easily located. For example, if a
cognate set has some words with an initial vowel and others
in which this vowel has been lost, and you feel that the succeeding phonemes of each word correspond, code the initial
vowels in a field which is left blank for the initial segment of the corresponding forms without the vowel.

Punch cards can be applied to bibliographical files.
Suggested fields are: alphabetical list of authors based
on a combination code suitable for sequence sorting, date
of publication, alphabetical listing of the language or
tribe, language classification, geographical area to which
the work applies, and direct coding of the subject matter--
phonology, grammar, etc.

6. Advantages

(a) Flexibility in maneuvering the cards into any desired
order.

(b) Speed for checking various hypotheses concerning complex interrelationships among various categories.

(c)   Speed in finding data and/or ordering a file.

(d)   Relative economy and simplicity of the equipment.

(e)   Utility for several types of analysis (see section 5).

(f)   Elimination of the need for duplicate cards by coding a single entry in many different ways, thereby allowing a wide variety of information to be retrieved from one file.

(g)   Ability to retrieve much information without alphabetical ordering, and hence its relative immunity from accidents and children.

(h)   Possibility of using relatively unskilled assistants for some of the fairly simple coding.

7.   Disadvantages

(a)   You must know what categories you want to represent before you can start. You must know some answers before you can decide what categories and coding are suitable for analyzing the particular problem.

(b)   The value of the system depends so much on careful planning, without which there is great potential for waste time and cards. It is very easy to lose time in developing and struggling to use an overly complex system of coding, or in sorting with an inefficient system. The most efficient use of punch cards requires experience with the many ways of finding desired information and ignoring that which is unwanted.

(c)   The usefulness of the system depends somewhat on the volume of data. If there are too many cards, it will take too long to sort them. That is, it will take more than ten times as long to process 10,000 cards as to process 1,000. This is because of the multiple handling needed to sort large bodies of data. (In such a case it might be better to investigate using computer facilities, if available.) On the other hand, if there are too few cards, it is usually easier to find the answer by simple inspection.

(d)   If this description of punch card systems leaves you cold, or if you find it quite difficult to follow, it would probably be more of a hindrance than a help.

Notes

1.   Three firms which manufacture the equipment are:
Royal McBee Corporation, Port Chester, New York 10573;
E-Z Sort System, 45 Second St., San Francisco, California
94105; Sands and McDougall Pty. Ltd., G.P.O. Box 4587,
Melbourne, Victoria 3001.

2.   Members of S.I.L. in Papua New Guinea have the use of
a 50-hole hand-operated punch in the Publications Department that punches holes along two edges of 3 by 5 inch
cards. However, the holes produced by this equipment are
rather close together and the small tongues of card between
adjacent holes soon weaken as the cards are used.

3.   S.I.L. members should inquire at their Technical
Studies Department for the best source of supply.

4.   However, before starting this procedure for a very
large file, you should consider making use of one of the
several computer programs that do a much more sophisticated
job of dictionary making. They provide for automatic re-
versal of vernacular-English files to English-vernacular
and provide for equivalents in several languages if desired.
S.I.L. members should inquire at their Technical Studies
Department for specific details.

Bibliography

Anonymous, 1962. "The Use of Punched Cards in Linguistic
    Analysis", Summer Institute of Linguistics, Grand
    Forks, North Dakota, mimeo, 8 pp.

Bee, Darlene, 1961. "The Punch Card System of Filing",
    in: *Workshop Papers of the Summer Institute of
    Linguistics New Guinea Branch,* mimeo, pp. 1-10.

Day, Colin, 1964. "The Use of Edge Punched Cards in
    Linguistic Analysis", British School of the Summer
    Institute of Linguistics, mimeo, 5 pp.

Grimes, Joseph E., 1959. "Huichol Tone and Intonation",
    I.J.A.L. 25:221-232, especially p. 232.

Pence, Alan, 1962. "Punched Card Filing for Linguists", *Oceania Linguistic Monographs,* 6:76-89.

Samarin, William J., 1967. *Field Linguistics,* Holt, Rinehart and Winston, New York, pp. 163-169.

Page Filing

Phyllis M. Healey

Of the several methods of linguistic file-keeping that have been advanced to date, the use of 3"x5" filing cards or slips has proved the most popular.[1] The great advantage of this system is that if the file is carefully kept, the entries of a dictionary file are almost in correct alphabetical order from the beginning. "Almost", because certain alterations due to revision of phonetics, phonemicisation, and greater enlightenment as to meaning are inevitable in time. Affixed forms can be entered together on one slip, and thus stems can eventually be identified, provided they do not get lost in the file through a wrong first guess as to the phonetic form of the stem.

However, several serious disadvantages have caused this system to become a bugbear to workers, especially those with children:

(a) The first and greatest disadvantage is the danger of thousands of small pieces of paper being accidentally disordered. A chance fall of the box containing them, a strong wind, or a small child may work havoc with hundreds of hours of hard work.

(b) A suitable container is another problem. The file expands quickly, outgrowing containers. Containers must be substantial to obviate the danger of the slips being scattered through getting too heavy for it.

(c) That raises a third problem, weight and bulkiness. A 3"x5" system and its container is heavy and awkward in shape thus providing headaches for mobile persons, who must often travel, yet want to take their materials with them.

(d) It is only too easy, as many 3"x5" users have testified, for useful words to be "lost" in the file for months or even years because they are not frequently seen. In fact, only one slip is visible at a time in this system, and thus valuable phonemic and morphemic clues that a comparison of words can afford are often missed.

On the other hand, the page file (also called flat filing) has hardly any of the disadvantages of the 3"x5" system. If it is kept in book form, disordering through

accident is impossible. If a loose-leaf book is used,
considerable expansion is possible without inordinate
weightiness, and these file books can be of the same size
and shape as other books. Thus all one's work materials
can be uniform, and therefore very compact for purposes
of packing and transportation. The danger of entries
being "lost" in a page file is greatly reduced, for each
time an entry is made, a whole page or more of phonetically
similar entries is presented to the eye. Phonemic and
morphemic clues can strike one even when they are not
being deliberately sought. And in addition, a more or
less unconscious vocabulary-learning process is going on
every time entries are sighted while others are being
made. The comparison of related forms is comparatively
easy, and the basic forms of stems and subtleties of
meaning can be obtained readily.

     One disadvantage of using page filing for a dictionary
is that the entries cannot be in correct alphabetical order,
although careful forethought can reduce the necessity for
arduous re-ordering to a minimum. Thus, some time spent in
re-alphabetizing is inevitable.

     This paper describes how the page filing method was
used in the field over a period of fifteen years as a tool
in the investigation of two very different languages.[2]
An attempt was made to reduce to a minimum any disadvantages
that the method might seem to have. Some unanticipated pitfalls were encountered, and ways of eliminating these are
discussed below.

Materials Used

     All stationery used in field work was the same size--
8"x10-1/2" quarto. A medium weight typing paper (called
"bank") was used for all purposes, including writing. All
linguistic files consisted of pages of this paper kept
in loose-leaf binders with fairly substantial covers.
There were separate data files for each member of the
team, a phonology file, two large dictionary files, and
several different grammar files. Linguistic reports and
papers were typed on the same size paper, and copies included in the relevant files. Apart from such reports and
some limited typing of data as it was collected, all entries
in all files were handwritten. Re-alphabetized pages of the
dictionary files were typed, however. It is suggested that
non-loose-leaf books are not at all practicable for dictionary work. Any expense involved in having adequate stationery
is well worth it.

Data Files

Each member of the team kept a couple of clip boards at various places around the house, so that utterances could be written down the moment they were heard. This day-by-day record was dated and kept in separate files for each member. It provided a marvelous source of spontaneous and idiomatic data for analysis and dictionary making.

Phonology File

Whenever any particular group of sounds became a problem, lists of the words containing each sound and lists of contrasting words were made out on sheets of paper. The same was also done for tone patterns. These were filed away together, and whenever new words containing these sounds or new instances of contrast were discovered they were promptly added to the lists. When enough data had been accumulated, this file was then used as the basis for careful checking and cross-checking with one or more informants until the analysis became clear.

English-Vernacular Dictionary File

A standard English Dictionary was taken, and the relative space taken by each initial CV and VC combination was roughly assessed. Blank paper was proportionately headed alphabetically. It is suggested that about 300-400 pages be used. This seems inordinately wasteful at first sight, but the pages soon fill up. It is very necessary to start big. It was found that starting with too few pages resulted before long in the necessity for a 4-fold expansion, with consequent re-writing.

Vernacular-English Dictionary File

As each new initial CV or VC was discovered, a new page was headed with the first two phonemes of the word, and it was entered thereunder. Thus the number of pages continued to expand until the possible initial CV combinations were exhausted. One bad oversight was made, however, for it was known that /a/ is the most frequent vowel (55%) in the language being studied. The Ca pages (i.e. ba, ka, da, etc.) soon became unwieldy. The solution to the problem proved to be the dividing of the Ca's into about 5 CaC pages in alphabetical order (e.g. bab-bac, bad-bag, bah-bal, etc.)

Eliminating the Pitfalls from Dictionary Filing

The lists on each page could have been much closer to
true alphabetical order had the words been arranged on the
page instead of just listed from the top downwards. This
was true for both English and Language sections. For
example, in the English section one page was enough for A
to AG, but it would have been better had words starting
with ab, ac, ad, ae, af, ag been appropriately spaced at
intervals down the page.

Centers of interest for both tribesfolk and worker
may result in some pages filling up much quicker than could
have been anticipated by reference to an English Dictionary,
e.g. the frequency of occurrence of natural species, forms
of rice, bamboo, rattan, etc. A suggested solution is the
setting aside of a whole page in the English section for
such things as 'bird', 'plant', 'rice', etc. as soon as the
beginning of such a situation is observed.

Some other initial CV combinations besides Ca, such as
/si/, turned out to be unexpectedly frequent in occurrence.
The solution in such cases is the same as for Ca, namely
adding successive pages of CVC's in alphabetical order.

The biggest difficulty with the page file is the necessity, ultimately at least, for re-alphabetization. Ways of
reducing this work to a minimum have been suggested. In comparing the two methods of filing, it should not be forgotten
that the 3"x5" file probably requires two drafts to get it
into true alphabetical order, because of revisions mentioned
above. It is submitted that two drafts can be sufficient for
the page file also, and that the initial draft need not be
such a burden as some have argued. A suggested method of
re-alphabetizing is to take some sheets of paper, and make a
list of stems of each initial CVC (or VCV, etc.) combination
as you come to it in the file. The stems are then numbered
(1, 2, 3, 4, etc.) in alphabetical order on the rough list.
This need take very little time. A dictionary in correct
alphabetical order can then be made by taking one stem at a
time and listing all the words based upon it that are found
in the original file. If several pages of original file are
involved in one re-alphabetization, it is suggested that they
be indicated (e.g. by a line between stems for each page
break) on the rough list for easier reference back to the
file. E.g. while alphabetizing the SI page(s), part of the
rough list may read:

sikig   (3)
sikal   (1)
siksik (4)
sikan   (2)

The typed re-alphabetized dictionary file should have
plenty of vertical space (1-2 inches) between entries
where later hand-written additions can be alphabetized.
Several copies of the typescript, kept in several places,
are an insurance against loss.

As each page is filled by later entries, and before
it gets out of alphabetical order, it can be retyped on
several pages, once again with wide spacing. Although
this retyping may seem rather tedious it refreshes one's
memory on all of the words and expressions involved. It
also gives an opportunity for checking the entries with a
language helper, for tidying up inconsistencies, and for
generally bringing the entries up to one's present standard
of knowledge, as indicated by a date at the head of each
page. Any changes that are made in the entries need also
to be made in the reverse half of the dictionary.

Examples and Cross-References

It is admitted that the page file cannot provide room
for examples in each case as can the 3"x5" without considerable expansion and loss of facility for visual comparison of
related entries. However, a minority of words only will require examples in the ultimate dictionary, and these can be
obtained from the references. It has proved absolutely
essential to record references to every significant occurrence in the data (e.g. A125.9 — Alan's data book, page 125,
9/10 of the way down the page). Several references are often
needed, especially in a monolingual situation, to establish
the exact area of meaning of a word. It has also proved
necessary to record each different occurrence of stem plus
verb affix, partly to establish the basic form of the stem,
partly to discover which set of verb affixes a particular
stem takes, partly to ascertain the meanings of the affixes
and the basic meaning of the stem (which often yields surprises). It is suggested that, in order to make a dictionary
usable, the set of affixes a particular stem can take should
be indicated in some way.

Alphabetical File of Lateral Morphemes

Because of the greater difficulty experienced in finding the meaning and usage of lateral morphemes, these were

filed separately from the stems, which comprised the dictionary. One page was taken for each "function word" (i.e.
non-affixable root), and one page for each affix, and all
examples of its occurrence were recorded in full along
with meaning and page reference. This eventually enabled
the meaning of the word or affix to be determined, and
also supplied examples of its syntactic usage.

File of Grammatical Constructions

For the first week or two of syntax filing no book was
employed. Pages were spread out vertically so that they
overlapped enough for just the heading of each to be seen
easily, and all were clamped together at the side with a
bulldog clip. One page was taken for each apparent construction type and suitably headed. Examples were listed below
in full with page references.

After a week or two it was noticed that very few new
constructions were being discovered, that the total number
that had been discovered was very limited, and it was then
possible to arrange the pages systematically in a book
according to the method of analysis, preceded by an index.

Re-ordering of this file many times is inevitable as
understanding of the true structure of the language increases,
and some reclassification of the examples is probably necessary.

Despite some weaknesses and pitfalls, the page filing
system does seem to be very workable, and has several
advantages over other systems.

Footnotes

1. The use of 3"x5" slips in linguistic analysis is
described in Eugene A. Nida, *Morphology: The Descriptive
Analysis of Words*, Ann Arbor, University of Michigan Press,
1949, pp. 195-205; and in Benjamin Elson and Velma Pickett,
An Introduction to Morphology and Syntax, Santa Ana,
Summer Institute of Linguistics, 1962, pp. 151-153.

2. I am indebted to R. S. Pittman for first suggesting
this method, and to him and H. B. Kerr for some of the
modifications that have been incorporated.

List of Words Suitable for Monolingual Eliciting

Alan Healey

Positions

above
on
under/below
beside
in/inside
outside
in front of
behind
between
near
far from

Directions

into
out of
up
down
over
across
along
upstream
downstream
oceanwards
landwards
towards
away from
north
east
south
west

Locations

top/upper
bottom/lower
side
edge
corner (inner, outer)

middle/center
front
back
here
there
this
that
left (hand side)
right (hand side)

Quantities

one
two
....
nine
ten
twenty
hundred
few
many
none
some
all
part/piece
half
whole
empty
full

Size

big
small
wide (path)
narrow (path)
thick (cloth)
thin (cloth)
long
short
tall/high

short/low
deep
shallow

Shapes

square (garden)
round (garden)
box-like
ball-like
straight
crooked
rough (stone)
smooth (stone)
sharp
blunt
rough (sea)
calm (sea)
hollow
solid

Descriptives

old (thing)
new (thing)
wet (cloth)
dry (cloth)
green (wood)
dry (wood)
cold (water)
warm (water)
hot (water)
good (fence)
bad/useless (fence)
good/edible (food)
bad/poisonous (food)
rotten (food)
hard/firm (ground)
soft (ground)
strong (rope)
weak (rope)
sweet
sour
bitter
hot tasting
loose
tight
level
sloping

vertical
leaning
silent (person)
talkative (person)
quiet (children)
noisy (children)
soft (call)
loud (call)
sick
well
quickly
slowly

Colors

clean
dirty
bright
pale/faded
dark
light
black
brown
yellow
white
blue
green
orange
red
purple

Postures

sit down
be seated
lie down
be reclining
stand up
be standing
kneel down
be kneeling
bend over
rise/get up
rest (when climbing)
wait

Motions

come

come in/up, etc.
go
go down/in, etc.
depart/go away
go home
walk
run
crawl
slip/slide
move along
fly
fall (from a tree)
swim
turn (oneself) (around, over)
float
sink
flow
flee/run away
hide (oneself)
jump (across, up)
pass
return/come back
roll
miss (a target)
stumble/trip
race (=contest)
nod (as a sign)
limp
alight/land (bird, plane)
bounce
echo
creep/stalk
overflow
spill
leak
dance

Moving Actions

give
take
steal
drop (something)
turn (something) (around, over)
throw (away)
drag (along ground)
carry (in arms, on shoulder,
        etc.)

bring
fetch (=go and bring)
take (there)
hide (something)
raise/lift up
put (down, in)
pick up
remove
take away from (someone)
send (something)
send (someone)
shake (something)
open (bag, door, eyes,
      mouth)
close/shut
stretch (rope, limb)
chase
catch (someone)
catch (a ball)
wave (something)
swing (something)
twist (thread)
lead (an animal)
leave behind
meet (on the road)

Manipulations

wash (hands, body, clothes)
rub
wipe
draw water
fill (a vessel)
empty out
split/chop (firewood)
tie (knot)
bind/tie up (a bundle)
untie (knot, bundle)
wind up (rope)
unwind
pinch
hit
kick
hunt
aim
shoot
fight
kill

ambush
fell/chop down
chop/cut (into lengths)
cut (rope)
cut (food) into pieces
butcher (an animal)
divide/share
break (rope, stick)
tear/rip
smash (bottle)
destroy (house, fence)
bend (a stick)
fold (cloth)
bore a hole
dig a hole
plant (seed, cuttings)
dig up (root crop)
pick (fruit, beans)
bury (something)
cover
uncover
wrap up
unwrap
whet (an axe)
sharpen (a stake)
press
squeeze
crush
push
pull
pierce/stab
weed (a garden)
mend/repair
sew
thread a needle
build (house, bridge, fence,
        boat)
make (bow, arrow, canoe)
"weave" (net bag, mat, bamboo
        wall)
tether (an animal)
sweep (floor)
paddle (a canoe)
steer (a boat)
peel
scrape
boil (food)
roast

cook
mix
pour
light (fire, lamp)
extinguish
point at
pile up
play (a game)
play/beat (drum)
spread out
show
examine
draw/sketch
paint
carve
comb (hair)
scratch (itchy spot)
touch/feel
hold
hang up
join
put (clothes) on
wear (clothes)
take (clothes) off
buy
sell
lose
search for
discover/find
mark
measure
count
try/attempt

Spontaneous Events

dry out
dissolve
melt
die
swell
(wood, fire) burns
wind blows
rain falls

Body Activities/Sensations

suck
drink

eat
chew (food, betel nut,
        sugar cane)
bite (piece off food)
swallow
blow (a fire)
breathe
sniffle
sniff/smell
blink
be sleepy
go to sleep
be asleep
wake up
be awake
listen/hear
watch/see
hurt/be sore
itch
sweat/perspire
be tired
be afraid
be angry
be hot
be cold
shiver
bleed
have fever

Oral Activities

speak
shout
call out
whisper
reply/answer
repeat/say again
sing
cry/weep
laugh
smile
hum
whistle
scream
hiccup
belch
sneeze
cough

snore
spit
yawn
(dog) barks
(rooster) crows

Persons

old man
old woman
man
woman
young man
young woman
boy
girl
baby

Body Parts

head
hair (of head)
face
forehead
ear
eye
cheek
nose
mouth
lips
teeth
tongue
jaw
chin
beard
nape
neck
throat
adam's apple
shoulder
arm
elbow (inner, outer)
wrist
hand
palm
thumb
finger
knuckle
finger nail

chest
breast
back
rib
backbone
waist
belly
navel
hips
buttocks
thighs
leg
knee
foot
sole
ankle
heel
toes
body hair
skin
blood
flesh/meat
fat
bone
feather
wing
egg
tail (of bird)
fur
tail (of animal)
tears

Natural Objects

sun
shadow
shade
moon
star
sky
cloud
wind
fog
rain
water
spring (of water)
river/stream
lake

lagoon
swamp
sea/ocean
shore
landing place
beach
bank (of river)
coral reef
island
stone
mountain
hill
valley
plain
ground
mud
dust
waves (of sea)
surf
cave
high tide
low tide
a flood

Plants

tree
branch
fork
trunk
stump
roots
bark (of tree)
leaf
flower
berry/fruit/nut
seed
forest/woods
rattan vine/cane
stick
grass
roofing grass
grassland vine
bush/shrub
moss
lichen
mushrooms/edible fungi
nettles

small swamp cane
shrub with large leaves (for
  ceremony or decoration)
(local) tobacco leaf
gourd
cucumber
sugar cane
taro
sweet potato
yam
manioc/tapioca/kassava
breadfruit
sago
red pandanus
nutty pandanus
corn
beans
banana
rice
coconut (palm)
betel nut/Areca nut
Areca Palm
black palm (for bows)
bamboo
leaf vegetables
and many others

Animals

earthworm
centipede
lizard
crocodile/alligator
turtle
snake
dugong
fish
eel
shark
octopus
crab
whale
bird
flying fox/fruit bat
bat
cassowary/emu/ostrich
tame pig
wild pig

wallaby/kangaroo
dog
rat
mouse
frog
leech
shell
snail
fowl/chicken
and many others

Insects

mosquito
fly
butterfly
moth
flea
louse
ant
termite
wasp
spider
scorpion
grasshopper
firefly

Manufactured Items

fire
smoke
embers/coals
white ash (undisturbed)
ashes (for baking food)
sparks
flame
charcoal
soot
smoking pipe
lime
salt
oil
torch/flare
flint for firelighting
friction firelighting
  equipment
ground oven
village
house

posts
floor
wall
roof
door
window
family house
men's house
menstrual house
steps/stairs/ladder
boat, canoe
outrigger canoe
raft
paddle
rope
twine
thread
knot (in rope)
trap (for birds, animals, fish)
fish net
hook (for fishing)
axe
adz
bird arrow
animal arrow
animal spear
bow
fighting club
fighting spear
fish spear
knife
fighting dagger
handle (of tool)
drum
jews harp
flute
conch shell
grass skirt
ear ornament
nose ornament
headdress
necklace
armband
wig/hat
bark cloth
mat
sleeping mat
net bag

basket
handle (of basket, bag)
a comb
mortar
pestle
cloth
needle
garden/farm
pole/stake
fence
shelter/bush hut
plate/bowl
road/path/trail
money
cost/price
wages/pay
hole (in wood, ground, wall,
     cloth, vessel)
crack
line/mark
point (of something)
a wound
nest (of bird)
and many others

460

Useful Expressions

Papua New Guinea Branch of the
Summer Institute of Linguistics

Greetings

Greetings upon arrival and responses
Leavetakings and responses
Greetings and leavetakings as you meet people on the trail

General Responses

Yes.
No.
Thank you.
O.K./That's alright.
That's good.
That's right.
That's wrong.
It doesn't matter.

Some Questions and Common Responses

What is that?   It is _____.
Whose _____ is that   It is _____'s.
Is that his?
Which _____ is it?   This one.
What is it like?   It's like that one.
Is it like this one?
Where is it?   It's here.
Is it on the _____?
Who is he?   He is _____.
What is his name?   His name is _____.
What did you say?/Say it
  again please.

Other Common Questions

What do you want?
What is the matter?
How did it happen?
Why is he angry?
Are you tired?

What are you doing?
Why are you doing that?
How did you do that?
Who did this?

Where are you going?
When will you come back?
How many days will it take?
Why didn't you come?
Where have you been/come from?
When did you arrive?
Why have you come?

Some Useful Replies

I don't know.
He isn't there.
I'm cooking food.
I'm reading a book.
I'm writing letters.
We're going to the market/trade store.
I'm coming back tomorrow/in a few days.
He went yesterday/in the morning/a long time ago.

Some Useful Statements

I need carriers.
I am thirsty/tired.
I'm full/I've had enough to eat.
I'm very sorry.
I like/don't like _____.
I want/don't want to _____.
I forgot to _____.

The baby is sleeping.
We're going to eat/sleep now.
We'll go (home) now.
We've finished making it.
You've worked hard/well.
You may keep it.
It's sweet/cold.
It's not very heavy/far.

Inquiries and Requests

May I come in?
May I go with you?
Will you come with us?
Let's all go together.
Come and eat with us.

Have you eaten yet?
Can you fix it?
Help me please.

Buying and Selling

Have you any bananas to sell?
How many do you have?
Are they ripe?
How much does it cost?

I want/don't want to buy them.
I have some/plenty.
Our bananas are all gone/finished.
That's enough.

Lending

When will you return it?
Return it tonight, please.
I'm not lending my axe any more.
I don't have any more nails.

Where is my _____?
Who borrowed my _____?

Commands

Come in.
Sit down.
Wait a little, please.
Hurry.

Come here.
Look at it.
Listen (to me).
Be quiet.
Stop it/Stop doing that.
Leave it alone.

Do it carefully please.
Do it now/later.
Do it like this/Do it this way.
Don't do it like that.
You do it.

Go and get it.
Give/hand it to me.
Would you give me some please?

Bring it here.
Put it down there.
Put it in the _____.
Pull/push it.

Household Instructions

Shut/open the door, please.
Sweep the floor.
Please light the fire.
Boil the water, please.
Throw all the rubbish out.
Please wash your hands first.
Bring me the one from the _____.
Don't pick the baby up when he cries.

Is the water boiling?
Will you bring me some water?
Will you wash our clothes?
Have you finished washing?
Hang the clothes out.
Are the clothes dry?
Bring the clothes in, please.

Language Learning

Please talk to me in Kamano.
How do you say _____ in Kamano?
What is this (thing) called in Kamano?
What does _____ mean?
When people say _____ what do they mean?

Please say it again./Please repeat it.
Say it more slowly, please.
What did he say?
You say it.

Is that correct?
Tell me when I make a mistake.

I don't understand.
I understand only a little.
I don't know how to speak Kamano.
We want to learn Kamano.

Medical

Are you sick?
How long have you been sick?

Have you been vomiting?
Do you have fever/cough/diarrhea/headache?
How long have you had _____?
Does it hurt?
Where does it hurt?
Are you getting better?

Hold the child, please.
Show it to me.
Open your mouth.
You need medicine/an injection.
It won't hurt.
Drink this./Swallow it.
Take (eat these--one in the morning and one at night.
Put a little of this on _____ each day.
Keep it clean.
Don't scratch it.
Come back tomorrow.

Family and Home

Is he your brother/father?
How many brothers and sisters do you have?
Is he kin to you?
Where do you live?

Weather

It's cold/hot today.
It's very cloudy.
Is it going to rain?
It's starting to rain./The rain is coming.

The sun is hot.
The moon is full.
The wind is strong.
The road is dry/slippery.

Progress Charts

These Progress Charts are designed for people who are following the Need-ordered Approach to the *Guide*, which is outlined on p. 25. Their purpose is to help you keep your work balanced, so you will not follow some particular interest to the neglect of other facets of language learning.

End of First Week

Units Completed: Tape file started ☐

1 ☐   2 ☐

What greetings can you respond to?

End of Second Week

Units Completed: _____   _____

List recordings and drills made:

What outings have you been on accompanied by vernacular speakers?

End of Third Week

Map of village started (5.1) ☐
Observations classified (5.4) ☐
Programed review system (pp. 318-321) is:
                                    suitable ☐   inadequate ☐
Are you and your partner Analysts or "Sponges"? (See
"Kinds of Learners" p. 26.)

Have discussed together how we can help each other. ☐
Comments on progress:

End of First Month

Dictionary File (7.4c, 7.4d) has been started:
                              English to Vernacular ☐
                              Vernacular to English ☐
                              Topical File ☐
Are you spending enough time out with people? _____
Are your discoveries being filed?   _____
Reviewing of drills is up to date ☐
Comments on progress:

End of Second Month in the Village   Date: _____

Dictionary File is up to date ☐

Reviewing of drills is up to date ☐

Have revised descriptions (11.4 h) ☐

Have started filing clauses in Grammar File (11.4g) ☐

Scan through the Classified List of Topics for Observation
and count how many sections you have completed _____

Do the same for Grammar Topics _____ and Phonology Topics
_____. Is you work ☐ well balanced?

                    ☐ imbalanced?

Are you spending enough time on conversation? ☐ Yes   ☐ No

                    on analysis?   ☐ Yes   ☐ No

Comments on progress:

If you feel you know a lot of words and structures but
cannot use them in conversation, pause now to make and
practice drills, then use what you learn in talking with
people. If you have neglected one area of your work,
concentrate on it for a while.

At the End of Each Month (after the second)

        Complete a row for each month you spend in the language
area. The columns are labeled as follows:

a. Dictionary is up to date (✓)
b. Revision of drills is up to date (✓)
c. Filing in Topical File and Grammar File is up to date (✓)
d. Scan through the Classified List of Topics for Observa-
    tion and count how many sections you have completed.
e. Number of Grammar Topics completed
f. Number of Phonology Topics completed
g. Work is well balanced (Y(es) or N(o))
h. Am spending enough time on conversation (Y or N)
i. Am spending enough time on analysis (Y or N)

Month	a	b	c	d	e	f	g	h	i	Comments

        Keep working your new discoveries into drills so you can
start to use them in conversation.

Classified List of Topics for Observation

Write the date against each section when you have made
the observation and filed the notes.

                                                          Date

(1) Ecology

     (a) Natural resources
          General impressions 1.1, 1.4

     (b) Geography and population
          General impressions 1.1, 1.4
          Map of neighborhood 5.1
          Extending the map 15.1a
          Further mapping 31.1c

(2) Technology

     (a) Subsistence
          Tools 4.1
          Foods 9.1
          Use of fire 18.1
          Animals, birds and fish 19.1
          Disease in crops or livestock 25.1
          Plants 28.1
          Daily routine 38.1
          Work patterns 39.1

     (b) Non-subsistence
          Dwellings 3.1a
          Tools 4.1
          Clothing 8.1
          Personal adornment 12.1
          Art 20.1
          Participating in creative work 27.1

(3) Kinship

     (a) Genealogies
          First genealogy 14.1b, 14.4d, and e
          Extending genealogy 15.1b, 19.2a

     (b) Kin categories and behavior
          Kin relationships and terms, Unit 13
          Affecting pronouns 24.4c (Note)
          Analyzing kin terms 39.3c, 4d, and 6b

Date

(4) Socio-Political System

  (a) The individual and others
        Greetings 2.1, 2.2, 2.4a, 2.6
        Division of labor 6.1, 14.1a
        Reciprocal gifts 8.1, 21.1
        Communal work and authority 16.1
        Role of animals in social gatherings
          19.1
        Patterns of marriage and residence
          19.4c
        Attitudes and social interactions
          23.1
        Recreation 24.1
        Sickness and health 25.1
        Methods of communication 29.1
        Visiting and hospitality 31.1a and b
        Singing and dancing 33.1
        Musical instruments and songs 34.1
        Authority and leadership, position
          of women and disciplining of
          children 36.1
        Birth 37.1b
        Initiation 37.1c
        Marriage 37.1d
        Death 37.1e
        Communal work, specialization and
          rewards 39.1
        Trading and money 41.1b
        Legal system 41.1d

  (b) Social units and their interactions 36.1
        Marriage 37.1d
        Death 37.1e

(5) Religion

  (a) Rituals and magic
        Use of fire in ceremonies 18.1
        Role of animals in ceremonies 19.1
        Sickness and health 25.1
        Plants and medicines 28.1
        General 32.1 and 41.1c
        From birth to death 37.1

Date

  (b) Beliefs
        General 32.1 and 41.1c
        About cause of death 37.1e

(6) Values

  (a) Etiquette and ethics
        Re dwellings 3.1a
        Re pointing 3.1b
        Standards taught to children 36.1

  (b) Goals in life
        People's interests 10.1, 10.2c
        Goals instilled in children 36.1

Grammar Topics

Each topic usually has several sections which touch on it. You should work through all the sections in one unit before leaving that topic. Write the date against each topic as you complete it.

Date

"What is this?" and nouns: 3.3, 3.6a

"What is that?" + equative clauses: 4.3-4.6

Verbs, phrase and clause structure: 6.3-6.4b

Person markers: 7.2c, 7.3-7.4b, 7.5-7.6, 8.2a

Possessives: 8. Preliminaries, 8.2b, 8.3-8.6, 9.2b

More on possessives, "Whose?": 9.3-9.6

"What are you doing?", "What did you say?", verbs: 10. Preliminaries, 10.2a and b, 10.3-10.4c, 10.5-10.6

Locationals and "Where?": 11.2b, 11.3, 11.4f, 11.5-11.6a

Yes/no questions and negatives: 12.2-12.6

Imperatives: 13.2-13.6

Kin terms: 13.2-13.6

Tense, "When?": 14.2b-14.4c, 14.4e-14.6c

Transcribing texts: 15.3a and b

Date

Transitive verbs: 15.2-15.6, 16.2

Numerals and "How many?": 16.3-16.6a

Intransitive verbs: 16.2-16.6b

Person markers: 17.4d

Verb "to be": 17.4e

REVIEW: When you have completed most of the above topics, work through Unit 17.

Recording a description or explanation: 18.2b

Aspect and mood/mode: 18.4a, 5b, 6b

Dependent and independent verbs: 18.3a, 18.4b, 5a

Verb paradigms: 18.4c

Allomorphic variation: 18.4d

Connectives: 18.4e

"Whom?" (with "Who?" and "Whose?"): 18.3b, 6a

"Why?" and "because": 19.2b-4b, 19.5 and 6

Emphatic mood: 20.2b-4a, 20.5 and 6a

Locative phrases: 20.5, 20.6a

"How?" and instrumentals: 21.3a-4a, 21.5 and 6a

Transcribing text: 21.4b

Prohibitions: 23.4c, 23.5, 23.6a

Subject pronouns: 24. (Preliminaries), 24.2, 5b

Duals and/or trials: 24.4b, 5b, 6b

Residue of pronouns: 24.4c

Object pronouns: 25.2a, 3, 4a, 6a and c

Testing recent discoveries: 25.5

Learning useful vocabulary and constructions from text: 25.6b and c

When most of the above topics have been completed, work through the Review Unit 26.

Benefactives and "For whom?": 27.3a-4a, 5a, 6a

Date

Translation practice--"of" constructions: 27.5b

Pronouns--frequency of usage: 28.2b

Hortatory constructions: 28.3a, 4a, 5a, 5b, 6a

Expanding vocabulary: 28.3b, 4b, 6b

How verb stems are formed: 28.4c

Expansion drill: 28.6c

Multi-clause sentences--same subject: 29.3a-4c,
5a-6d

Sentence analysis: 30.4c

Drill in conversation and a game: 30.6b

Multi-clause-same-subject sentences in non-
indicative moods: 31.3a-6a

Descriptives and comparative constructions
32.3a-4c, 5, 6b and c

Constructions with more than one descriptive:
33.3a and b, 4a and b, 6a

Demonstratives: 33.3c, 4c, 6c

Comparative constructions: 33.6b

Time clauses: 34.3a, 4, 6b and c

Multi-clause-different-subject sentences:
34.3b, 4, 5, 6c

When you have completed most of the above topics, work
through Unit 35.

Tense changes: 35.5a

Descriptives: 35.5b

Accompaniment: 36.3a

Locative phrases: 36.3b

Other moods: 37.3, 4a, 5, 6a
i.e. desiderative: 37.3b
      purpose: 37.3c
      reason: 37.3d
      conditional: 37.3e
      causative: 37.3f

Vocatives and exclamations: 38.2b, 4b

Date

Adverbs, intensifiers, "How?" and conjunctions:
38.3, 4a, 5, 6

"New information" structures: 39.2

Embedded clauses: 39.3a and b, 4a-c, 6a

Determining morpheme classes: 40.4b

When you have completed most of the above topics, work
through Unit 40. Then go back and finish any relevant topics
you have not marked off. Then turn to Unit 41, "How to
continue language learning" on p. 252.

Phonology Topics   Date

Write the date against each topic as you complete it.

Initial mimicry and making friends: 1.2-1.3,
1.5-1.6

Greeting friends and mimicry, intonation types:
2.2, 2.4b

Intonation and mimicking a text: 3.4, 3.6b and c

Mimicry: 4.2, 4.6b

Visiting and mimicry: 5.2, 5.6

Record and mimic another text: 6.2

Rhythm system: 6.4c

Conversation: 7.2a and b, 7.6c

Conversation with person morphemes: review
7.6b, 8.2a

Mimicry and intonation: 8.2c

Conversation and mimicry: 9.2

Intonation contours: 10.4d

Phonemic interpretation: 11.4a-e

Using pictures in conversation: 12.2a

Articulation practice: 12.6b

Intonation of imperatives: 13.4, 13.6

Articulation practice for vowels: 13.6c

Articulation practice for stops: 14.6d

Date

Conversation, greetings and memory: 15.2

Watching for other intonation patterns: 15.2b

Articulation: 15.6c

Vowel articulation: 16.6d

Mimicking a text: 16.6e

CV patterns: 17.4a

Uniting allophones and separating phonemes:
17.4c

Tracking, conversation and further practice:
17.6

REVIEW: When you have done most of the above categories, work through Unit 17.

Conversation practice while gathering
genealogical data: 19.2a

Articulation practice—same manner of
articulation: 20.6b

Articulation practice: 21.6b

Tracking: 22.2a

Continuing phonemic analysis: 22.4b

Assessing evidence for tone: 22.4c

Intonation contours: 23.2a and b, 23.4a and b

Articulation — vowel clusters: 23.6b

Checking intonation of memorized expressions:
24.2, 4a

Articulation — consonant clusters: 24.6c

Tracking discussion: 25.2b

Practicing supra-segmental contrast: 25.6d

When most of the above topics have been completed, work
through the Review Unit 26.

Phonemic analysis: 26.4c

Check list: 26.4d

Date

Pitch, stress, and length: 26.4f

Context forcing drill: 26.6b

Articulation--2-syllable words: 27.6c

Articulation--3-syllable words: 28.6d

Intonation patterns: 29.2a, 4d

Articulation--4-syllable words: 29.6e

Length, stress, and pitch: 30.4b

Articulation--5-syllable words: 31.6b

Learning a text: 32.6e

Articulation of words in frames: 33.6d, 34.6d

Learning a song: 34.6e

When you have completed most of the above topics, work through Unit 35.

Starting phoneme statement: 35.4b

Recording your own pronunciation: 37.6b

Intonation contours with vocatives and exclamations: 38.4b

When you have finished most of the above topics, work through Unit 40, then go back and finish any relevant topics you have not marked off. Then turn to Unit 41, "How to continue language learning" on p. 252.

Classification for Cultural Observations

When your "anthropology" file becomes thick and cumbersome, subdivide it according to your guesses as to meaningful categories for your language group. The following six categories (expandable to twelve) may be useful.

(1) Ecology

    (a) Natural resources
    (b) Geography and population

(2) Technology

    (a) Subsistence (agriculture, hunting, foods, etc.)
    (b) Non-subsistence (houses, clothing, weapons, art, etc.)

(3) Kinship

    (a) Genealogies
    (b) Kin categories and behavior

(4) Socio-political System

    (a) The individual's relationship to others (division of labor, initiation, marriage, reciprocal gifts, leadership, etc.)
    (b) Social units and their relationships (clan, village, alliance, etc.)

(5) Religion (including illness and death)

    (a) Rituals and magic
    (b) Beliefs (world view, nature of man, spirit beings, etc.)

(6) Values

    (a) Etiquette and "good" versus "bad" behavior
    (b) Goals in life and characteristics of a good person

GLOSSARY

actor: the one carrying out the action of the verb.

affix: a morpheme that is added to a stem to form a word. It may be a prefix, suffix, or infix.

agreement: grammatical harmony between two or more words in a phrase or clause such that they reflect the same number, case, person, or gender.

allomorph: if a particular morpheme has two or more forms, depending on its environment, each of those forms is called an allomorph.

allophone: an individual phoneme often has several variants in pronunciation, each of which is called an allophone.

animate: that group of things which are generally "alive" in an animal sense as opposed to those things (inanimate) which are not usually thought of in this way. What nouns belong in which category depends on a speaker's culture, how he views his world, and how he classifies its parts.

aspect: the feature of verbs or verb phrases in some languages which shows whether the action is momentary, continuous, repetitive, habitual, etc.

attribute: that part of a phrase which describes the central part (or head) of the phrase. (Example: In *young man*, *young* is the attribute and *man* is the head of the phrase.)

benefactive: that form of verb or clause which denotes that the action is in the interest of another person.

bilingual: knowing and speaking two or more languages.

bound form: a morpheme or allomorph of a morpheme which cannot stand alone as a word but must occur attached to (bound to) another morpheme. (Example: In the Miniafia word *enan* 'he is going' *e-* is the bound form of the free pronoun *i* 'he'.)

causative: a particle or affix which indicates that one person causes another person to perform an action.

comparative: expressive of degree in an adjective or adverb, usually in the sense of "more than" or "less than".

complementary distribution: two similar features of a language are said to be in complementary distribution if the first occurs only in a certain environment and the second occurs only in another completely different (non-overlapping) environment.

<u>concord</u>:   see agreement.

<u>conditional</u> construction: a construction of two clauses in
    in which one of the actions must actually take place be-
    fore it is possible for the other one to take place.   In
    English, the word *if* appears in the conditional con-
    struction.

<u>conjunction</u>:   a word whose basic function is to connect two
    words, phrases, or clauses.   Some languages have conjunc-
    tive affixes instead of free conjunctions.

<u>construction</u>:   a string of words which belong together be-
    cause of their grammatical interrelationships.

<u>contoid</u>:   any speech sound which is not a vocoid.   In any
    given language almost all contoids function as consonants.

<u>CV</u> pattern: the arrangement of consonants and vowels within
    a syllable or word.   The CV pattern demonstrated by the
    one-syllable word *ban* would be consonant-vowel-consonant,
    or CVC.

<u>declarative</u>:   the mode (mood) of a verb or sentence that
    simply states a fact.   See also indicative.

<u>demonstrative</u>:   a small class of words that designate a
    particular object (or objects) as distinguished from
    others, and which usually indicate the nearness of that
    object.   (Examples: *these rocks, that house*.)

<u>dependent</u> verb or clause: a verb or clause which depends
    upon another for support in expressing some features of
    its action.   (Example: *Having eaten, they departed*.   In
    this sentence, *having eaten* depends on the rest of the
    sentence to specify the subject and tense of the action
    of eating.)

<u>desiderative</u>:   that mode of a verb which expresses desire
    that an action should take place.

<u>dual</u>:   a special form of plural that includes only two
    persons as opposed to other forms of plural which might
    include three or more.

<u>dubitative</u>:   expressing doubt.

<u>embedded</u> clause: a clause which occurs within the framework
    of a larger clause, usually filling a slot that is typi-
    cally filled by a noun phrase.

<u>emic</u>:   significant, functional, distinctive, contrastive.

<u>equative</u> clause: a clause in which one phrase of the whole

is balanced by the other phrase in a manner that equates the two. (Example: *Your brother is a good swimmer. Your brother* may be equated with *a good swimmer, is* being a stative verb commonly used as a connector in such clauses in English.)

ergative system: a grammatical system in which the subject of a transitive verb is marked by the ergative case, whereas the subject of an intransitive verb and the object of a transitive verb are both marked by the nominative case.

etic: having an undetermined significance and function; without regard to distinctiveness or contrast.

exclusive: a plural pronoun that excludes certain parties (usually the second person) but includes others. (Example: *aki* 'we (but not you)'.)

filler: a grammatical element that occurs in a grammatical slot.

frame: a concise grammatical construction in which one part may be changed by substituting other words or phrases. Frames are particularly useful for comparing the pitch patterns of words in language study, and for drill exercises in the initial stages of language learning.

free form: a morpheme or allomorph of a morpheme that may comprise a word that can be uttered in isolation. (Example: In the word *national, nation* is a free form in that it may be uttered as an independent word; *-al*, however, does not have such independence and is therefore not a free form.)

function morpheme: a morpheme that shows the part played within the sentence by another morpheme, word, or construction. Prepositions and conjunctions are function morphemes.

gender: when a class of words (usually nouns) is divided into grammatical subclasses which are partly semantic and partly arbitrary, these subclasses are generally referred to as genders. (In Spanish, for example, all nouns are assigned to one of two genders, masculine or feminine.) The subclass of the noun which occurs as head of a noun phrase or as subject of a clause is the basis of agreement within that construction.

glide, vocoid: two vocoids that occur one immediately after the other in a word in such a way that the pronunciation of the first flows or blends naturally into the second.

The boundary between them thus becomes blurred.

homophonous: sounding the same but having different meanings.

hortatory: the mode (mood) of an utterance that is advisory or exhortative in nature. (Example: *Let's go.*)

imperative: the mode (mood) of an utterance which is a command. (Example: *Go away!*)

inanimate: the opposite of animate. Generally, those things which the speaker of the language does not regard as "alive" in an animal sense. The nouns found in this class vary somewhat from language to language.

inclusive: those pronouns which do not exclude the hearer in their plural forms. (Example: In Miniafia, the pronoun *it* means 'we' including the hearer (we and you). *Aki* also means 'we', but does not include the hearer (we but not you).)

independent verb or clause: a verb or clause that is complete in itself, expressing action without the need of a helping verb or another clause.

indicative: the mode (mood) of a verb or sentence that expresses the reality or fact of an action or state. (This may be contrasted with interrogative and conditional.)

infix: an affix that is attached within a word instead of before (prefix) or after (suffix) it.

inflected: (a word that) undergoes change, usually involving the addition of affixes, to indicate changes in gender, case, person, number, tense, aspect, etc.

instrument: a noun phrase expressing the thing used in carrying out an action.

intentive: that form of a verb or verb phrase which expresses intention to perform an action.

interpretation: determining, for a given language, whether a particular sound is functioning as a consonant or as a vowel, and whether a particular sequence of sounds is functioning as a single phoneme or as a cluster of phonemes.

interrogative: a word or sentence which asks a question rather than stating a fact.

intransitive: when a verb is incapable of accepting a grammatical object it is described as intransitive.

kernel sentence: a basic form of sentence from which many other kinds of sentences may be derived by transformation.

lingua franca: a language other than the speakers' native language which serves for general communication between people from diverse language groups. Often called a trade language.

locative: a word or phrase used to describe the location of a person, thing, or event. (Example: *The car is in the garage. In the garage* is a locative phrase referring to the physical location of the car.)

minimal pair: two words in a language which have different meanings and which differ from one another phonetically in only one sound. Commonly used to demonstrate phonemic contrast.

mode (mood): the speaker's attitude to what he says and his expectation as to how the person addressed will respond, as indicated by a morpheme within his utterance. E.g. indicative, dubitative, imperative, interrogative, etc.

modifiers: those words within a phrase which describe in some way the head word of the phrase. (Example: In *the old man, old* is a modifier describing *man*.)

monolingual: using only one language. This term may be used to describe either a person who knows only one language, or a method of language learning and data collecting in which only the language being studied is used.

morpheme: the smallest segment of speech that has meaning. (Example: *oxen* is composed of two morphemes: *ox* 'a type of animal' and *-en* 'plural'.)

morphophonemics: a study of morphemes which deals with the phonemic variants of a morpheme and where each variant occurs.

paradigm: a set of inflected (affixed) forms of a word arranged so that the changes from one form to the next can be clearly seen. Paradigms are often used to study verb formation where the change of an affix may signal a change in tense, subject, number, object, etc.

participle: a verb form which may be used as an adjective and has the characteristics of both verb and adjective. (This term is sometimes used loosely as a label for some particular kind of dependent verb.)

passive voice: the distinctive feature of a type of clause in which the person or thing to which the action is done is expressed as the subject. (Example: *The car was polished by Jim. The car* was acted upon by Jim, yet *the car* is subject of the clause.)

484 GLOSSARY

person: the particular party referred to by a pronoun or person affix. We commonly speak of three persons: first person (*I, we*), second person (*you*), and third person (*he, she, it, they*). In some languages these distinctions are expanded to show inclusion and exclusion of the second person from the first person plural pronouns.

phone: any individual speech sound without regard to how it fits into the sound pattern of a particular language.

phoneme: a significant speech sound which is used in communication to distinguish one word from another. (Example: The *p* and *f* in English pat and *fat* are two different phonemes.)

pitch: the absolute musical pitch of a syllable in speech.

portmanteau morpheme: a morpheme, often of only one phoneme, which conveys two or more distinct meanings simultaneously. (Example: French /o/ 'to the (masc.)' instead of */a lə/.

prefix: a morpheme which goes in front of the stem to which it is attached. (Example: In English *re-* is a prefix in *retell*.)

reciprocal verb or clause: showing mutual action by two or more actors on each other.

reduplication: the practice in some languages of repeating a portion or all of a morpheme to change the information carried by the morpheme. (Example: In Miniafia: *akif* 'I swam', *akifukif* 'I am swimming'.)

reflexive verb or clause: if a verb's action is "reflected" back so that the subject also becomes the object of the verb, it is called reflexive. (Example: *He cut himself.*)

root: a morpheme which is not an affix.

slot: the privileges and features of occurrence of a particular word or larger item within a grammatical construction. (Example: In *The boy ran away*, *the boy* is the filler of the subject slot of an intransitive clause.)

stative: a verb or clause expressing a state rather than an action.

stem: the nucleus of a word to which inflectional affixes may be attached. A stem may consist of a single root, two roots forming a compound stem, or a root and a derivational affix forming a derived stem.

stress: special emphasis or speech power that is given to a

syllable within a word so that it is louder than the other
syllables in that word.

subminimal pair: two words that have different meanings and
that differ in only two (or at most three) phonetic aspects. (Example: English *mission* and *vision* differ by
/m/ versus /v/ and by /š/ versus /ž/.) Compare with
minimal pair.

suffix: an affix that is attached to the end of a word.

superlative: that form of an adjective or adverb that denotes the highest degree of that quality. (Example:
good, better, best all speak of a degree of excellence,
but *best* refers to the highest degree of that quality.)

suprasegmental: a phonetic feature of a word other than the
segmental sounds (consonants and vowels). Examples of
this are pitch and stress.

suspect: sounds and sequences of sounds which vary in the
way they behave from language to language are called
"suspect" because their behavior needs to be interpreted
afresh in each language. See interpretation.

tagmemic: having to do with the theory of grammar that describes a construction as a string of tagmemes.

temporal: pertaining to time.

tone: the relative musical pitch (highness or lowness) of a
syllable in speech.

transform: the form of a sentence resulting from the process
of transformation.

transformation: the process of shifting from one sentence
to another closely related sentence containing the same
nouns, verbs, and adjectives, and having the same or very
similar meaning. (Example: *Bill saw the robber* → *The
robber was seen by Bill* or *Bill did not see the robber*.)

transitive: a verb which is capable of having an object.

trial: a pronoun which represents exactly three persons (as
opposed to dual or plural pronouns).

vernacular: one's native language (mother tongue), the language one learns in infancy as the language of his own
culture or group.

vocative: an attention-getting word or short sentence which
is addressed directly to the particular person to whom
one wishes to speak.

vocoid: any central resonant oral speech sound. In any
given language most vocoids function as vowels.

INDEX

Abstracts, 43, 374-375 (see
    also Adjectives/De-
    scriptiyes and Ad-
    verbs/Manner words)
    meaning of, 382-383
Accompaniment/Coordinate
    223-5
Activities
    observing (see Ob-
        serving)
    participating/sharing,
        76, 95, 110, 126,
        149, 153, 173,
        196, 216, 235,
        323, 344, 365
    photographing, 136
Adjectives/Descriptives,
    202-5, 208-10, 220,
    225, 249, 374-375,
    452-453
Adornment/Decoration, 91,
    136, 253
Adverbs/Manner words, 236-7,
    240, 249
Affixes, 427
    benefactive, 174-8
    case-marking, 59, 118
    charts, 63
    combinations of, 69, 257
    contrast marking, 238
    embedded clause, 242-6
    filing of, 257, 440, 446,
        450-1
    meaning of, 278-279
    negative, 93
    noun, 117, 143, 154-6,
        174
    order, 129, 187
    person, 55-63
    possessive, 66-70, 72-5
    pronoun, 55-61, 63, 174
    verb, 60, 79, 93-4,
        96-9, 103-107, 113,
        118, 128-131, 134,
        137-8, 143, 151,
        167-8, 174, 181,

186-7, 197-200,213-4,
    229-232, 236, 237
    vocative, 236
(see also Eliciting, Verb
    modes)
"after", 186, 216
Agreement/Concord, 81, 113,
    167, 205, 249, 257,
    312-3
Allocating
    choice of area, 20-1
    time, 27, 35, 110-1, 115
Allomorphs, 129, 312, 313,
    405-406
Allophones, 164, 351, 406
    (see also Free variation,
        Mutually exclusive
        distribution)
"although", 256
Analysis
    phonology, 85-6, 122, 161,
        164-6, 192, 219, 350-
        2, 404-405, 420-422
    length, pitch, and stress,
        166, 192 (see also
        Length, Pitch, and
        Stress)
    sentence, 193
    (see also 263 and Categories
        4 and 5 in Units)
"and", 43, 47, 238
Animate/Inanimate, 58, 79
Animals, birds and fish, 132,
    180, 458
Anthropology, 34, 49, 442, 447
    (see also Category 1 in the
        Units)
Antonyms, 202-3, 367-368, 373,
    374, 382
Art, 136, 253
Articulation (see Pronunciation
    and Drills - phono-
    logical)
Aspect (see Verbs, aspect)
Association (see Accompani-
    ment/Co-Ordinate)

Authority, 116
Back translation, 357
Basic expressions (see Expressions, useful)
"because", 134-5, 256
"before", 213
Behavior, standards of, 222, 254, 277
Benefactive (see Eliciting, Verb modes)
Birds (see Animals, birds and fish)
Birth, 228
Body parts, 66, 116, 256, 456-457
Buildings (see Houses)
"but", 237
Carving/Woodwork (see Art and Tools)
Causative (see Eliciting, verb modes)
Ceremonies, 422
    birth, 228
    death/burial/mourning, 212, 229
    healing, 157, 212, 254
    initiation, 126, 228
    religions, 126, 132, 180, 201, 207, 252-4
    wedding, 149, 228
Charts,
    genealogical, 105, 408-410
    phonetic, 85, 122, 147, 164
    pronoun, 62-3
    verb affix, 129, 187, 198
Check lists
    kinship, 134, 246
    phonetic, 165-6
Checking, 23 (see Category 5 in Units)
    "cycle check", 384-385
    dictionary, completeness of, 239

elicited response, 356
    pronunciation, 94, 162, 166, 168, 234, 418-420, 425
    text, meaning of, 356-357, 361, 383-386
    using tape recorder for, 284, 350, 401, 403, 420
Children, 173, 222-3, 408, 443
    using in language learning, 38, 168, 171, 194, 300-302
Classes and Subclasses
    descriptives, 203
    morpheme, 249
    noun, 70, 117, 160 (see also Nouns)
    numerals, 117
    pronouns, 59, 160
    word, 249, 358, 366-367, 376, 377, 440
Clauses, sequences of, 127, 130, 186-7, 199, 215-6, 230-2
    different actors, 214-6, 231-2
    embedded, 242-6
    interclause relationships, 130, 231-2
    joining features of, 130, 230-1
    same actor, 186-7, 189, 197, 215-6, 230-1
Clauses, types of,
    dependent (non-final) 79-80, 113, 128-9, 187
    descriptive (stative), 209
    embedded, 242-6
    equative/equational, 42-3, 47
    expanded, 208
    expressing emotion, 256
    final (independent) 79-80, 112-3, 128-9
    intransitive, 53, 118-9, 182
    motion, 85, 96-8, 159, 181

stative (descriptive),
209
temporal, 213
transitive, 112, 116,
159, 182, 205
(see also Eliciting, verb
modes)
Clusters (phonetic),
drills with, 152, 156,
200
phonemic interpretation
of, 85-6, 121,
147, 164
Clothing, 65, 91
Collocations (see Eliciting)
Colors, 202, 428, 453
Coming of age, 201 (see
also Initiation)
Commands/Imperatives,
(see Eliciting, verb
modes)
Communication (methods of),
185
Comparatives, 203, 210, 237
Complementary Distribution,
122, 164
Concord (see Agreement/
Concord)
Conditional (Contrafact-
ual), 231, 256
Conjunctions and Connec-
tives, 43, 47, 130,
230-1, 237, 257
Context forcing drills,
167-8, 205
Contoids, 85-6, 121-2,
147, 164-6
drills with, 107, 138-9,
144, 152, 156,
161-2, 179
Contrast, phonetic, 122,
147, 164-5, 179, 192,
219, 350-2, 399-407,
420, 421, 448
Contrastive phonological
drills, 161-2
167-8, 205
Conversation (see Cate-

gories 2 and 6 in Units)
in language learning, 22,
46, 55, 71, 76, 91,
103, 126, 132, 137,
163, 180, 186, 191,
201-2, 204, 207, 213,
218, 223, 236, 242,
248, 254-5, 259, 261,
282, 286, 303, 322,
324, 344, 426
(see also articles in
Appendix on learning
monolingually, and
Language Learning in
relation to Focus)
inner conversation, 142
taping, 38, 42, 110, 213,
242, 423-4,
using for data gathering
137, 173-4, 197, 201,
(see also Pronunciation and
Tracking)
Counting (see numerals)
Culture/Customs (see Category
1 in the Units)
European culture contact
and change, 37, 153,
185, 252-3
Culture stress and shock, 327-
343
CV patterns, 85, 121 (see also
Contoids, Vocoids, and
Phonology)
Daily life, 235 (see also
Recreation, Work)
Dancing, 207
Data, books, 17, 43
files, 448
obtaining, 344-360
processing of, 134 (see
also Filing)
Death, 201, 229, 254
Decoration (see Adornment/
Decoration
Demonstratives, 208-10, 220
Dependent (medial, non-final)
verbs
(see Verbs, dependent)

249
Descriptives (see Adjectives/
    Descriptives)
Desiderative (see Eliciting,
    Verb modes)
Dialects, 21, 197, 222, 257,
    399, 404, 405
Dictation of text material
    without tape recorder,
    112, 159, 174
Dictionary, 43, 49, 93, 249,
    425, 427-8, 439-42,
    447, 448-50, 466
Difficult sounds, 164-6
    drills, 107, 156, 161,
        168, 170, 179,
        200, 234
        (see also Pronun-
        ciation)
Directional (see Locational)
Discipline, 223, 254
Division of labor, 46, 52,
    102, 136, 173, 207,
    212, 222, 235, 241-2,
    252
Drills, 23 (see Category 6
    in Units)
    design of, 307, 419
    practice of, 416
Drills, grammatical, 307-
    317, 411
    agreement, 81, 167-8,
        312-3
    comparative/superlative
        constructions, 210
    context forcing, 167-8,
        205, 312
    contraction, 314-15
    correlation, 312
    deletion, 314-15
    different subject, 216
    dual/trial, 156
    equative clauses, 47
    expansion, 182-4, 210,
        227, 313-4
    frame and substitutions,
        60-1, 74-5, 80, 88,
        100, 105, 205, 227,

234, 243, 308-9
    integration, 316
    locational, 88, 226
    multi-clause sentence,
        186-7, 199, 315-6
    multiple context forcing,
        312-13
    multiple substitution, 309
    multiple system, 310
    progressive, 313
    progressive substitution,
        309
    prohibition, 152
    question-and-answer, 44,
        80, 93-4, 130, 160,
        226, 310
    reduction, 314-15
    selection, 309
    sequence of events, 215-6
    stimulus-response se-
        quence, 158, 247,
        316-7, 419
    substitution (see frame
        and substitutions)
    system, 309-310
    tail - head linking, 216,
        313
    transform(ation), 61, 80,
        100, 106-7, 131,
        189, 199, 216, 310-
        312
    utterance-response (see
        stimulus response)
    verb, 120
Drills, phonological
    clusters, 152, 156, 200
    contoids, 107, 138-9,
        144, 152, 156, 161-
        2, 179
    contrasts/contrastive,
        144, 161
    difficult sounds, 107,
        156, 161, 168,
        170, 179, 200, 234
    intonation, 206, 210,
        216, 234
    length, pitch, stress,

161, 179, 184, 195, 200, 206, 210, 216
vocoids, 101, 107, 120, 144
vocoid glides, 152
(see also Pronunciation and Tapes for drills)
Drums, 185
Dual/Trial, 155
Dwellings (see Houses)
"Echo" conversation, 303
Ecological setting/environment, 31, 362, 469, 477
Eliciting/Elicitation, 22-3, 353, 355, 365-75
(see Category 3 in Units)
accompaniment/association, 223-4
adjectives/descriptives, 202-5, 208-10, 220, 225, 249, 374, 375, 452-53
adverbs/manner words, 236-7, 240, 249, 374, 375
aggregate constructions, 175-6
"and", 43, 47, 238
antonyms, 202-3, 367, 373, 374
benefactives, 174-8
"but", 237
by situation, 354, 369-370, 373, 384-5,
collective terms, 367
collocations, 353, 358, 373, 375-83
color words, 202
comparative constructions, 203
conjunctive devices, 43, 47, 130, 230-1, 237
contrastive, 353
demonstratives, 42-3, 47, 208, 249
descriptives/adjectives,

202-5, 208-10, 220, 225
embedded clauses, 242-6
emotions, 256
exploratory, 353
"for whom?", 175
genealogical data, 102, 105, 244, 408-10
generic terms, 366-367
grammatical material, 352-356
greetings, 14, 37-40, 110, 460
hortatory constructions, 181
"how?", 142-3 (instrumental), 237 (manner)
"how many?", 117-8
"if", 231, 270
instrumental, 143
intensifiers, 237
interrogatives/questions, 34, 42-3, 47, 53, 72, 77, 79, 83-4, 91-4, 103-4, 117-8, 127, 133, 142-3, 175, 237, 324, 355, 357, 460-4
(see how, what, etc.)
kinship terms and genealogies, 98, 102
linguistic data, 344-60
locational, 85-6, 224, 249
manner words/adverbs, 236-7, 240, 249, 324, 361, 375-86, 450
meaning, 218, 223
mode/mood (see verb modes)
multi-verb sentences, 127, 214, 230-2
names, 32-3, 35 (see also Names)
negatives, 91-4, 181, 198, 256
nouns, 43, 154, 366-68, 456-59
meaning of, 376-80
numerals, 117, 452
"of" constructions, 175-6

"or", 238
paradigmatic, 356
part-whole, 367
positional morphemes, 224
possessives, 66-8, 72-3,
    127-8, 155
pronouns, 55-63, 158, 354
questions, 355, 357, 362,
    363, 365, 391-2
    (see interrogatives)
relationals, 375, 383
synonyms, 372, 373, 375,
    394
systematic, 355
temporals/time words and
    expressions, 103-4,
    213
transformations, 389-98
verbs, 53, 77-8, 79-80,
    112, 118, 150, 245
    (see also verb
    modes and Useful
    expressions) 368-73,
    453-6
verb modes, 98
    benefactive, 174-8
    causative, 231-3, 256,
        368, 377-8
    conditional, 231, 233
    contrafactual, 256
    desiderative, 230,
        232, 256
    emphatic, 137
    hortatory, 181-3, 200
    imperative, 96-8, 151,
        370, 462-3, 464
    indicative, 186-7
    intentive (purposive),
        229-30, 232, 256
    interrogative, 53, 77,
        91-4, 133, 198
        (see also "what?",
        "when?", etc.)
    intransitive, 53, 118
    passive, 256
    purposive (intentive),
        229-30, 232, 256
    reason, 231-3, 256

    reciprocal, 256
    reflexive, 285
    transitive, 112
verb tenses, 104
vocabulary, 43, 255, 283,
    365-75, 452-59
"what?", 79
"what doing/saying?", 53,
    77, 268, 277
"what is this/that?", 42-
    3, 47, 268, 277, 355
"when?", 103-4, 270
"where?", 83-4, 269
"who?", 34, 127, 130, 269
"whom?", 127
"whose?", 72, 127, 131
"why?", 133, 363
"with", 223-4
"yes/no", 91-2
Embedded clauses, 242-6
Emotions, how to express,
    256
Emphasis/Emphatic, 114,
    137-8
Equational/Equative clauses
    46-7
Equipment, 17-19
Ergative, 118
Etiquette, 41, 299, 477
European contact (see
    Culture)
Events, 43, 369-74, 455
    (see also Verbs)
    meaning of event words
        (eliciting), 380-2
Exclamations, 236, 239
Exclusive, 58, 62-3
Expansion drills, (see Drills)
Expansion of clause, 208
Expressions, useful, 14-5, 58,
    194, 220, 249, 323,
    460-4
Family life, 235, 252-3, 464
Farewells (see Greetings)
Fauna, 180
Feasts/Festivals, 132, 201,
    423 (see also Cere-
    monies)

Fertility rites, 201
Filing, instructions for,
        23, 43, 248, 257
    (see also Category 4
    in Units)
  anthropology, 49, 95
        191, 248
  charts (see Charts)
  dictionary, 49, 93, 249,
        439-42, 448-50
  grammar, 54, 73, 86, 93,
        138, 167, 194, 248,
        257
  phonology, 434-8, 448
  programed review cards,
        318-21
  tapes, 38-9
  topical, 50, 73, 87,
        93, 138, 167,
        194, 219, 248
Filing, methods of, 49, 86
  flat page, 446-51
  punch card, 429-45
  three-by-fives, 32, 166,
        273, 278, 282,
        427-8, 446
Final/Independent verbs and
    clauses (see Verbs)
Fire, 126
Fish, 132, 180
Flat page filing (see
    Filing, methods of)
Flora, 180, 457, 458
Fluency, 22 (see Category 2
    in Units)
Focus, Language Learning in
    relation to, 297-306
Food, 71
Formulas (tagmemic), 73
Frame drills (see Drills),
    364
Free variation/fluctuation,
    122, 164, 405, 406
Function morphemes, 353,
    357, 392, 426, 451
Funerals (see Death and
    Ceremonies)
Games/Recreation, 153

Gardens, 31, 126, 235, 241
Gender system, 58, 113, 154,
    205
Genealogies, 102, 105, 244,
    408-10
Gestures, 83, 146, 185, 426
Giving
  gift exchange, 65, 141
  help, 95, 242
Glides, vocoid, (see Vocoids)
Grammar, 471-74
  conclusions (see Cate-
        gories 4 and 5 in
        Units)
  filing (see Files/Filing)
Greetings and Farewells, 14,
    37-40, 109-10, 277
Handicrafts, 46, 126, 136,
    153, 173, 212, 242
Harris pair test, 165, 399-
    407
Health/Hygiene, 157, 252-3
Hidden/Secret talk, 212, 255
Homophonous pairs, 165, 278,
    399, 402
Hortatory (see Eliciting,
    verb modes)
Hospitality, 196 (see also
    Visiting)
Houses, 41, 55
"how?", 142-4 (Instrumental),
    237 (manner), 386
"how many?", 117-8
Humming pitch, 351-2, 420
Hygiene (see Health)
"if", 231, 270
Imperatives/Commands (see
    Eliciting, verb modes)
Inclusive/Exclusive, 58-9,
    62-3
Independent (final) verbs
    (see Verbs)
Indicative (see Eliciting,
    verb modes)
Indirect object, 174
Indirect (quoted) speech,
    245-6
Informants (see Language

helpers)
Initiation, 228
Instrumental, 143-4
Intensifiers, 237
Intentive/Purposive (see
    Eliciting, verb modes)
Interpretation (in phonemic
    analysis)
    (see Analysis, phono-
    logy)
Interrogatives (see Elicit-
    ing, interrogatives and
    Drills, question-and-
    answer)
Intonation, 38, 44, 66, 80,
    99, 150, 166, 185-6,
    239, 299, 420
    (see also Pitch and
    Tracking)
    drills (see Drills,
        phonological -
        intonation
Intransitive, 53, 118-9, 182
Irregular verbs, 79, 93, 123
"it is a....", 43
Joining features between
    clauses (see Con-
    junctions)
Kinship, 469, 477
    chart, 134, 246
    groups, 222
    obligations and privi-
        leges, 95
    terminology, 33, 96, 246,
        256, 377
    (see also Genealogies and
        Eliciting, kinship
        terms)
Language
    bibliography on language
        learning, 295-6
    choice of name for, 21
    learning, 26-7, 285-306,
        322-326
    helpers, 16, 23, 48, 52,
        260-2, 281-2, 287,
        345-9, 350, 419,
        421, 423

(see also Children,
    using in language
    learning and Training
    assistants)
monolingual learning, 28,
    32, 42, 47, 53, 56,
    58, 72, 77, 209, 214,
    267-84, 352-6, 452-9
styles, 257
types of learner, 26
use of bilingual speakers,
    14, 16, 56, 58, 77, 92,
    105, 110, 133, 232
written, 262
Laws/Legal system, 254
Leisure, 52, 325
Length, phonetic, 119, 166-
    7, 192, 420
    (see also Drills,
    phonological)
sentence, 193
"let's...." (see Eliciting,
    verb modes, hortatory)
Lexicon (see Dictionary)
Life cycle, 228
Listening, 31, 55, 268-9,
    286, 299
Locational, 85-6, 138, 224-
    6, 243-4, 452
    drills, 88, 226
Loops (see Tape loops)
Magic (see Ceremonies)
Manner words (see Adverbs)
Maps, 20, 49, 75, 197, 466
Marriage, 228-9, 252-3
Matrix (see Charts)
Meaning, 365, 375
    checking, 383-6
    finding, 356, 357, 358,
        451
    (see also Eliciting)
Medicine, 157, 252, 463-4
Memorizing, 40, 206, 216,
    325, 364 (see also Ex-
    pressions, useful)
Mimicry, 31-2, 38, 42, 45,
    52, 55, 66, 72
    tape recording for, 42,

52, 110, 416
418-20 (see also
Text, listening and
mimicking and
Tracking)
Minimal pairs (see Analysis,
phonology)
Modifiers (see Adjectives
and Adverbs)
Money/Payment, 141, 242, 253
Monolingual approach (see
Language, learning-
monolingual)
Mood/Mode (see Verbs)
Morphophonemics, 249, 257,
405
Motion clauses (see Clauses)
Multi-verb/clause sentences,
130, 186-7, 199, 214-6,
231-2, 242-6
drills, 186-7, 199,
315-6
(see also Clauses, se-
quences of)
Music/Musical instruments
212-3, 252-3
Mutually exclusive/Comple-
mentary distribution,
122, 164 (see also
Analysis, phonology)
Names (of people), 32-3,
54, 88, 90, 109,
114, 196, 269
Negatives, 91-4, 181,
198, 256, 370
Non-final verbs (see Verbs,
dependent)
Non-suspect CV patterns, 85
121 (see also Contoids,
Vocoids, and Phonology)
Notational devices (transform), 395-7
Nouns, 43, 154, 181, 183,
249
noun classes, 70, 117
noun phrase, 53-4,
204-5
attributes of, 378-80

Numerals/Numeral adjectives,
116-9, 227, 452
Object (grammatical)
direct object (noun, pro-
noun, phrase), 62-3,
112, 158-60, 204-5
drills, 159-60, 182, 205
embedded clause, 242-5
indirect object, 174-5
Obligatory/Optional, 69
Obligatory possession, 73
Observing (see Category 1 in
Units), 22, 357, 469-71
animals, birds, fish, 132
art, 136
attitudes and social in-
teractions, 149
clothing, 65
communal work and author-
ity, 116
culture change, 252
daily life, 235
dancing, 207
dwellings, 41
ecological setting of
language group, 31
fire, 126
flora, 180
foods, 71
gestures, 83
gift exchanges, 141
greetings, 37
indigenous legal system,
254
kin relationships, 95
life cycle, 228
methods of communication,
185
musical instruments, 212
patterns of work, 241
people's interests, 76
personal adornment, 91
pointing, 41
reactions by research as-
sistants to travel,
261
recreational activities,
153

religious beliefs and
    practices, 201, 253-
    4
sickness and health, 157
social organization, 222
tools, 46
trading, 253
village routine and
    leisure times, 52
visiting, 196
work load, 102
"of" constructions, 175-8
Optionality, 395-6, 397
"or", 238
Orders
of adjectives, 210
of verb affixes, 129
Page filing (see Filing,
    methods of)
Pair test (Harris), 165,
    399-407
Paradigms (see verbs)
Partner, working with, 26,
    47-8, 50, 53, 66, 75,
    77, 96, 112, 118, 125,
    147, 168, 170, 174,
    192, 216, 226, 231,
    235, 237, 243
Part-whole relationship, 377
Passive, 256, 390
Payment (see Money)
Person morphemes, 55-63, 123
Phonemics statement, 219
    257
Phonetic check lists, 164-6
Phonetic symbols, 39
Phonetic work chart, 85,
    122, 147, 164
Phonology, 474-6
analysis, 85-6, 122, 161,
    164-6, 192, 350-2,
    420-22, 438
charts, 85, 122, 147, 164
drills (see Drills, pho-
    nological)
filing, 434-8, 448
Photography, 136
Phrase

coordinated, 238
descriptive, 208-10
noun, 53-4
Pictures/sketches, 91, 271,
    278, 283, 351-2, 372,
    400
Pitch, 54, 119, 147, 166-7,
    192, 299, 351, 420,
    448
drills (see Drills,
    phonological)
how to check, 166-7
Plants (see Flora)
Plurals, 118, 154-6, 208
Pointing, 41, 267
Portmanteau morphemes, 69
Positional morphemes, 85-6,
    224, 452
Possession/possessive, 66-75,
    127-8, 155, 175-8, 354
drill, 74
Preparations for language
    learning, 13-9
Prepositions (see Positional
    morphemes)
Programed Review Cards, 318-
    21
Progress charts, 465-76
Prohibitives, 151
Pronouns, types of
benefactive, 174-5
demonstrative, 42-4, 47,
    208
indirect object, 174-5
in locational phrase, 225
object, 62-3, 157-60
personal, 55-63
possessive, 62-3, 66-75,
    127
residual, 155
subject, 55-63, 189
(see also Eliciting, pro-
    nouns and Charts,
    pronoun)
Pronunciation, 89, 94, 101,
    107, 120, 138, 144, 152,
    156, 161, 168, 179, 184,
    195, 200, 206, 210, 216,

234, 249
(see also Drills, phono-
   logical, Mimicry and
   Tracking)
Punch card filing (see Filing,
   methods of)
Purposive/intentive (see
   Eliciting, verb modes)
Quantity (see also Adjectives
   and Numerals)
Questions, 169, 357, 362-3,
   383, 384, 386, (see
   also Eliciting, inter-
   rogatives, and specific
   question words what?,
   whose?, etc. and Drills,
   question-and-answer
Quoted speech, 245-6
Reason, 229-33, 256
Reciprocal, 256
Recreation, 153
Reflexive, 256
Relationals, 43, 375 (see
   also Function morphemes)
   eliciting functions of,
   383
Religion and Religious ceremonies, 201, 253-4,
   470-1, 477
Rhythm, 32, 42, 54, 89, 166-
   7, 184, 200, 210, 420
Rituals (see Ceremonies)
Secret/hidden talk, 212, 255
Sentences
   analysis, 193
   kernel, 390
   length of, 193
   multi-clause, 127, 130,
      189, 197, 199,
      214-6, 220, 230-2
   word-plus-prop, 394
   (see also Clauses)
Sex, 35, 46 (see also Di-
   vision of labor)
Shaman, 252
Sickness, 157, 252
Singing, 212, 216
Social groupings, 222, 470,

477
Songs (see Singing)
Sorcery, 33, 229, 253-4
Spatial relationships, 377
Spirits/Supernatural, 126,
   132, 180, 201, 207,
   252-4
   (see also Ceremonies)
Spontaneous expressions, 229
   (see also Expressions,
   useful)
Stative (see Clauses)
Stress, 54, 119, 166-7, 192,
   299, 420
   stress timing, 54
   drills (see Drills, pho-
      nological)
   how to check, 166-7
Stress-Producing Factors in
   Cultural Adjustment,
   327-43
Subclasses (see Classes)
Subject, 55-63, 186, 188-9,
   205
   drills, 61, 216
   embedded clause, 242-5
Superlatives, 203, 210
Supernatural (see Spirits)
Suprasegmentals, 119, 161
   (see also Length,
   Pitch, Stress, Tone)
Surveying where to live,
   20-1
Suspect pairs/groups/sounds/
   sequences (see also
   Analysis, phonology)
Syllables, 86, 147, 165-7,
   192, 206, 210
   syllable timing, 54
   drills, 179, 184, 190,
      200, 206, 210, 216
Synonyms, 358, 372-3, 394
Taboos, 33, 132, 201, 422,
   424
Tagmemic formulas, 73
Tail-head linking drill, 216
Tape loops, 45, 194, 216,
   415-6, 419-20

Tape recorders
    care of, 19, 416-8
    disadvantages in use of
        426
    features to look for in
        411-12
    use of, 284, 346, 350,
        401, 403, 411-26
Tapes
    filing of, 38-9
    for drills and vocabulary
        learning, 44, 60-1,
        74, 80, 88, 93-4,
        100, 106-7, 130,
        148, 160-2, 178,
        183-4, 189, 199
        206, 227 (see also
        Drills)
    for music, 212-3, 216
    for text (see Text)
    for tracking (see
        Tracking)
    splicing, 414-5
Temporals/Time words and
    expressions, 103-4, 188
    clauses, 213
    drills, 189, 215-6
Tense, 104-7, 129, 187-8,
    220
    drills, 105-7, 189,
        215-6
    elicitation, 104
Testing, 23 (see Category 5
    in Units), 421-2
Text, 422-5
    adapting when transcribed,
        258-9
    constructions from, 393-4
    conversation, description,
        narrative, 42, 110,
        127, 174, 387-8
    drills (see Tapes, for
        drills and vocabu-
        lary learning)
    listening and mimicking
        for language learn-
        ing, 16, 38-9, 120,

        138-9, 179, 190, 193,
            204, 261
    memorizing, 206, 210
    transcribing, 23, 110-1,
        158-9, 174, 193, 261-
        3, 424-5
    transformations from, 393
    using for analysis, 160,
        187, 258, 263
    without a tape recorder,
        112, 174, 262
"that/this is...", 43, 47,
    208
Things, 43 (see also Nouns)
"this is..." (see "that/
    this is...")
Three-by-fives (see Filing,
    methods of)
Time words (see Temporals)
Tone, 147, 351-2, 411, 440,
    448 (see also Pitch)
Tools, 46, 55
Topical file (see Filing)
Tracking, 42, 48, 52, 83,
    124, 146, 149, 157,
    163, 180, 185, 191,
    248, 323, 420
Trading, 136, 253
Training Assistants, 256-
    7, 347-9, 399
Transcribing text (see Text)
Transforms/transformations,
    61, 80, 159, 189, 197-8,
    216, 389-98
    drills, 61, 80, 100, 106-
        7, 131, 189, 199,
        216, 310-2
Transitive, 112, 116, 159,
    182, 205
Translating, 239-40, 247,
    249, 259, 426
Useful expressions (see Ex-
    pressions, useful)
Variation
    of allophones (see Free
        variation)
    of constructions, 154

of verbs, 187
of word order, 396, 439
Verbs
  affixes (see Affixes,
      verb)
  allomorphic variation,129
  aspect and mode/mood,
      128-31, 188 (see
      also Eliciting, verb
      modes)
  being/existing, 123, 204,
      224
  dependent, 79-80, 113,
      128-9, 187, 310,
      315
  drills, 120
  elicitation of, 53, 77-8,
      79-80, 112, 118, 150,
      245, 355-73, 453-56
  independent/final, 79-80,
      112-3, 128-9, 310,
      315
  intransitive, 53, 118-9,
      182
  irregular, 79, 93, 123
  mode/mood (see Eliciting,
      verb modes)
  motion, 85, 96-8, 159,
      181
  paradigms, 129, 187, 214,
      262, 283-4, 356,
      387-8, 411, 422
  participles, 186
  stems
      formation of, 182
      identification of, 182
  tense, 104-7, 129, 187-9,
      215-6, 220
  transitive, 112, 116,
      159, 182, 205
Vernacular, using, 23, 57
    325, 344 (see also
    Language, monolingual
    learning)
Visiting
  etiquette of, 41, 196,
      282
  instructions for, 37, 49,

52, 71, 109, 121,
133, 142, 146, 149-
50, 171, 196, 201,
223, 273, 275, 282,
344
Visitors, 196-7
Vocabulary
  eliciting and gathering,
      43, 255, 283, 361-
      386 (see also
      Eliciting)
  filing, 43, 239, 439-42,
      447-50
  lists for phonemic ana-
      lysis, 180, 420-2
  memorization of 364
Vocative, 236, 239
Vocoids, 39, 85-6, 119,
    121-2, 147, 164-6, 219
  drills with, 101, 107,
      120, 144, 152, 161,
      179, 200
  glides, 152
"want to...", 230, 232, 256
"what?", 79, 386
"what doing, saying?", 53,
    77-8, 112, 118, 150
    268, 277
"what is this, that?", etc.
    42, 47, 112, 154, 268,
    277
"when?", 103-4, 270, 386
"when", 127, 186, 213-5
"where?", 83-4, 269, 355,
    386
"while", 213
Whistling
  in communication, 185
  in pitch analysis, 351,
      420
"who?", 34, 127, 130, 269,
    355, 386
"whom?", 127, 130
"whose?", 72, 127. 131
"why?", 133-5
"with", 222-3
Words
  new words, 357, 361,

365-75, 452-9
word classes, 249, 365-6,
    376, 377
word order, 53, 395, 403
Work, 102, 116, 235, 241
    (see also Division of
    labor)
Work charts (phonology), 85,
    122, 147, 164
Writing/written style, 185,
    262
"yes/no", 91-4

Printed by the S.I.L. Printing Department
Ukarumpa, E.H.D., Papua New Guinea